HISTORIC PHOTOS OF
MEMPHIS

TEXT AND CAPTIONS BY
GINA CORDELL AND PATRICK O'DANIEL

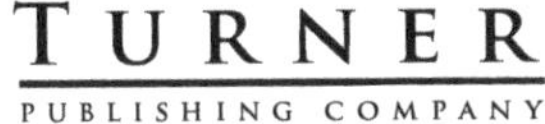

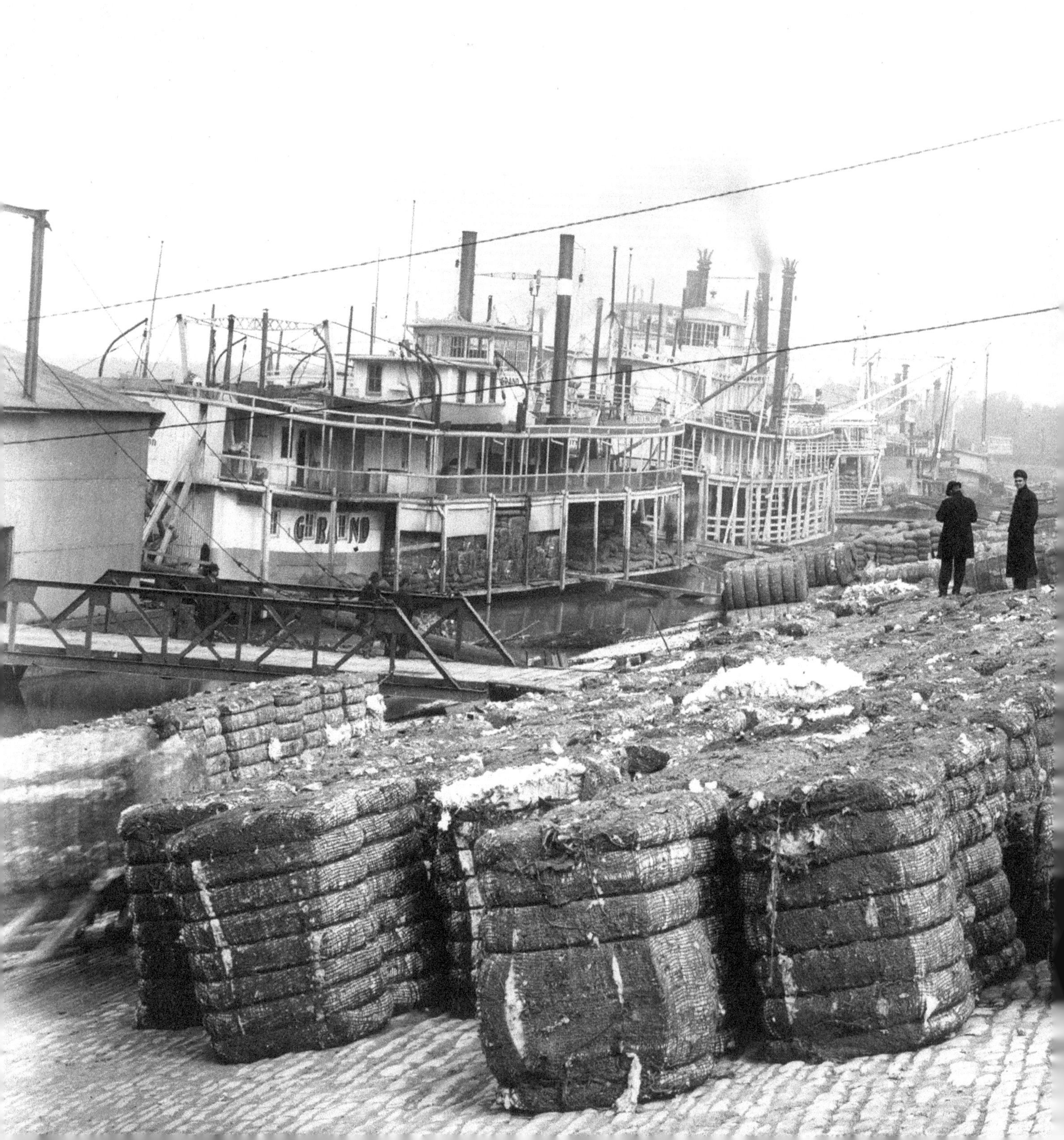

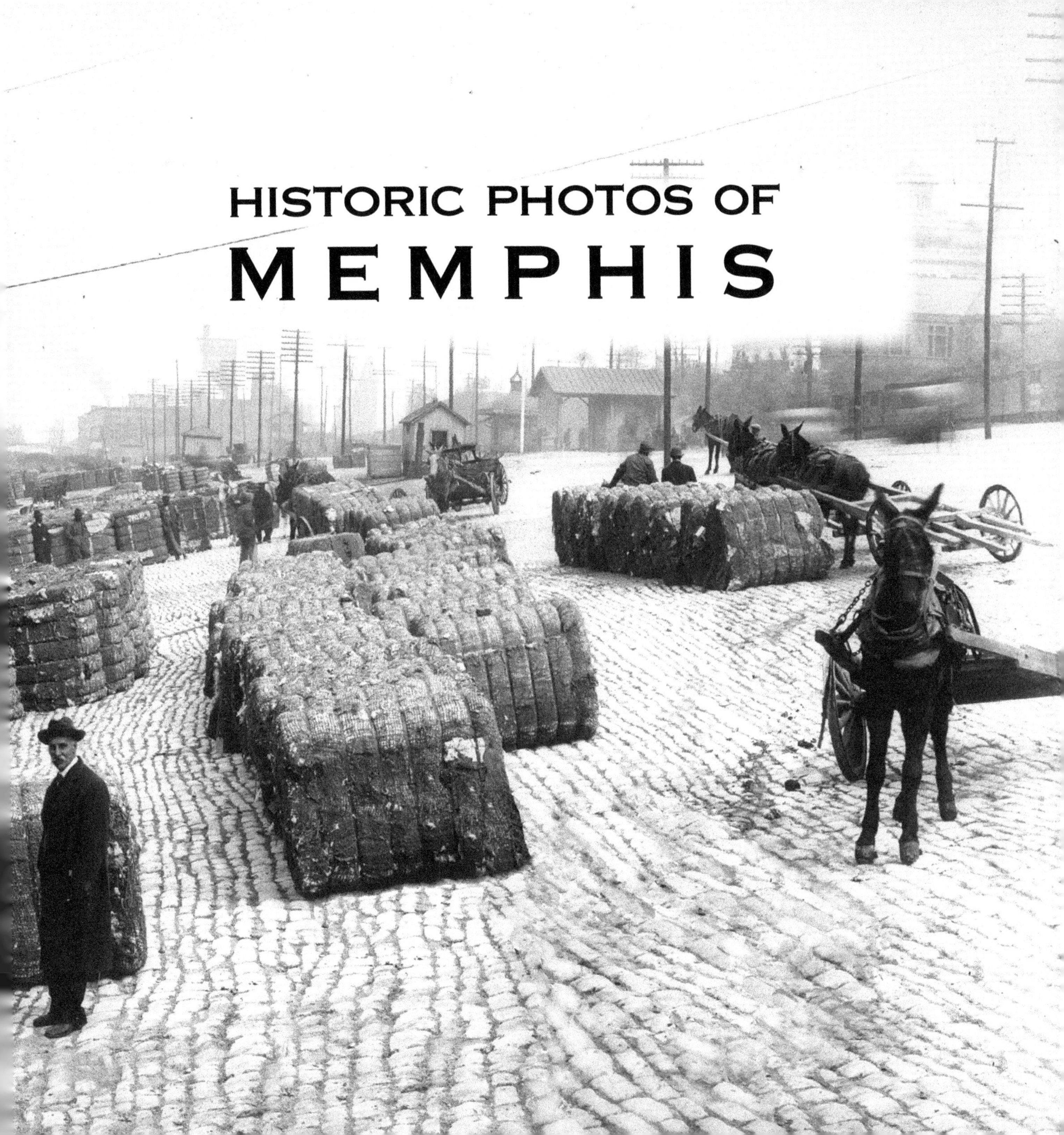

HISTORIC PHOTOS OF
MEMPHIS

Turner Publishing Company
www.turnerpublishing.com

Historic Photos of Memphis

Library of Congress Control Number: 2006902320

ISBN-13: 978-1-59652-261-9
ISBN: 1-59652-261-5

Printed in the United States of America

ISBN 978-1-68336-913-4 (hc)

Contents

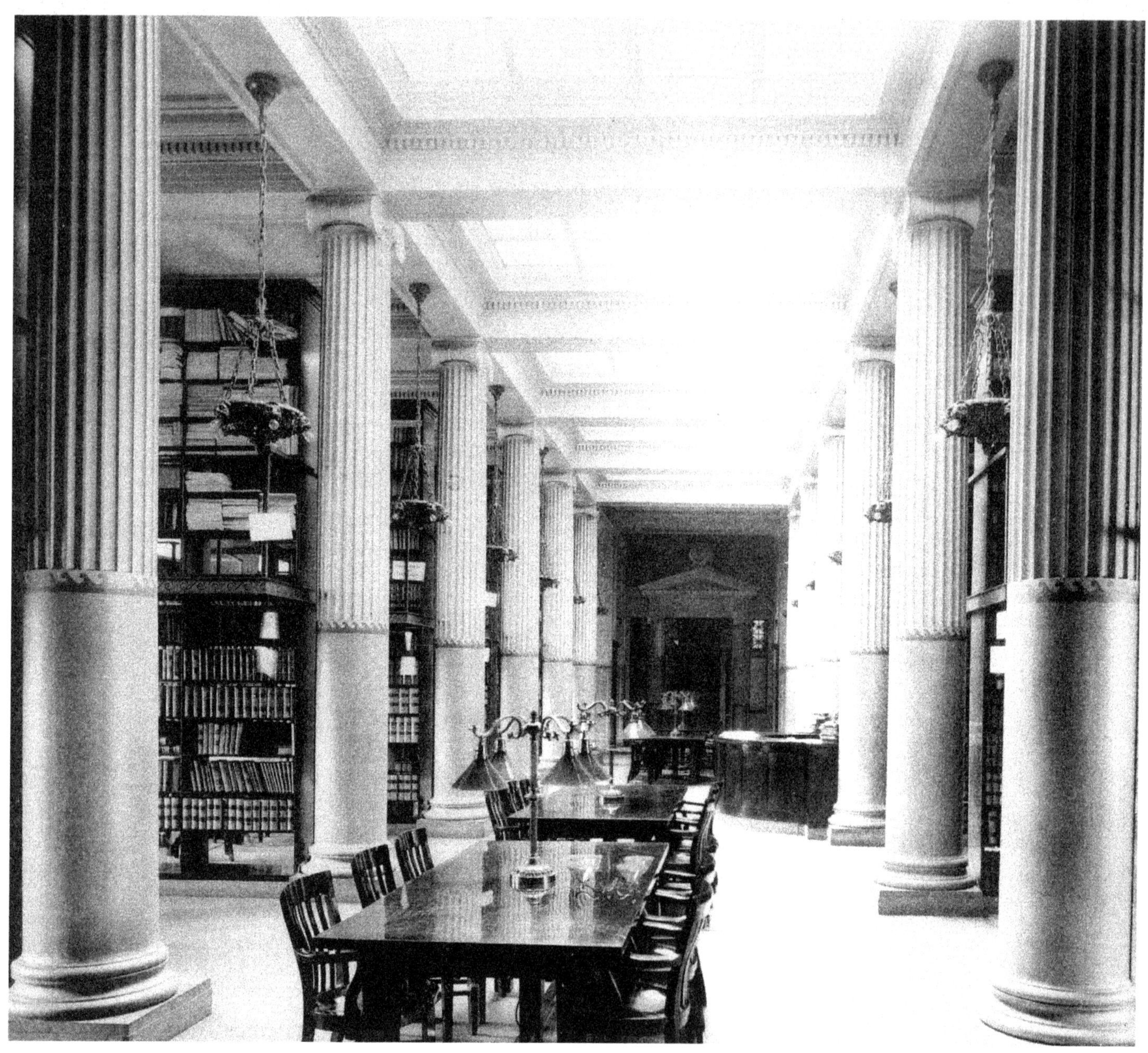

Interior of the Shelby County Court House law library, 1913.

Acknowledgments

This volume, *Historic Photos of Memphis,* is the result of the cooperation and efforts of many individuals, organizations, and corporations. It is with great thanks that we acknowledge the valuable contribution of the following for their generous support:

First Tennessee Bank
Memphis Light, Gas & Water
Memphis Public Library

We would also like to express our gratitude to Dr. Wayne Dowdy for providing research and contributing in all ways possible.

And finally, we would like to thank the following individuals for their valuable contribution and assistance in making this work possible:

Dr. Jim Johnson, Memphis and Shelby County Room, Memphis Public Library
Patricia LaPointe, Memphis and Shelby County Room, Memphis Public Library
Dr. Jim Johnson, Senior Manager, History Department
G. Wayne Dowdy, Archivist, History Department
Patricia LaPointe, Curator, Memphis and Shelby County Room
Betty Anne Wilson, Assistant Director for Library Advancement

Kim Cherry, Vice President of Corporate Communications, First Horizon National Corporation

Preface

Memphis has thousands of historic photographs that reside in archives, both locally and nationally. This book began with the observation that, while those photographs are of great interest to many, they are not easily accessible. During a time when Memphis is looking ahead and evaluating its future course, many people are asking how do we treat the past? These decisions affect every aspect of the city – architecture, public spaces, commerce and infrastructure – and these, in turn, affect the way that people live their lives. This book seeks to provide easy access to a valuable, objective look into the history of Memphis.

The power of photographs is that they are less subjective in their treatment of history. While the photographer can make decisions regarding what subject matter to capture and some limited variation in its presentation, photographs do not provide the breadth of interpretation that text does. For this reason, they provide an original, untainted perspective that allows the viewer to interpret and observe.

This project represents countless hours of review and research. The researchers and authors have reviewed thousands of photographs in numerous archives. We greatly appreciate the generous assistance of the archivists listed in the acknowledgements of this work without which, this project could not have been completed.

The goal in publishing this work is to provide broader access to this set of extraordinary photographs that seek to inspire, provide perspective and evoke insight that might assist people who are responsible for determining Memphis' future. In addition, the book seeks to preserve the past with adequate respect and reverence.

The photographs selected have been reproduced using multiple colors of ink to provide depth to the images. With the exception of touching up imperfections caused by the damage of time, no other changes have been made. The focus and clarity of many images is limited to the technology and the ability of the photographer at the time they were taken.

The work is divided into eras. The history of Memphis is recorded in some of the earliest known photographs from pre-Civil War to modern Memphis.

In each of these sections we have made an effort to capture various aspects of life through our selection of photographs. People, commerce, transportation, infrastructure, religious institutions and educational institutions have been included to provide a broad perspective.

We encourage readers to reflect as they go walking in Memphis, along the riverfront or through the Peabody. See the riverboats that once lined the Mississippi and many buildings, long since demolished, that lined Front and Main streets. It is the publisher's hope that in utilizing this work, long time residents will learn something new and that new residents will gain a perspective on where Memphis has been, so that each can contribute to its future.

—Todd Bottorff, Publisher

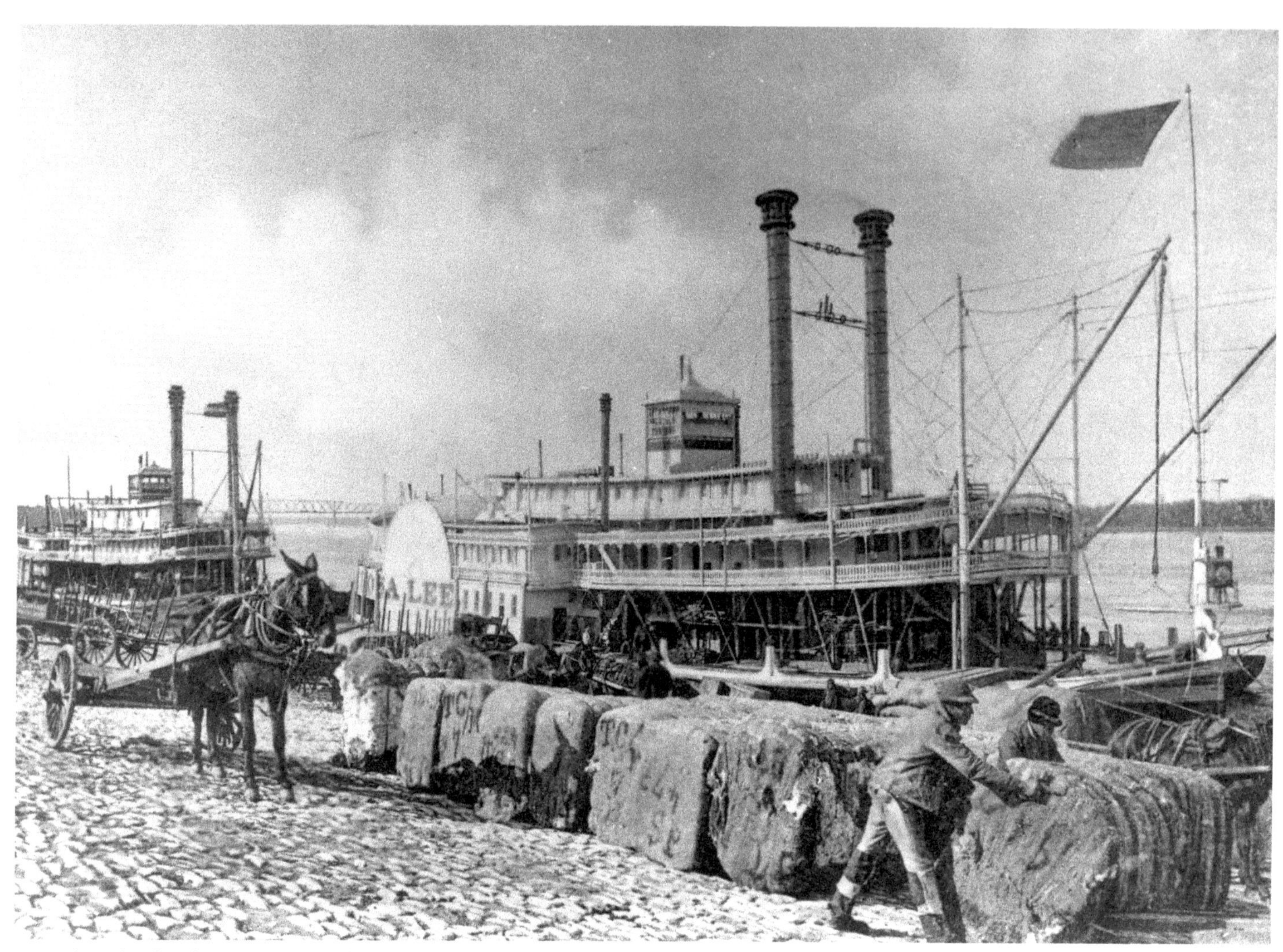

Memphis wharf with steamboats docked and ready for loading of goods.

Pre-Civil War to the Turn of the Century

1860-1899

Memphis had developed considerably because of river trade by the second half of the nineteenth century. The city's commercial importance increased when the Memphis and Charleston Railroad was completed in 1857, linking the Atlantic Ocean and the Mississippi River. The city's population in 1860 was ten times greater than it had been just twenty years earlier largely due to an influx of Irish and German immigrants. Before the Civil War, Memphis was a vibrant and important city.

The city was occupied by Federal forces in June 1862 following the Battle of Memphis. Fortunately, the brief naval engagement left the city largely undamaged and the business community continued to thrive even under occupation. As the city adjusted to life after the Civil War newcomers continued to flock to the city.

Memphis was a haven for thousands of displaced former slaves. Their presence, along with the predominantly African American Federal occupation force, led to a shift in the city's racial makeup causing resentment among many former Confederates. Tensions erupted into a three-day race riot in 1866 leaving many dead and injured. Despite adverse circumstances in the wake of this tragedy, African Americans managed to maintain a foothold in the fabric of the growing city. As time went on, many made social, political and economic advances rarely seen in other Southern cities.

The 1870s were difficult times for Memphis. The city suffered a series of devastating yellow fever outbreaks in the1860s and 1870s, but the worst outbreak was in 1878. Thousands died, while many others fled the city never to return. Falling property values and reckless management of city finances led the city to declare bankruptcy and to loose its charter in 1879.

The end of the nineteenth century marked a period of renewal for Memphis. In 1880, state-appointed officials took control of the city and cleared debts, improved sanitation and rebuilt the political infrastructure. Cotton and the growing hardwood industry contributed to the economic recovery. Other improvements included the discovery of artesian water in 1887, the construction of the Frisco Bridge across the Mississippi River in 1892 and the first public library in 1893. Also in 1893, home rule for Memphis returned and the South's first African American millionaire, Robert Reed Church, Sr., purchased the first city bond. Memphis continued to grow with the opening of the Porter Building in 1895, which was the city's first modern skyscraper, and the opening of Church's Park and Auditorium, the city's first park and entertainment center for African Americans, in 1899.

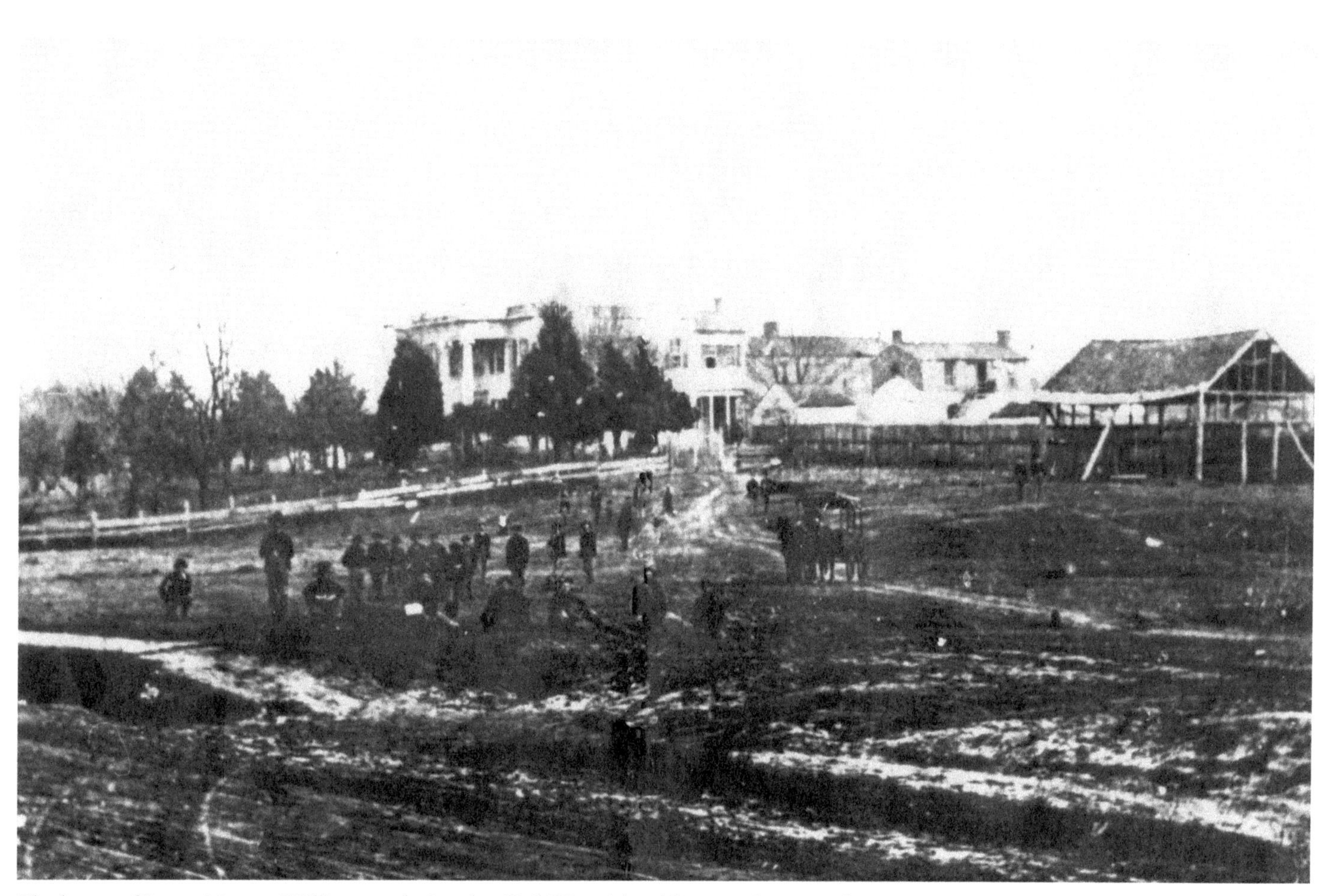

The home of James Monroe Williamson during the Civil War with soldiers on the grounds.

The Hunt-Phelan House. The home was built between 1828 and 1832 on Beale Street and was headquarters to General Leonidas Polk during the Civil War. After the war, the Freedman's Bureau ran a school on the property.

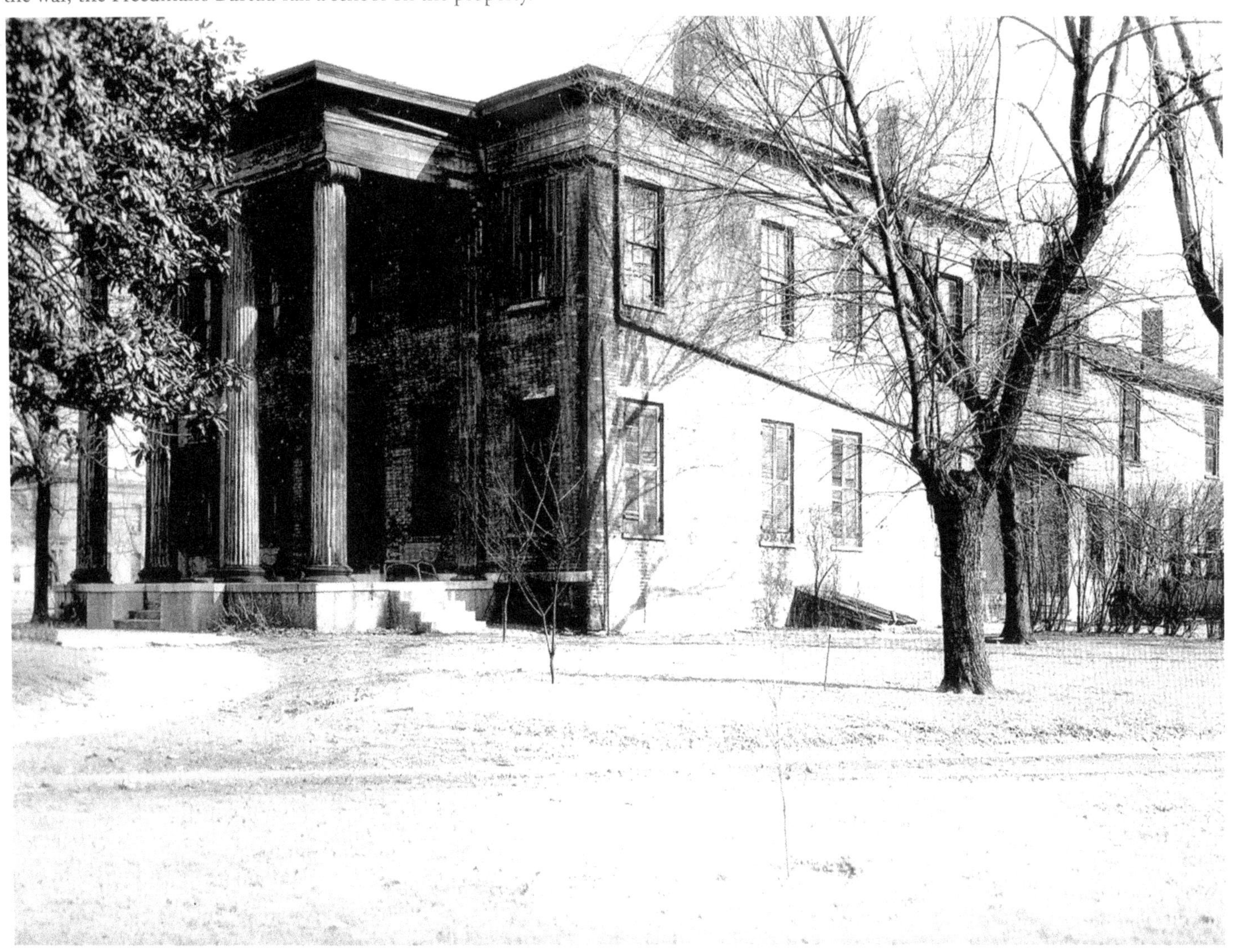

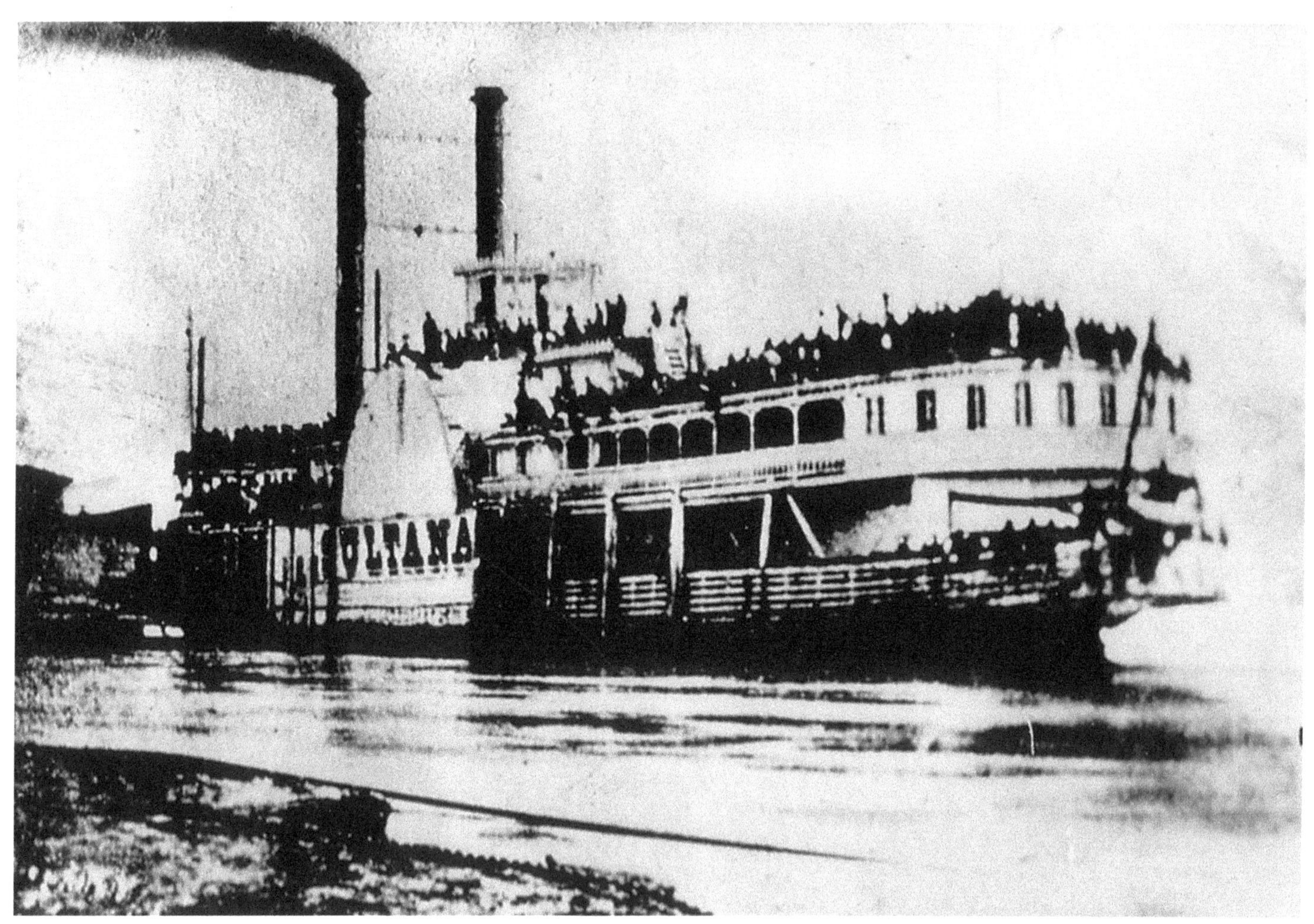

This is the last photograph taken of the *Sultana*. It was destroyed when the boilers exploded shortly after leaving Memphis on April 27, 1865. The sinking of the *Sultana* was the worst maritime disaster in American history.

Frederick H. Cossitt and family, 1884. A gift of $75,000 from Cossitt's estate made the founding of the first free public library in Memphis possible.

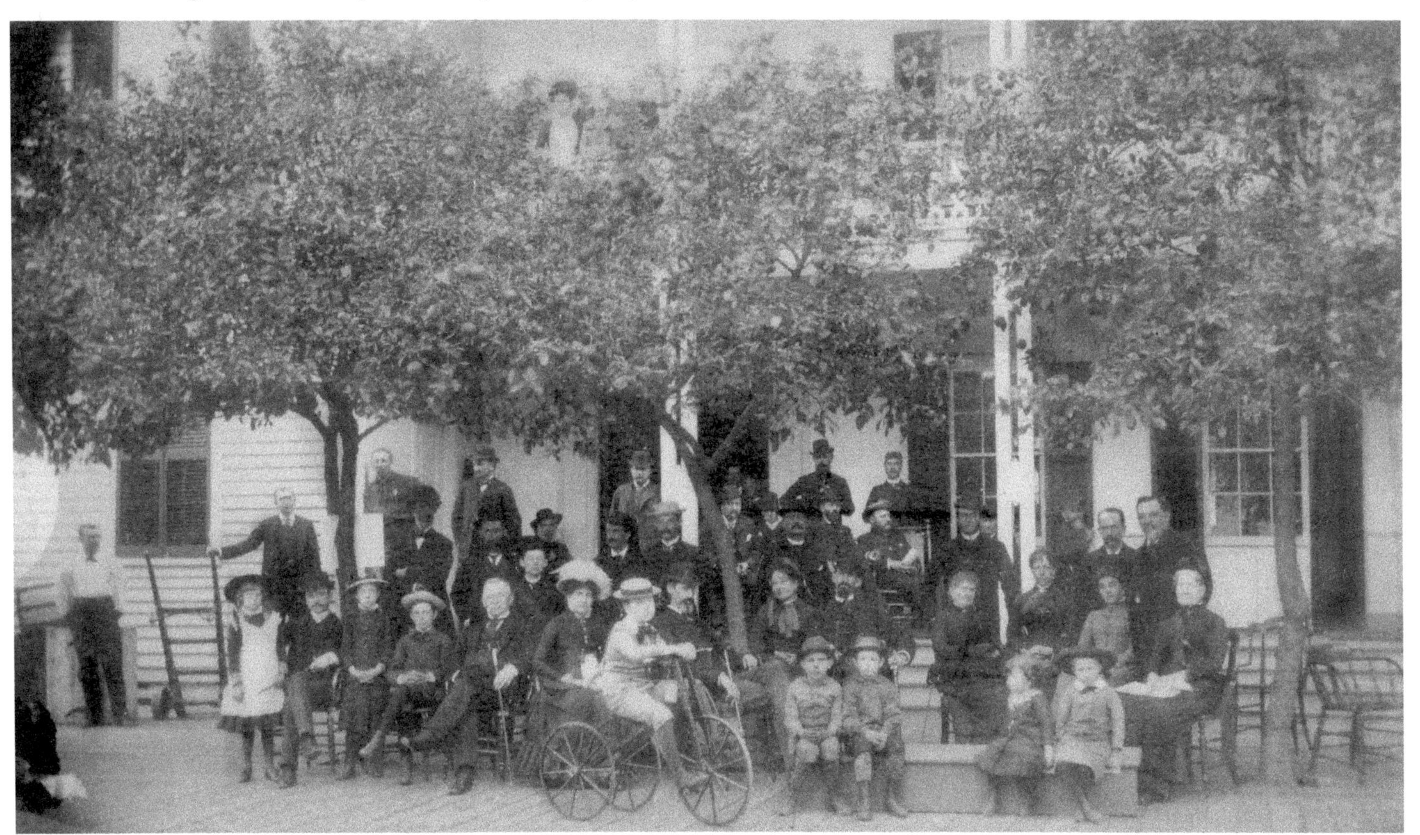

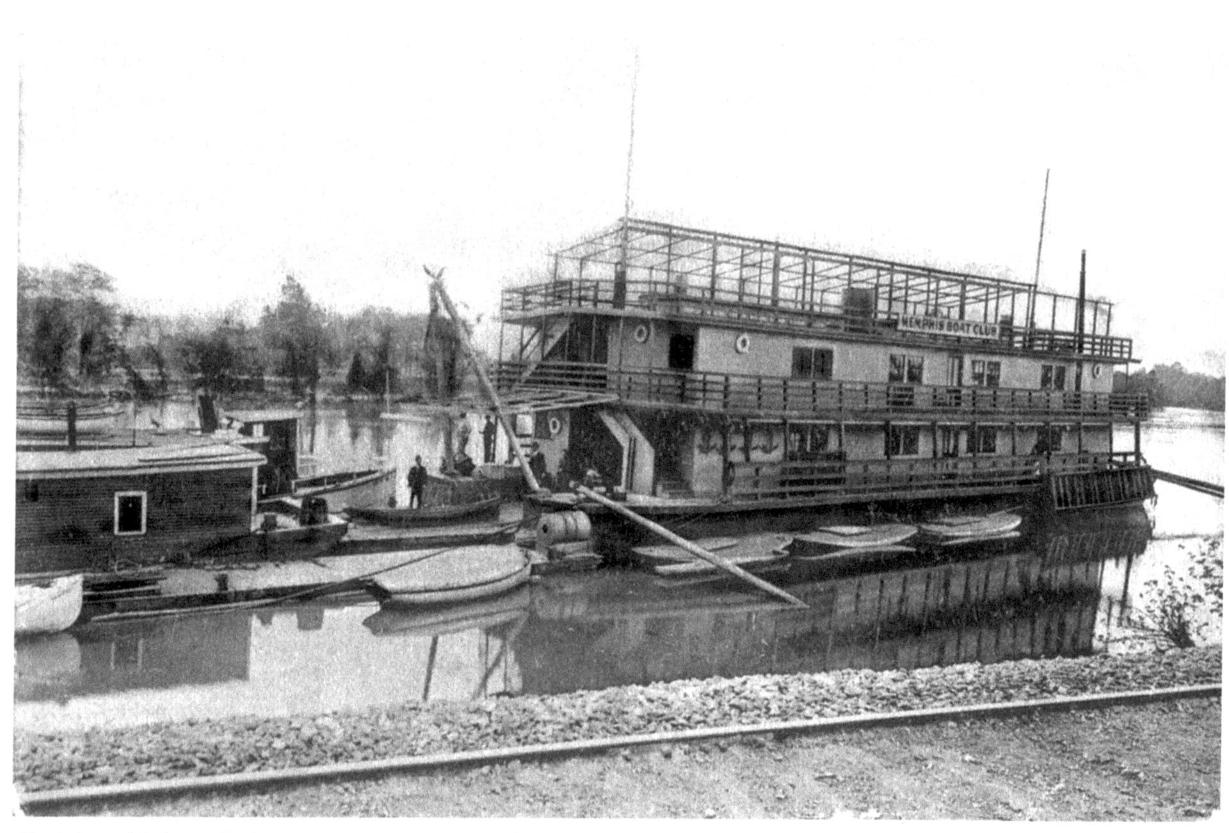

The Memphis Boat Club was organized in 1901 to foster participation in rowing, boating and yachting.

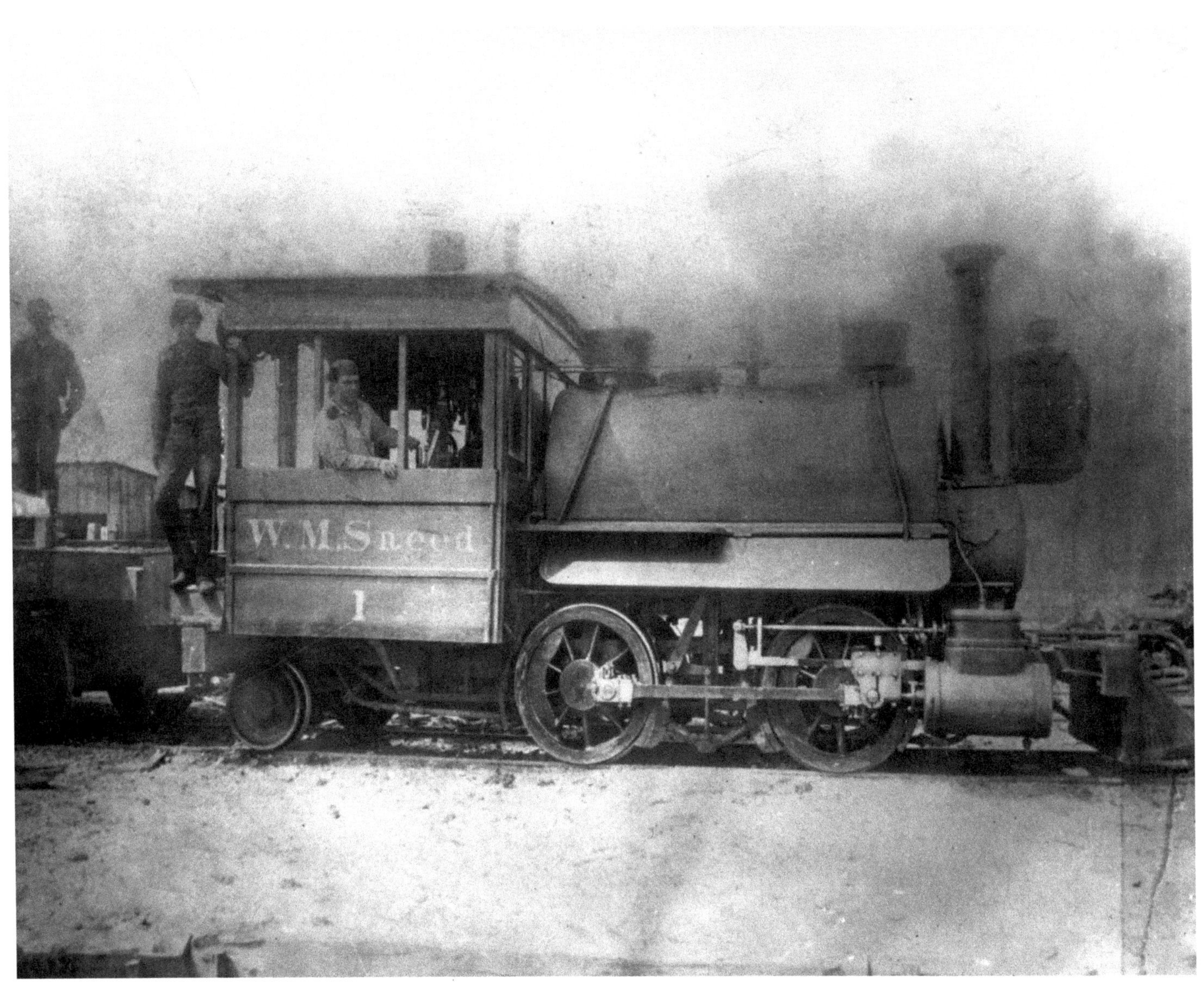

Illinois Central Railroad, East End Dummy Line, 1888.

Equitable Building, 1890s.

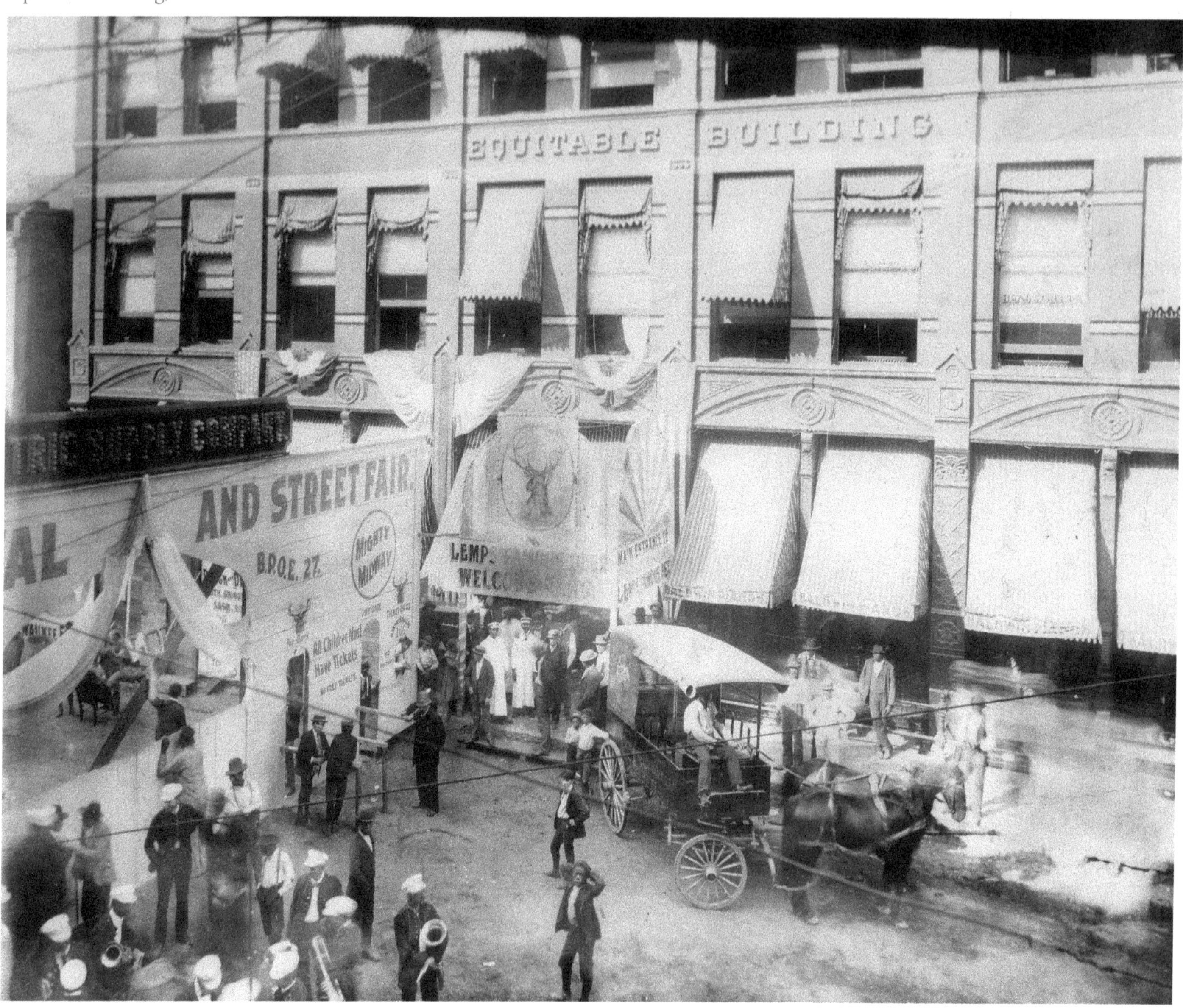

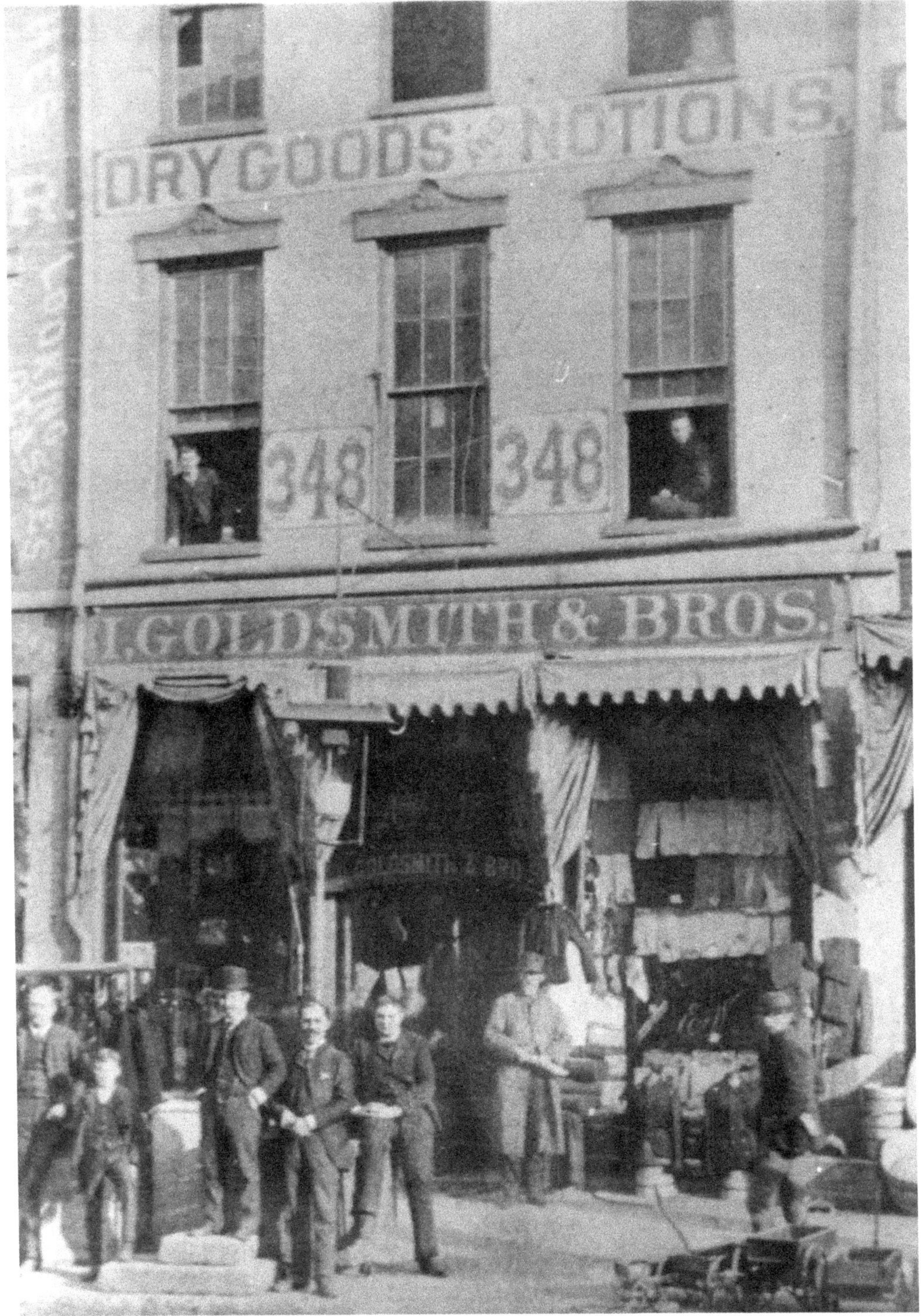

Goldsmith's Dry Goods Store at 348 Main Street, 1880s.

The Great Bridge, later named the Frisco Bridge, during construction, 1891.

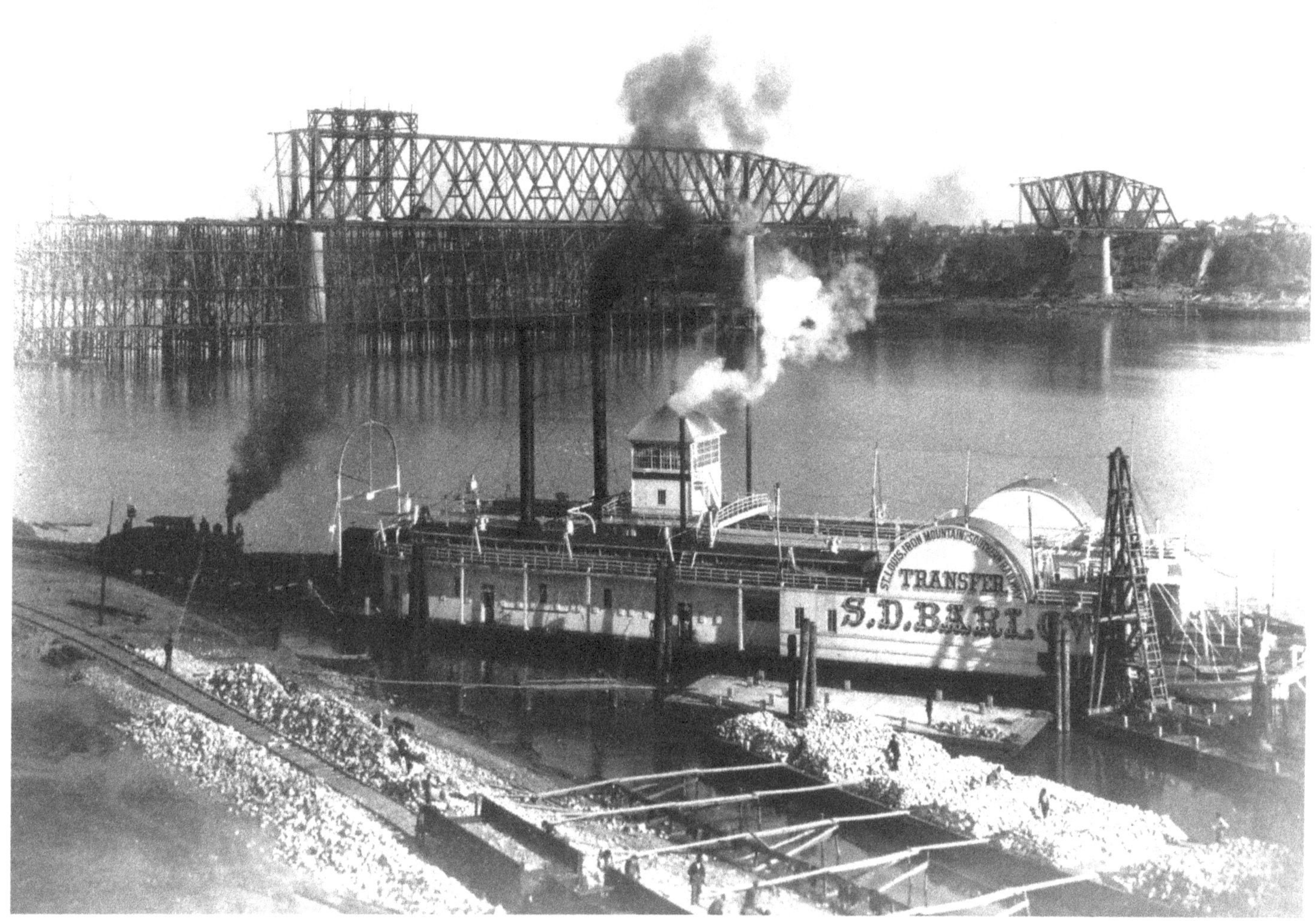

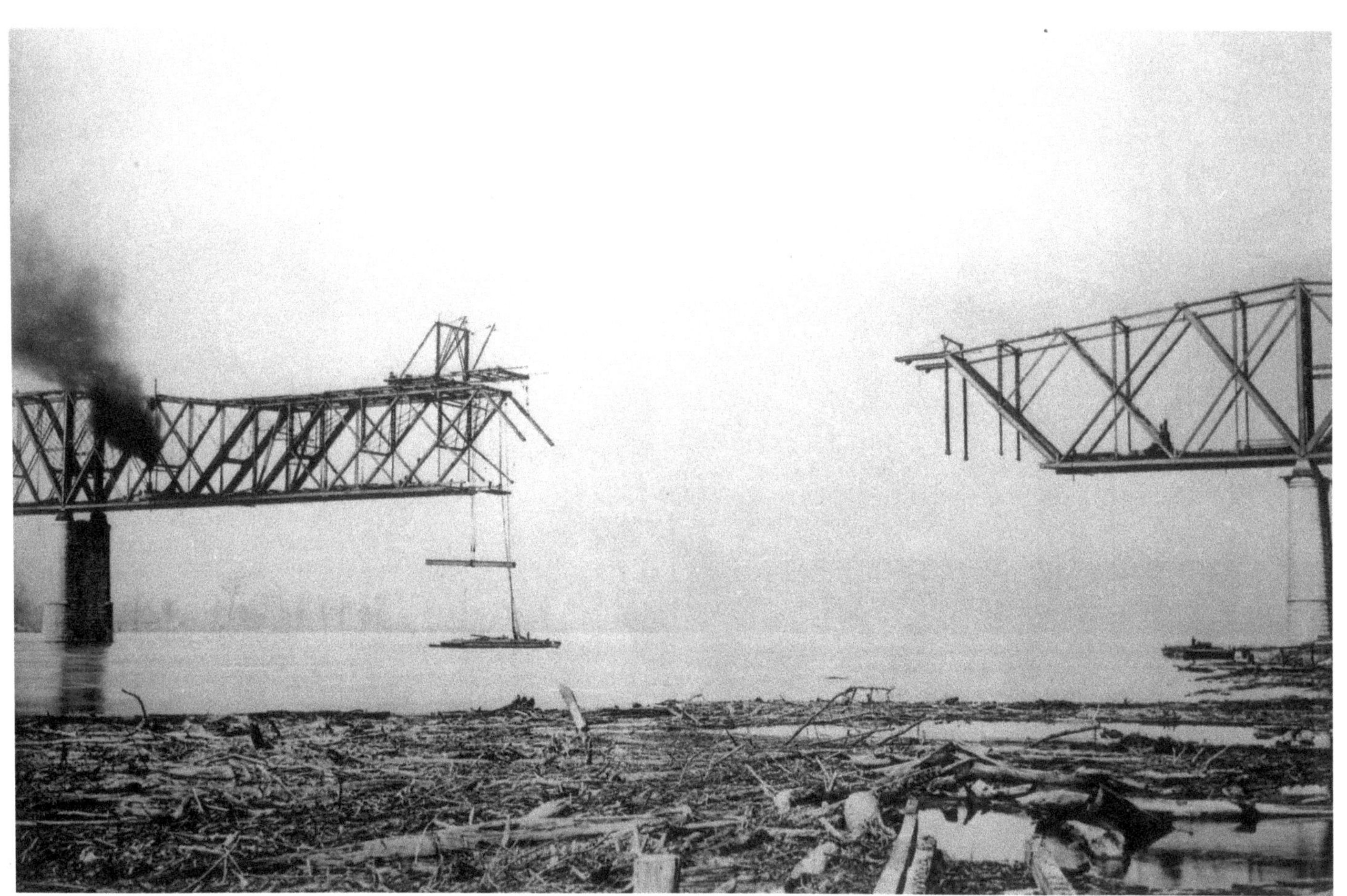

Erection of the east intermediate span of the Frisco Bridge, March 2, 1892.

Belle of the Bends at Memphis, circa 1899.

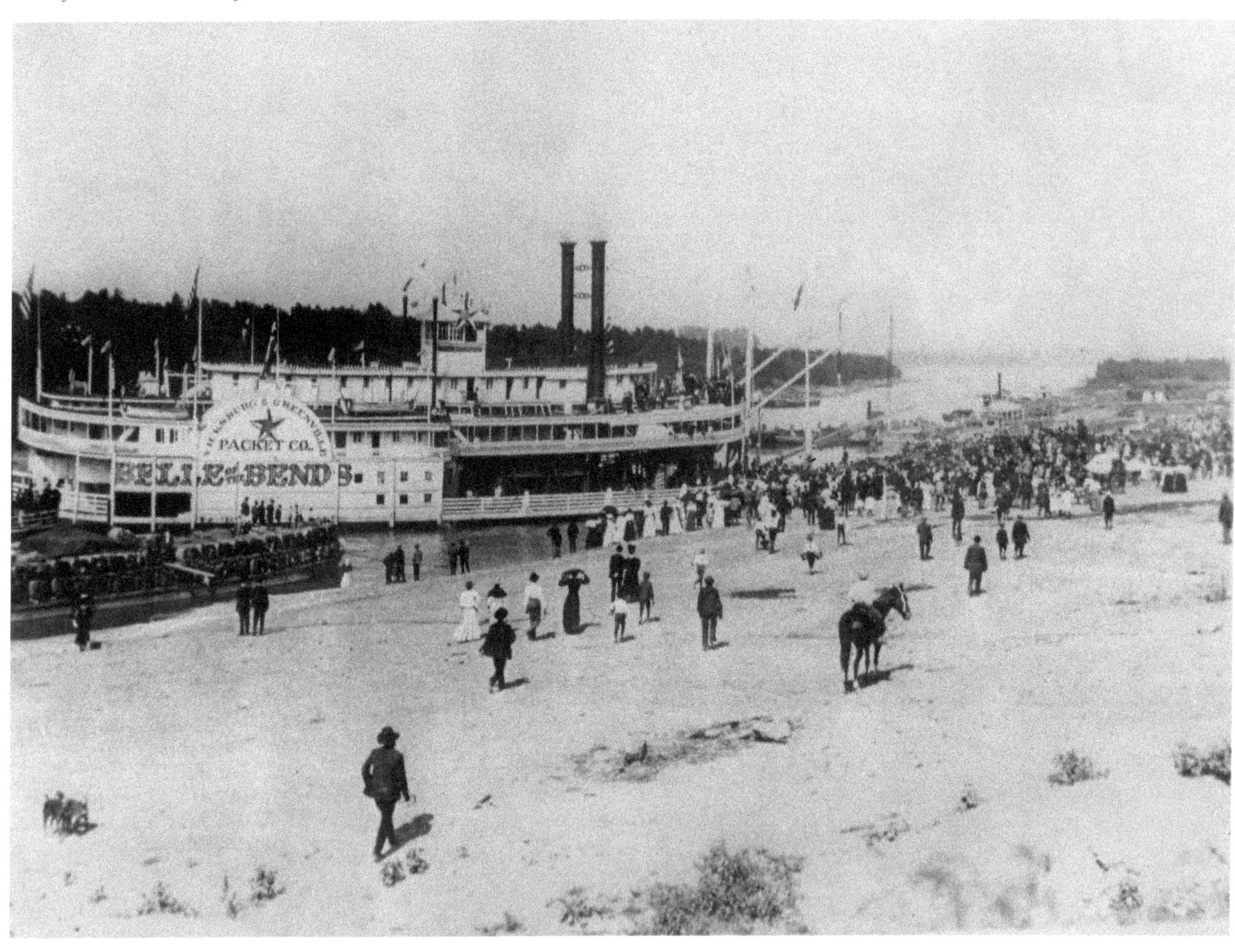

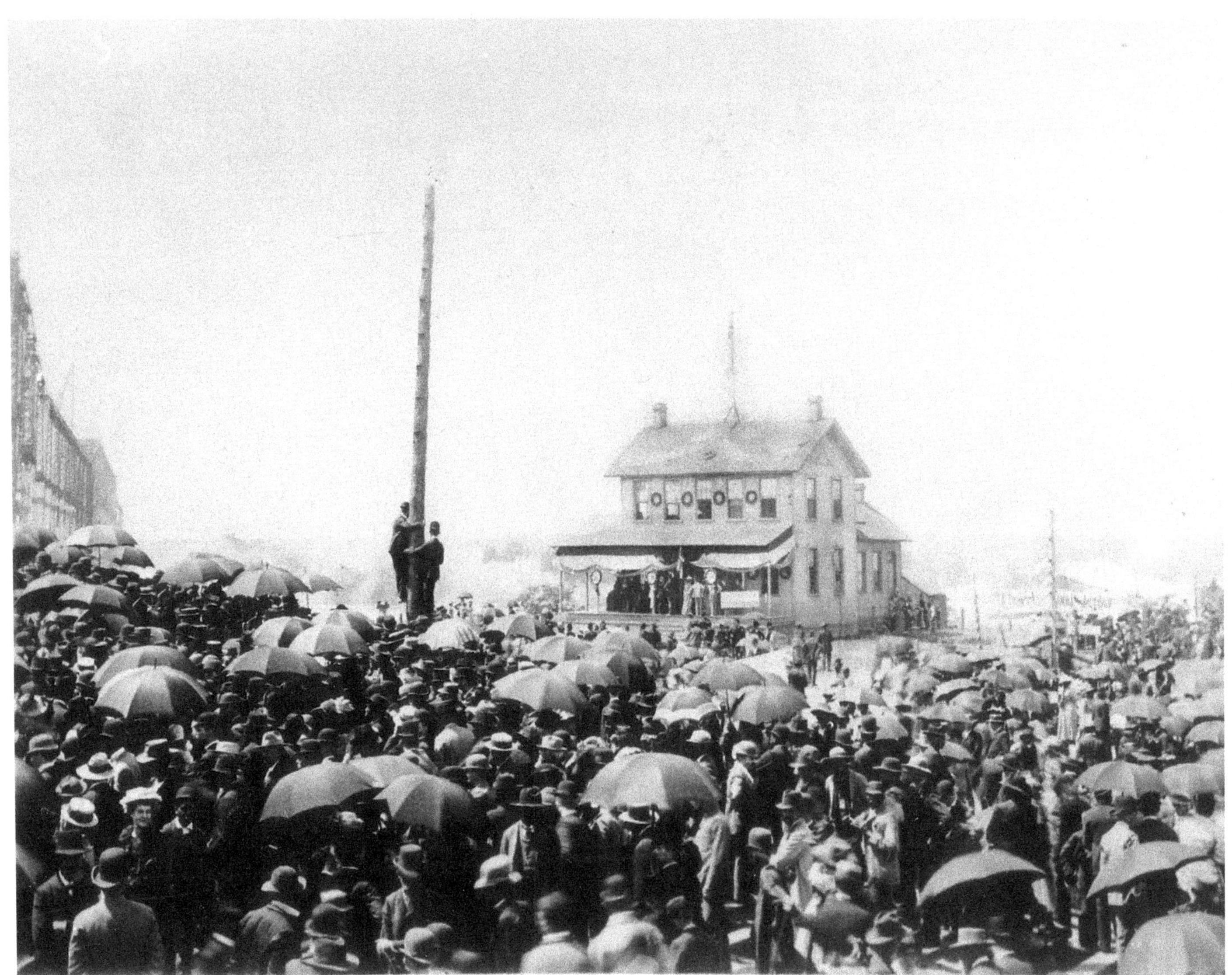

Opening of the Great Bridge at Memphis on May 12, 1892. The bridge was only the second to span the Mississippi River, after the Eads Bridge was constructed at St. Louis in the 1870s. After the bridge was purchased by the St. Louis and San Francisco Railway in 1903, the name was changed to the Frisco Bridge.

Scene from South Memphis, circa 1899.

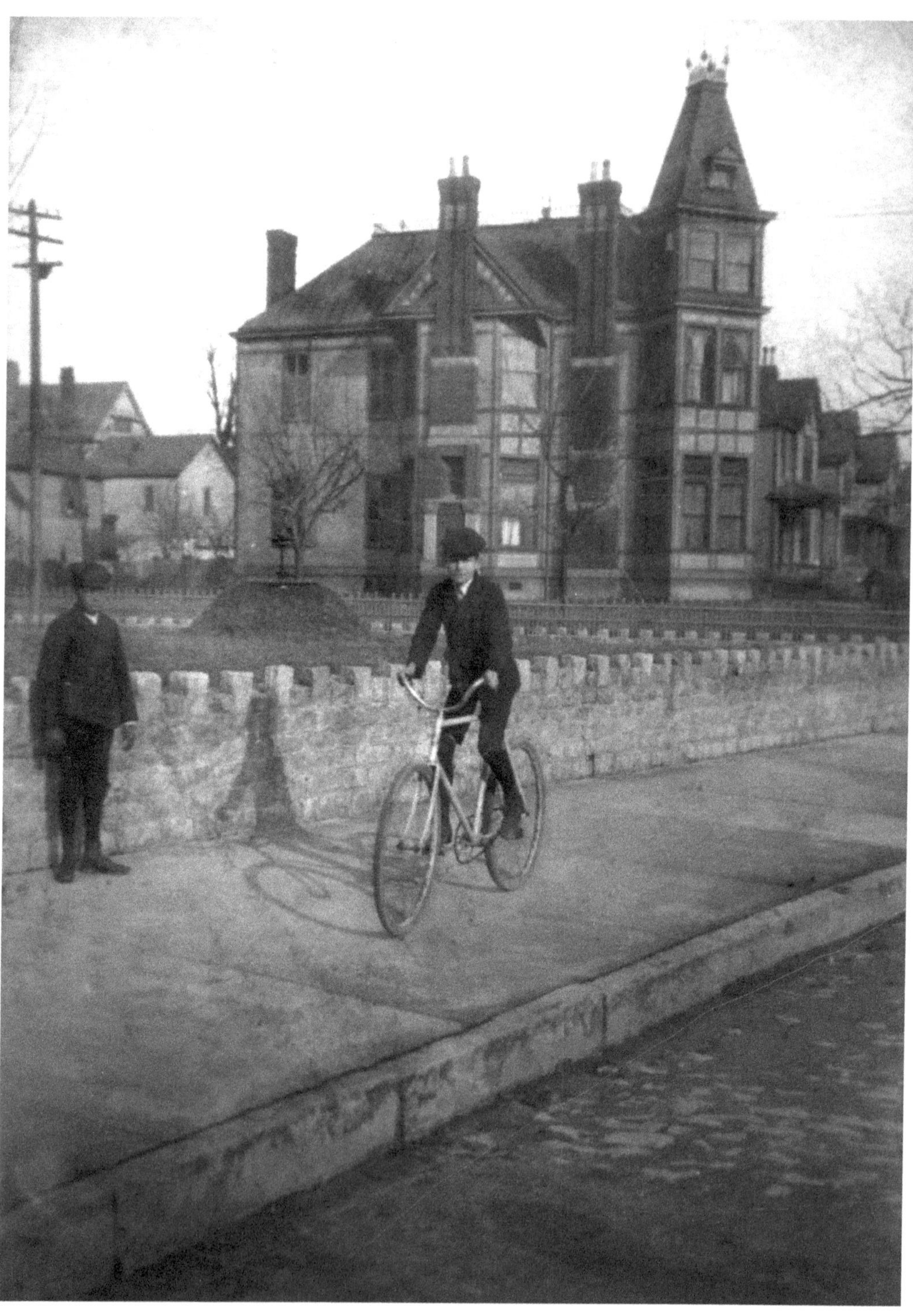

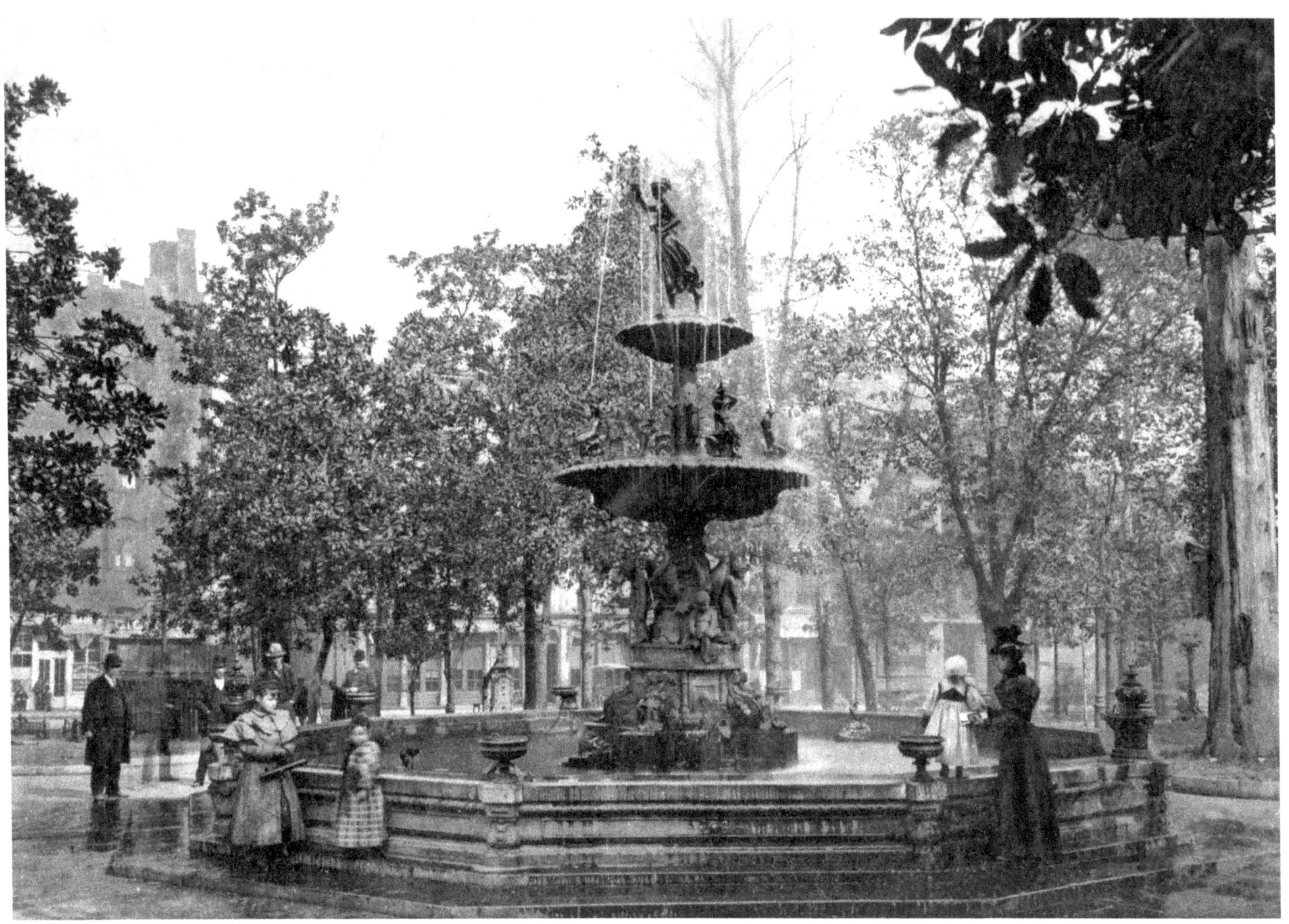

Court Square in 1895. The park is one of the four public squares originally designated in 1819. The fountain was erected in 1876 in honor of the nation's Centennial.

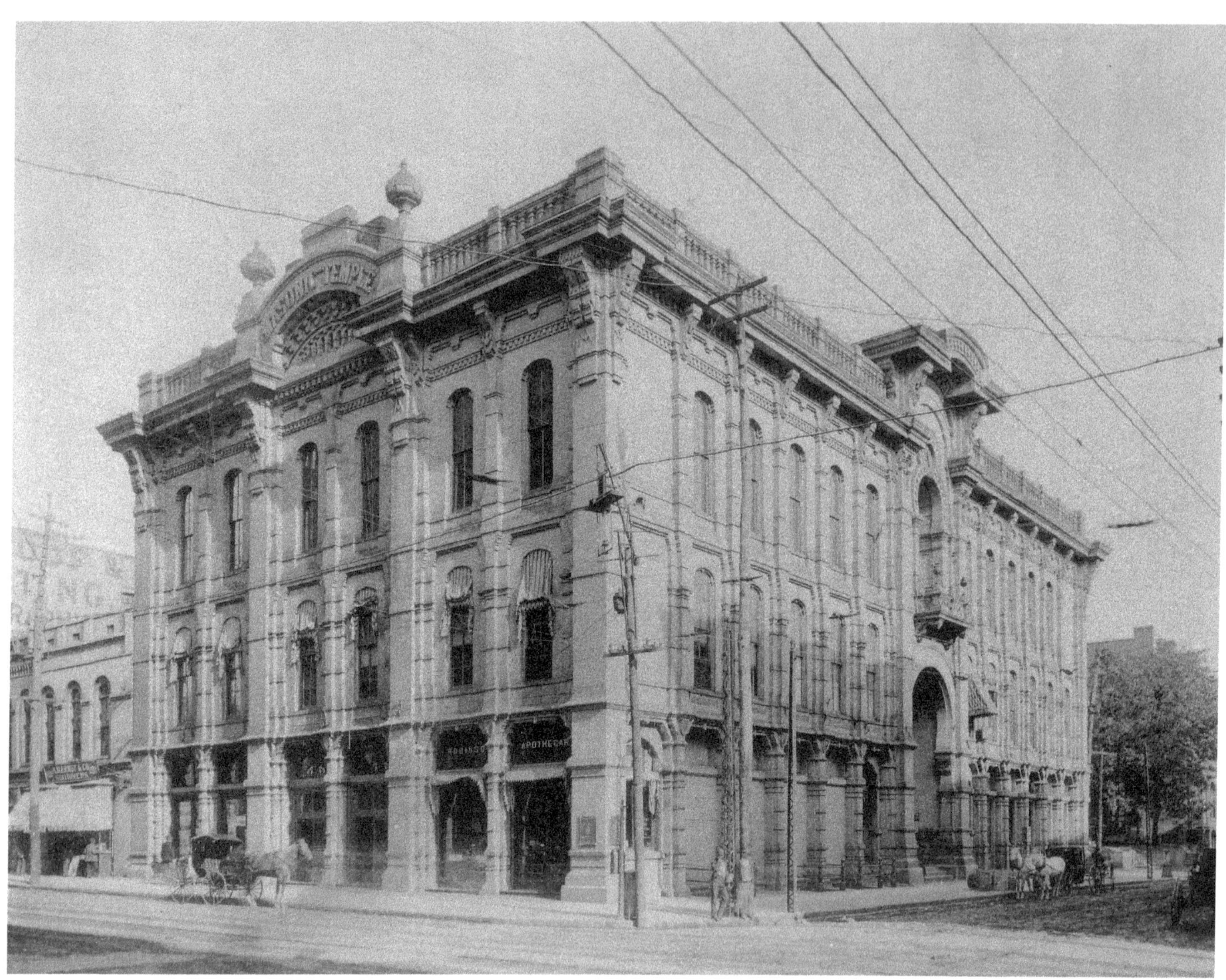

Masonic Temple at the corner of Madison and Second Street, 1895.

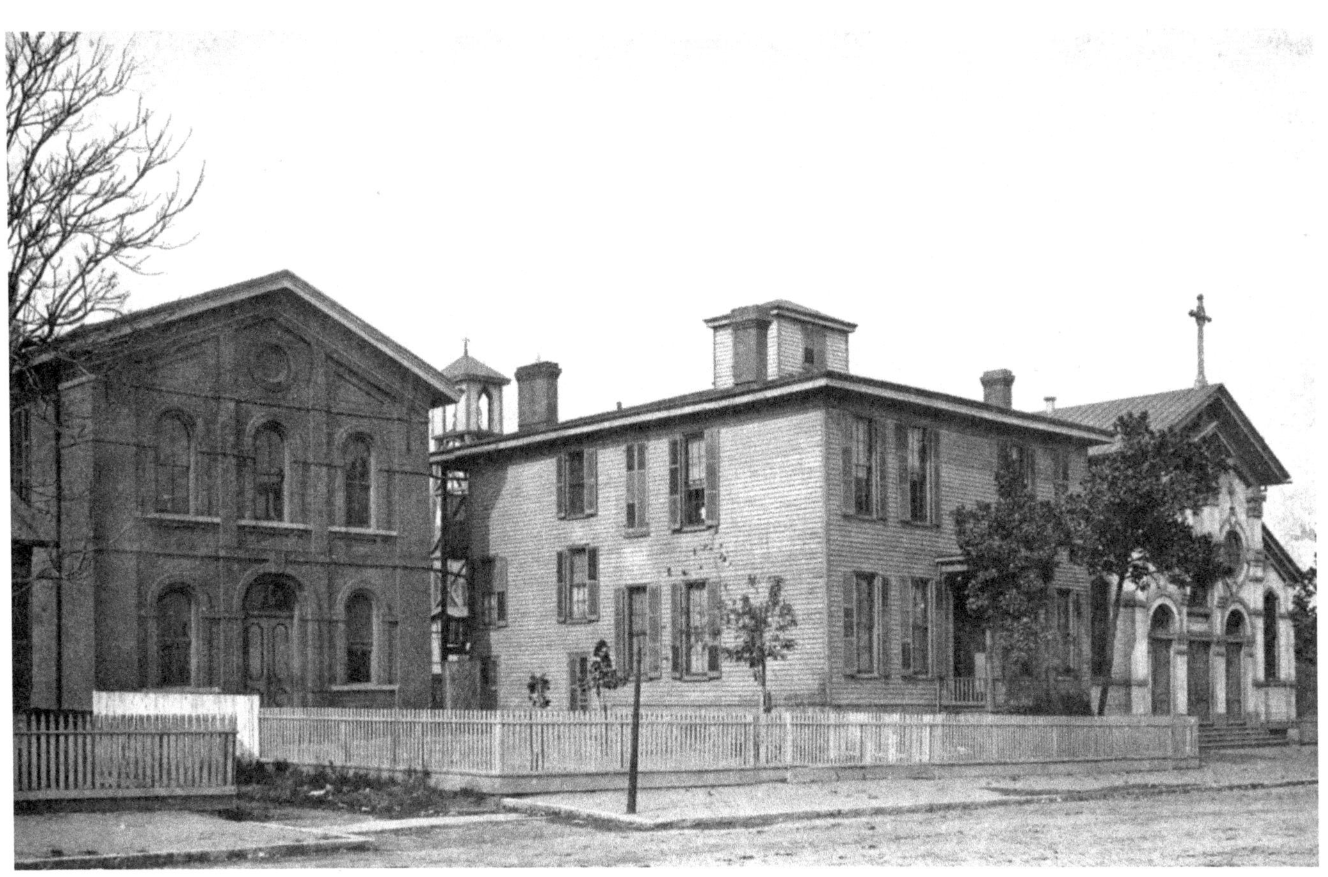

St. Brigid's Catholic Church, 1895. It was built in 1870 and served the largely Irish population of the Pinch District for many years.

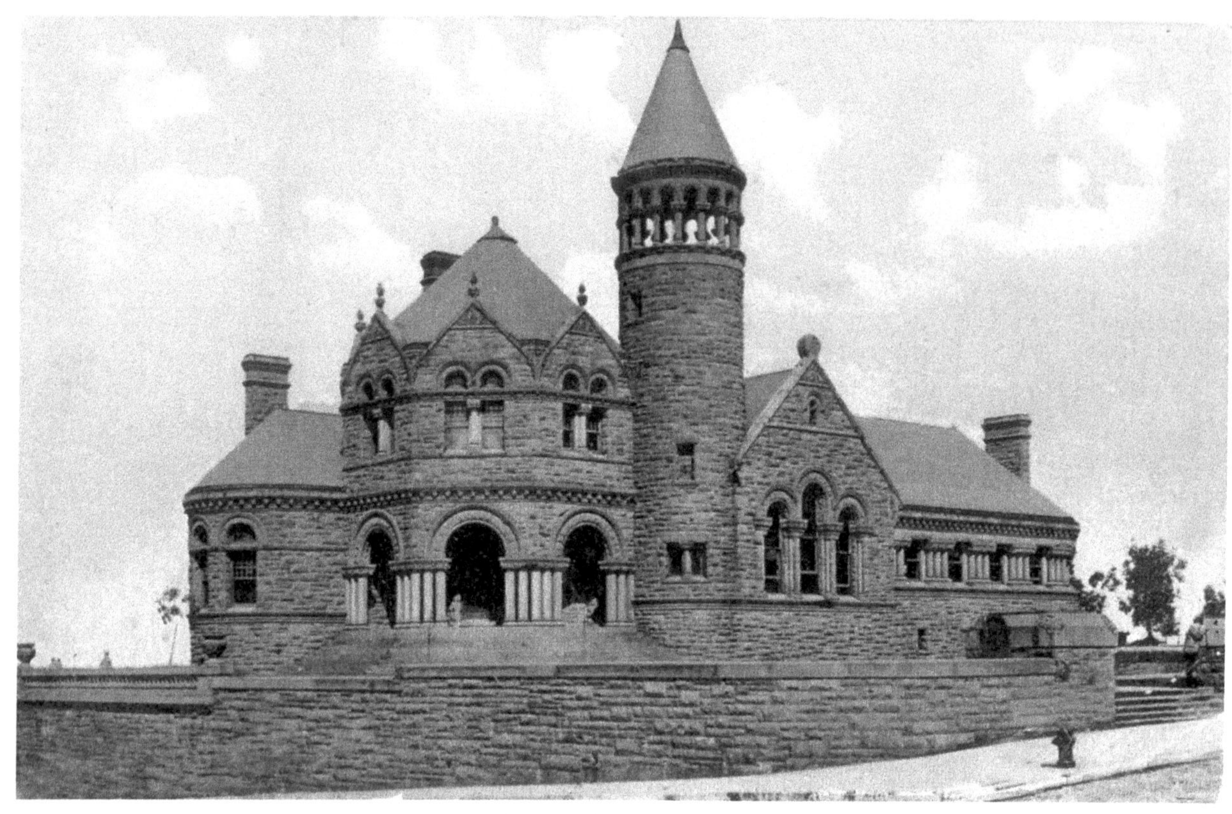

Cossitt Library, the city's first free public library, opened in 1893. It was financed by the heirs of dry goods magnate Frederick H. Cossitt. The original building featured a round tower and a triple-arched entry.

Workmen laying streetcar tracks on Main Street, 1891.

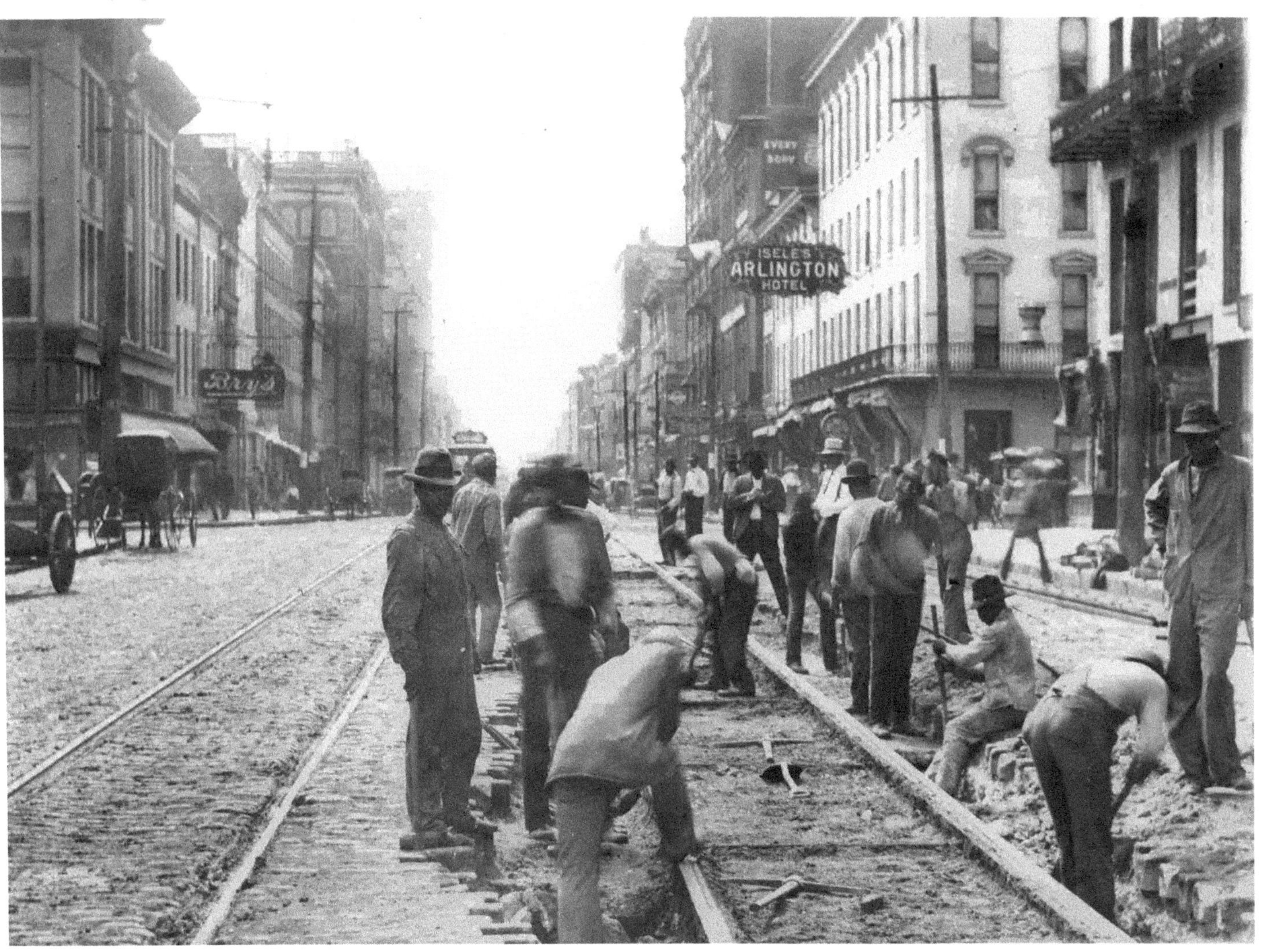

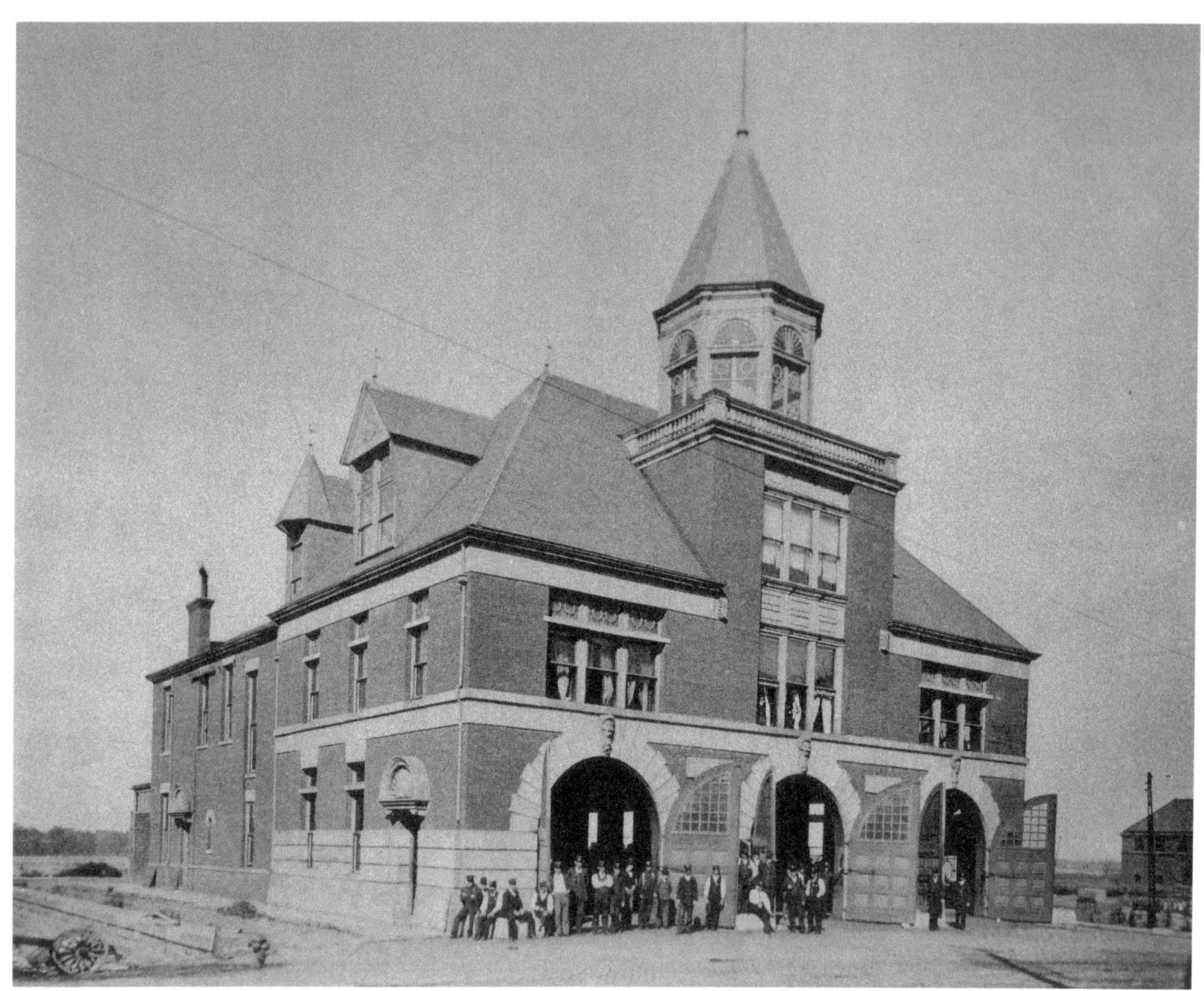

Fire Department Headquarters, 1895.

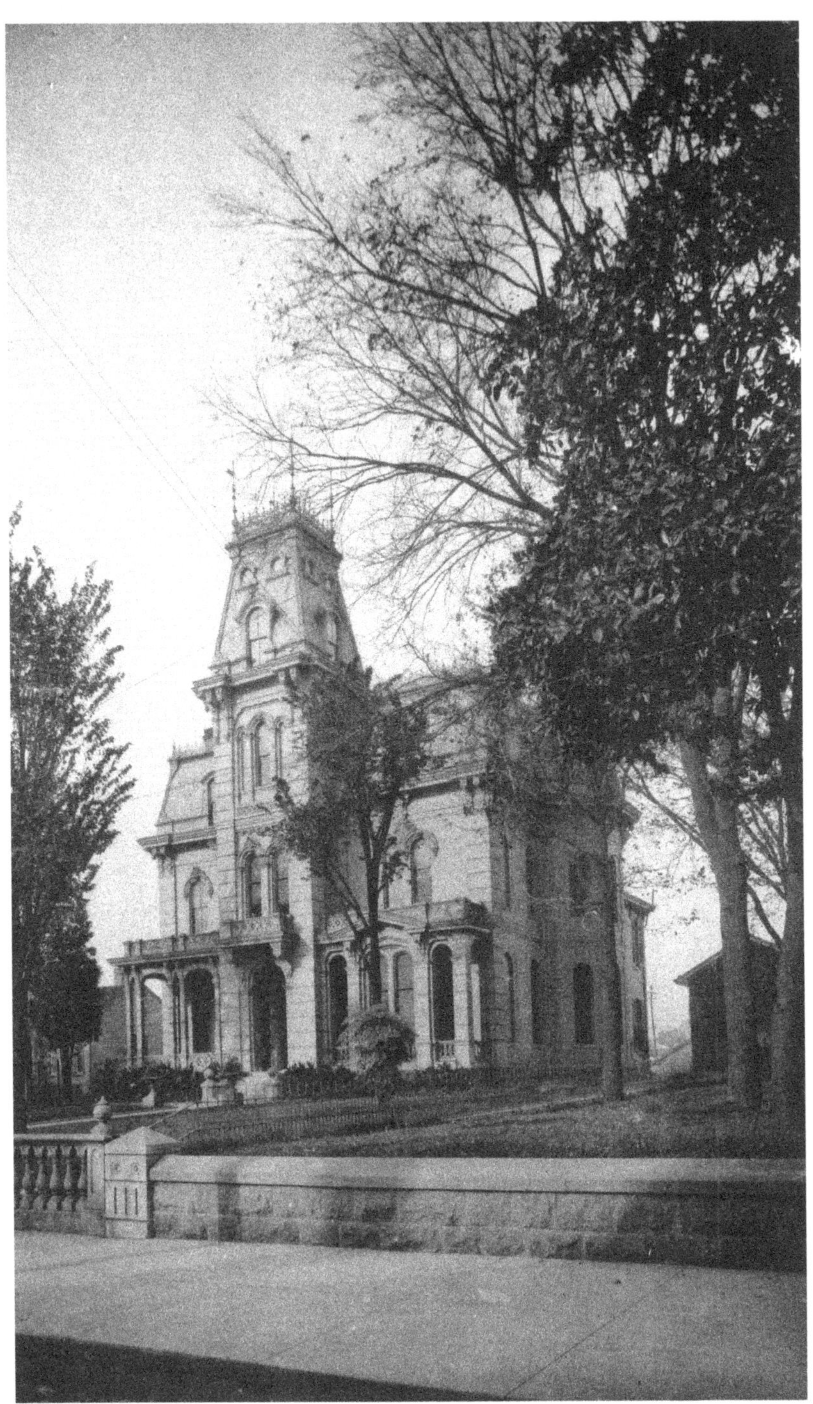

Cotton merchant Noland Fontaine's mansion at 340 Adams, 1900.

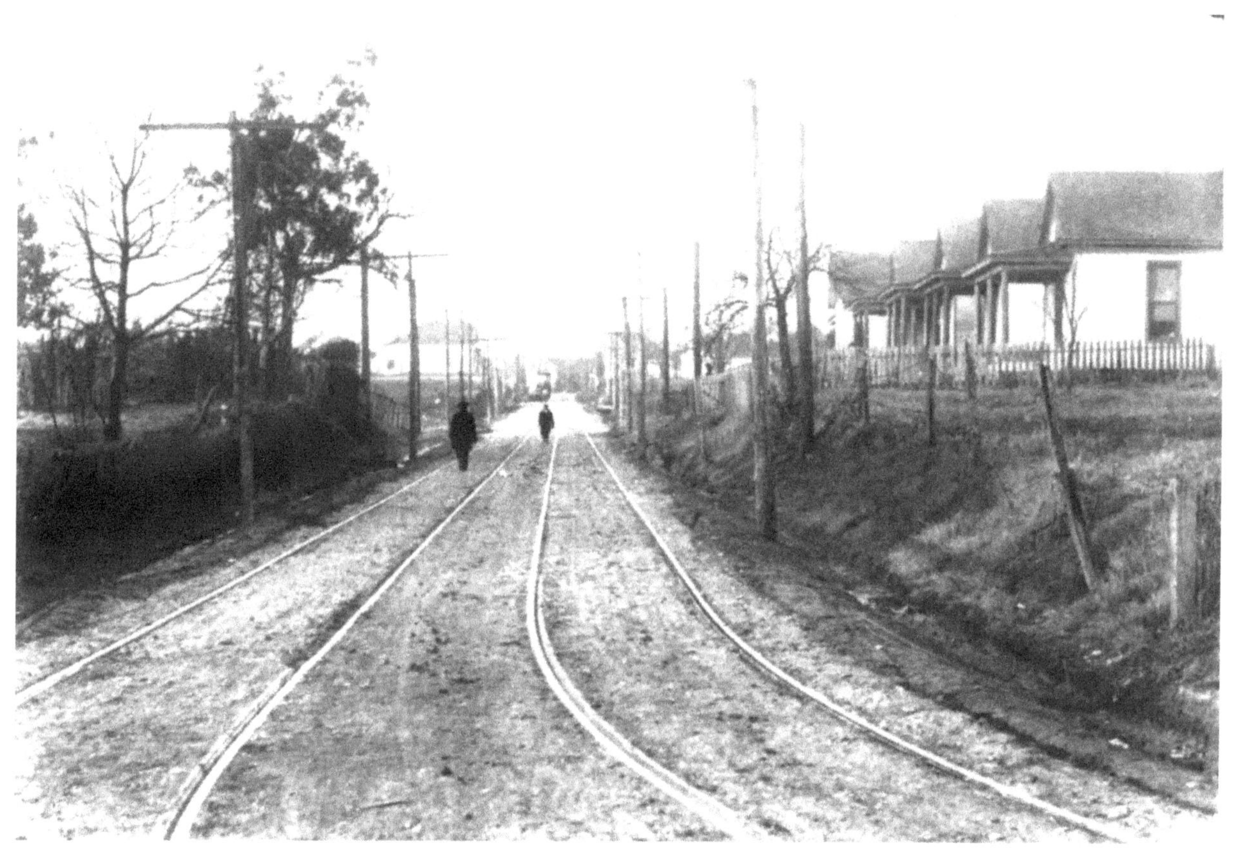

Scene on Latham Avenue at Trigg, looking North to McLemore Avenue, circa 1895.

Memphis firefighters, circa 1890.

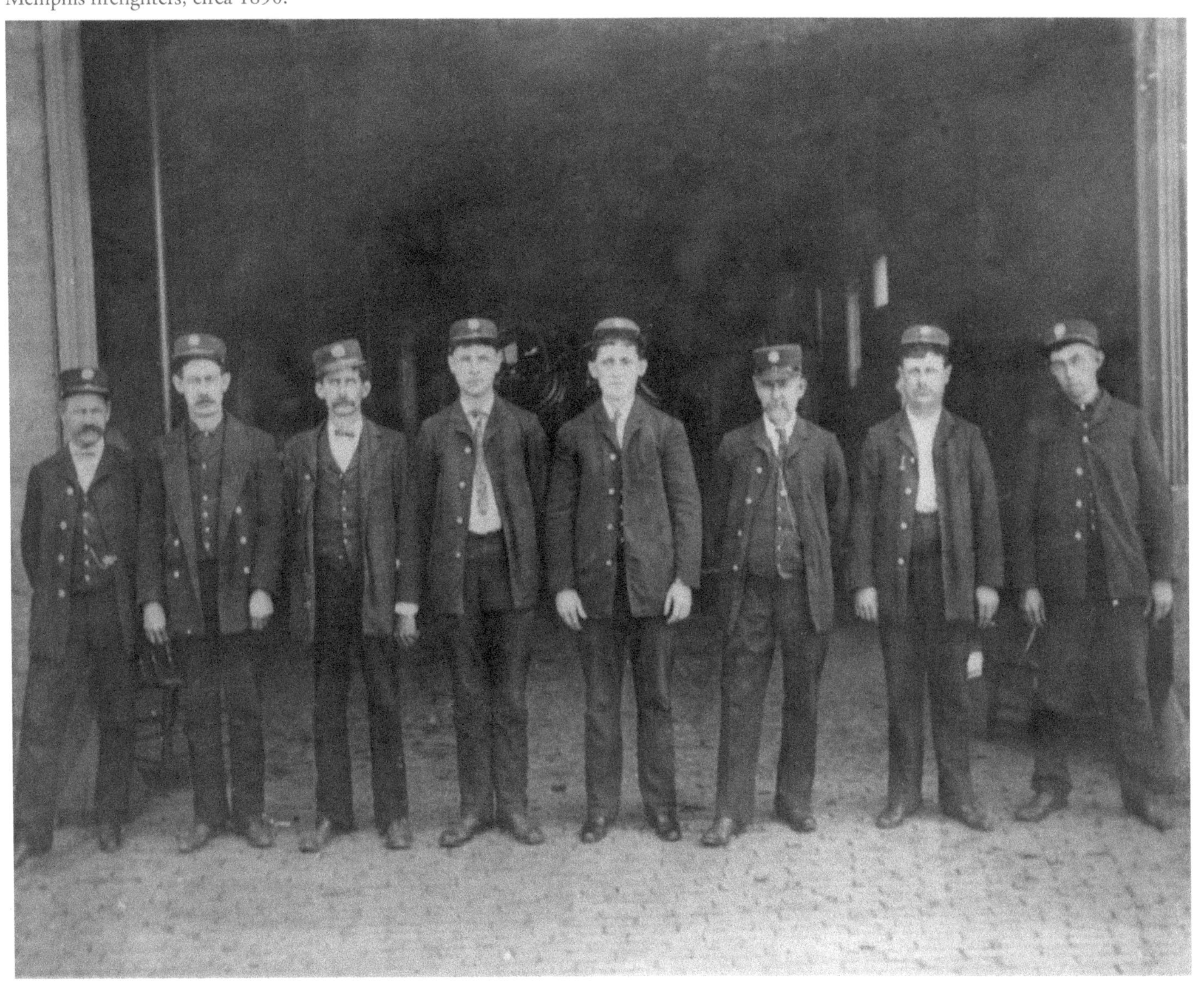

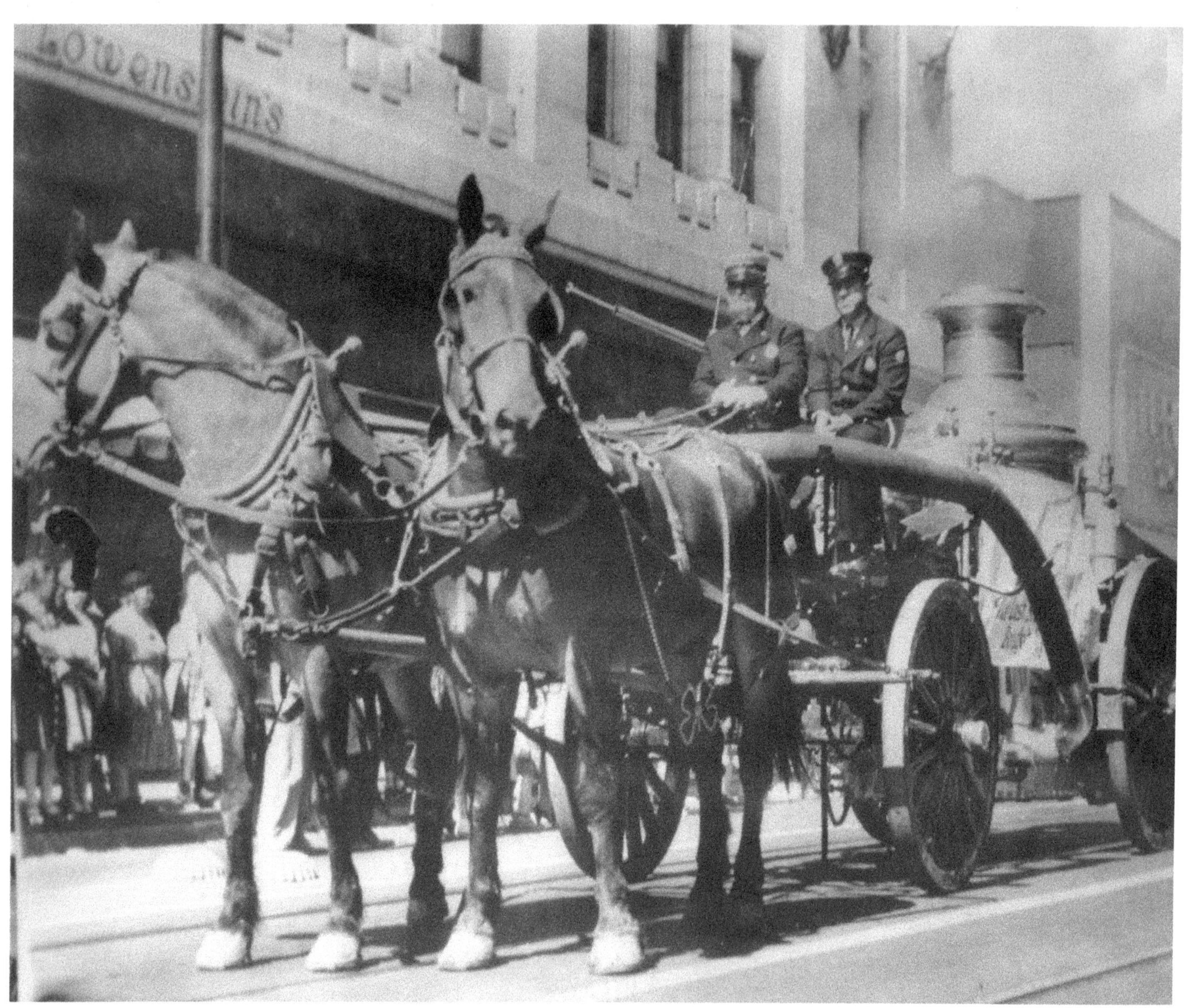

Early fire engine.

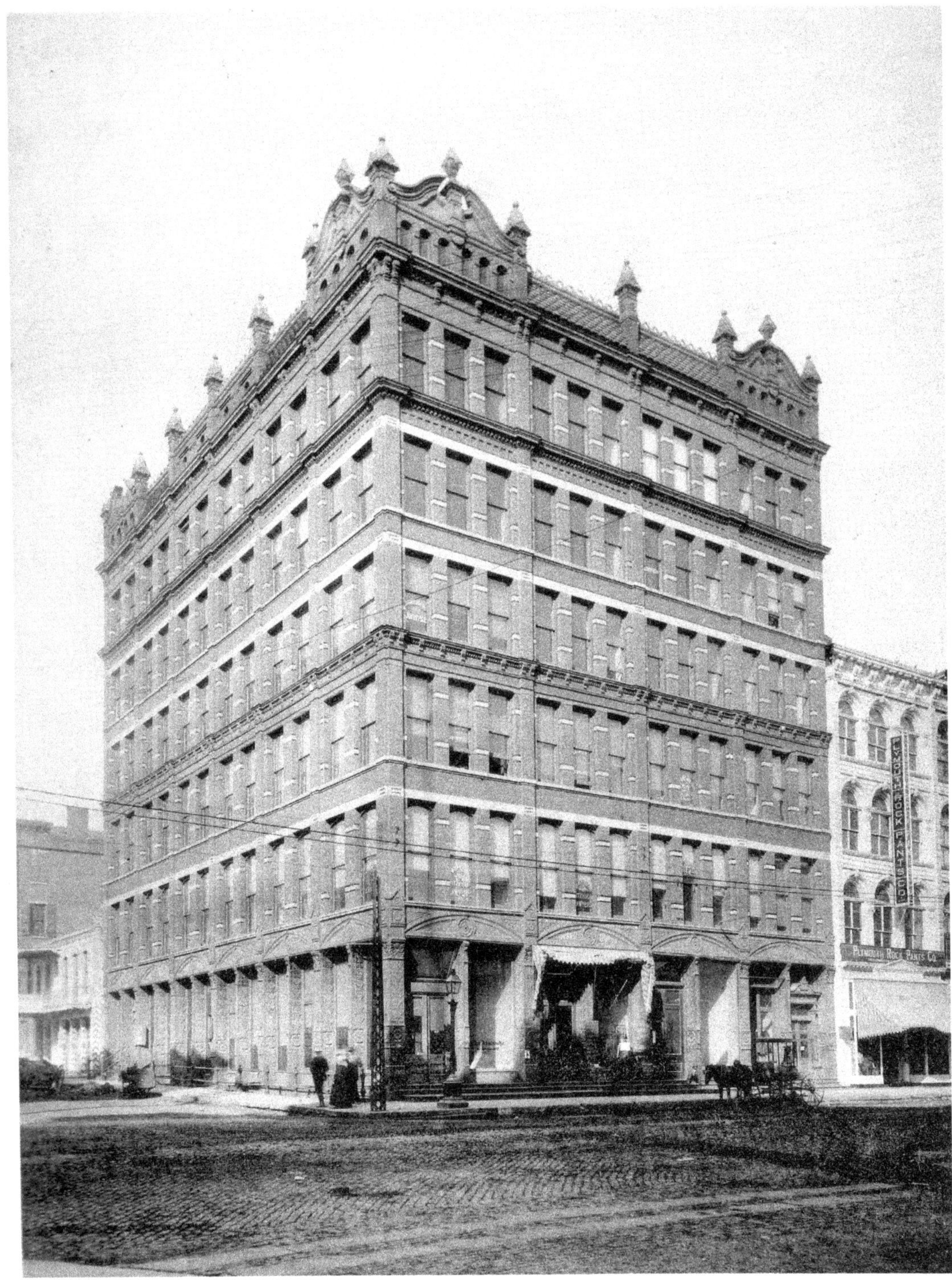

The Appeal Building, 1895. The building originally opened as the Collier Building in 1889, and in 1900 became the home of the Memphis newspaper The Appeal.

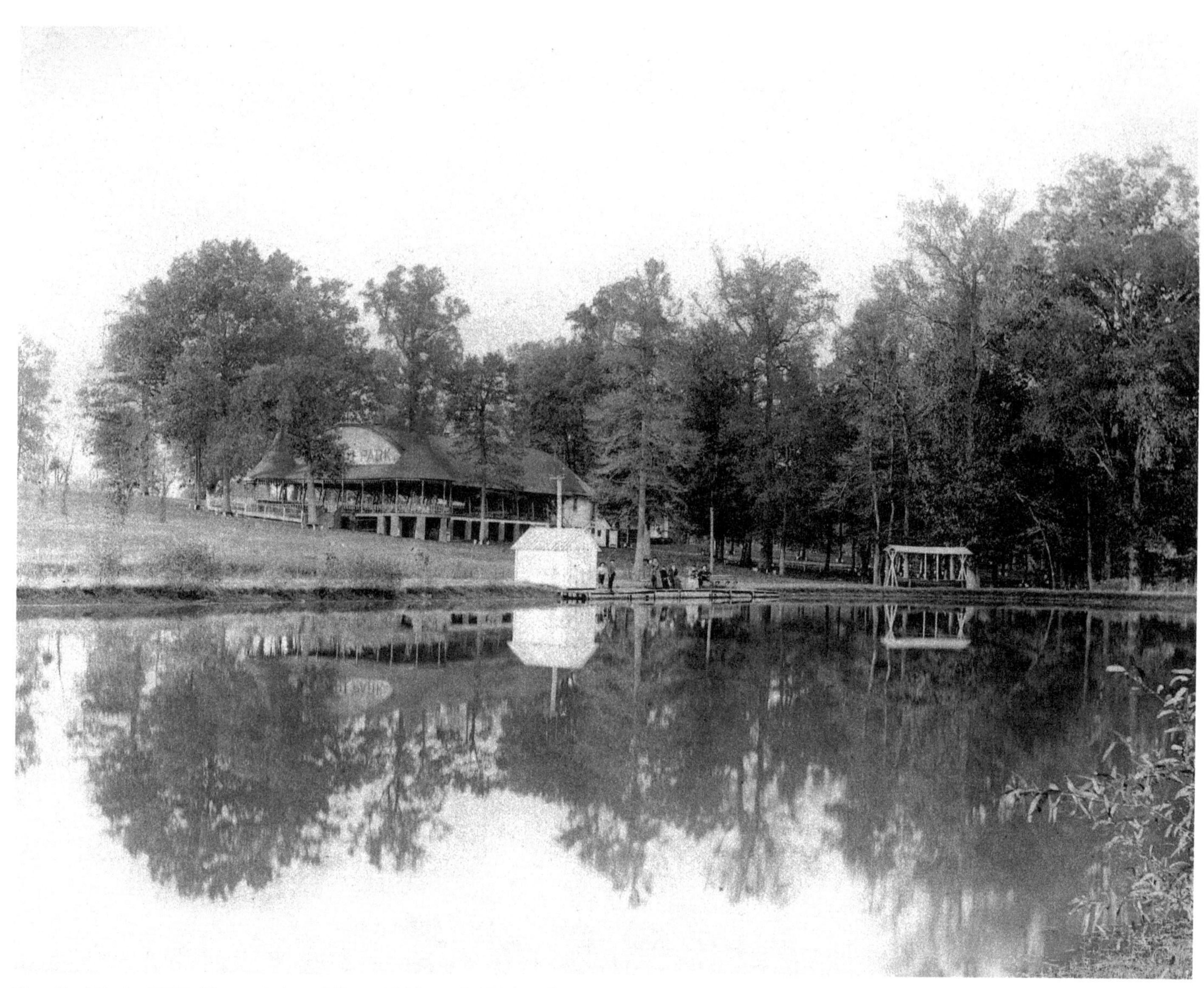

East End Park, 1895. The park lasted from 1889 until 1913 and was a favorite gathering place of the local German community.

Tennessee Brewing Company at 477 Tennessee Street, 1895.

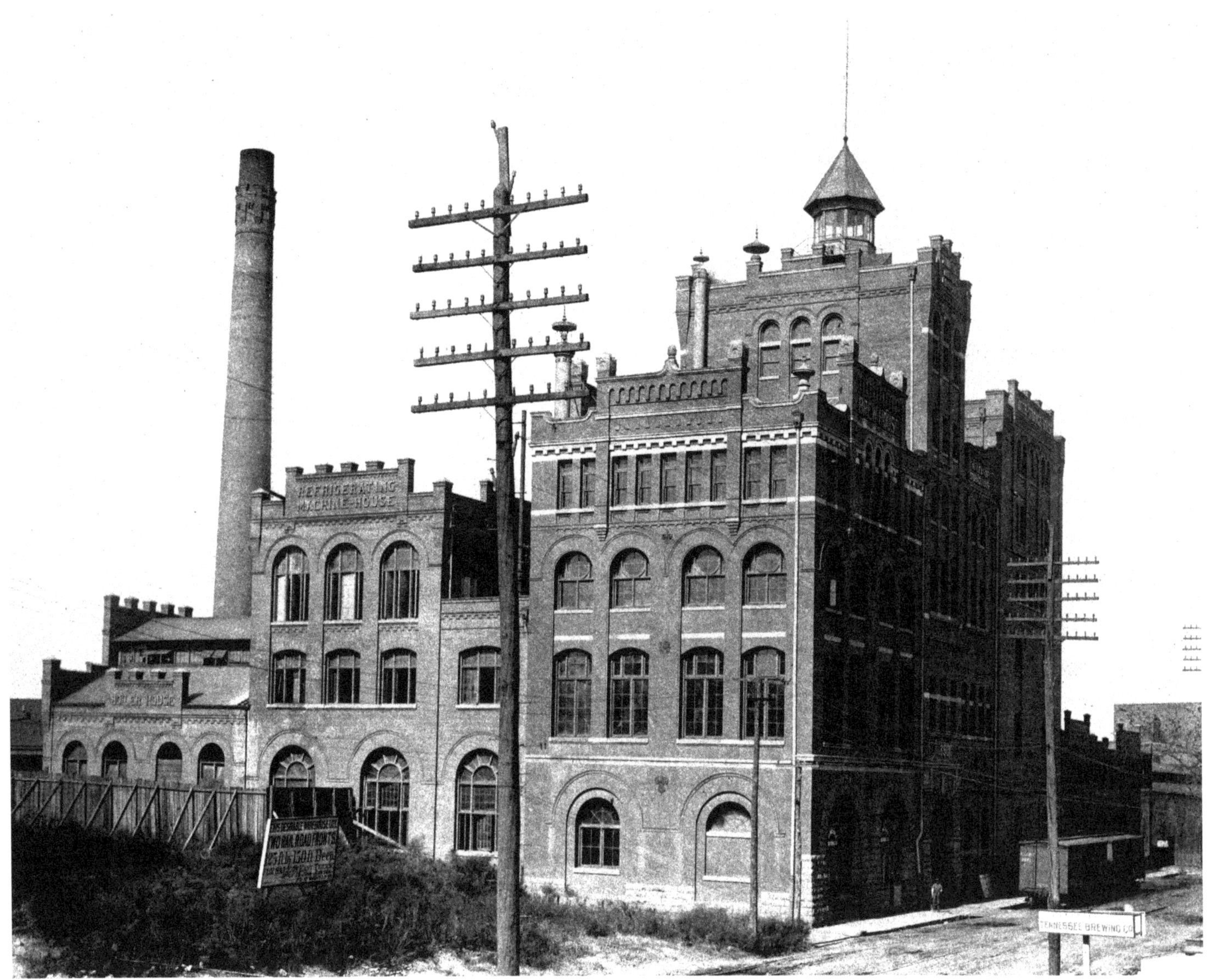

Residence of cotton merchant Napoleon Hill, 1900.

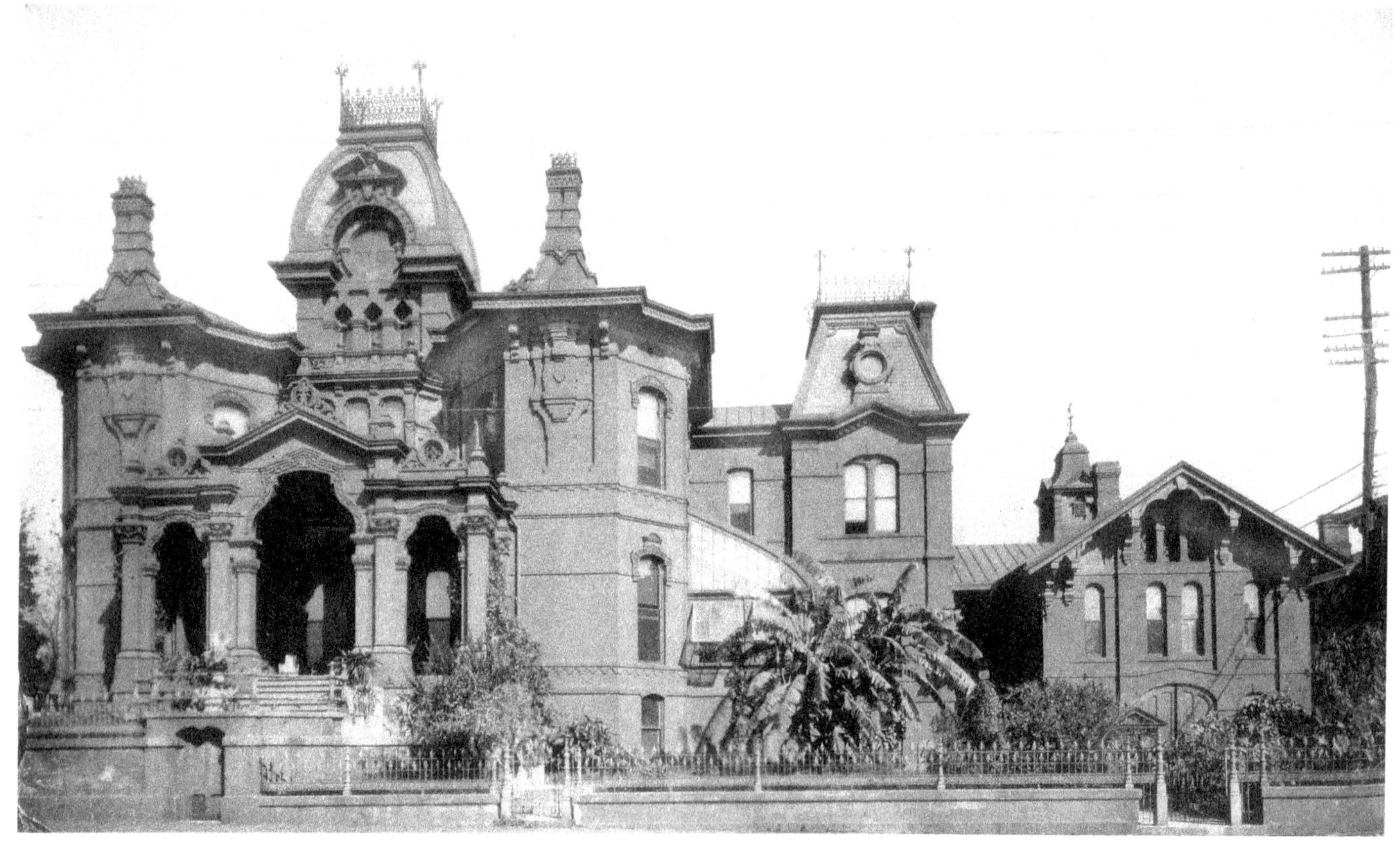

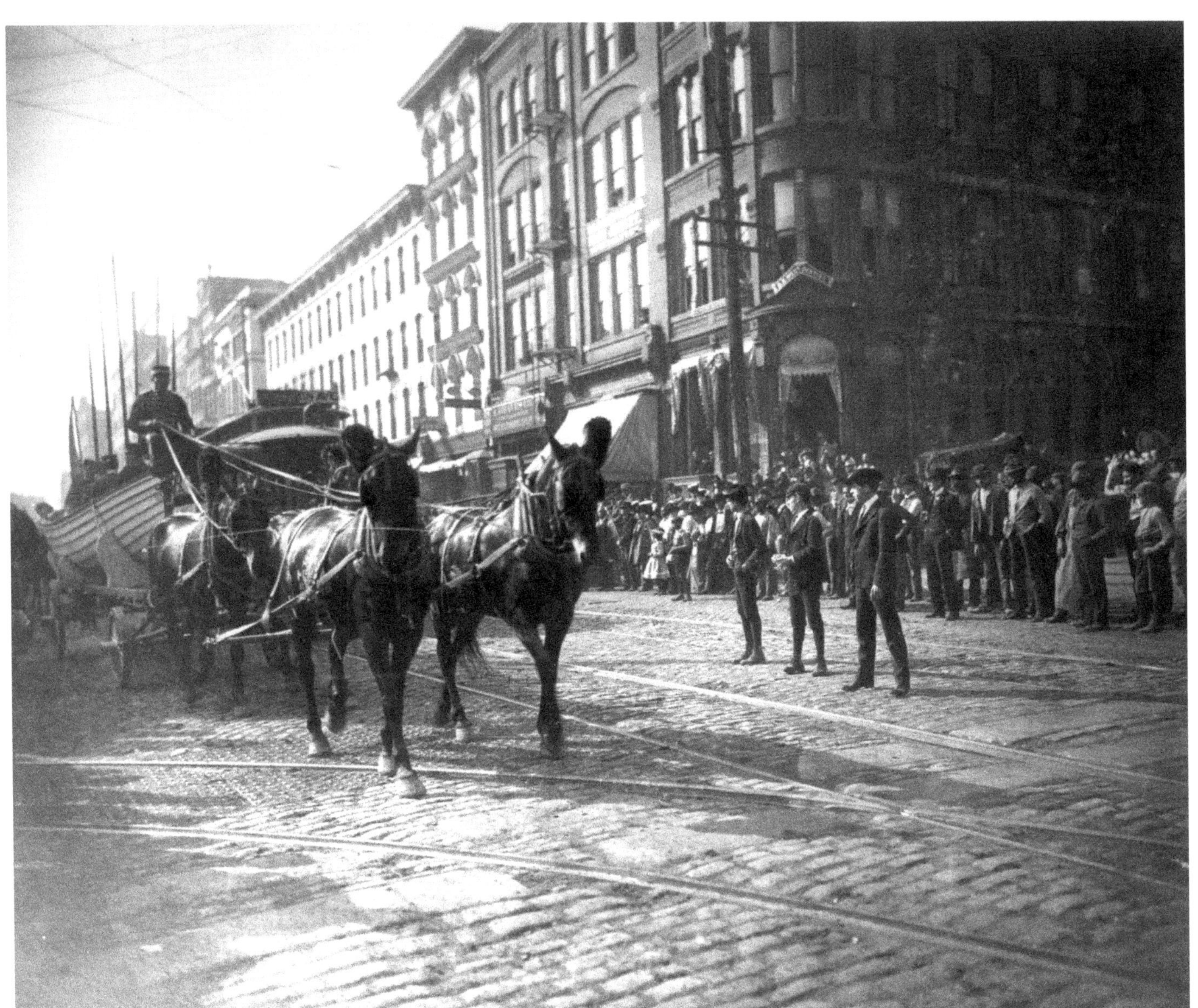

Main Street, 1880s.

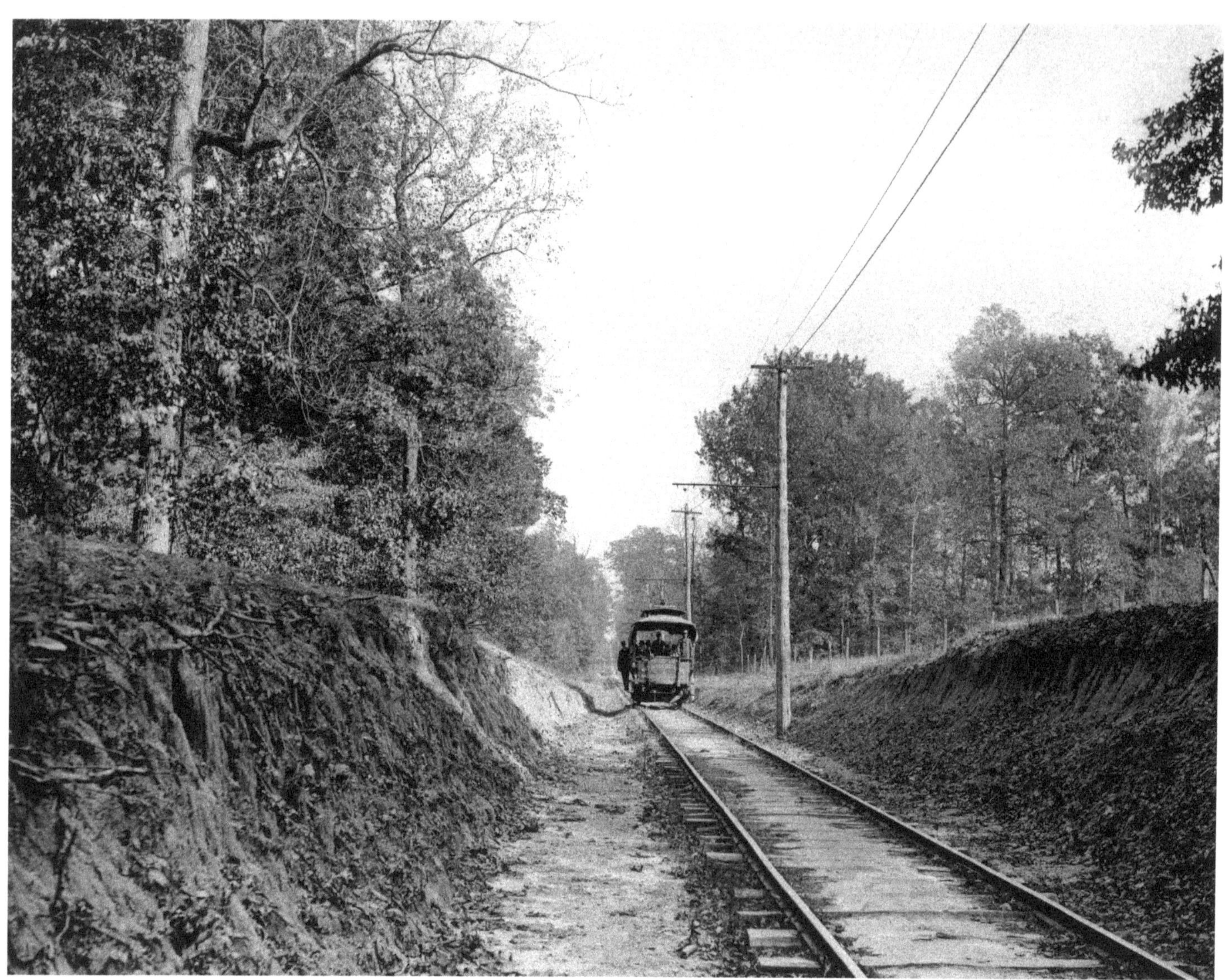

Raleigh Springs Car Line, 1895. A railroad was built to this popular resort in 1871 then replaced by an electric street car line in 1891.

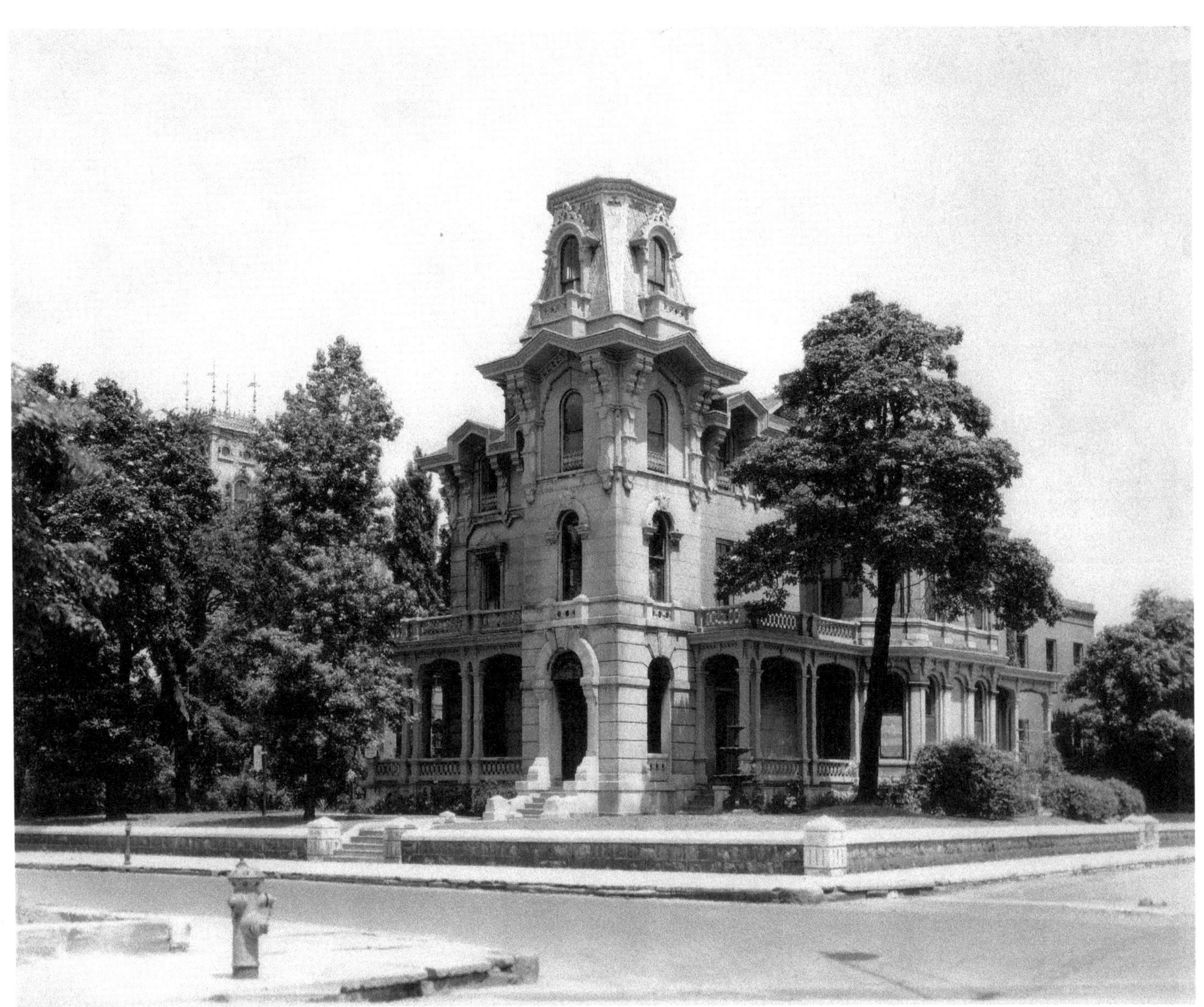

The James Lee House in Victorian Village.

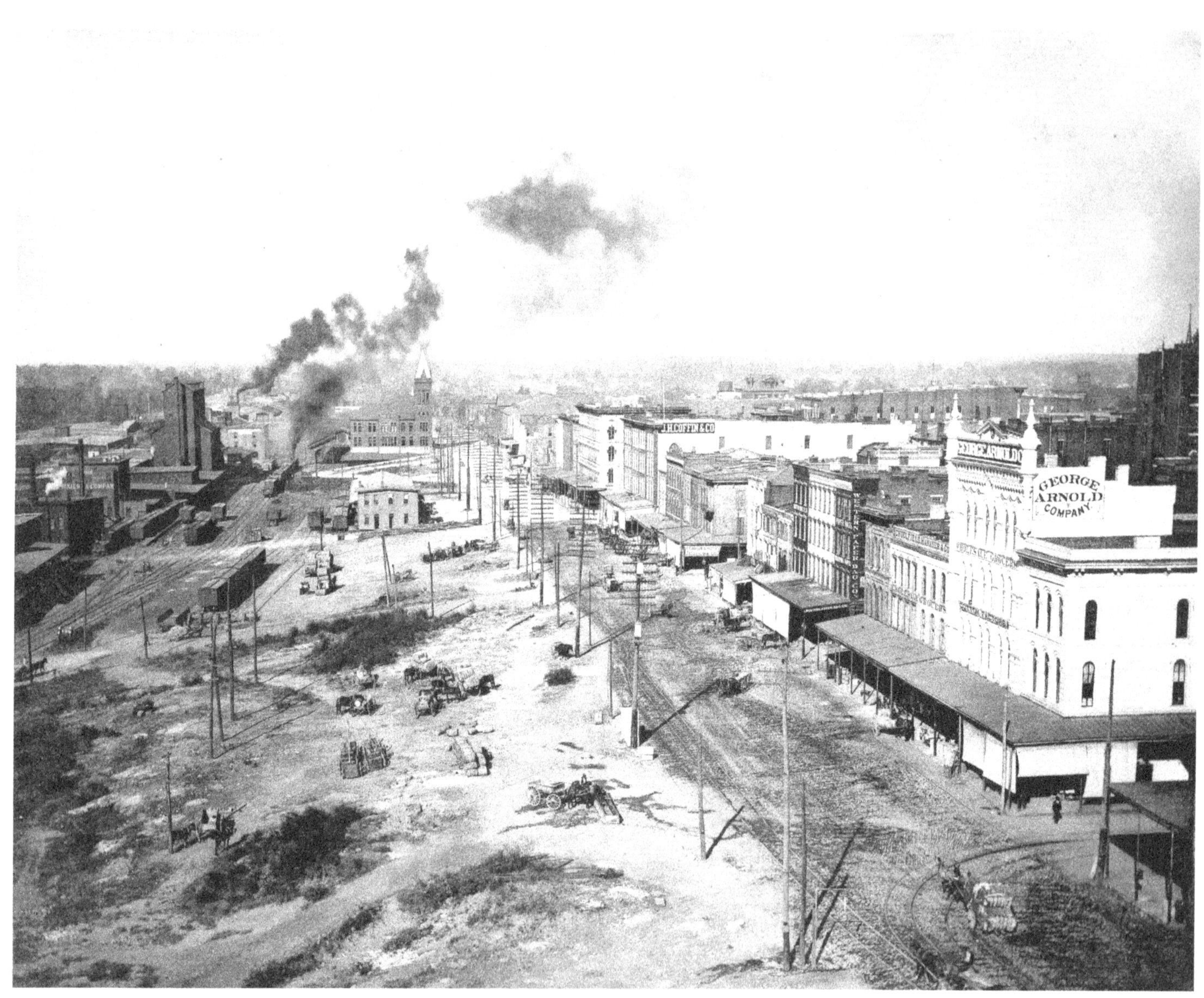

View of Front Street from the Government Building, circa 1895.

Orgill Brothers on Front Street.

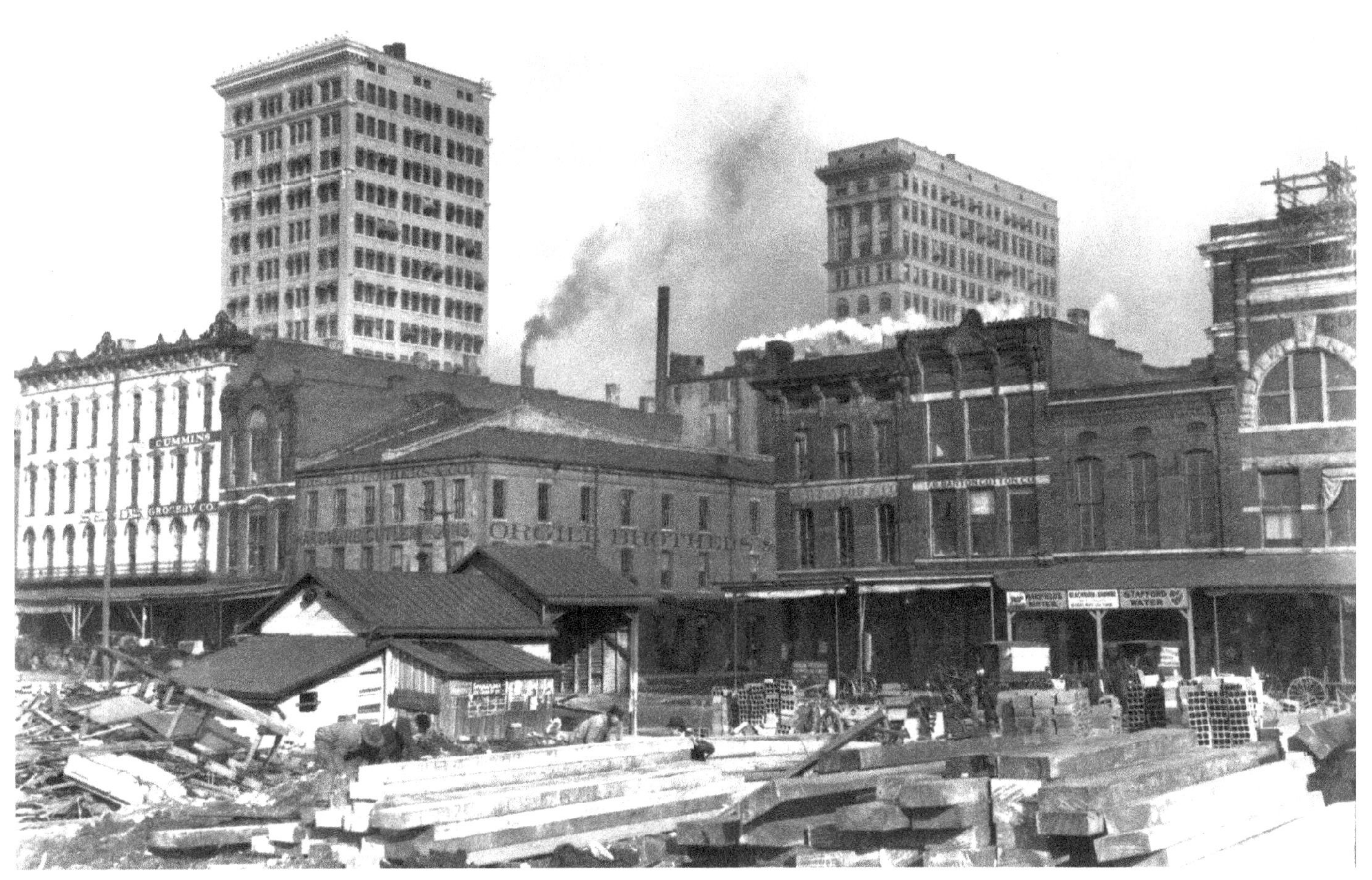

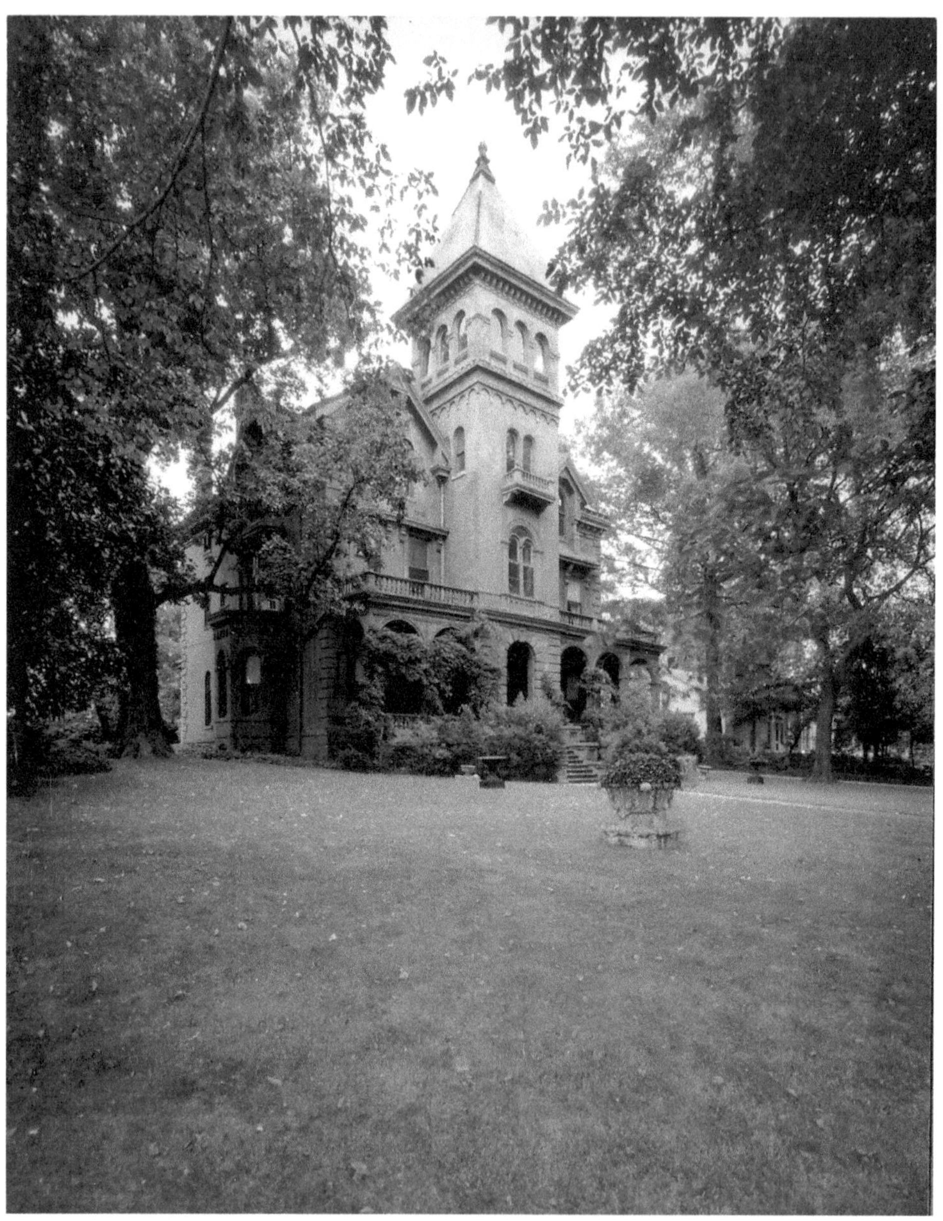

The Mallory-Neely House at 652 Adams Avenue in Victorian Village. The house was built in the 1850s and additions were made in the 1870s and 1880s.

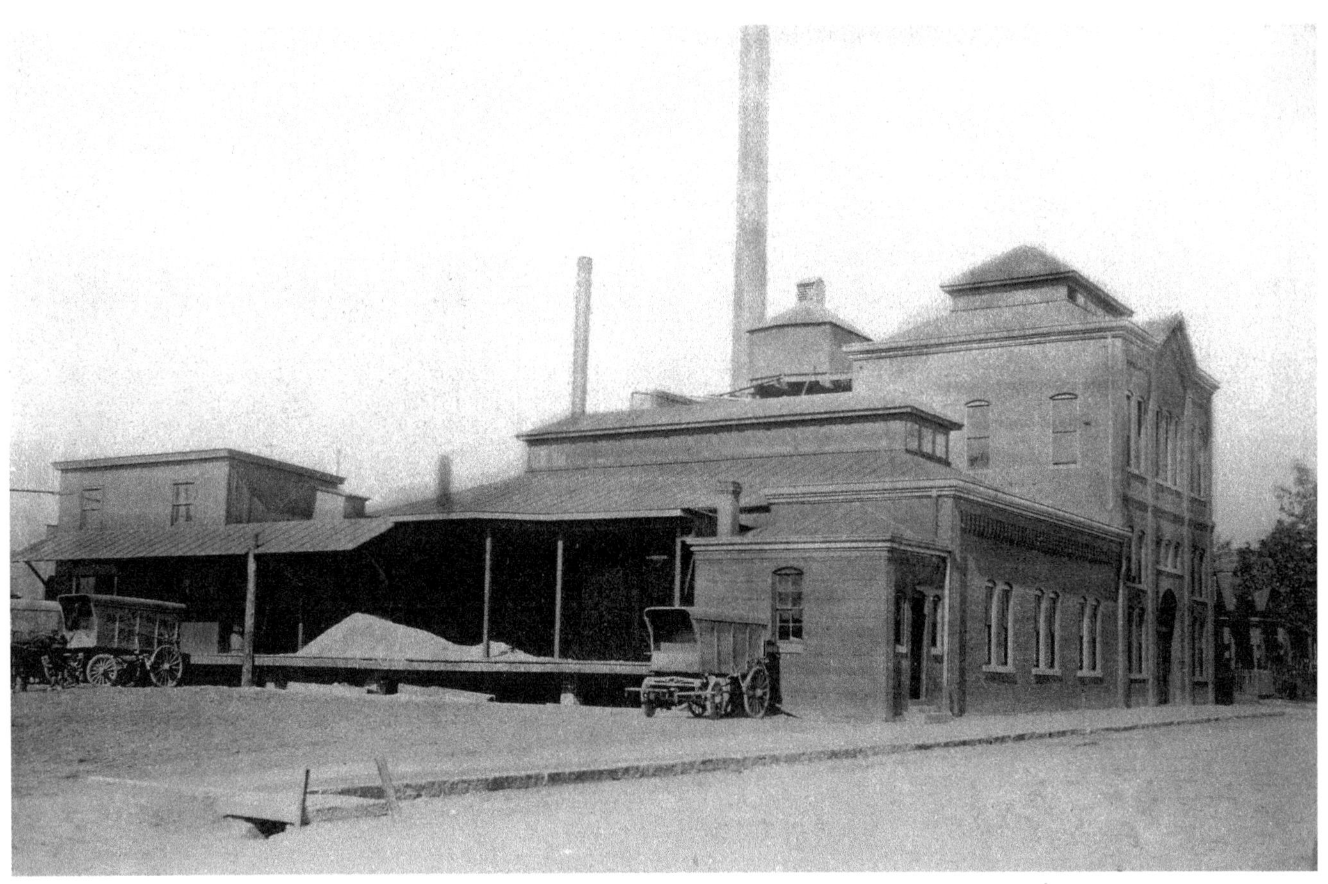

Bohlen-Huse Ice Company. John Bohlen began operating the City Ice House before 1855. Originally, ice was cut from frozen northern lakes and stored in the company's underground ice houses. Later, artificial means were used to produce ice from local artesian water.

The Magevney House at 198 Adams, built circa 1833. Irish-born Eugene Magevney was a teacher and real estate entrepreneur. His home was the site of the first Catholic Mass, Marriage, and Baptism in Memphis.

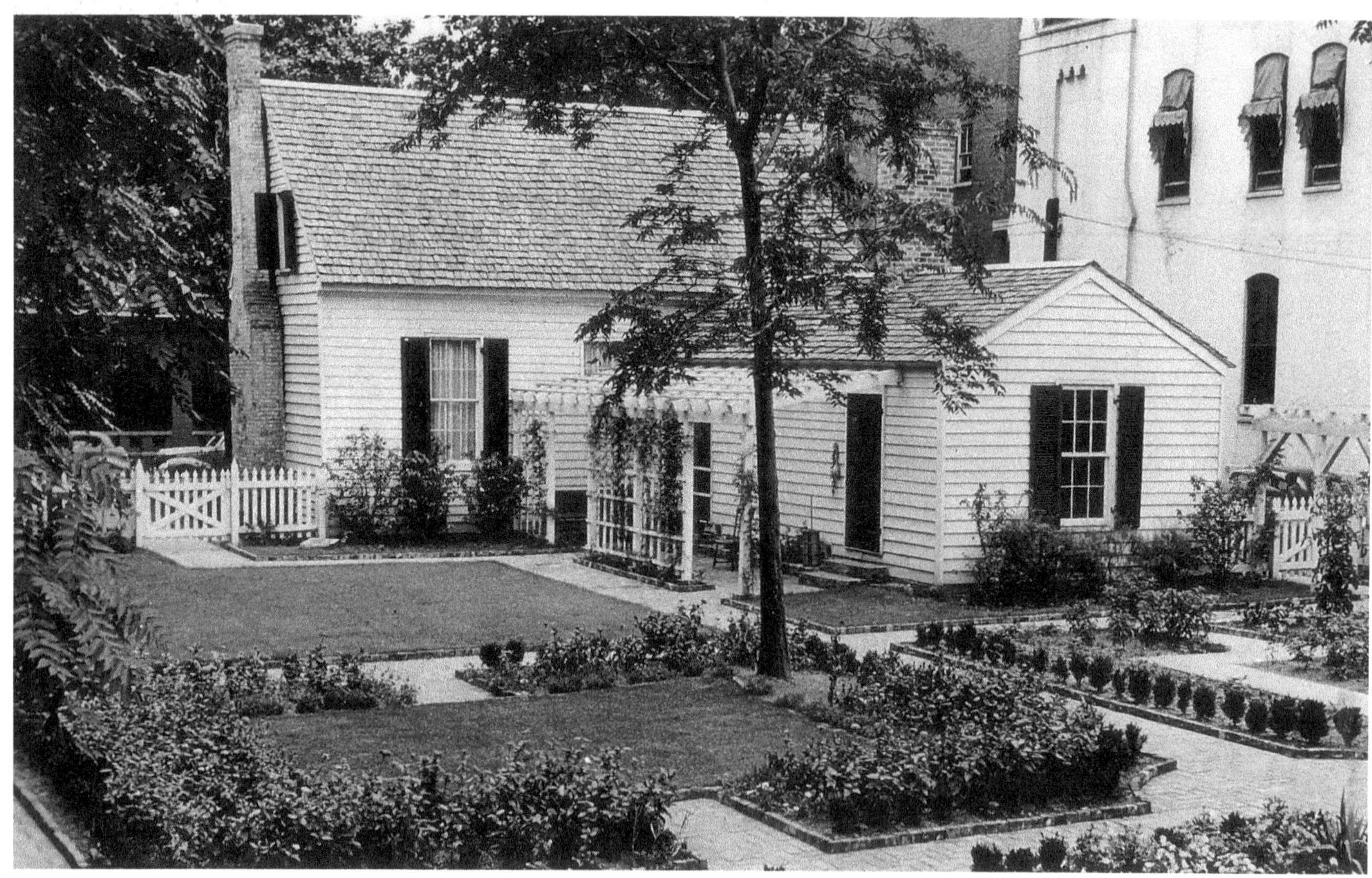

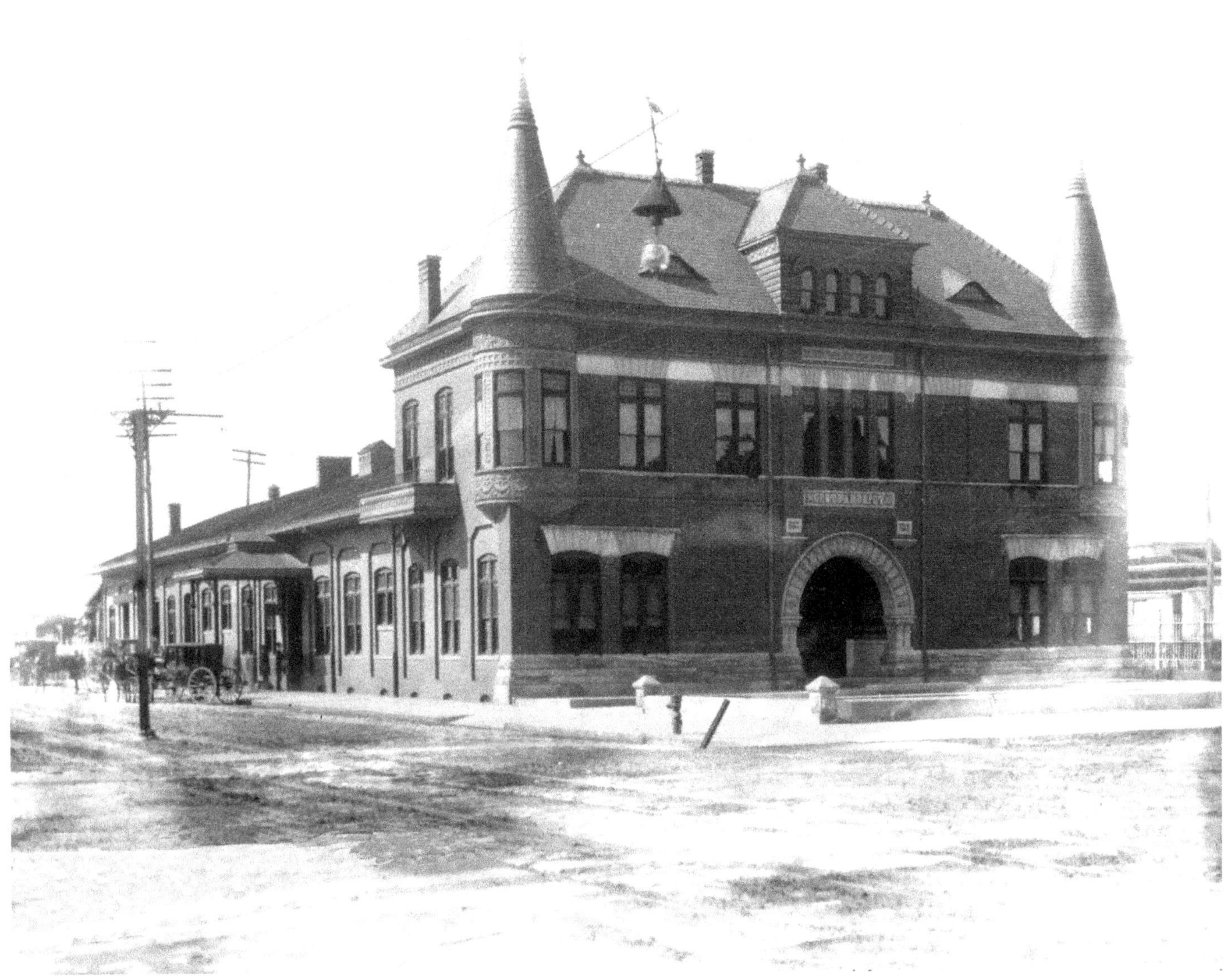

Illinois Central Railroad Depot, 1899.

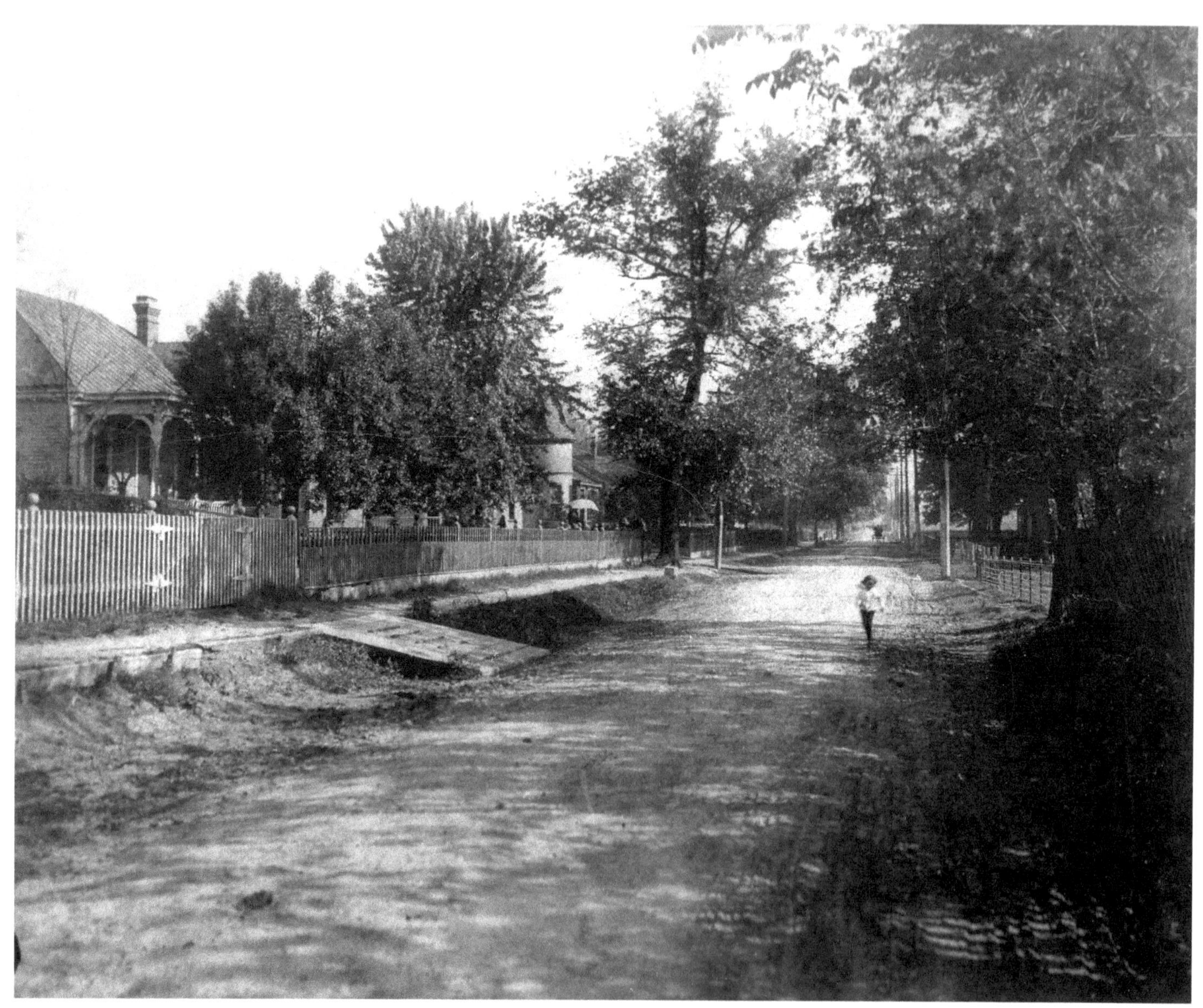

McLean Avenue, circa 1890.

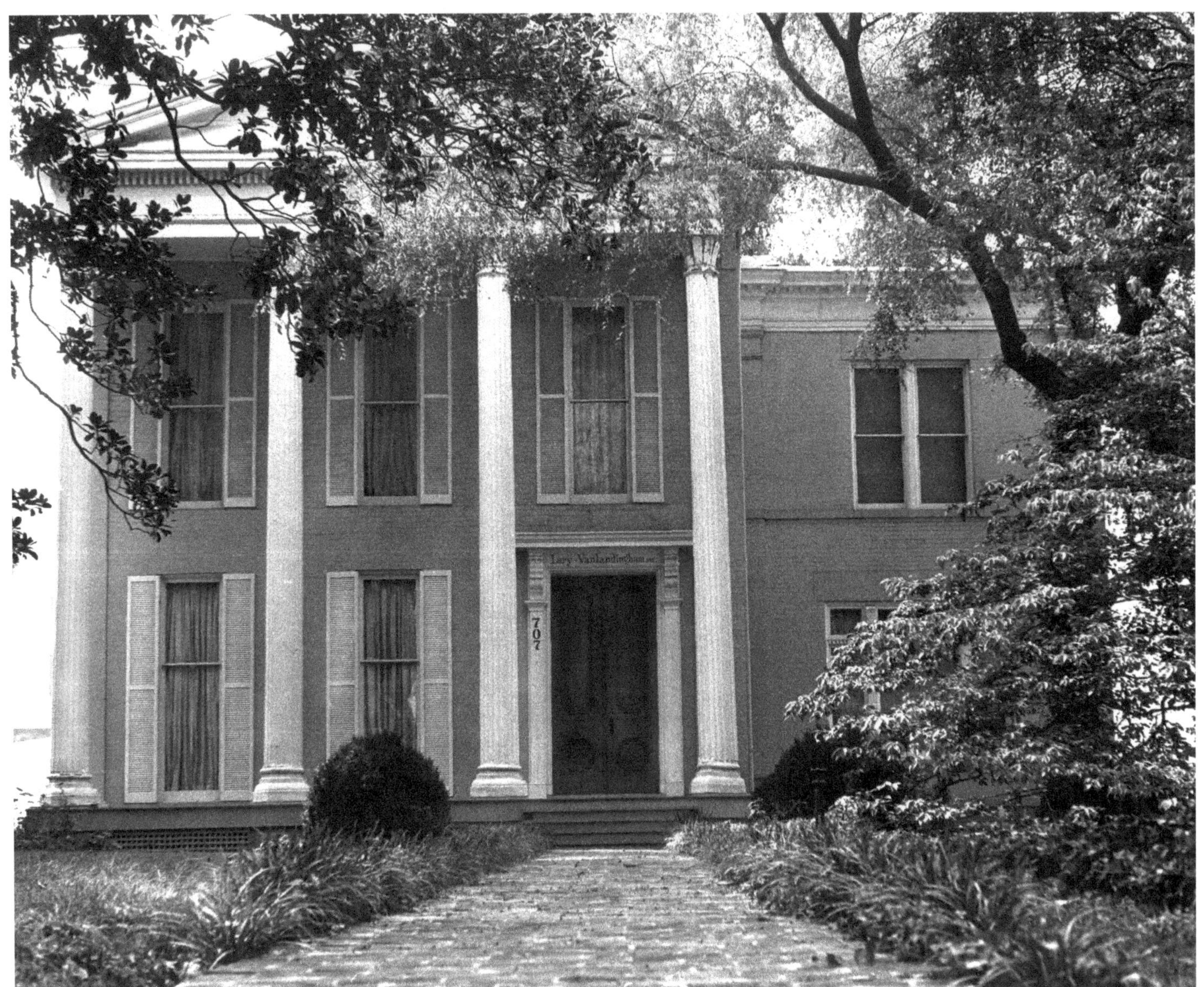

The Pillow-McIntyre House at 707 Adams in Victorian Village. Built in the 1850s, the home once belonged to Civil War General Gideon Pillow. The Free Art School of the Memphis Art Association held classes in the home from the 1940s to the 1960s.

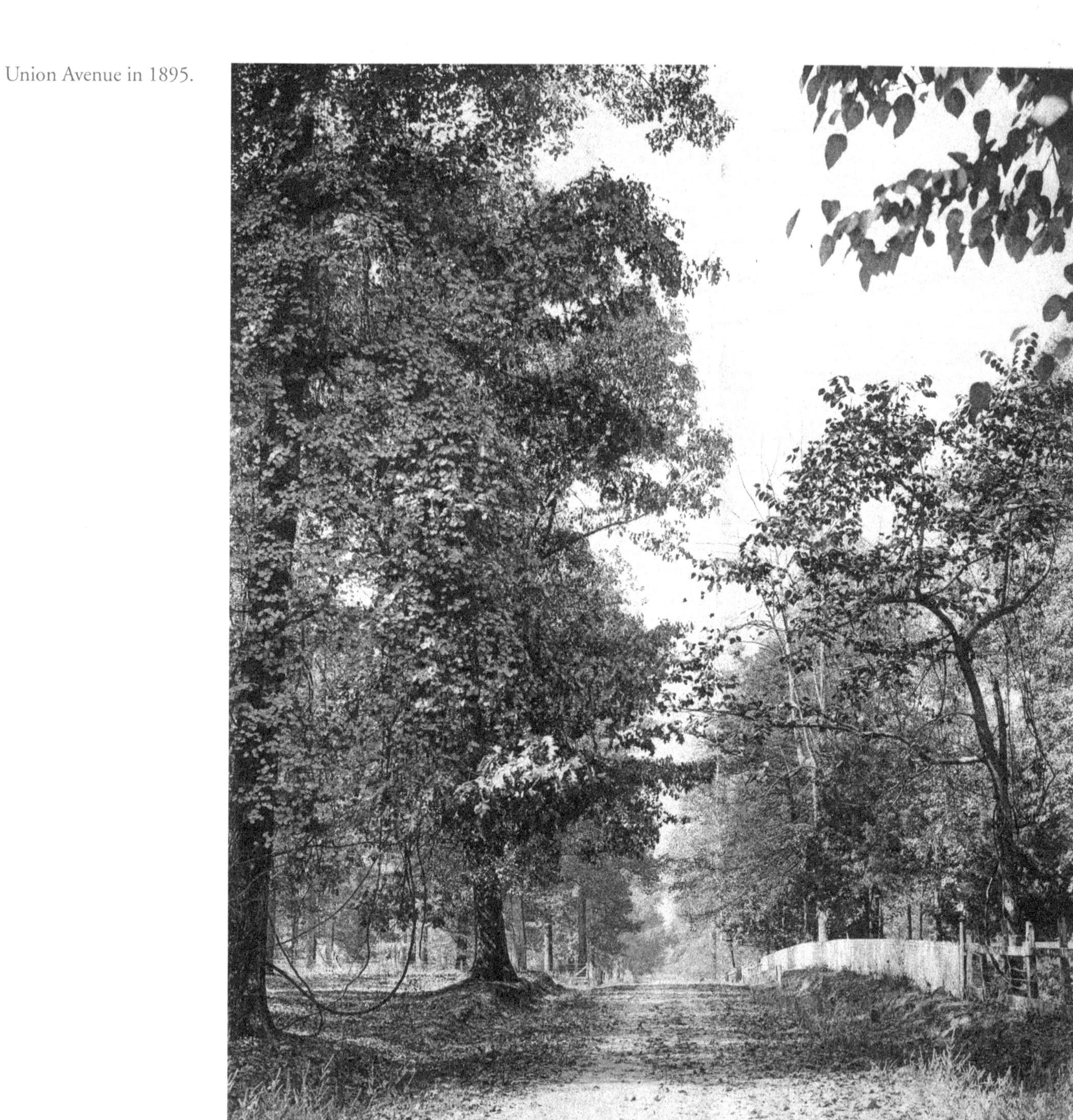

Union Avenue in 1895.

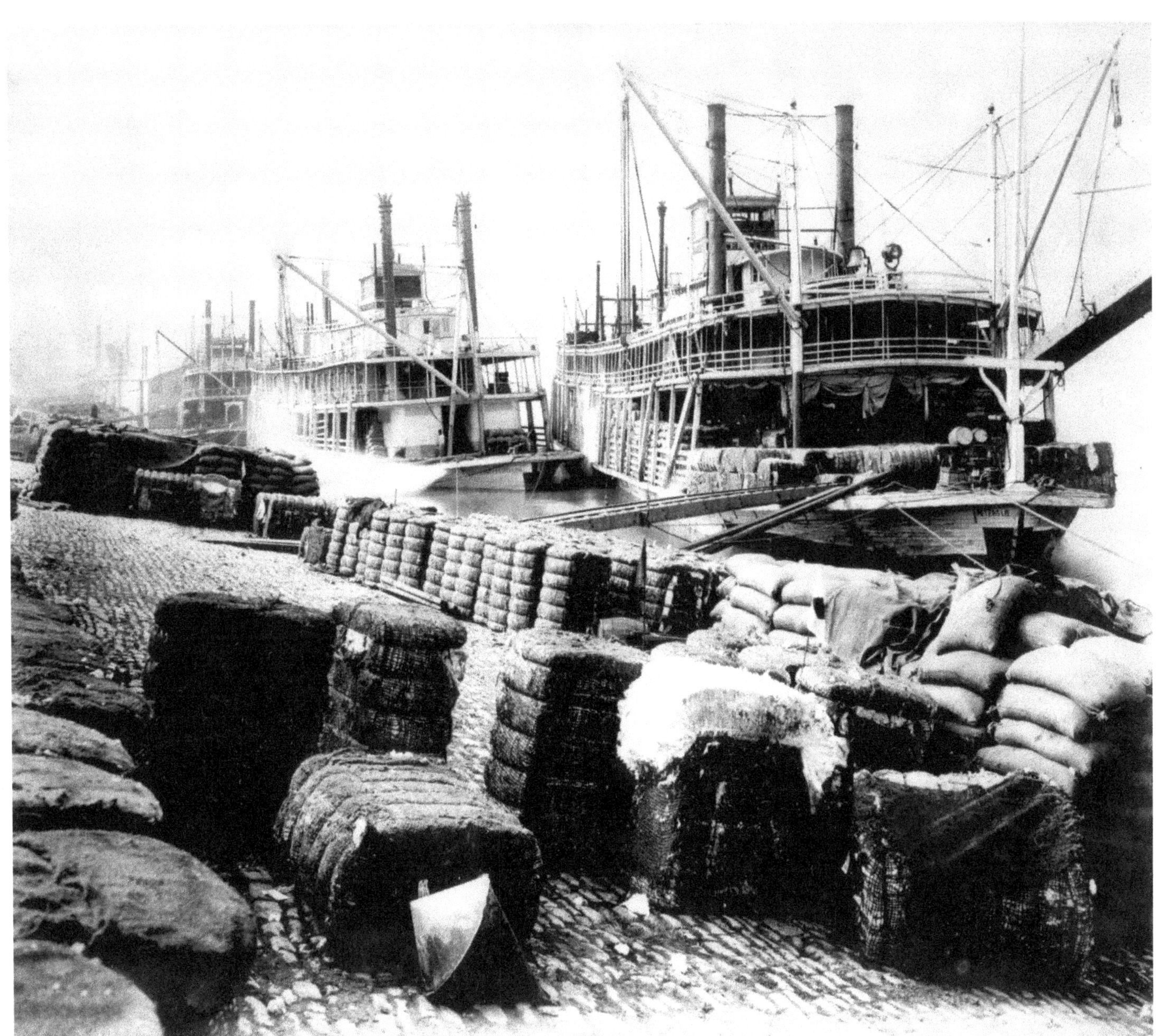

The *Peters Lee* shipped freight between Cincinnati and Memphis from 1904 through 1913.

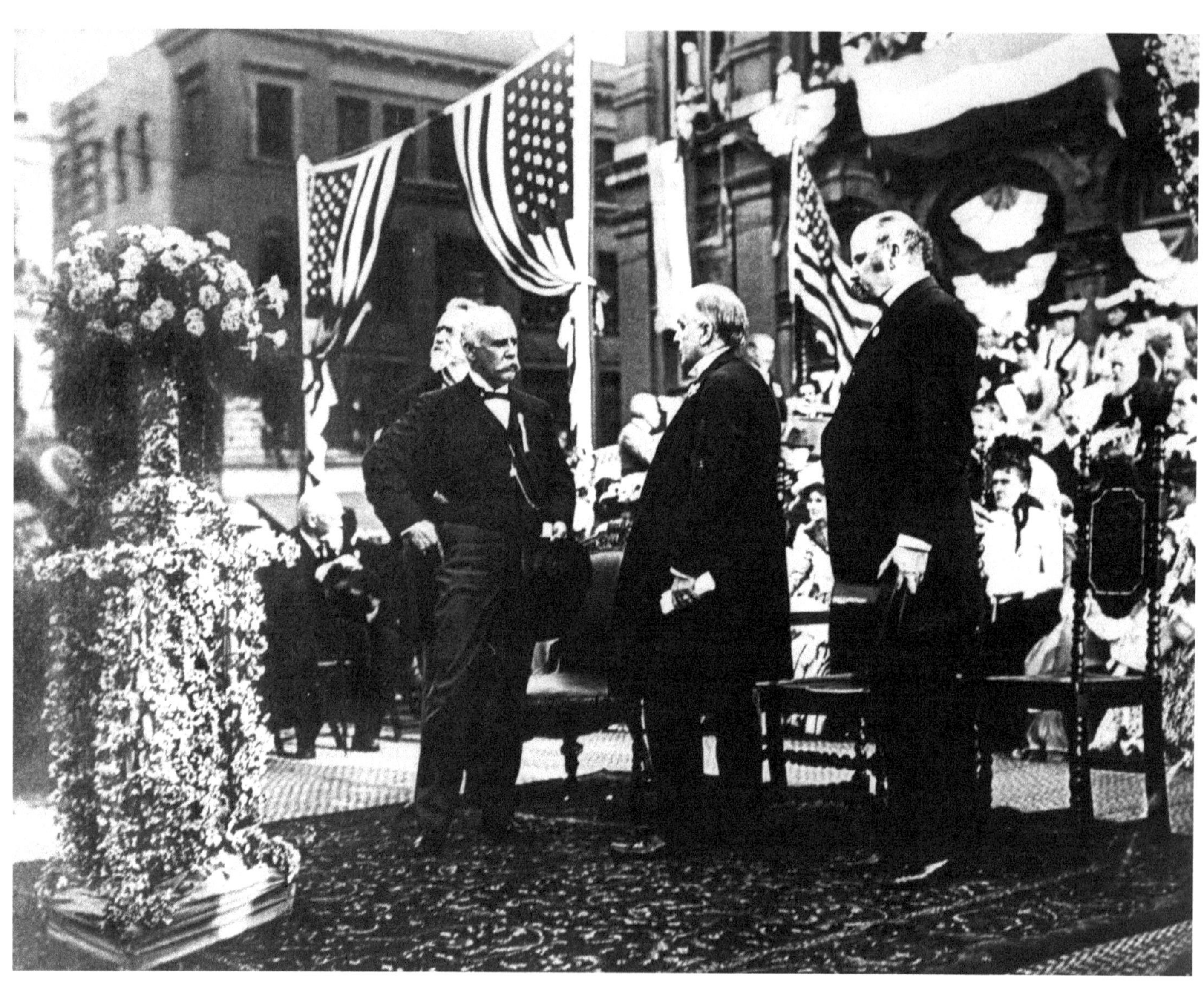

President William McKinley being greeted by Memphis Mayor J.J. Williams in Court Square on May 1, 1901.

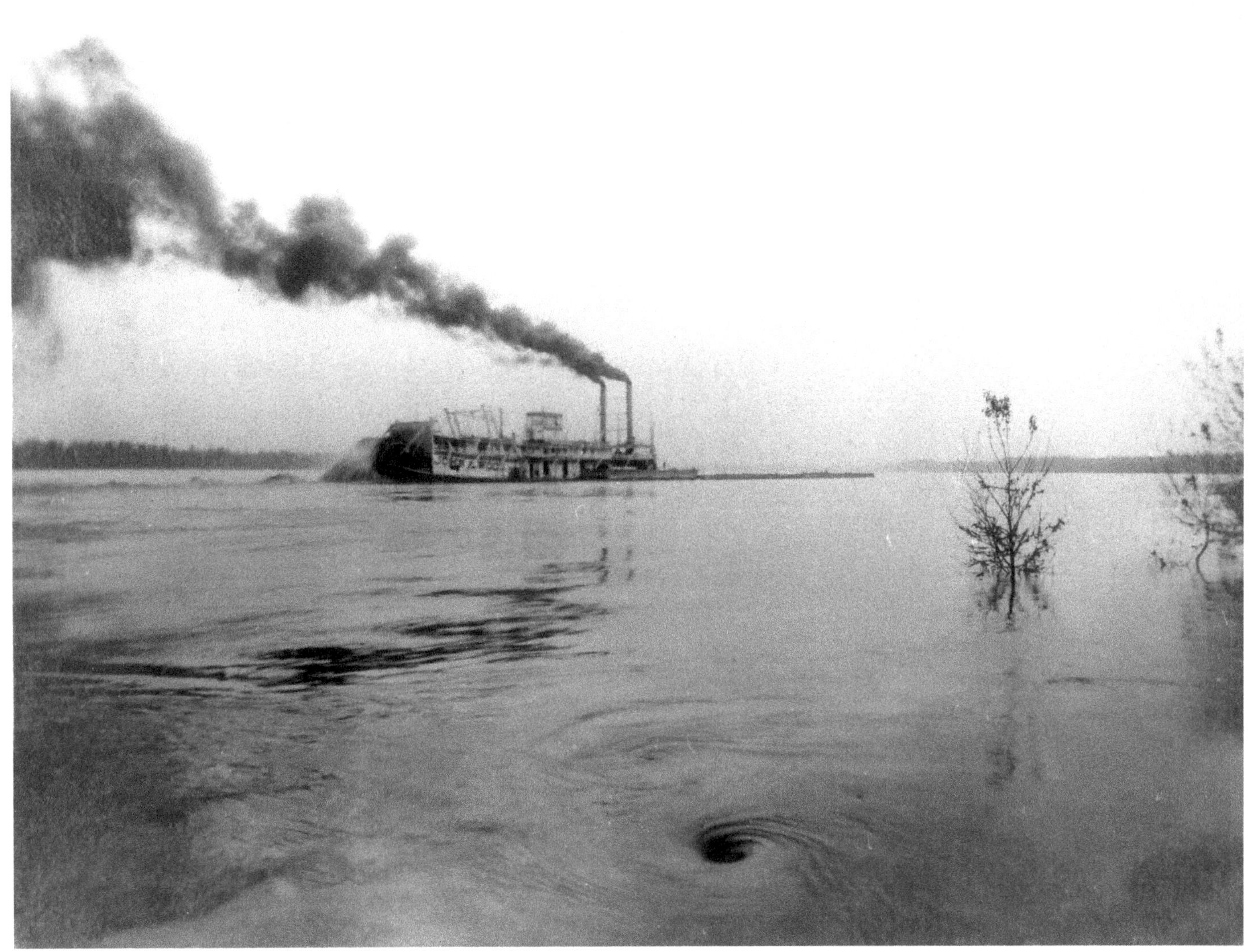

A small whirlpool forms in the Mississippi River with the steamer *John A. Wood* in the background.

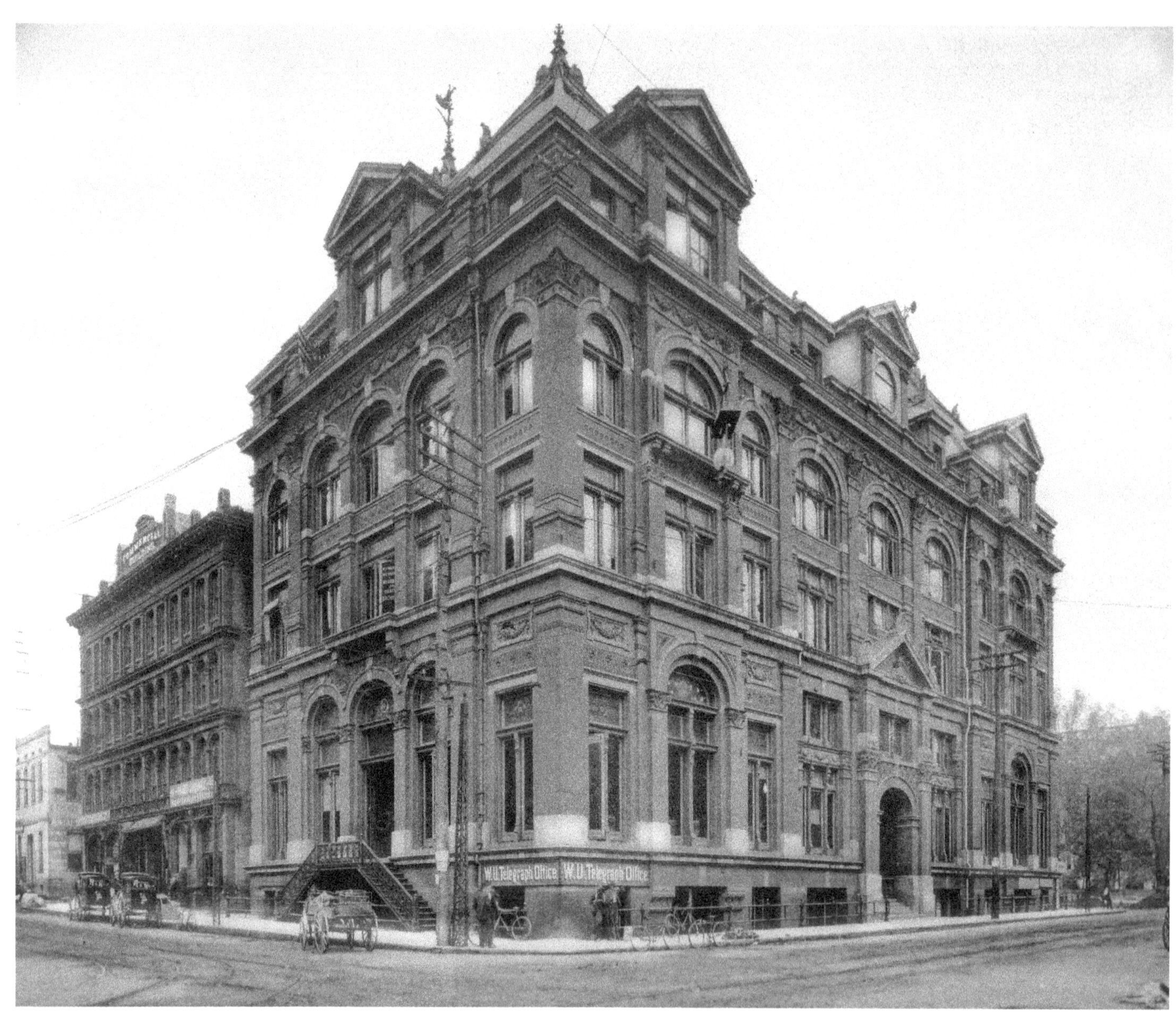

The Cotton Exchange Building at the corner of Madison and Second, 1900.

The steamer *Katie Robbins*, circa 1890.

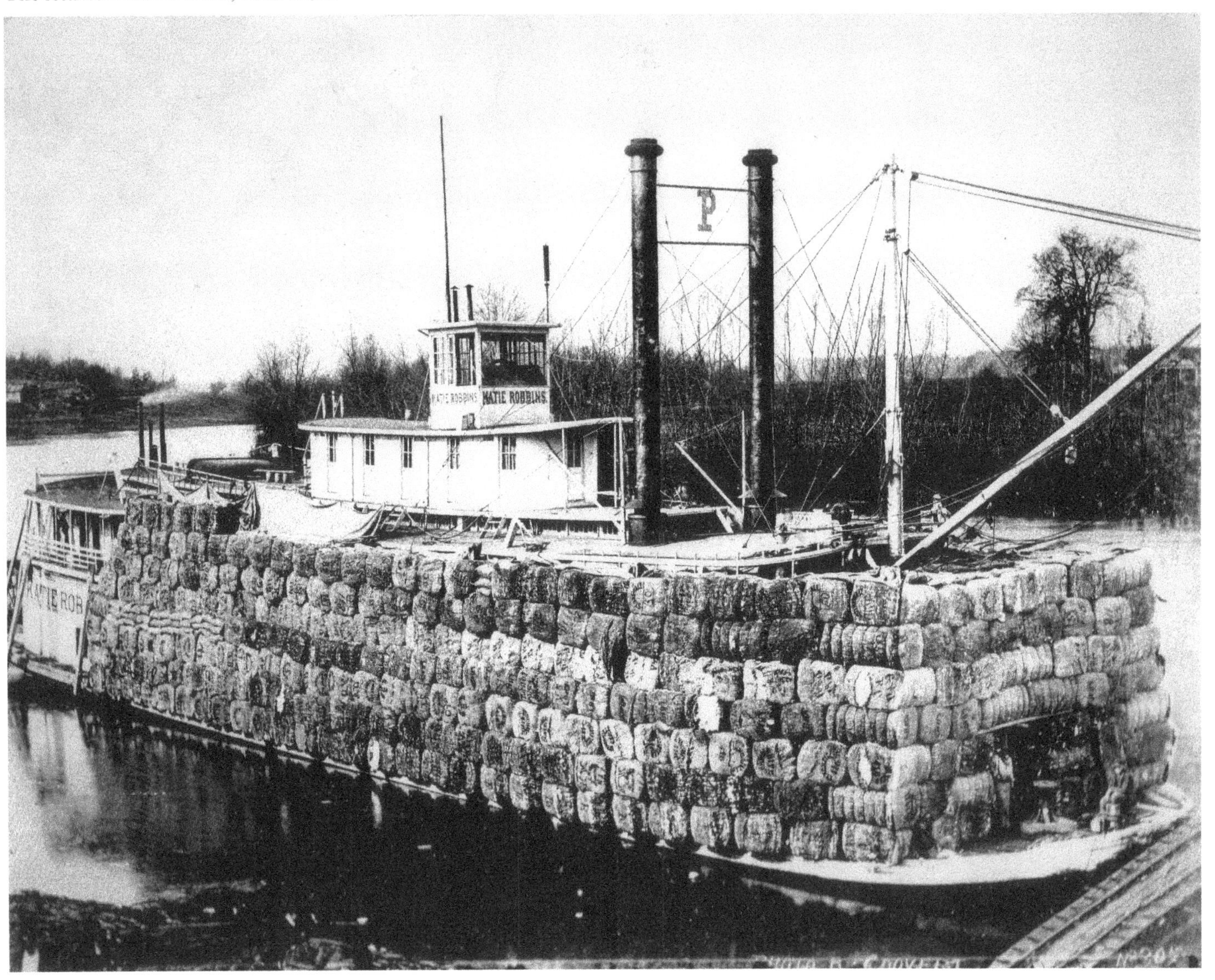

At the turn of the century, Memphis prided itself as the "hardwood capitol of the world."

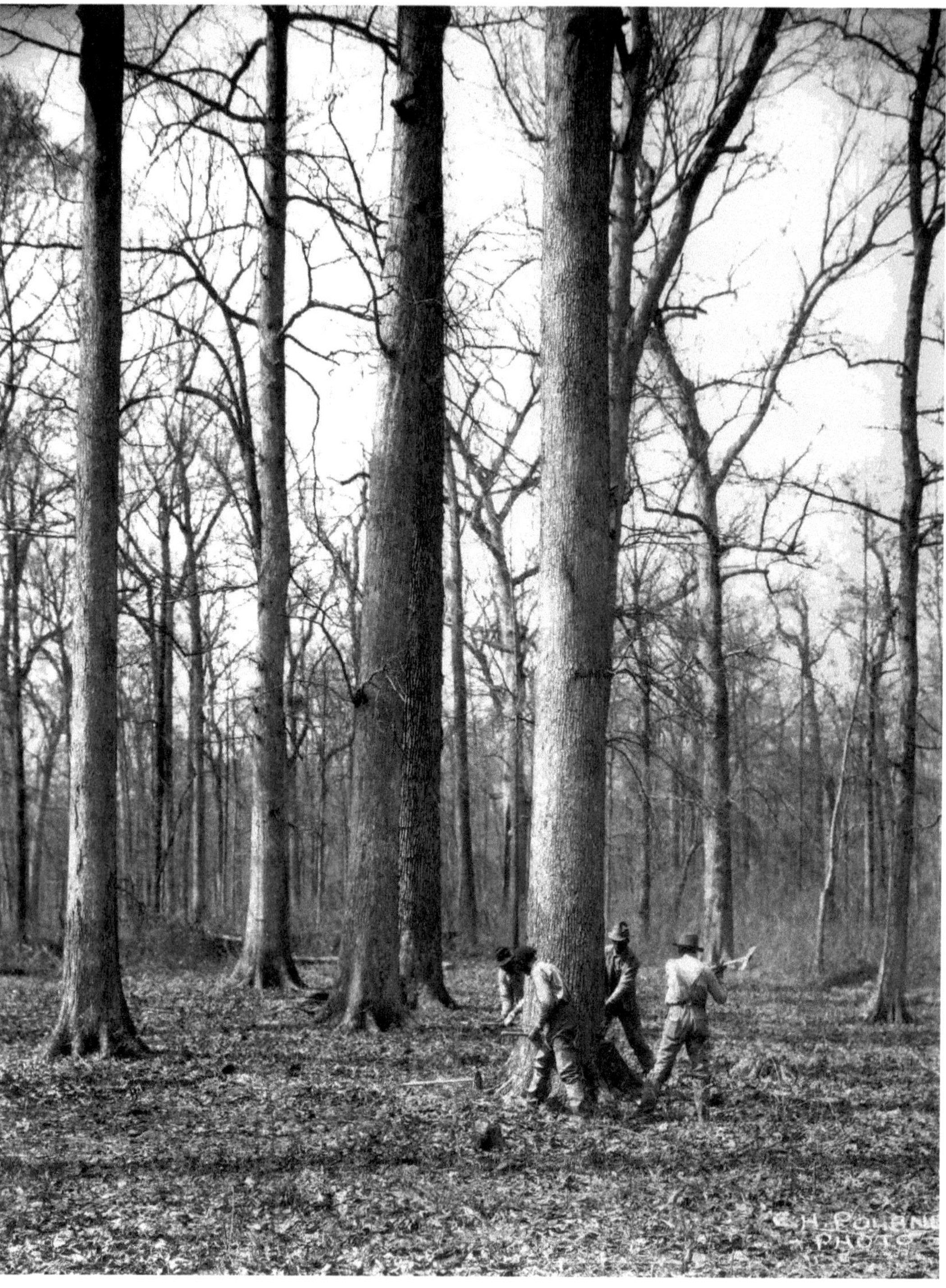

Memphis at the Turn of the Century

1900-1919

Memphis proudly claimed to have the world's largest cotton and lumber markets, the country's largest inland river port and the largest railroad center in the South at the turn of the century. Reform-minded citizens' organizations fought the new city government's impulse to fall back on cronyism and inefficiency. There were some improvements, but in general, local leadership generally lacked decisiveness. This pattern of inaction ended with the ascension of Edward Hull Crump, who dominated Memphis politics through the 1950s.

Flooding was an ever-worsening problem in the early twentieth century especially in the Mid-South. Continuing deforestation and the resulting erosion made these seasonal events life-threatening disasters. The worst floods hit in 1912, 1913, 1927 and 1937. Not only did the waters find their way into parts of Memphis, but the city had to accommodate thousands of refugees from surrounding areas.

Despite facing bigotry and inequity, African Americans managed to make significant economic and political advances beginning in the 1900s. Robert R. Church, Jr. formed the Lincoln League in 1916 to encourage voter registration and in 1917 he organized the local chapter of the NAACP. Uniting in these organizations was beneficial to the African American community as Church and others were able to take advantage of Crump's need for votes to gain concessions from the political machine.

Improvements and innovations characterized this period as well. The opening of the Overton Park Zoo in 1906 and the founding of the park system in 1911 was followed by a movement to build safe public playgrounds in 1915. There were numerous advancements in education including the merging of The University of Tennessee Medical School with Memphis Hospital Medical College. Central High School was built in 1911 and The West Tennessee State Normal School, forerunner of the University of Memphis, opened the following year.

Beale Street had been a melting pot of Italians, Germans, Irish, Jews and African Americans, among others, but by the 1900s, it was known as a center of African American culture in the South. The street was home to numerous Black-owned businesses and offices, including physicians, dentists, lawyers, undertakers, teachers, photographers, barbers and insurance companies. Yet it was music, most notably the Blues, which made Beale Street famous.

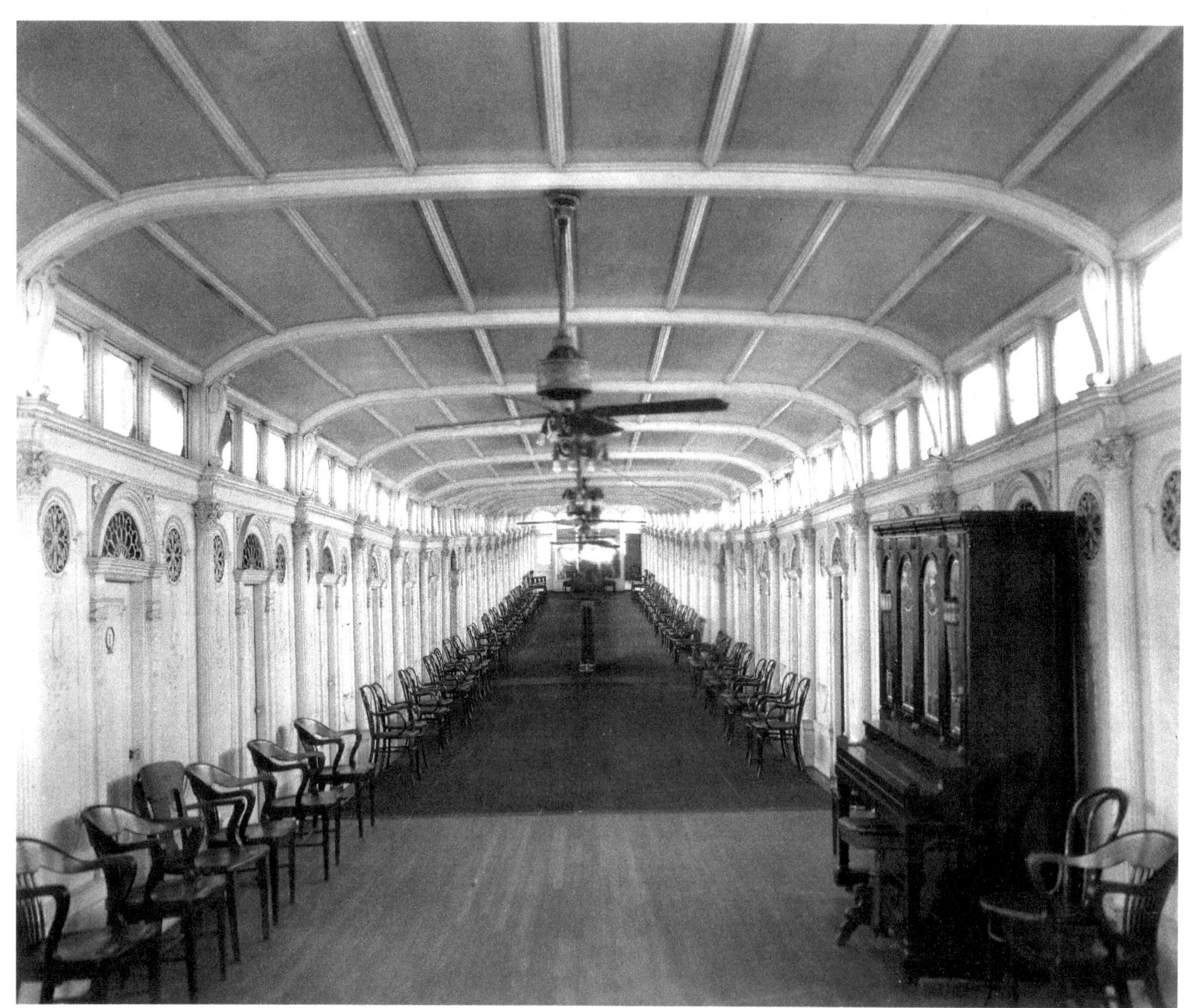

Interior of the *Kate Adams III*, circa 1903.

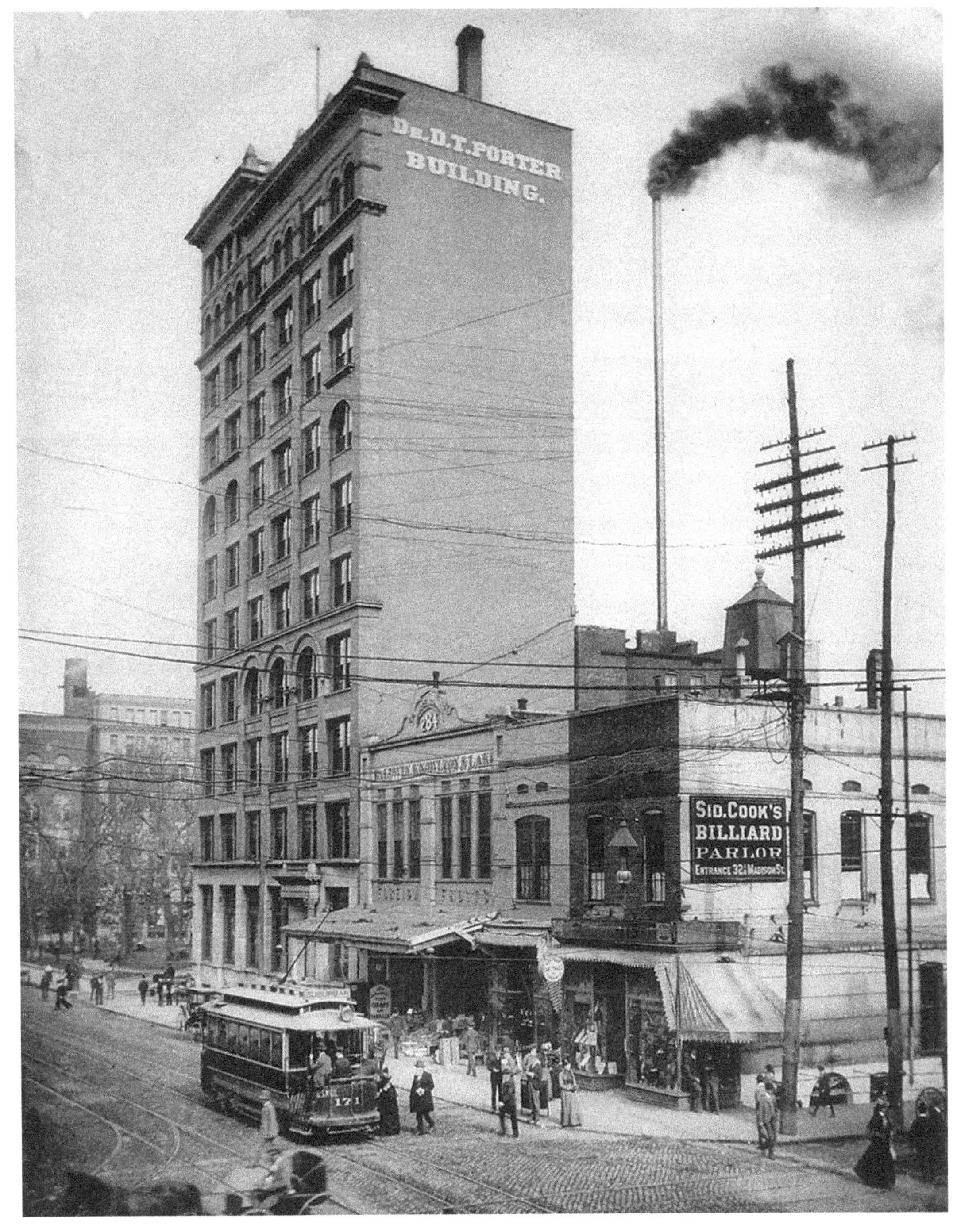

Scene on Main Street, 1900.

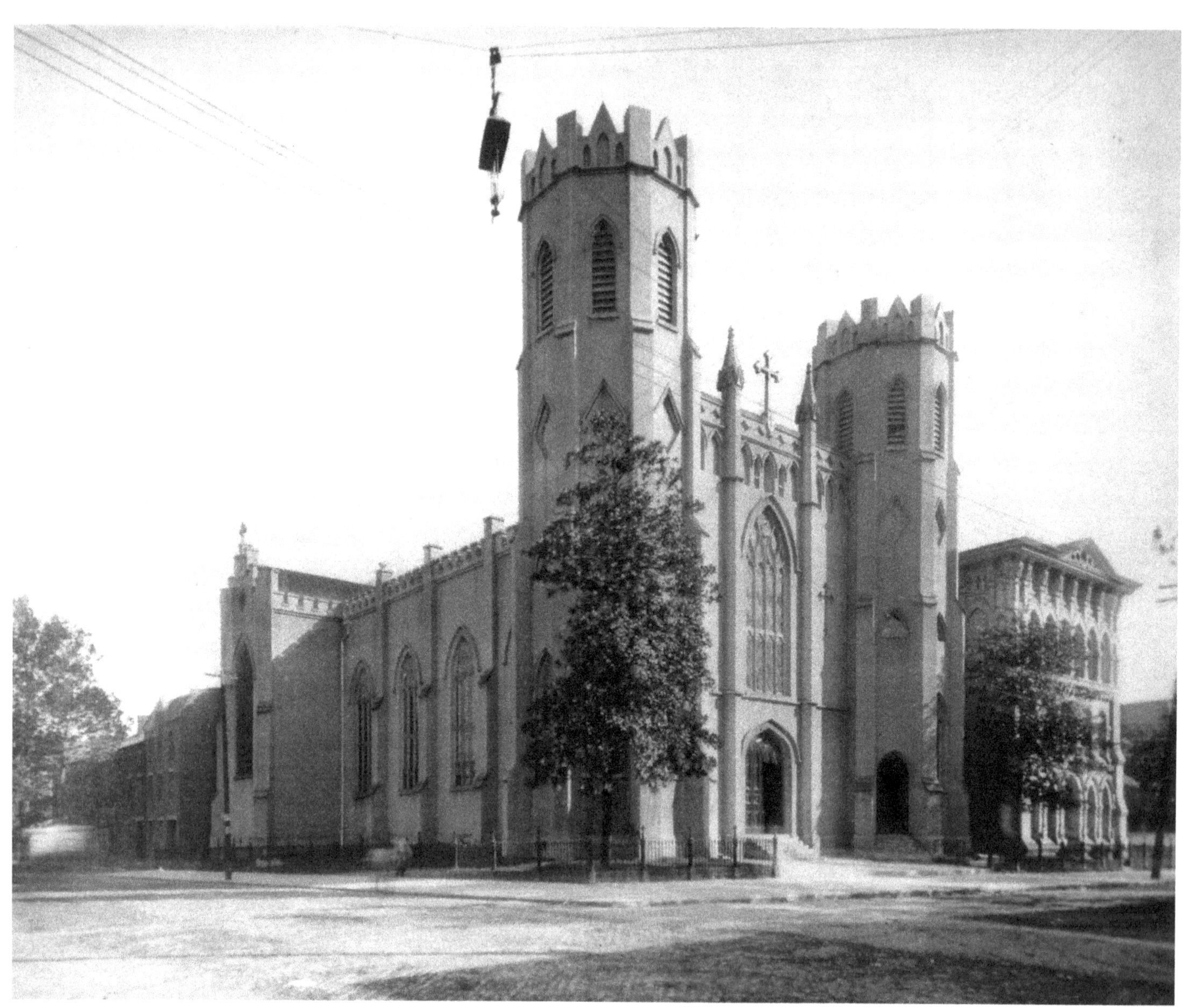

St. Peter's Catholic Church, 1900. Completed in 1855, this was the first Catholic Church in Memphis.

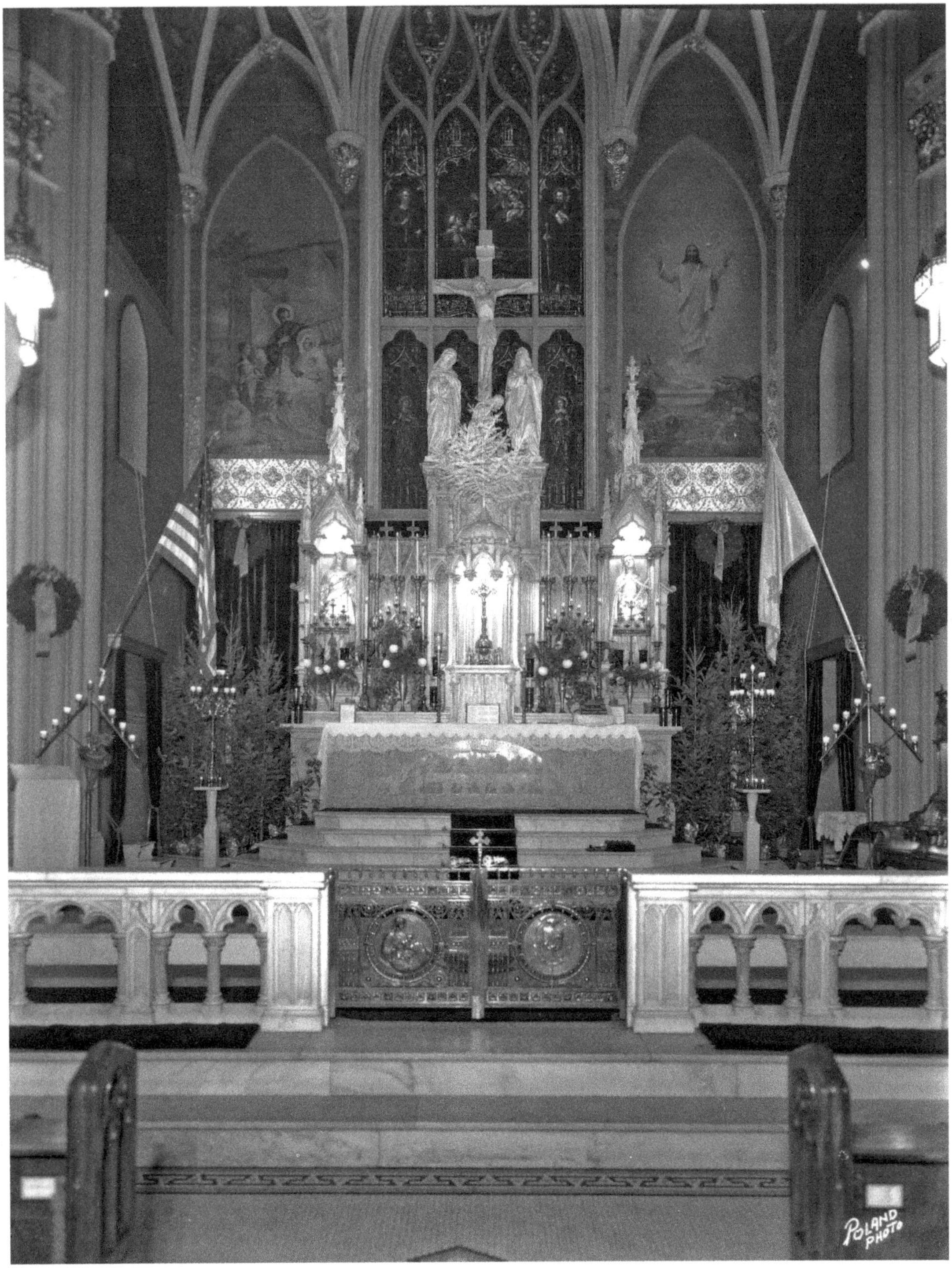

Interior of St. Peter's Catholic Church.

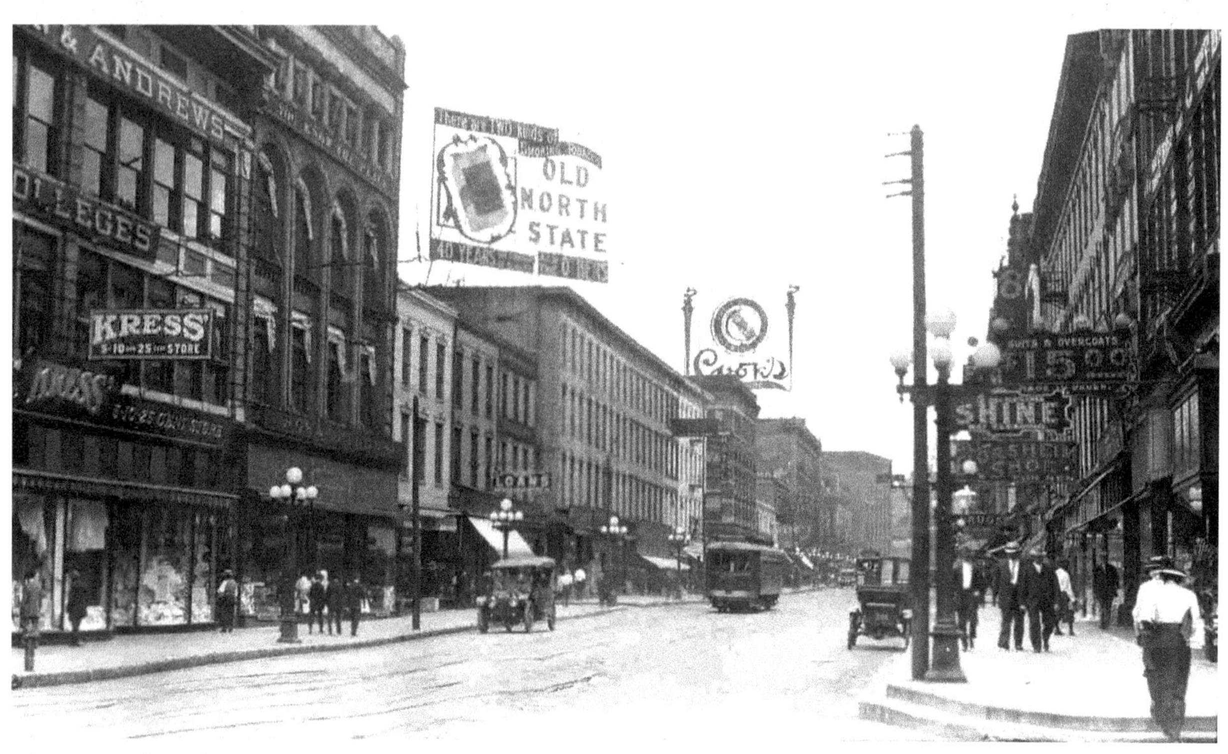

The corner of South Main and Union, circa 1910.

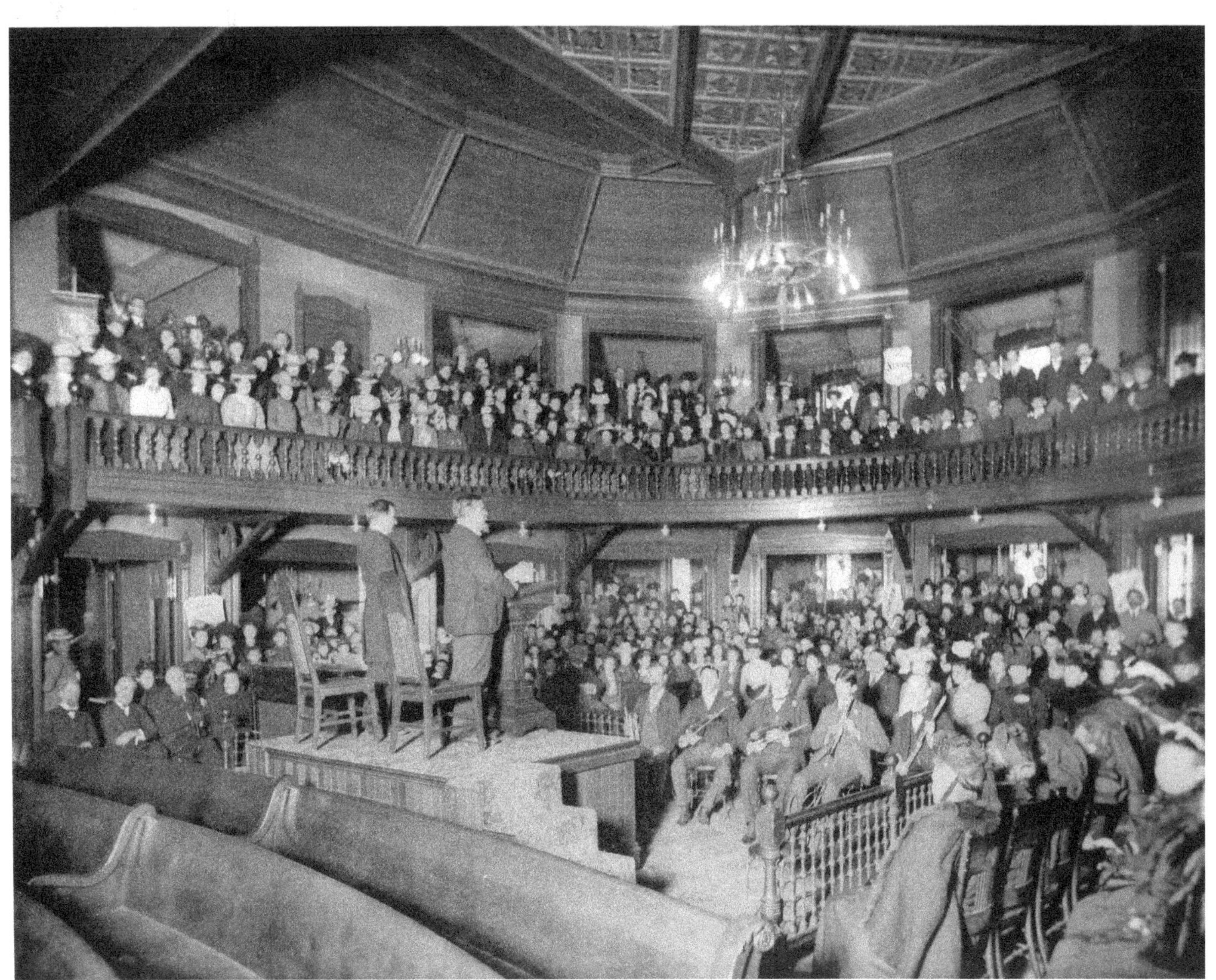

Interior of First Methodist Episcopal Church Sunday School, 1900.

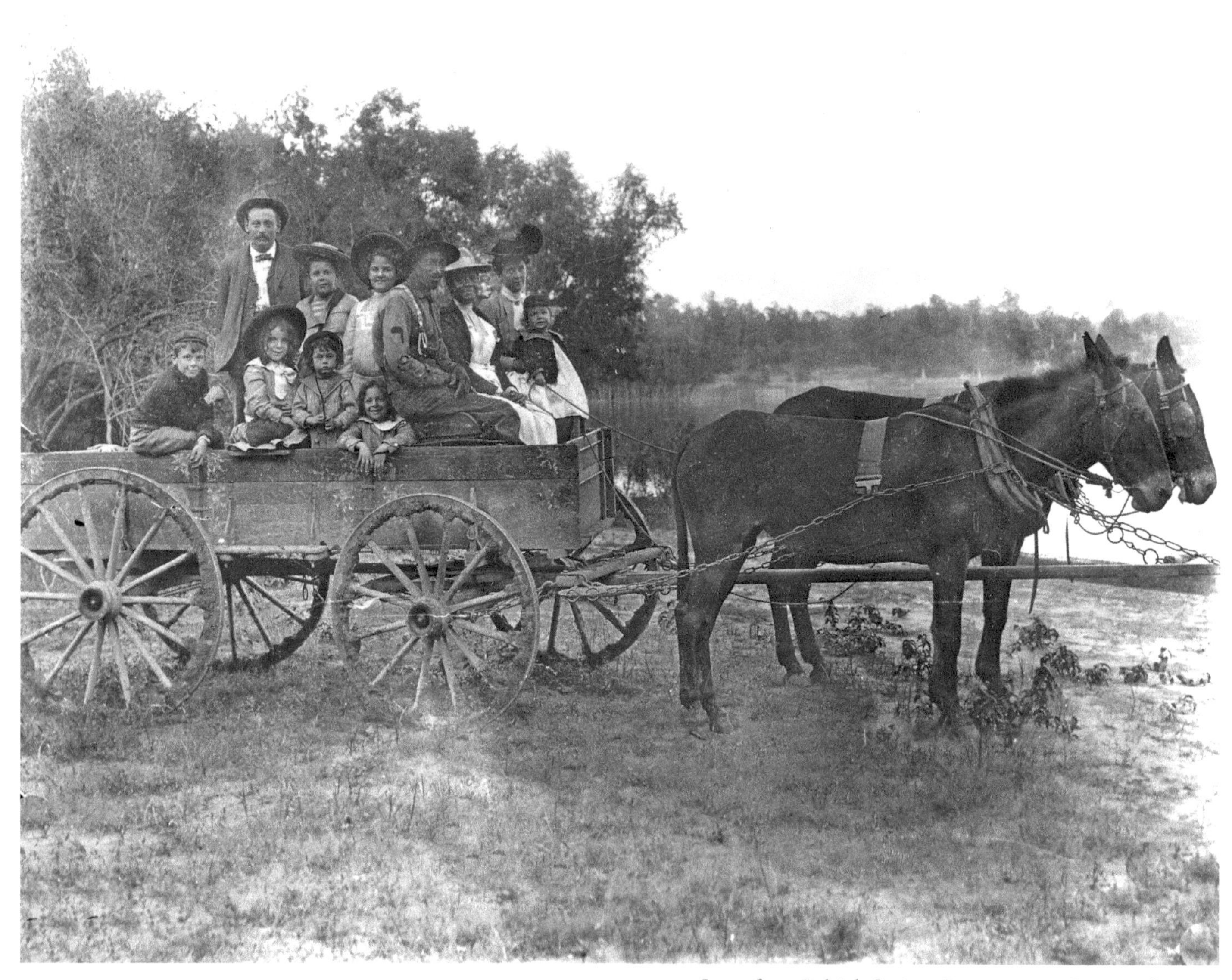

Scene from Raleigh Springs Resort, 1902. Its natural spring water made it a popular destination for Memphians.

Raleigh Springs Resort, 1900.

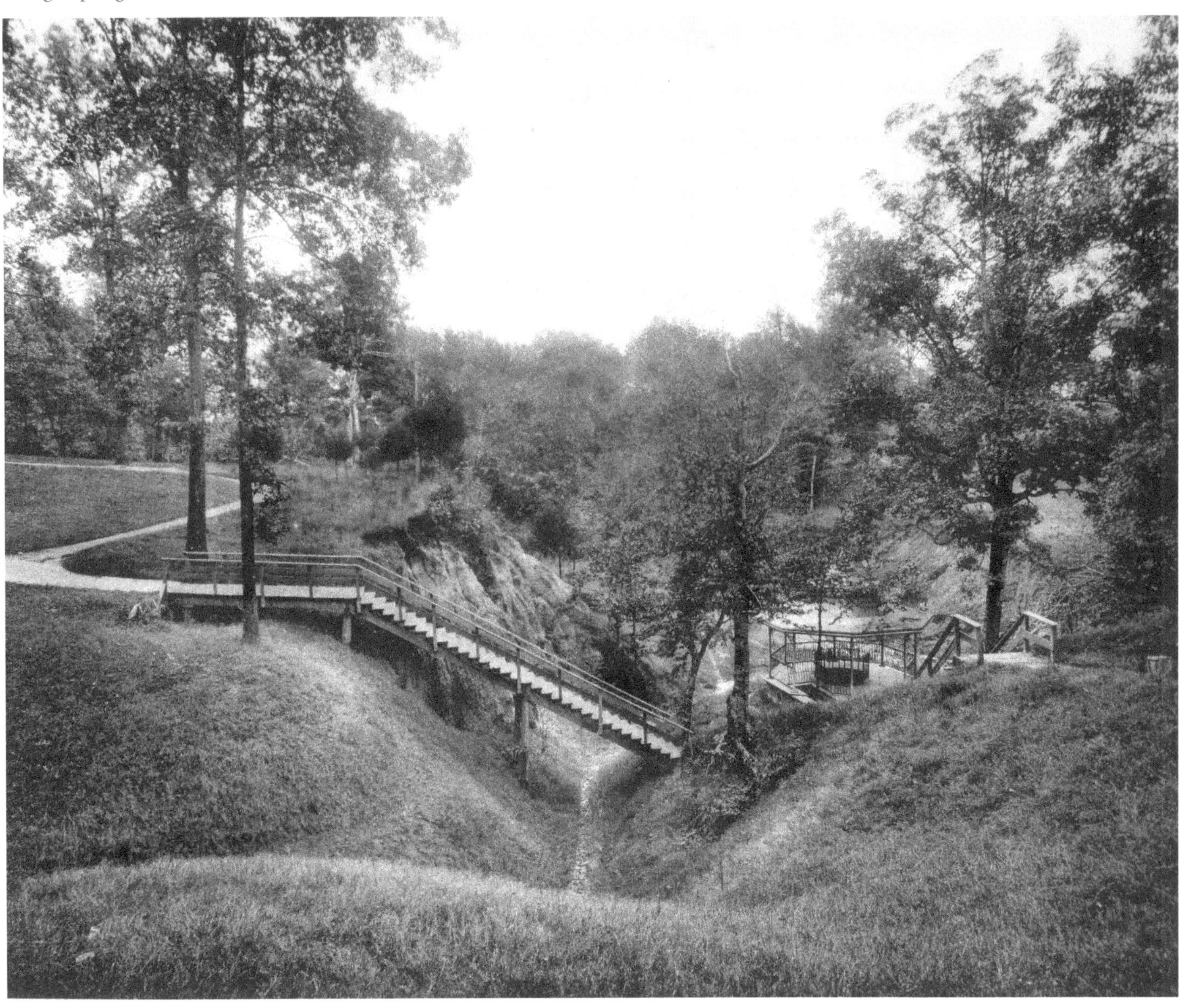

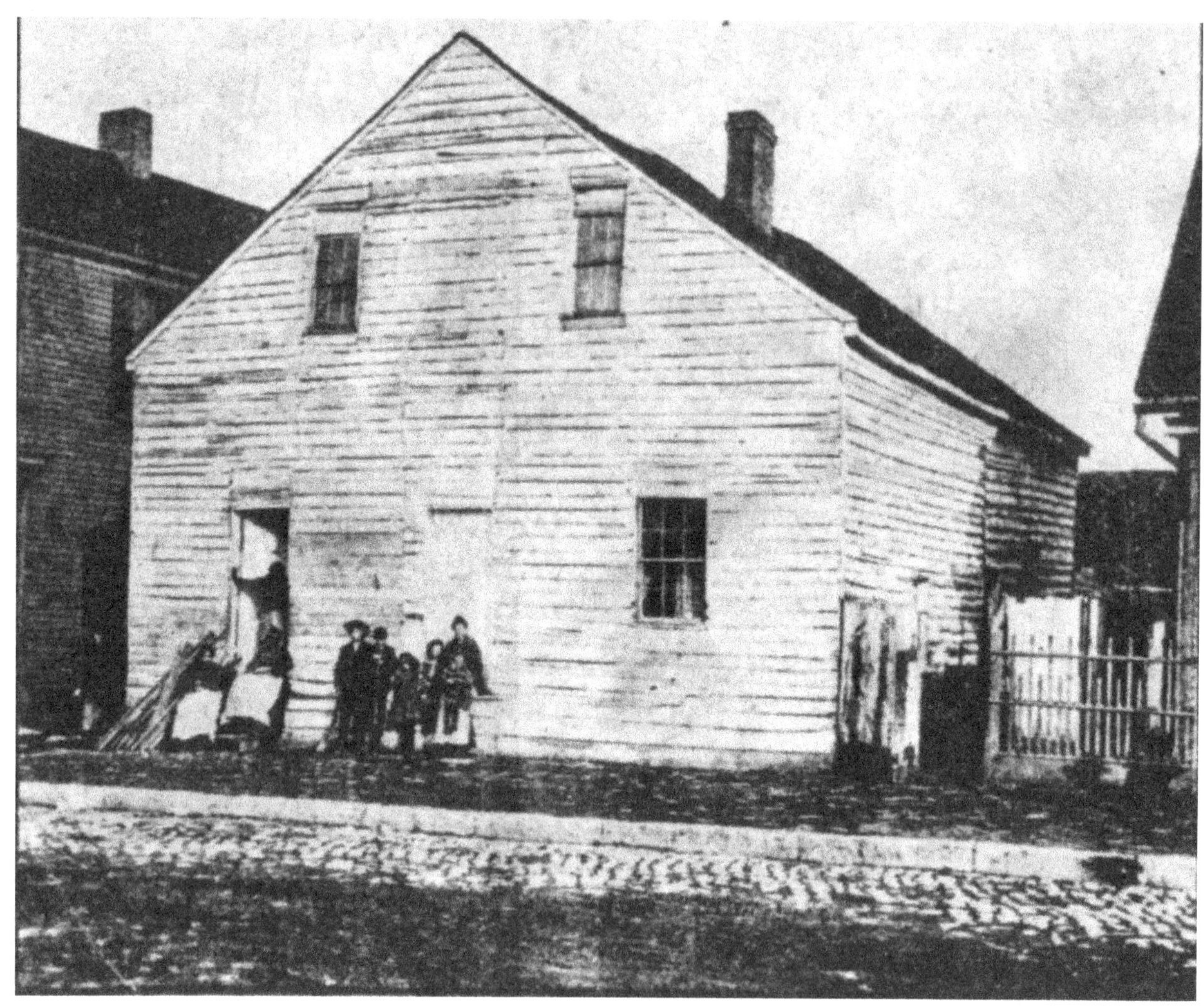

Irishman Paddy Meagher, owner of the Bell Tavern, arrived at the Chickasaw Bluff around 1813. His many guests included Andrew Jackson, Isaac Shelby and David Crockett.

A mule-drawn Coca-Cola wagon driven by Landan Smith. Mack's Saloon, which was operated by Charles McClelland, appears in the background.

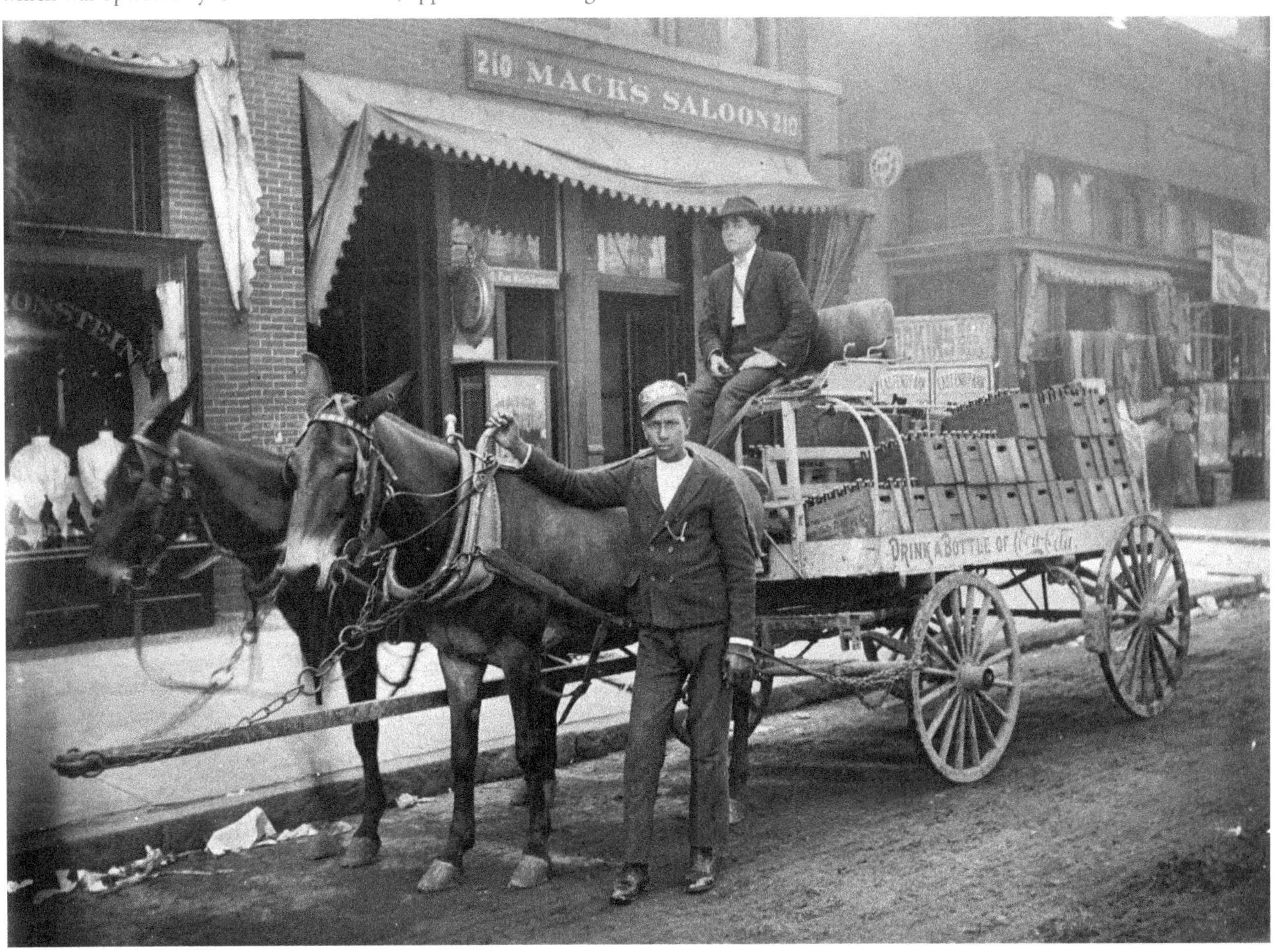

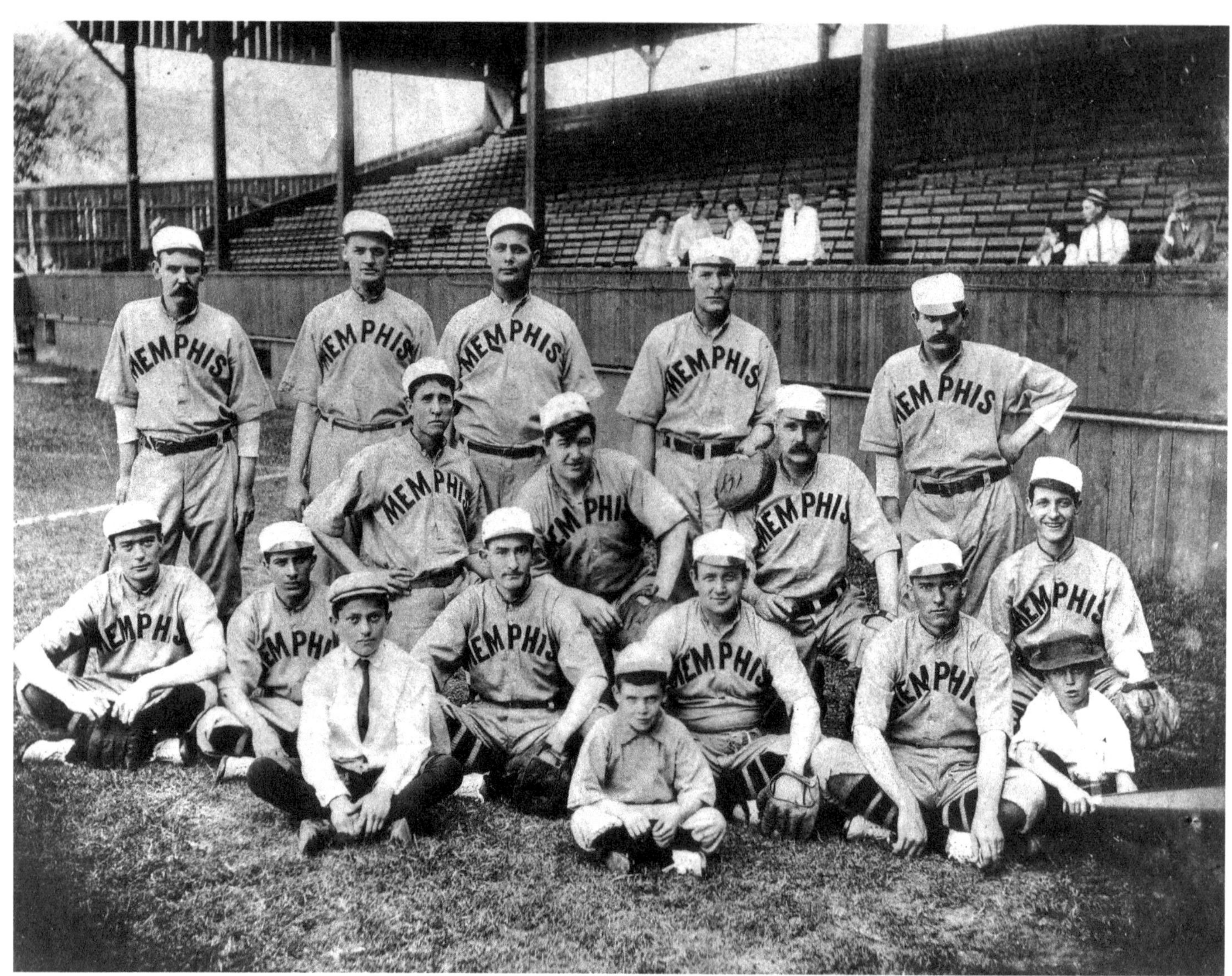

A local baseball team, 1900s.

Horseracing at Montgomery Park, circa 1900.

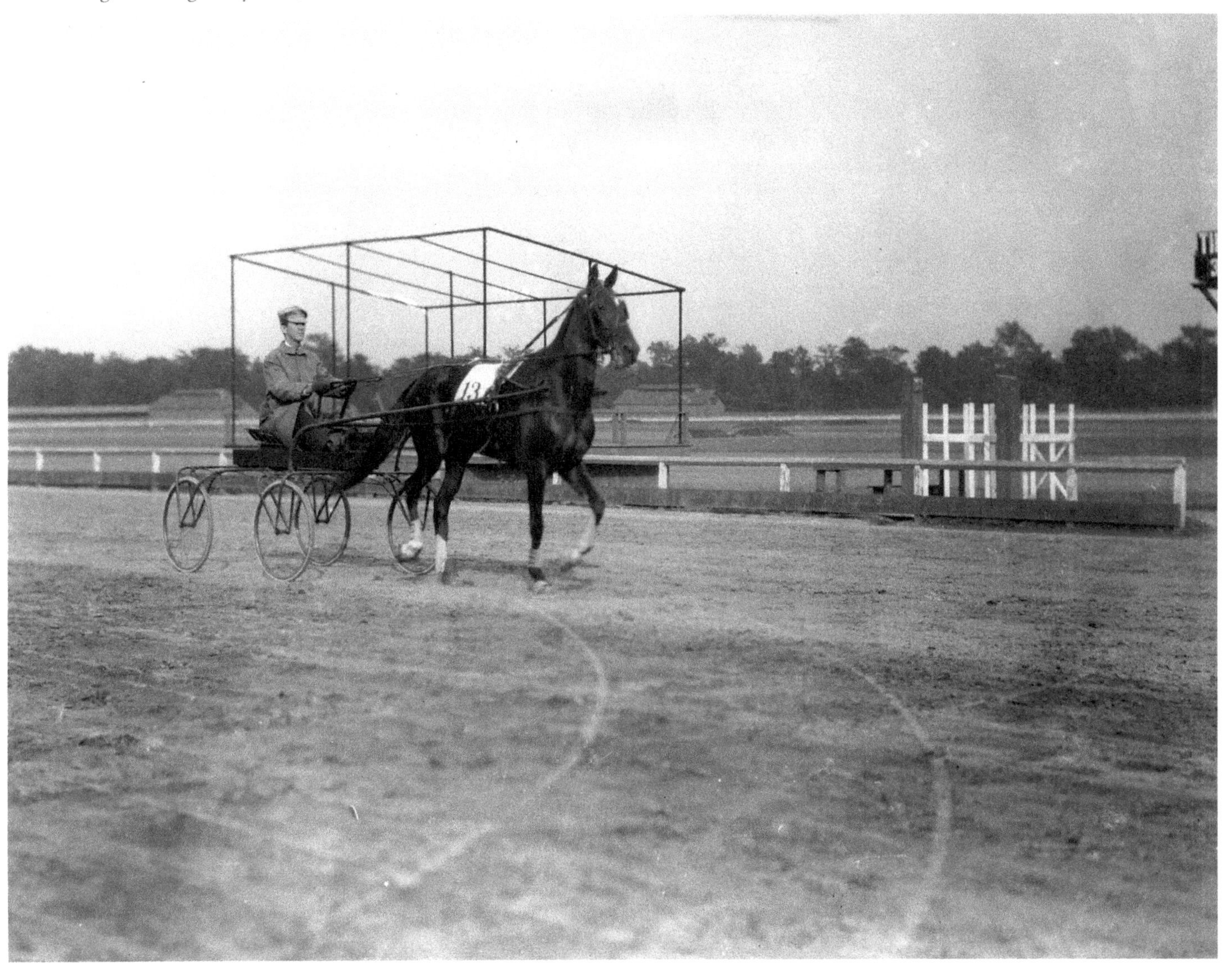

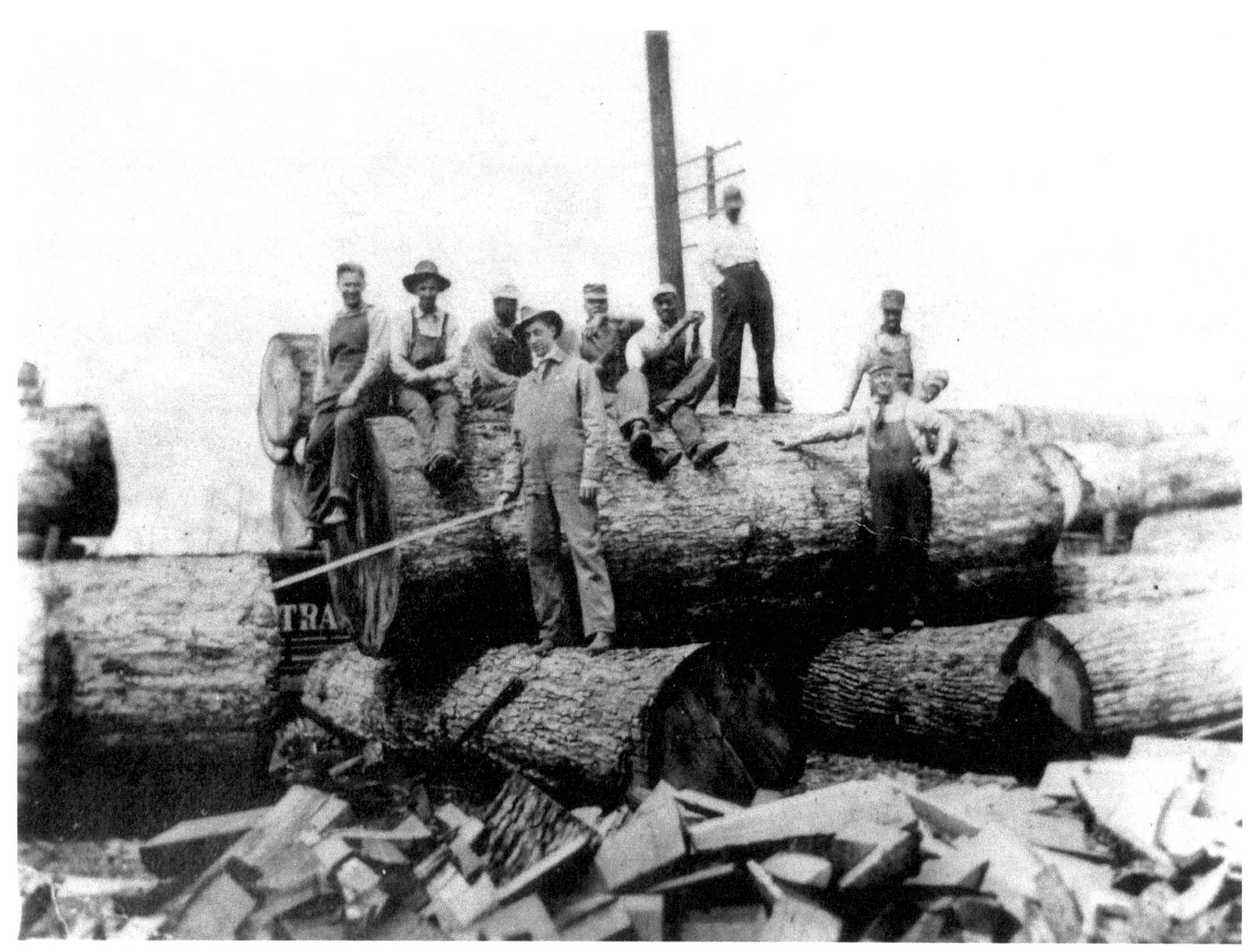

Nickey Brothers Lumber Company, 1908. A.B. Nickey's business, which he opened in 1866, lasted through the 1980s. One of the largest fires in Memphis history broke out at the company's Summer Avenue facility in 1964 and destroyed a number of warehouses.

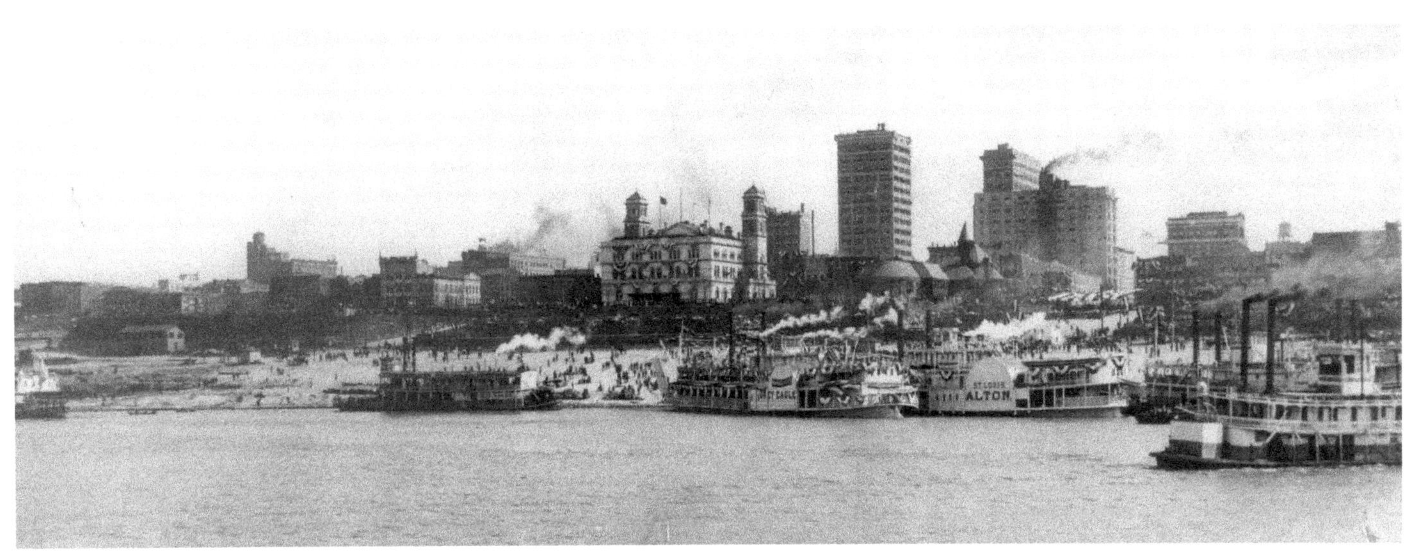

The steamboats *Grey Eagle* and *Alton* docked at the waterfront at Memphis, 1909.

Photo on following page: T. H. Hayes and Sons Funeral Home employees next to Beale Street First Baptist Church. Hayes came to Memphis in 1879 and opened his business at the suggestion of Robert R. Church.

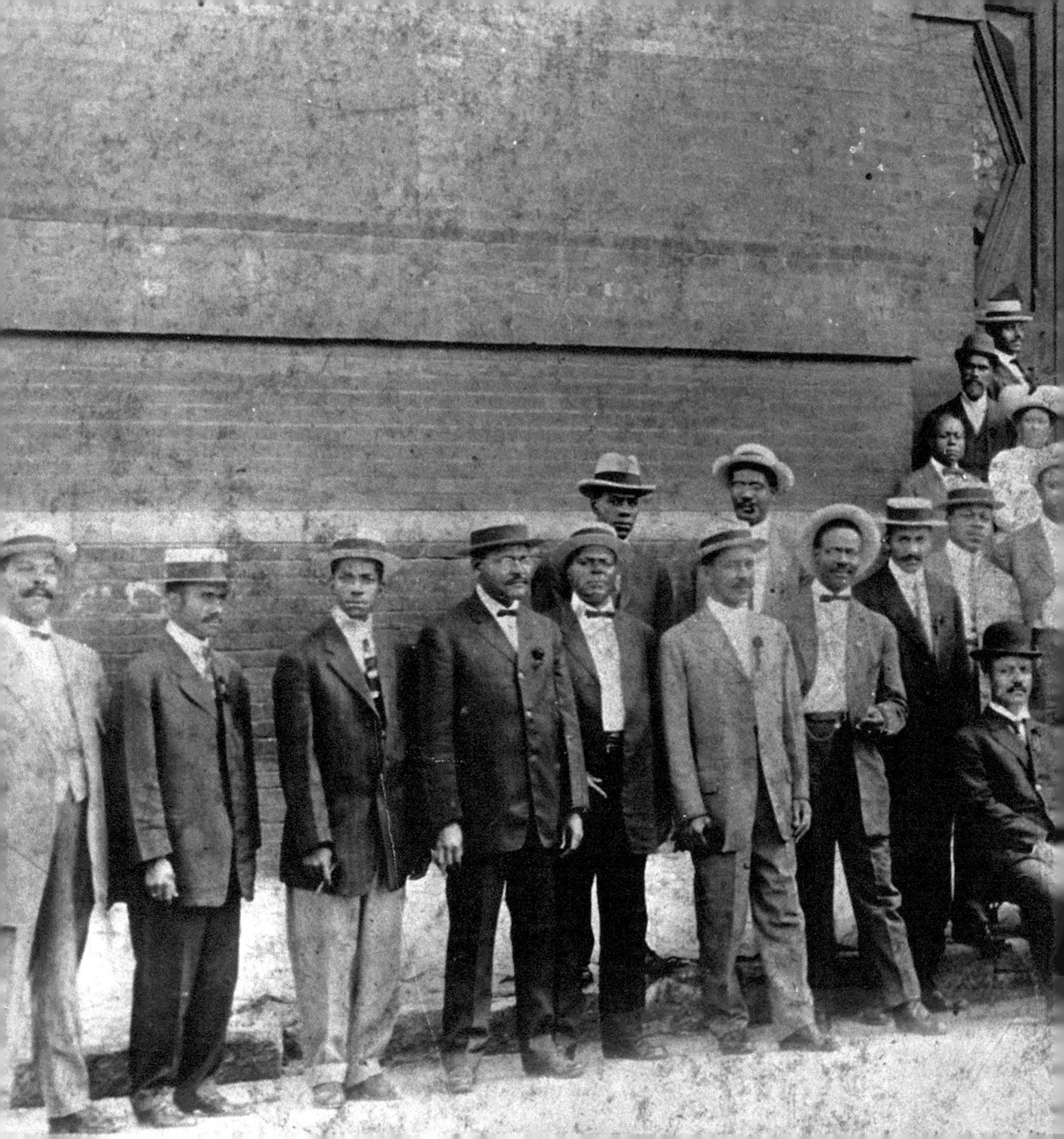

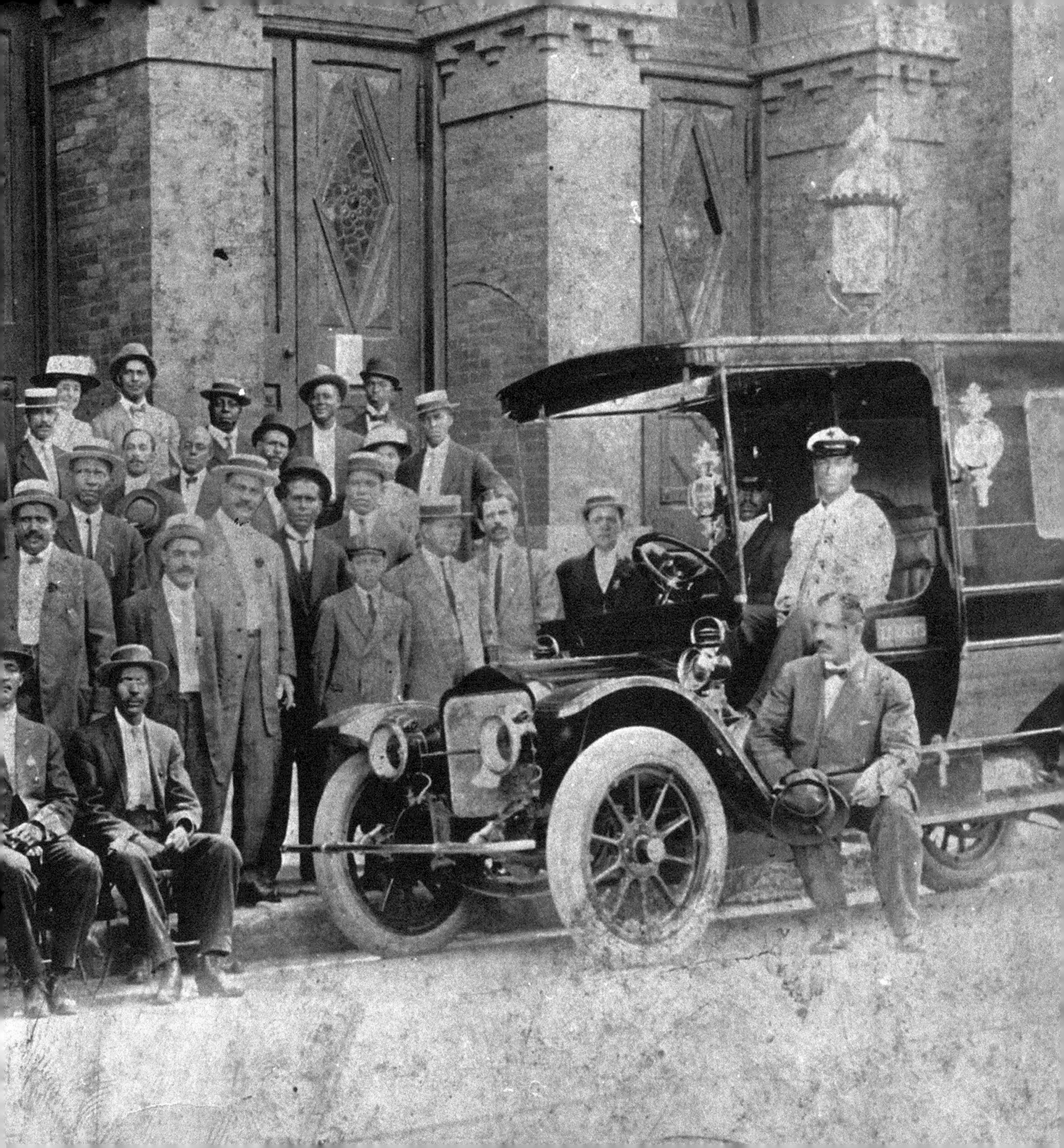

Scene on Main Street near Court Square.

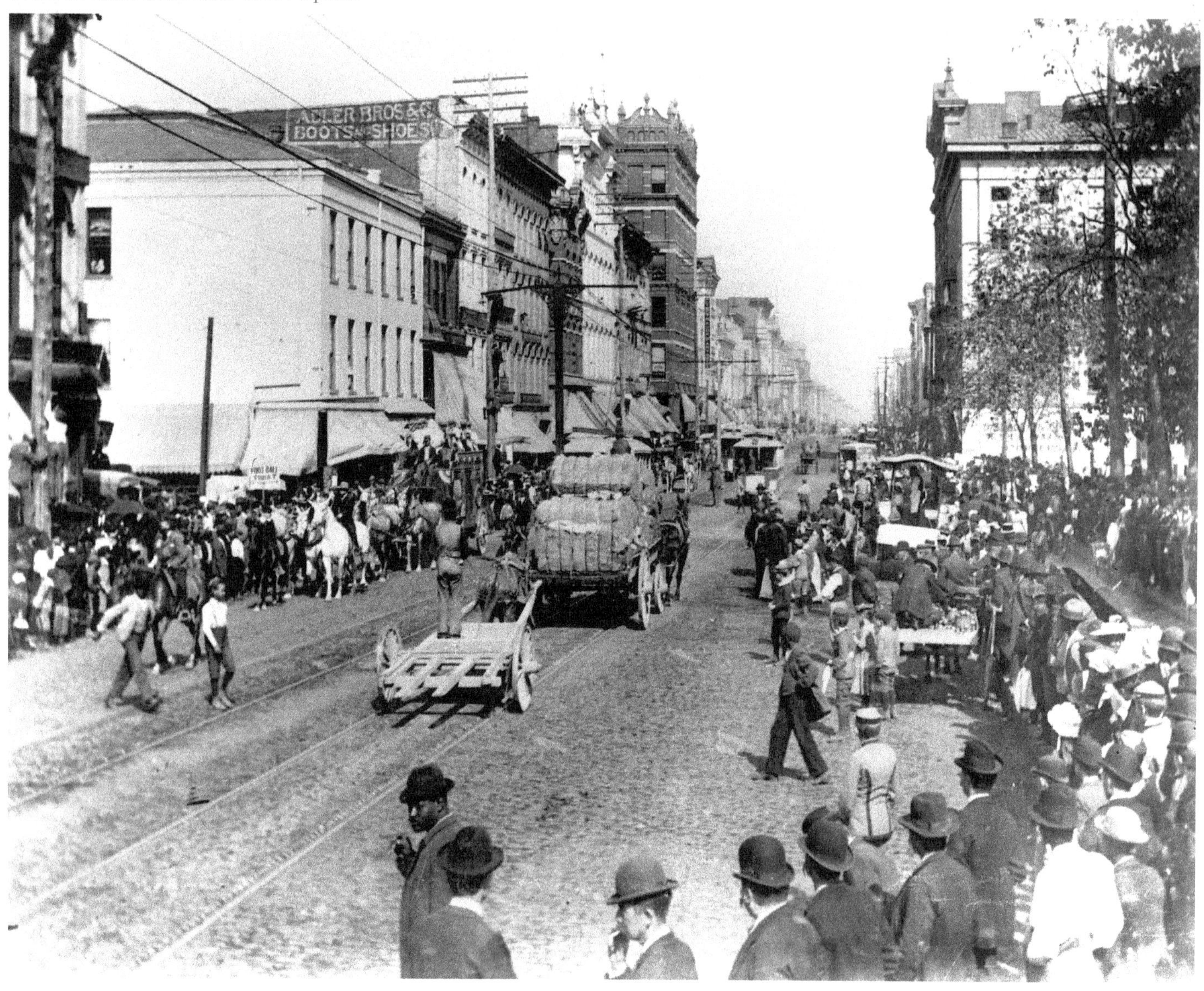

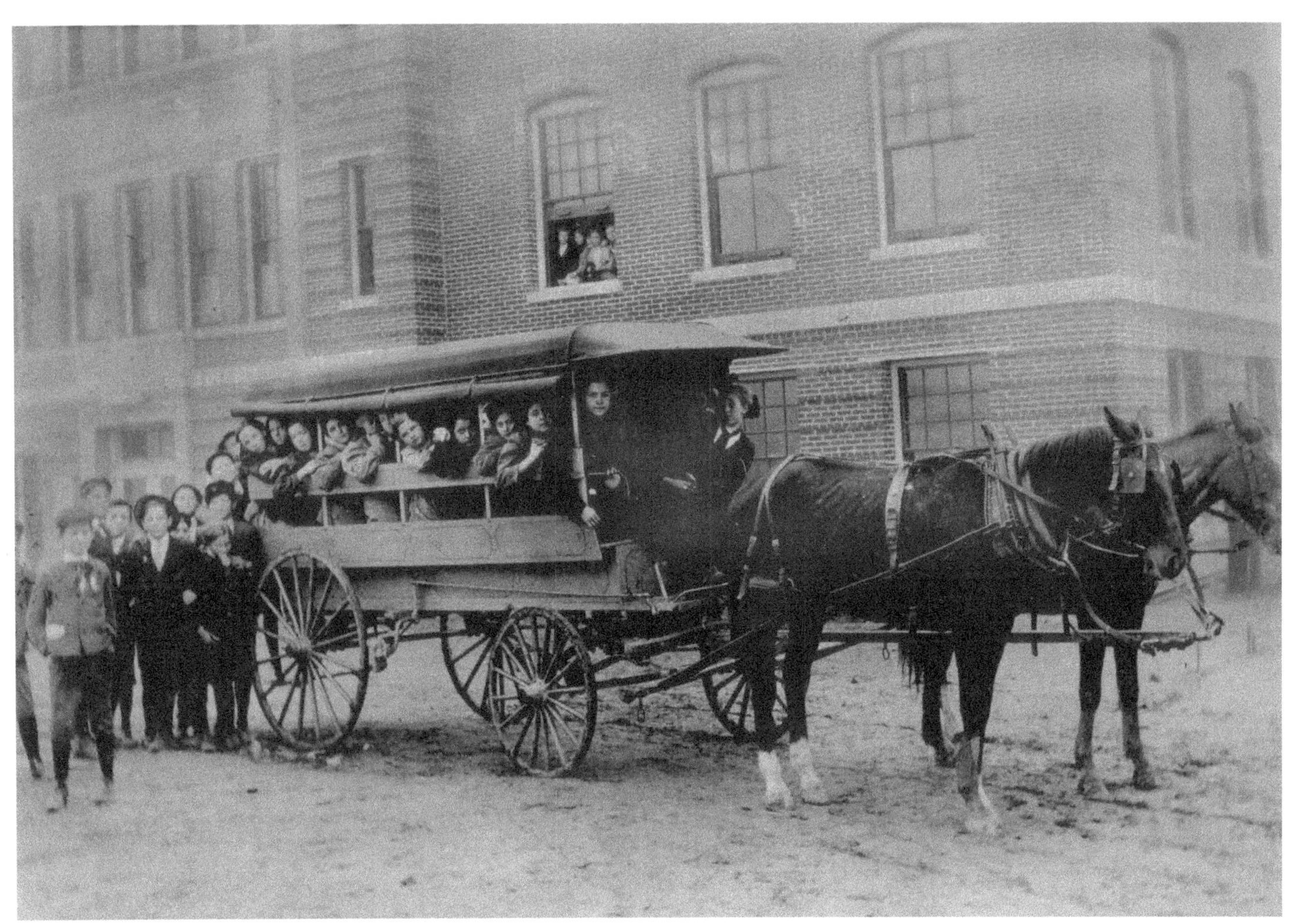

The first schoolbus in Memphis.

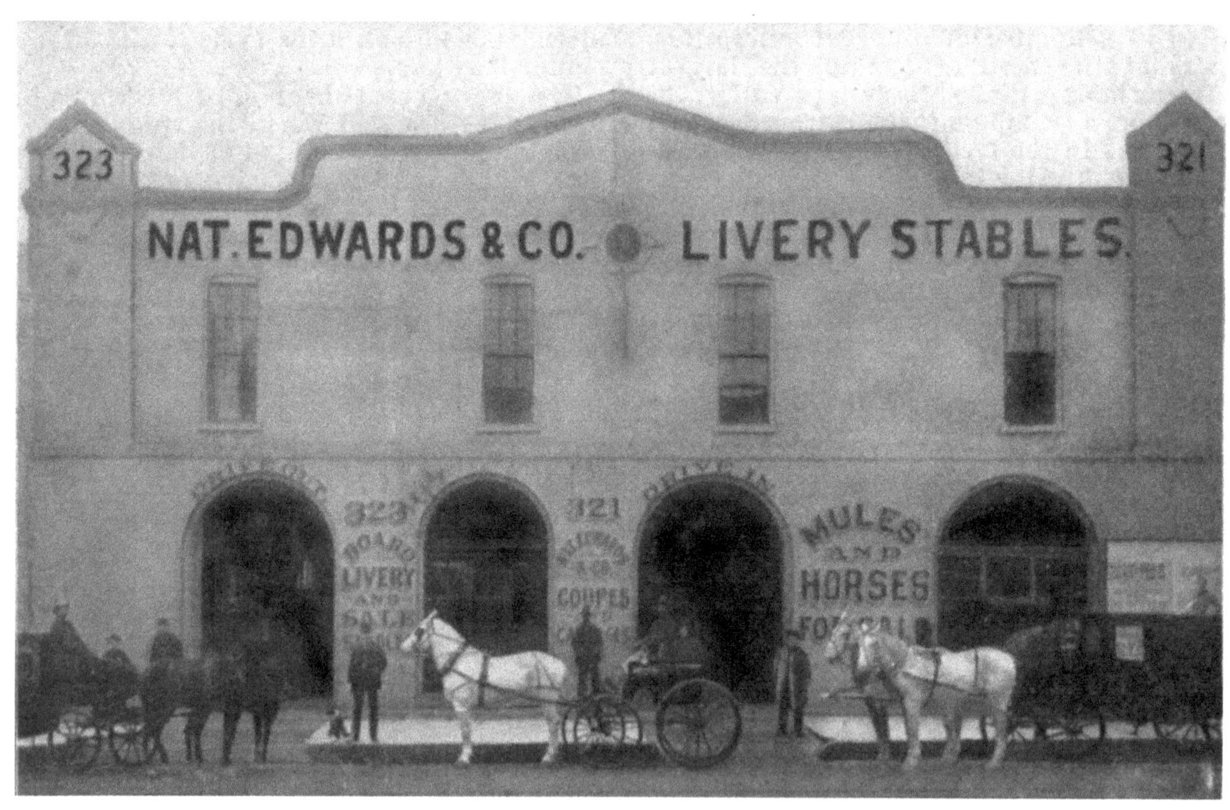

Nat Edwards and Company Livery Stables.

Grover Cleveland Sherrod, who went on to serve as the U.S. District Attorney General for the 13th District, in his grocery store, circa 1910.

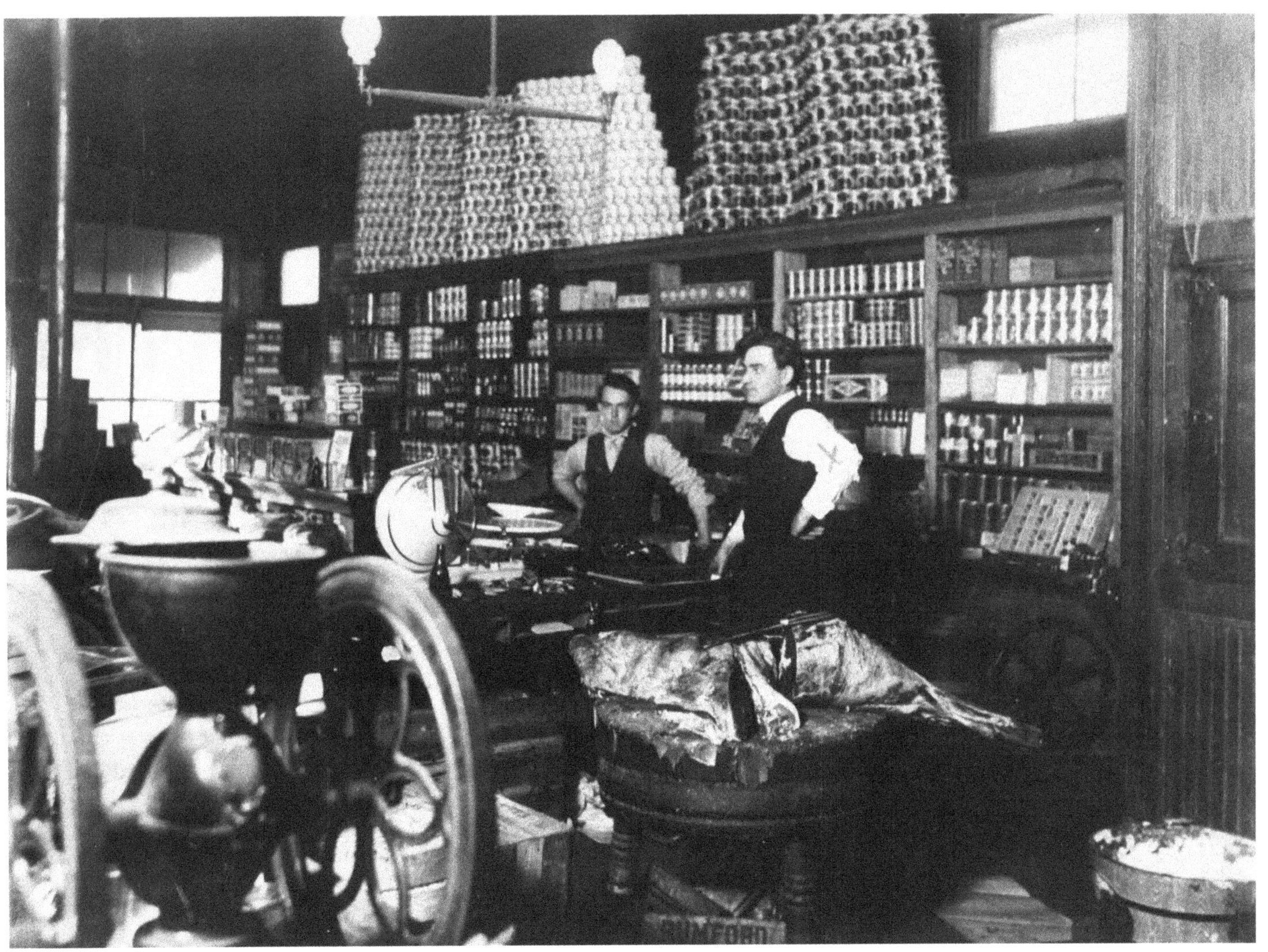

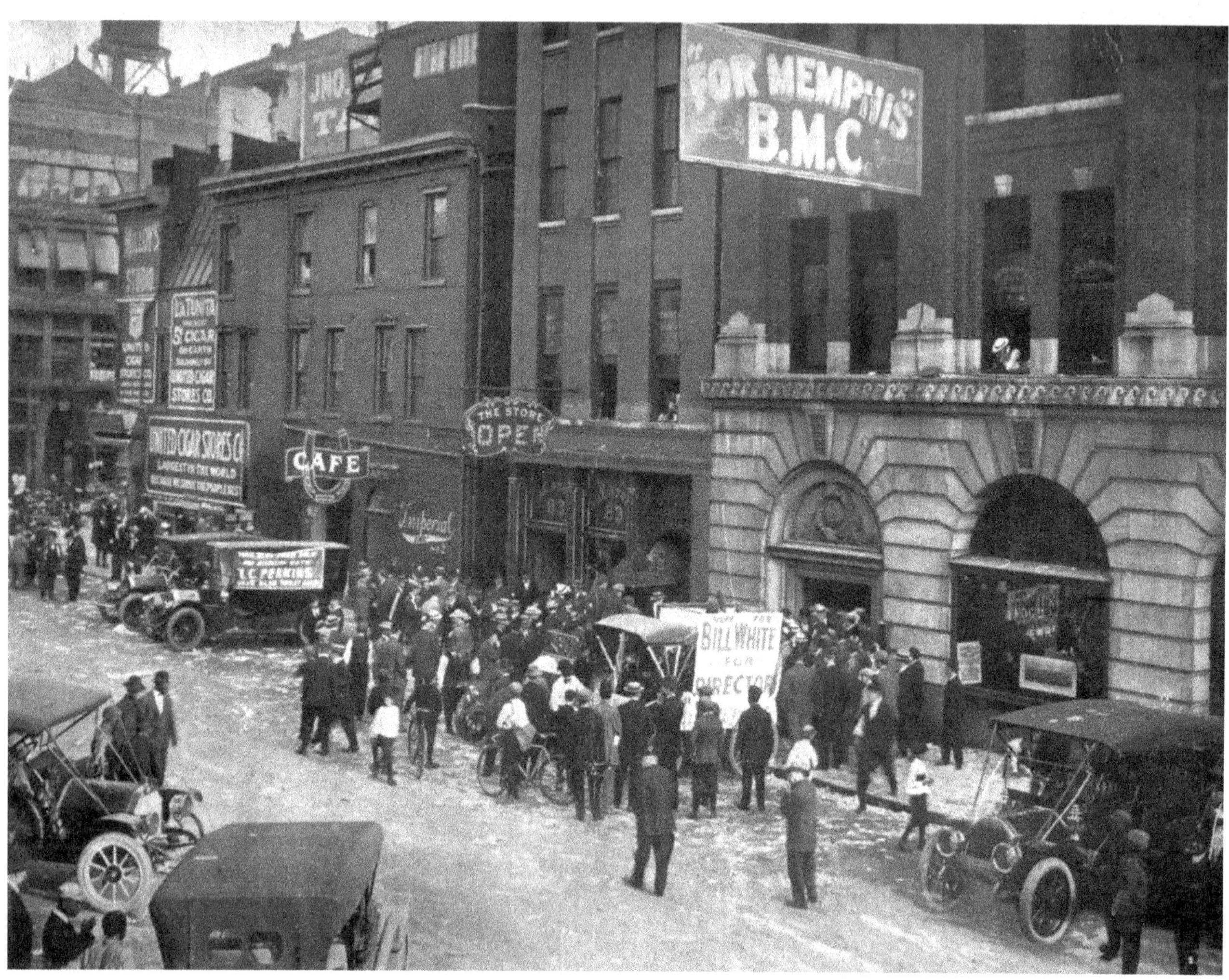

Business Men's Club election, 1911. The organization was founded in 1900 and moved into the building pictured at 81 Monroe in 1907. Beginning in 1913, the building was the headquarters for the Memphis Chamber of Commerce.

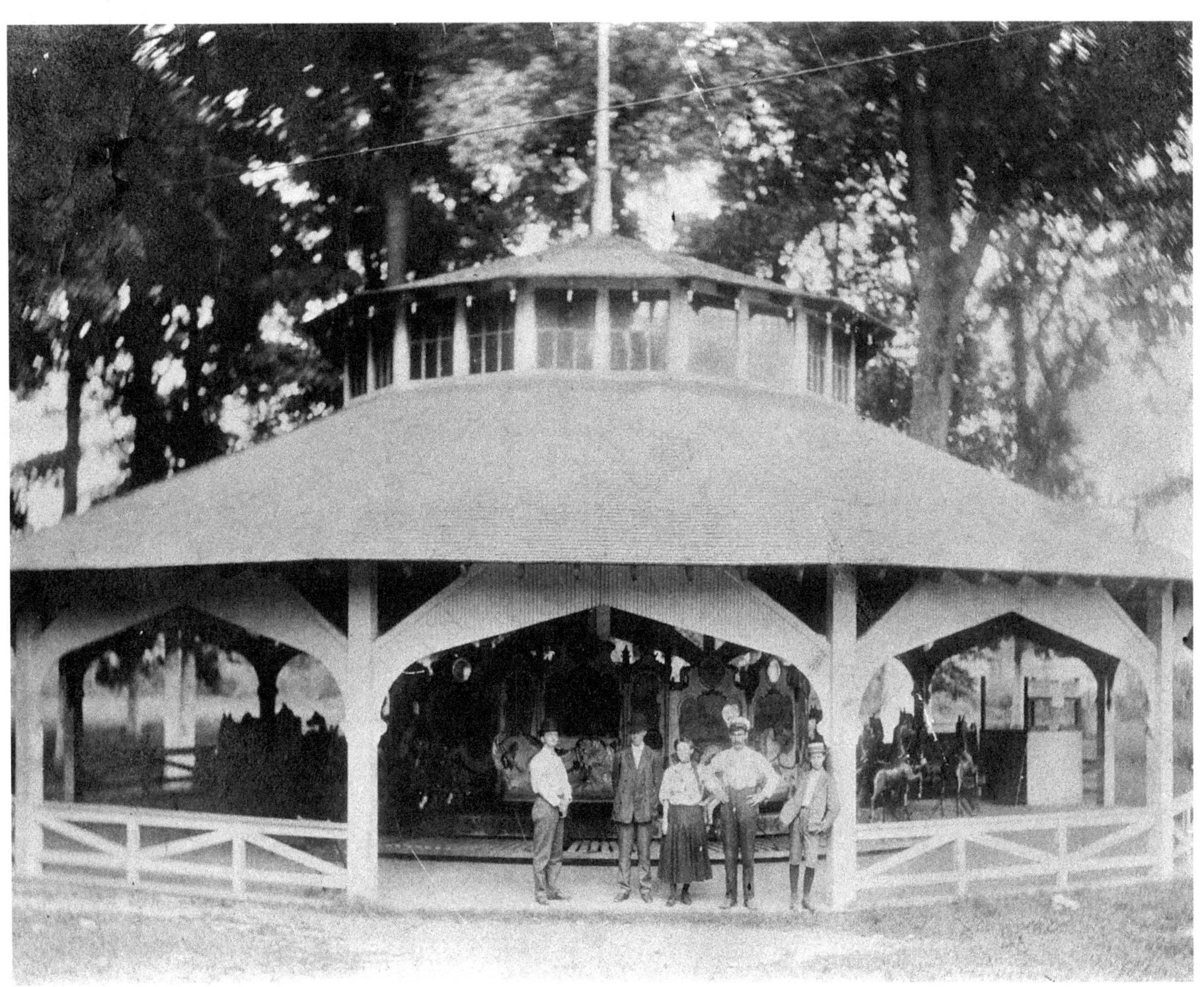

The merry-go-round at East End Park, 1911.

Main Street, 1912.

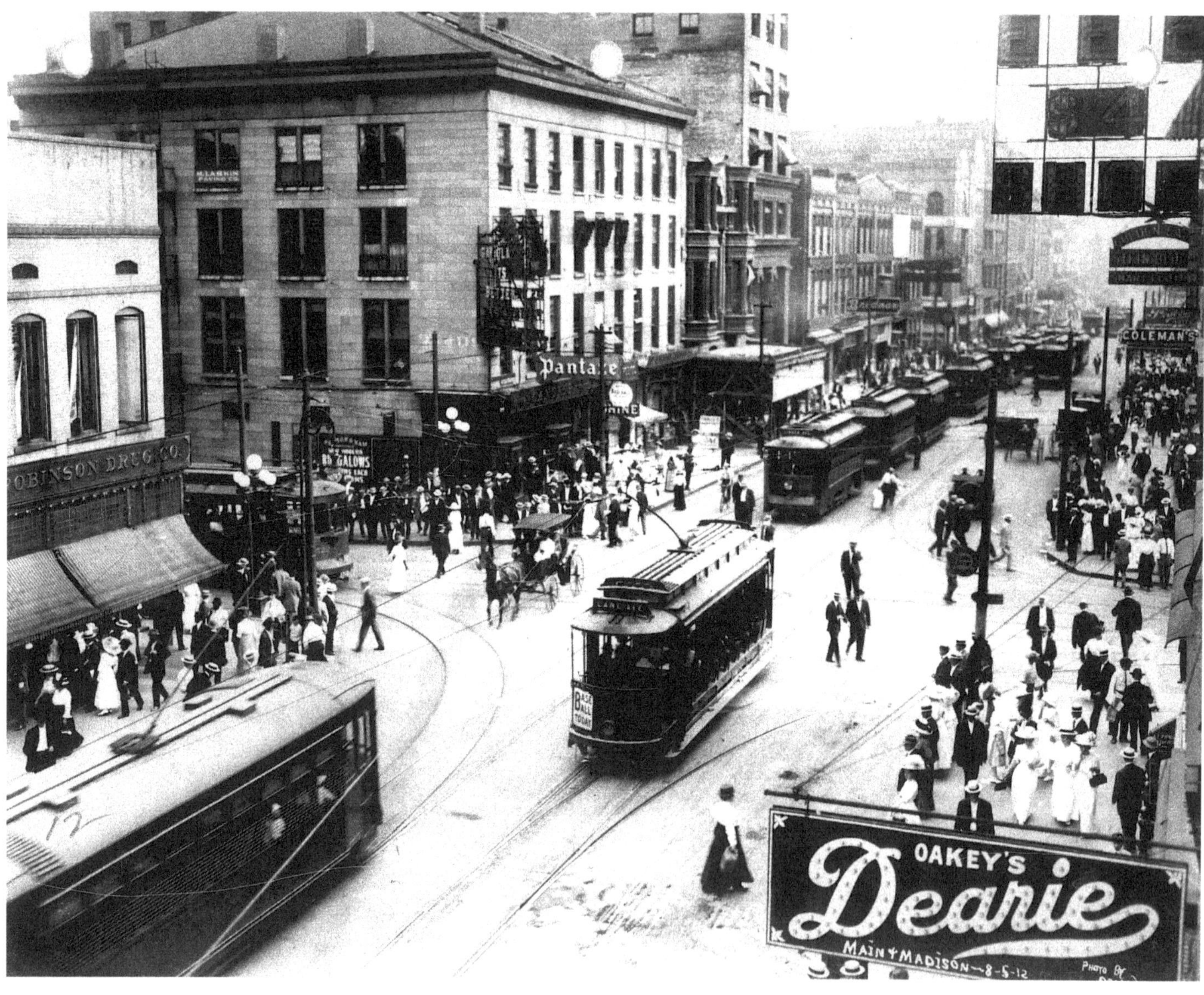

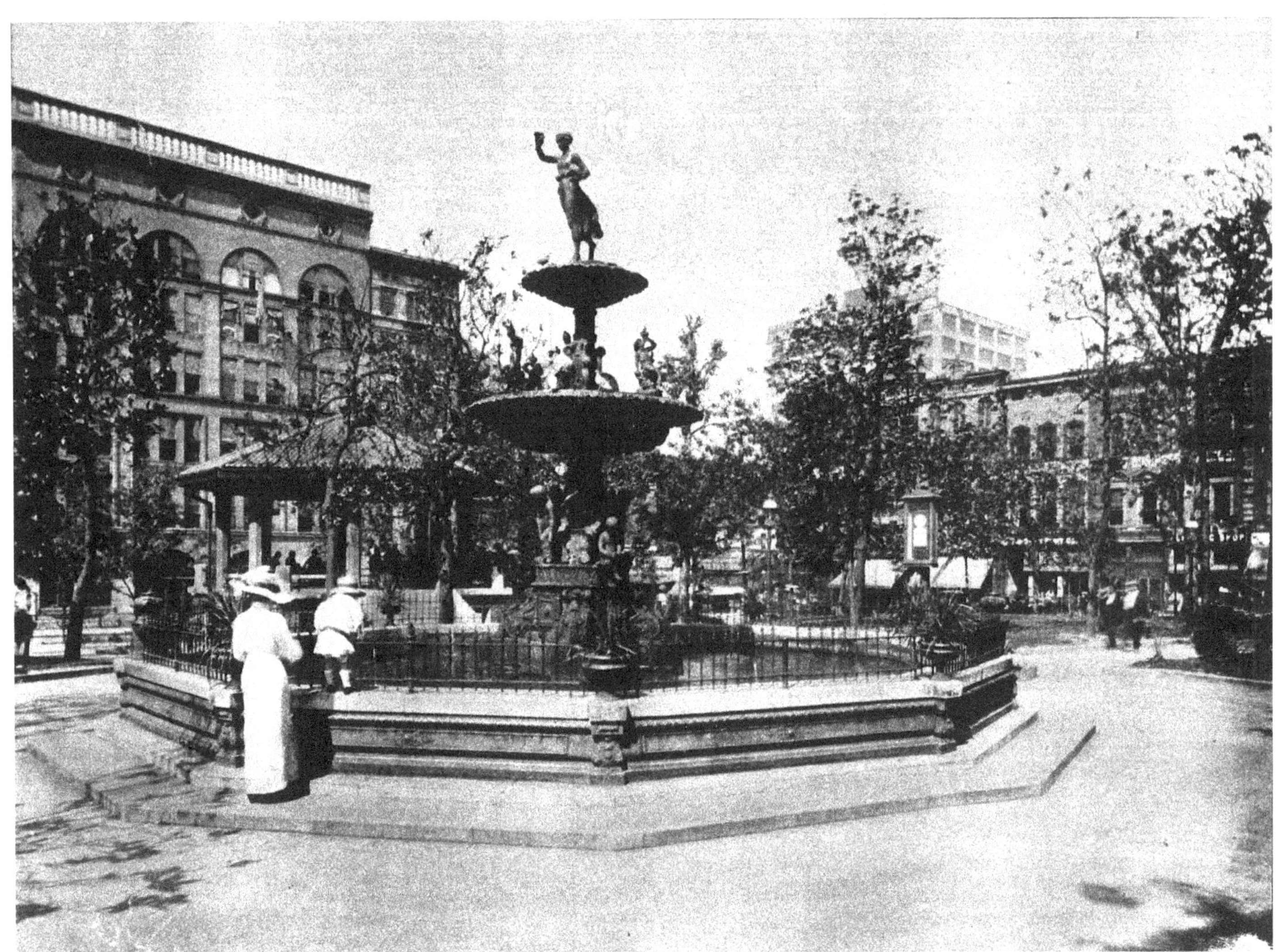

Court Square Fountain, 1912.

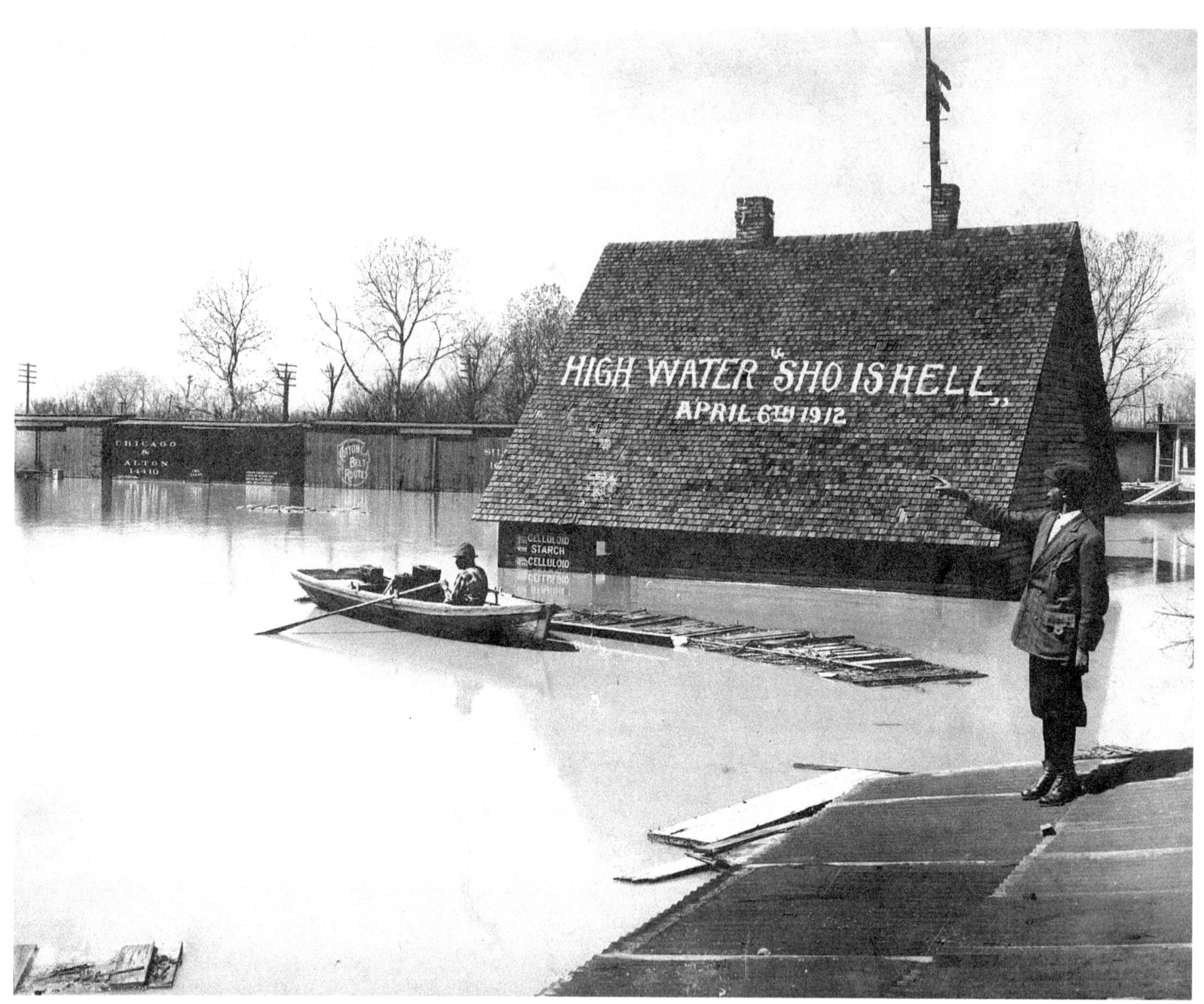

Scene from the 1912 Mississippi River flood. Memphis was relatively safe from high water, but some low-lying areas in the city became susceptible to rising back water as flood levels worsened at the beginning of the 20th century.

Memphis was a haven for Mid-South flood refugees. Facilities such as "Camp Crump," pictured here in 1912, were set up in the city to house refugees.

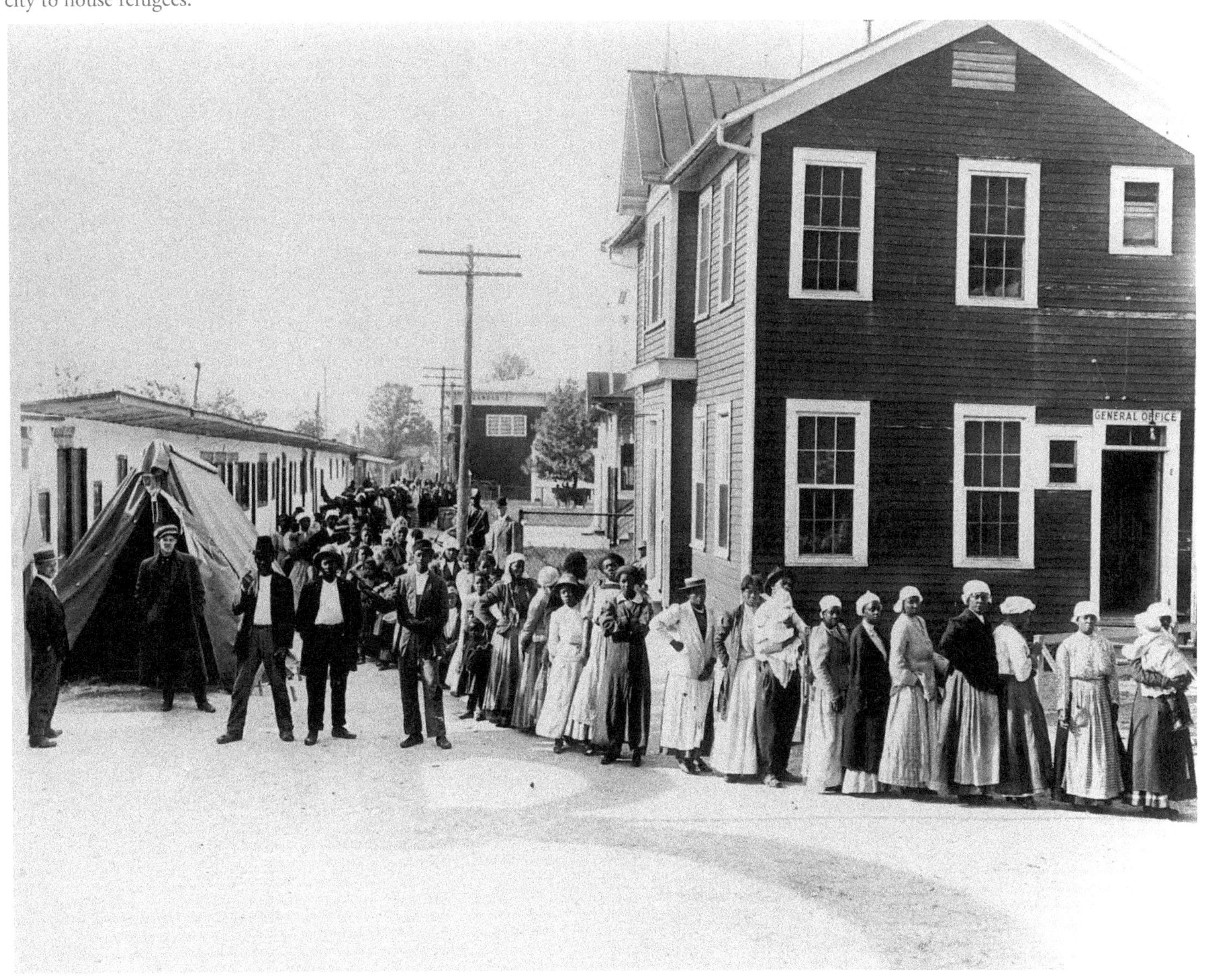

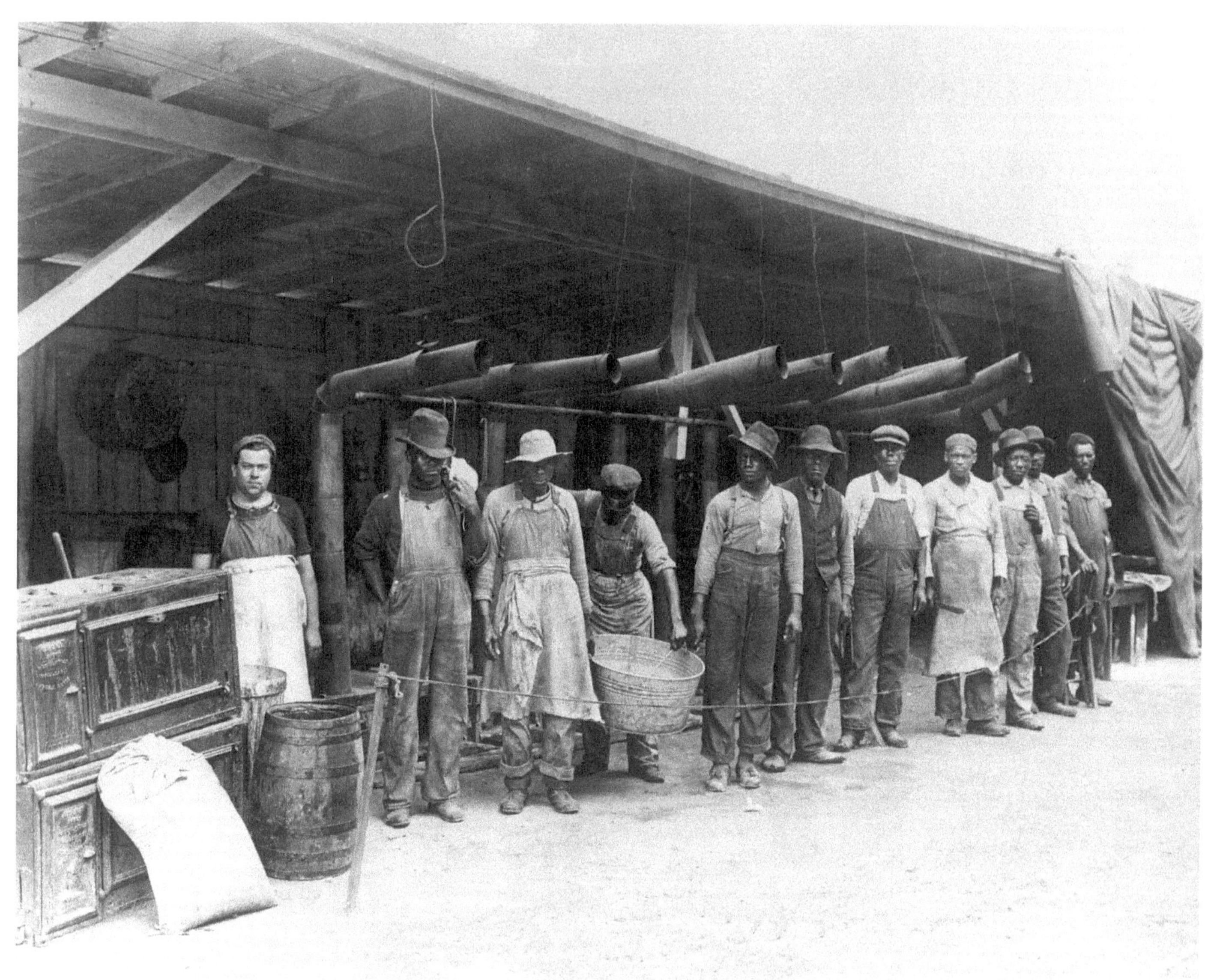

Camp Crump Refugee Camp, 1912. Refugees were often required to perform manual labor in return for assistance.

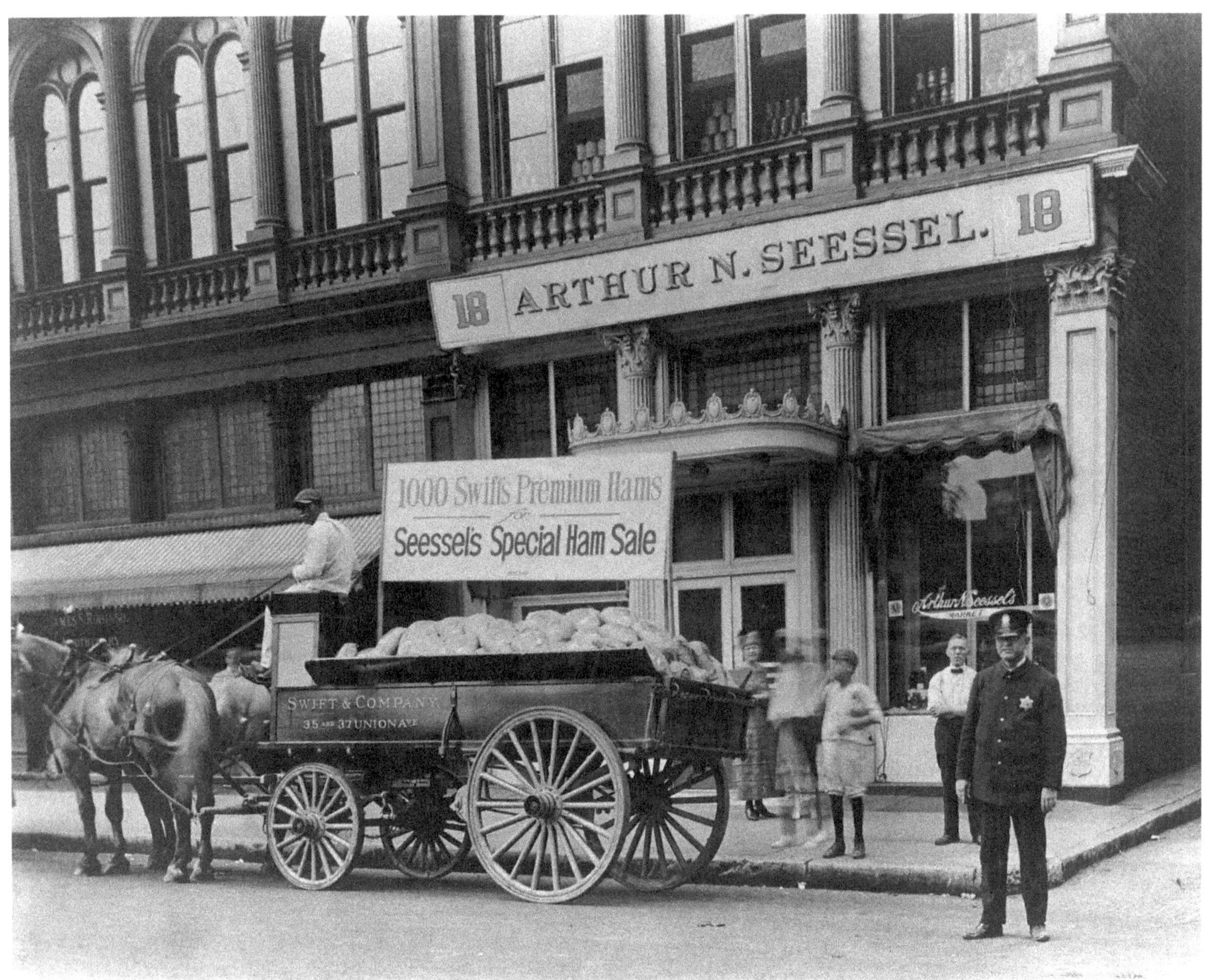

German-born Henry Seessel arrived in Memphis in 1857 and began a butcher business. In 1917, his grandson Arthur opened a full-line grocery, pictured here at 18 North Second. The Seessel family owned a chain of grocery stores which lasted until 2002.

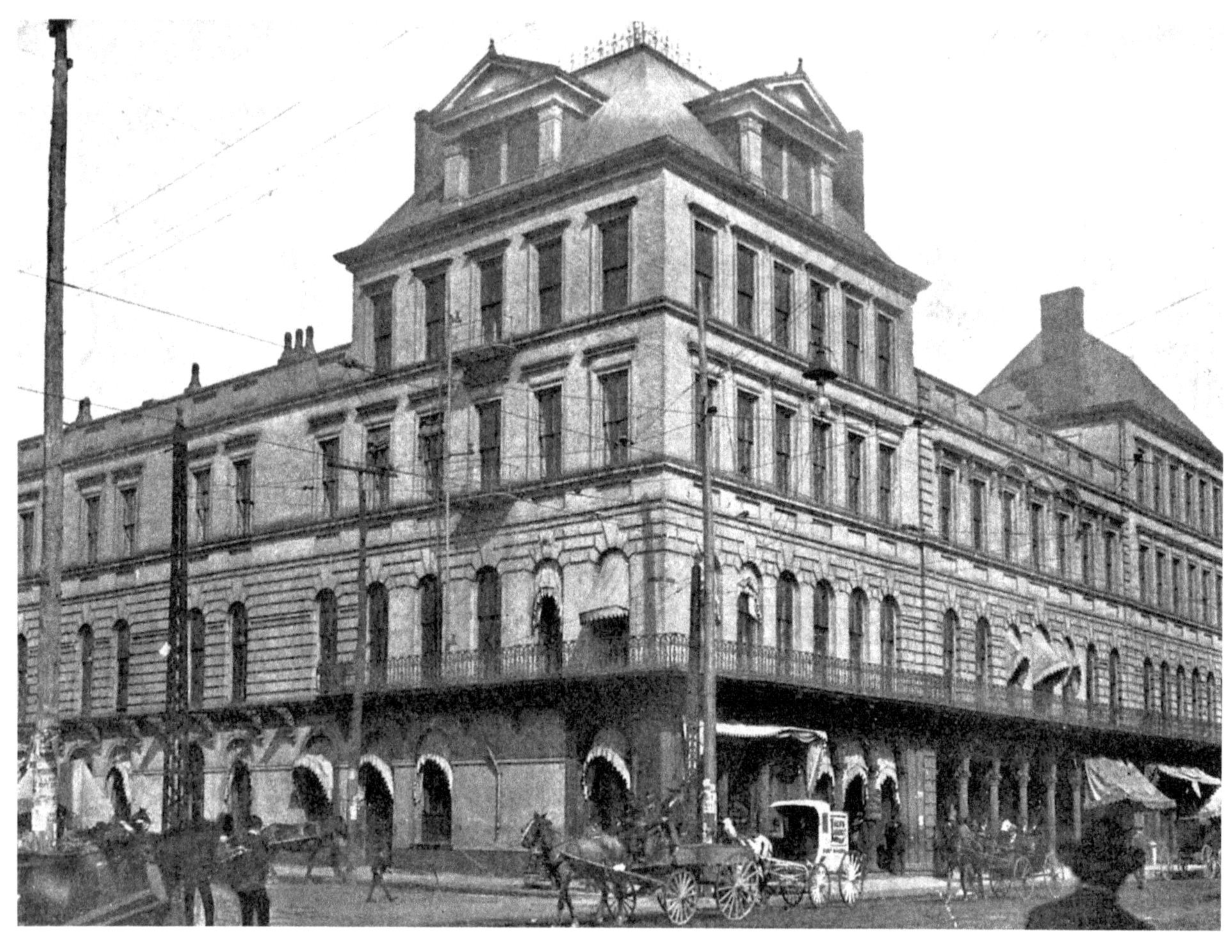

The Shelby County Court House, circa 1890. The Overton Hotel at Main and Poplar Avenue was completed in December 1860. It was sold to the city in 1874 and used as the Shelby County Courthouse until 1909.

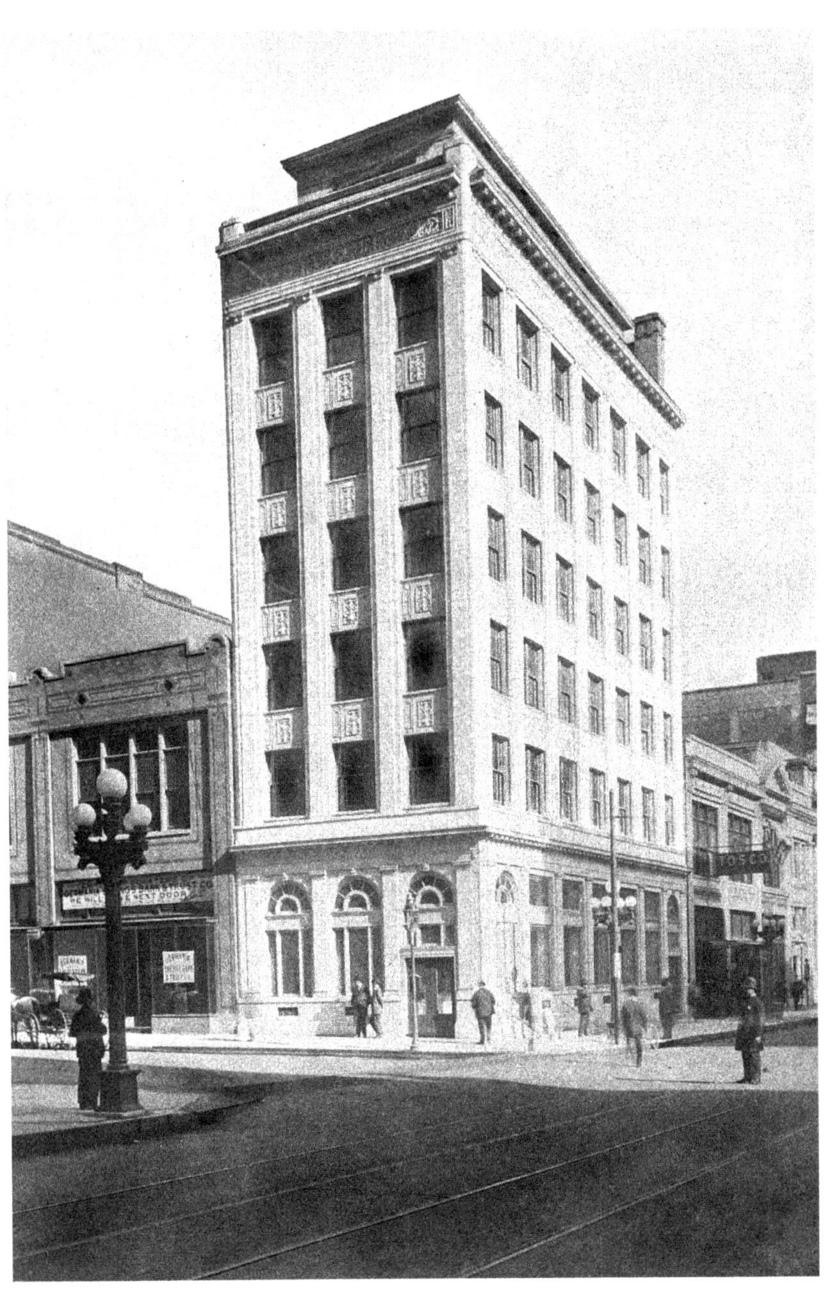

The Germania Bank Building at Second and Madison Avenue, 1913.

Beale Street and Hernando, circa 1915.

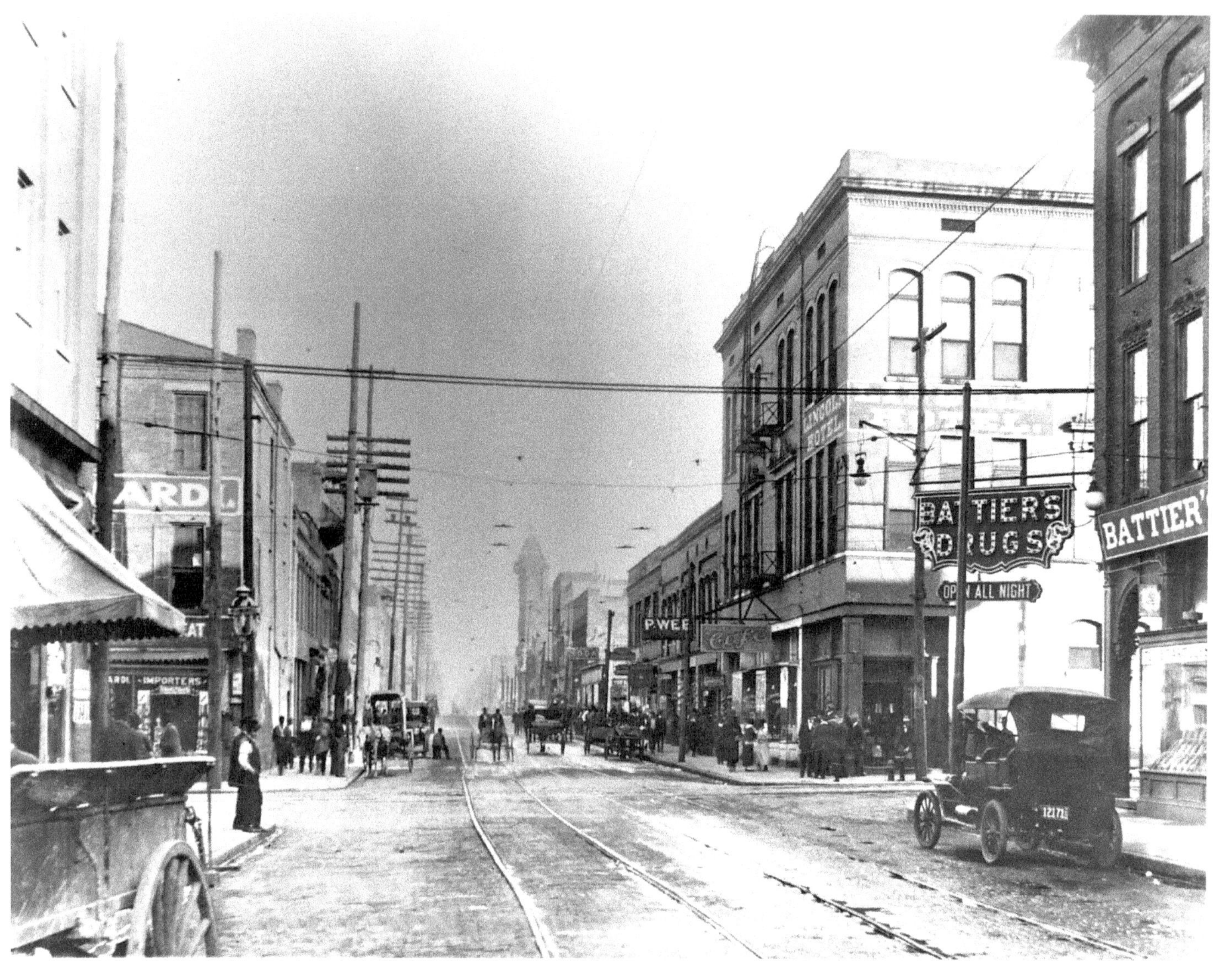

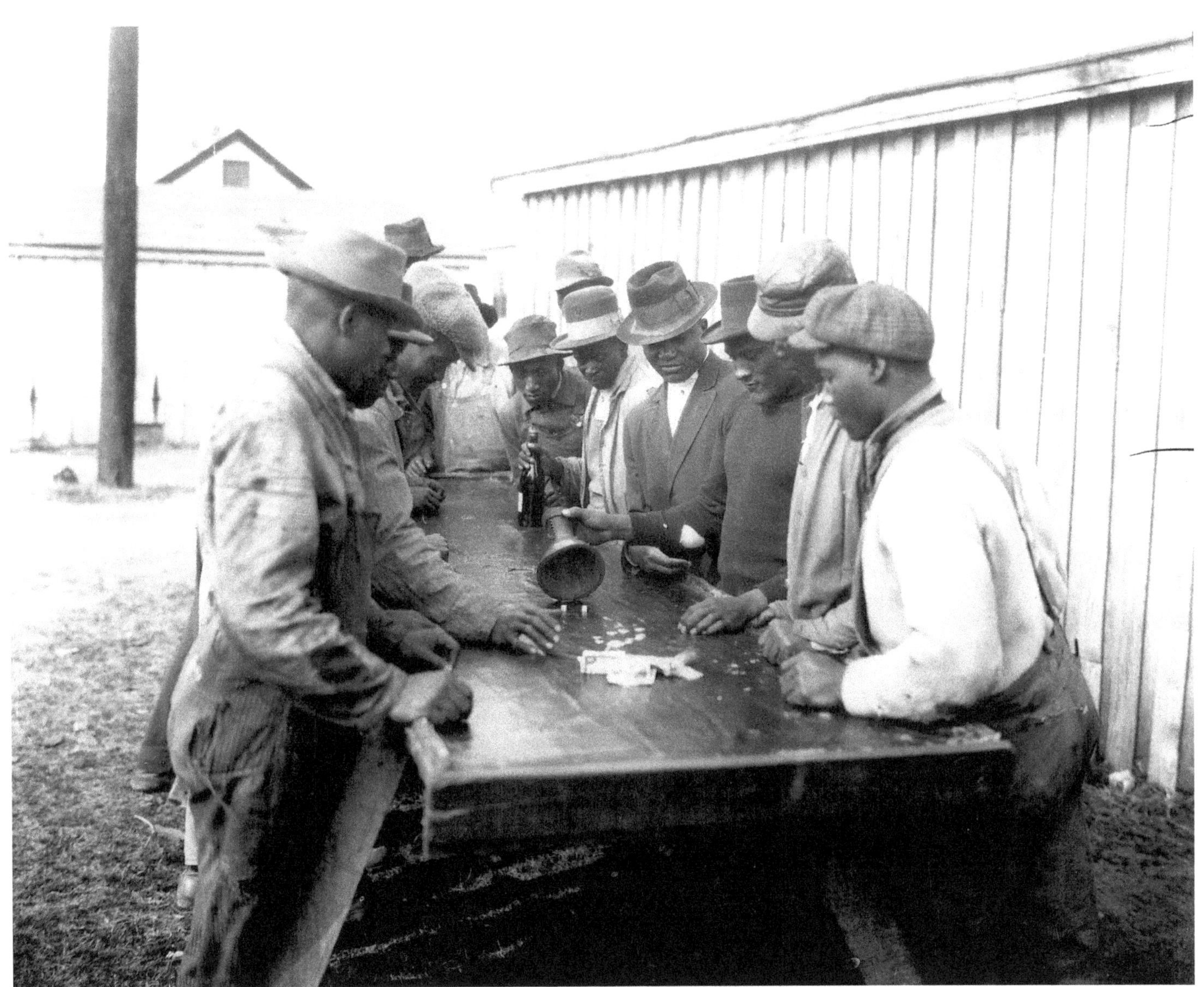

Mayor David "Pappy" Hadden supposedly created the Hadden's Horn as a way to ensure people could not cheat when throwing dice.

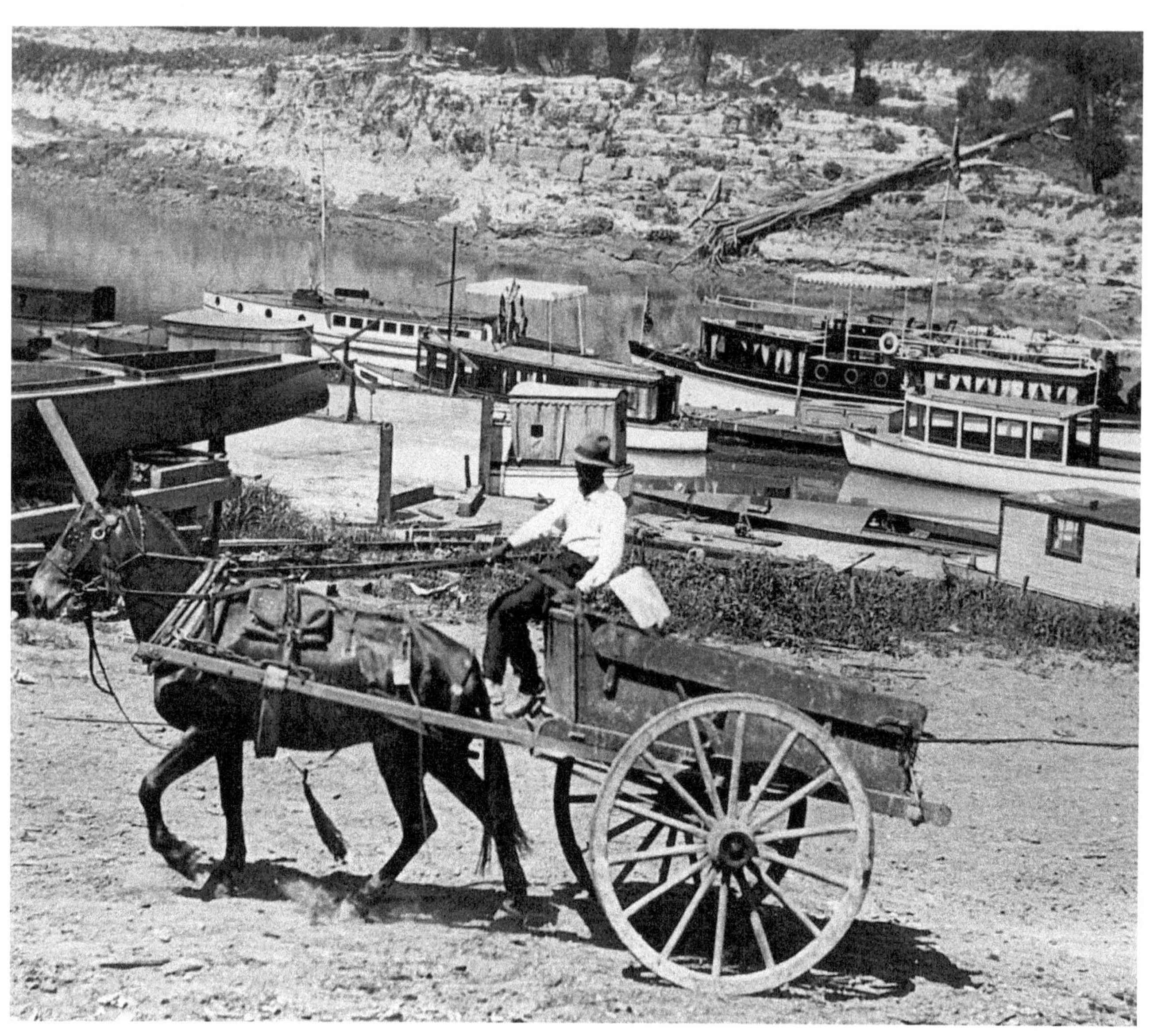

Scene on the bank of the Wolf River at the Gayoso Oil Works.

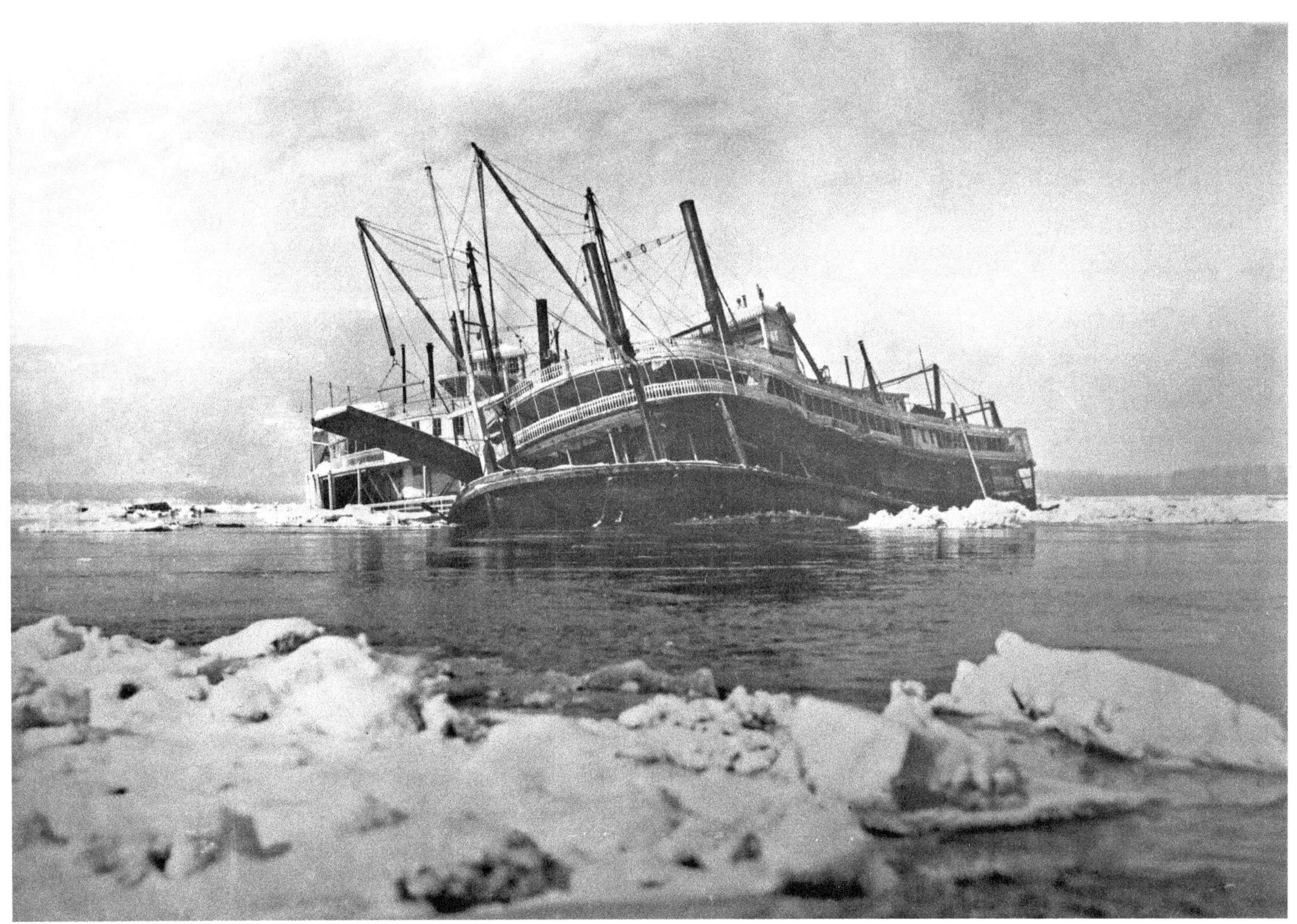

The *Georgia Lee* and the *Desoto*, which was formerly called the *James Lee*, were two of the vessels destroyed when the Mississippi River froze in January 1918.

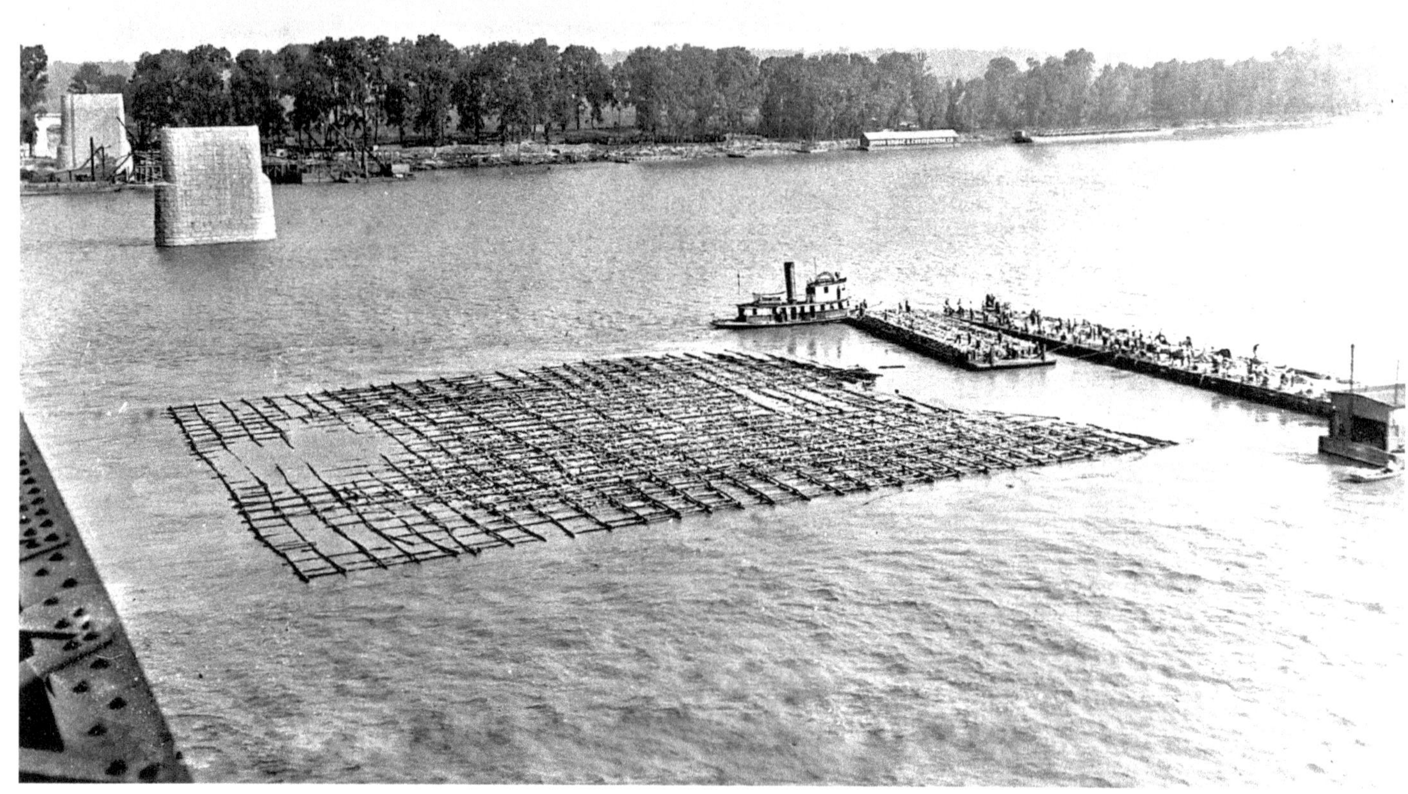

Mats such as the one pictured here were used to stabilize the river bed for the construction of the Harahan Bridge in 1914.

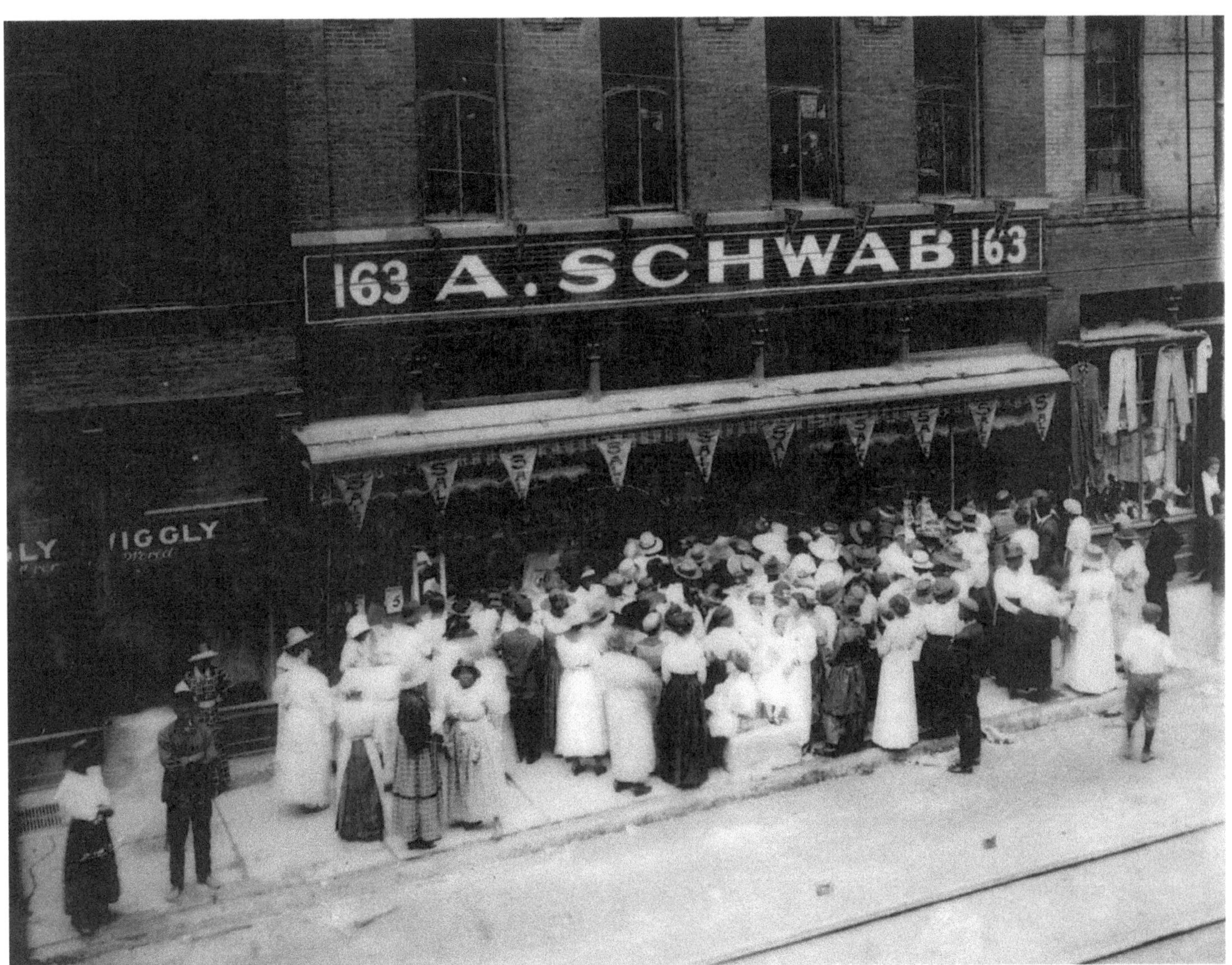

In 1912, Abraham Schwab moved his dry goods business from 149 to 163 Beale Street to accommodate his growing business. Schwab's has been in business on Beale since 1876.

The Cordova Hotel at the corner of Third and Madison.

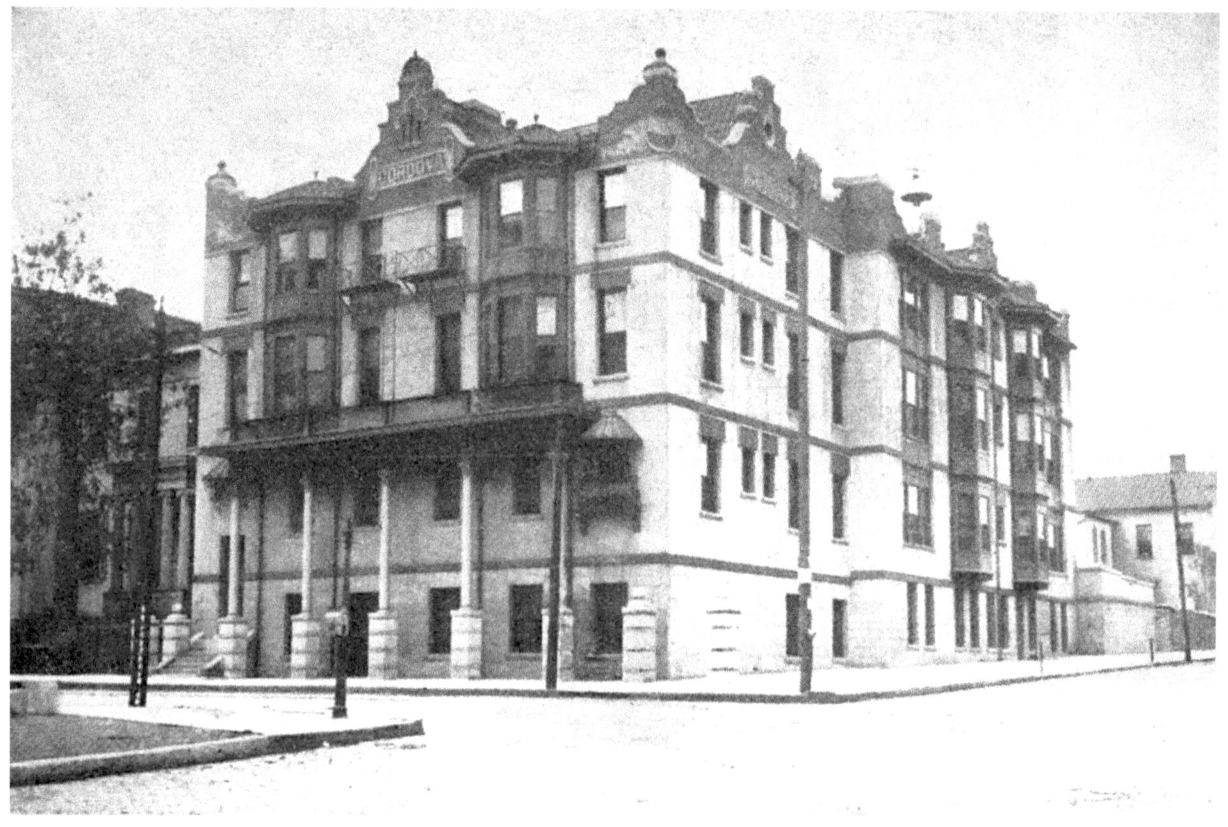

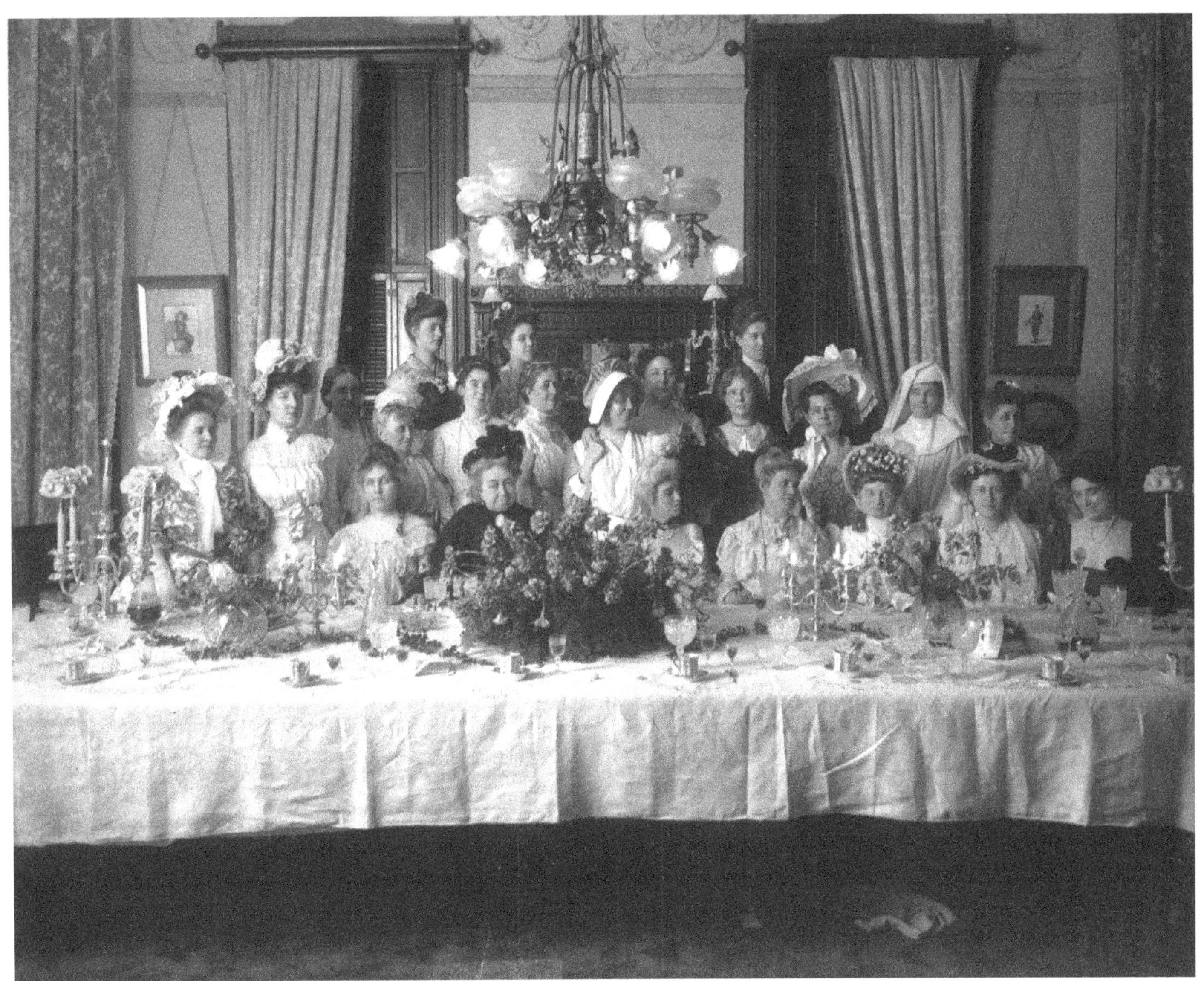

Members of the Memphis Woman's Club, 1904. The Woman's Building at Jefferson and Third opened in 1898 in the building occupied by the Post Office during the Civil War. It was the scene of Memphis society's most exclusive balls and the home of studios where Memphians learned music and the latest dance steps.

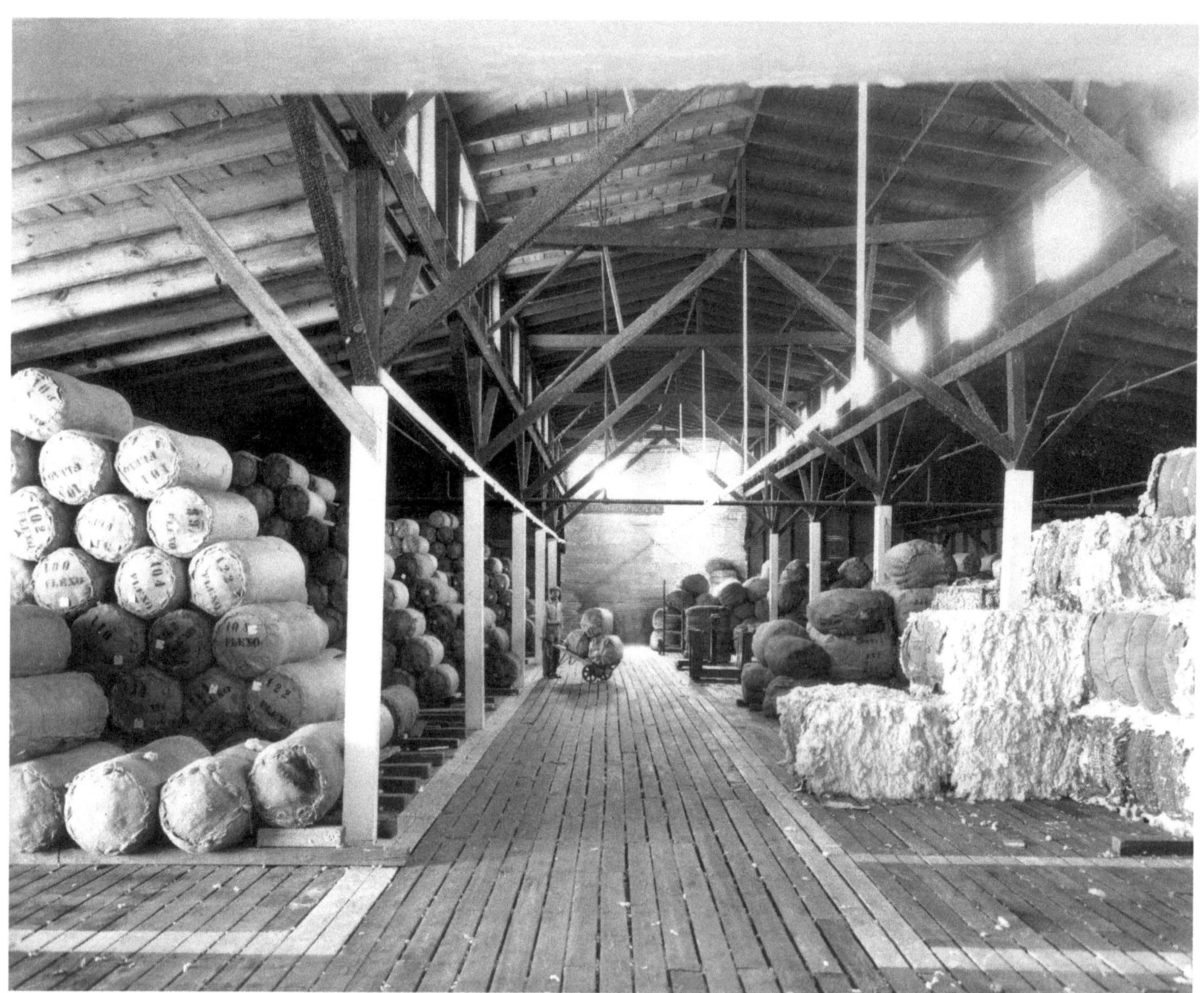

Interior of a cotton warehouse.

The Thriving Metropolis

1920-1939

The 1920s and 1930s marked a time of remarkable change in Memphis. Many small suburban streetcar towns including Binghamton, Normal and Highland Heights became part of the city. Unfortunately, these sudden changes blurred the lines between residential and commercial properties. In response, the City Planning Commission was formed in 1921 to regulate newly created zoning ordinances, which were later redefined by the Bartholomew Plan of 1924. The Commission's success made Memphis a model for other American citys' planning efforts.

New public construction projects were undertaken as well. The General Hospital added an isolation wing in 1922 and a separate maternity wing in 1924. Also in 1924, Ellis Auditorium was constructed as a venue for conventions, concerts, sports and other entertainment. The newest incarnation of the Orpheum Theatre opened in 1928, replacing the Grand Opera House. Southwestern College was built in 1925 and Memphis Technical High School was completed in 1929. Post-war improvements in aviation brought about the need for the Municipal Airport, which would later prove to be as important as river and rail transportation.

Memphis was the scene of a number of remarkable events in the 1920s. The Universal Life Insurance Company, one of the largest black-owned insurance companies in the nation, was founded in 1923. Tom Lee saved the lives of thirty-two people when the Norman capsized near Memphis in May 1925.

As the Great Depression struck in October 1929, agricultural prices fell and Memphians suffered dearly. In response, local businessmen founded the Cotton Carnival as a way to raise spirits and restore faith in the cotton industry. The success of the Mardi Gras-like festival made it into a permanent annual event.

In the midst of the Depression, one event helped transform Memphis into a modern city. The Tennessee Valley Authority was established in 1933 as part of President Franklin Roosevelt's New Deal program to provide plentiful and inexpensive electricity. E.H. Crump campaigned tirelessly to persuade Memphians to join TVA. His efforts paid off in 1934 when the results of a special election gave officials the authority to purchase the local electrical system from its private owners and link it to the larger network. The process was completed in 1939 when the city purchased the local utility company and renamed it Memphis Light, Gas and Water Division.

Cotton bales being unloaded from a riverboat.

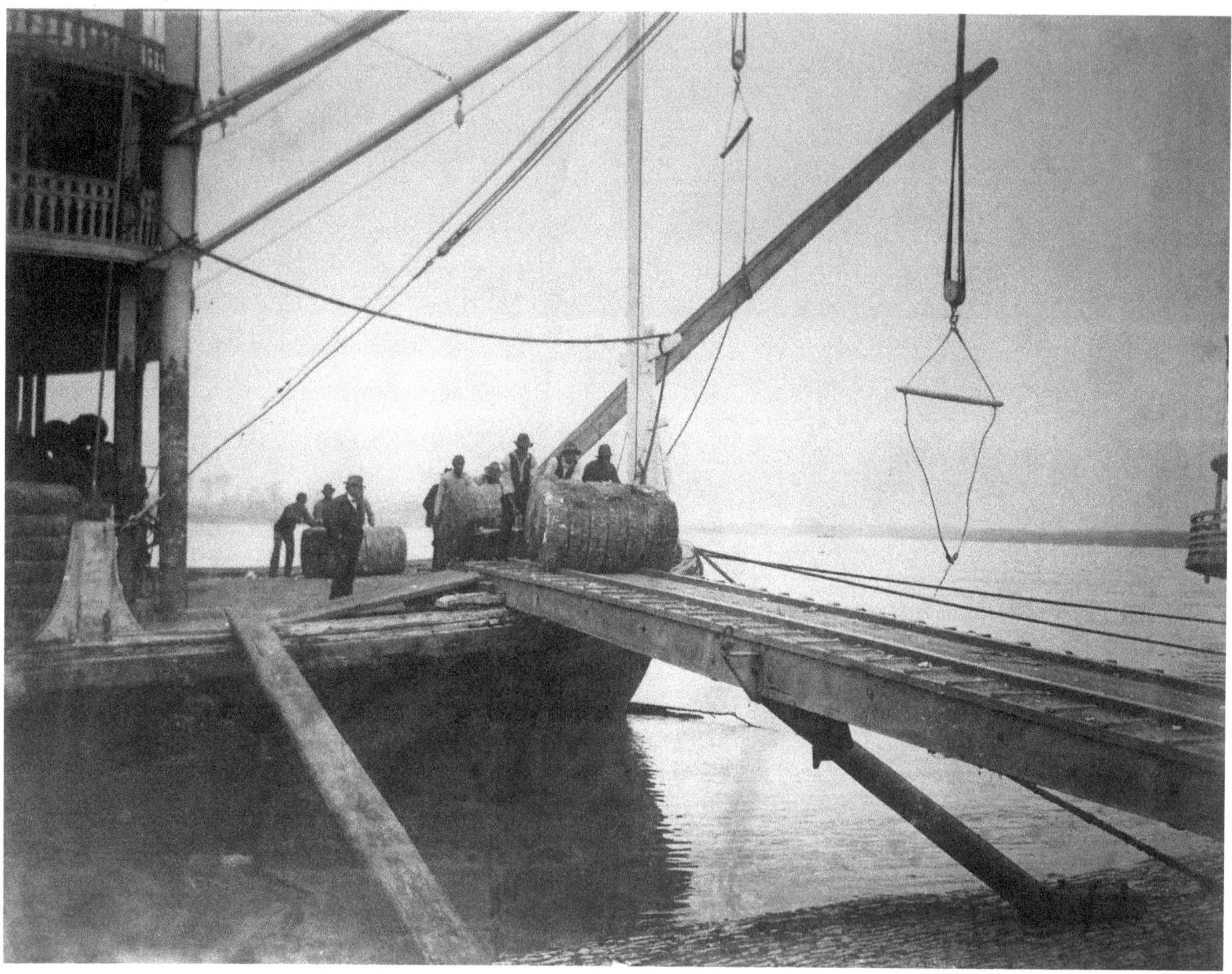

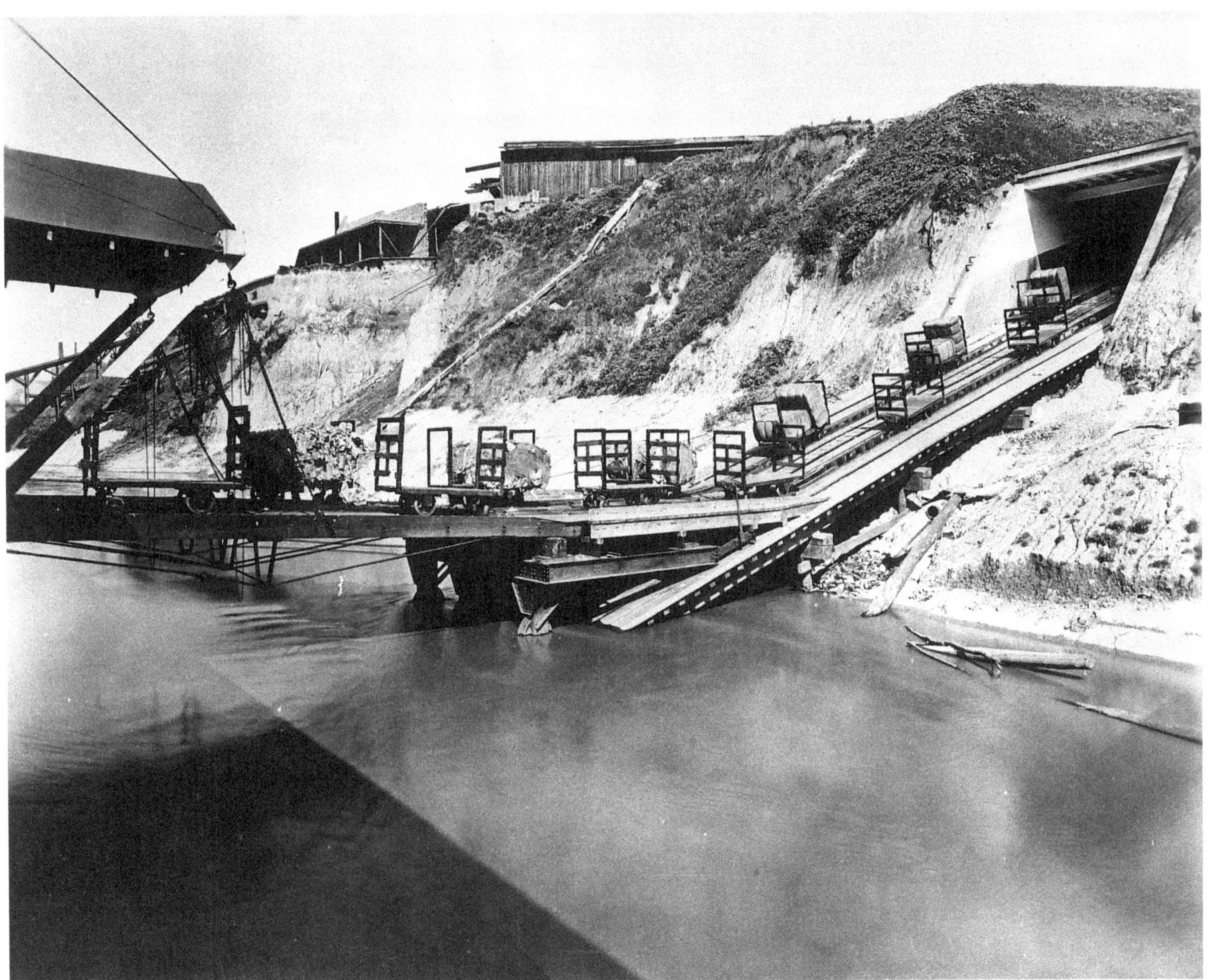

Thousands of tons of products such as cotton, charcoal and canned goods were shipped via barge on the Mississippi River by the Federal Barge Line through the Port of Memphis.

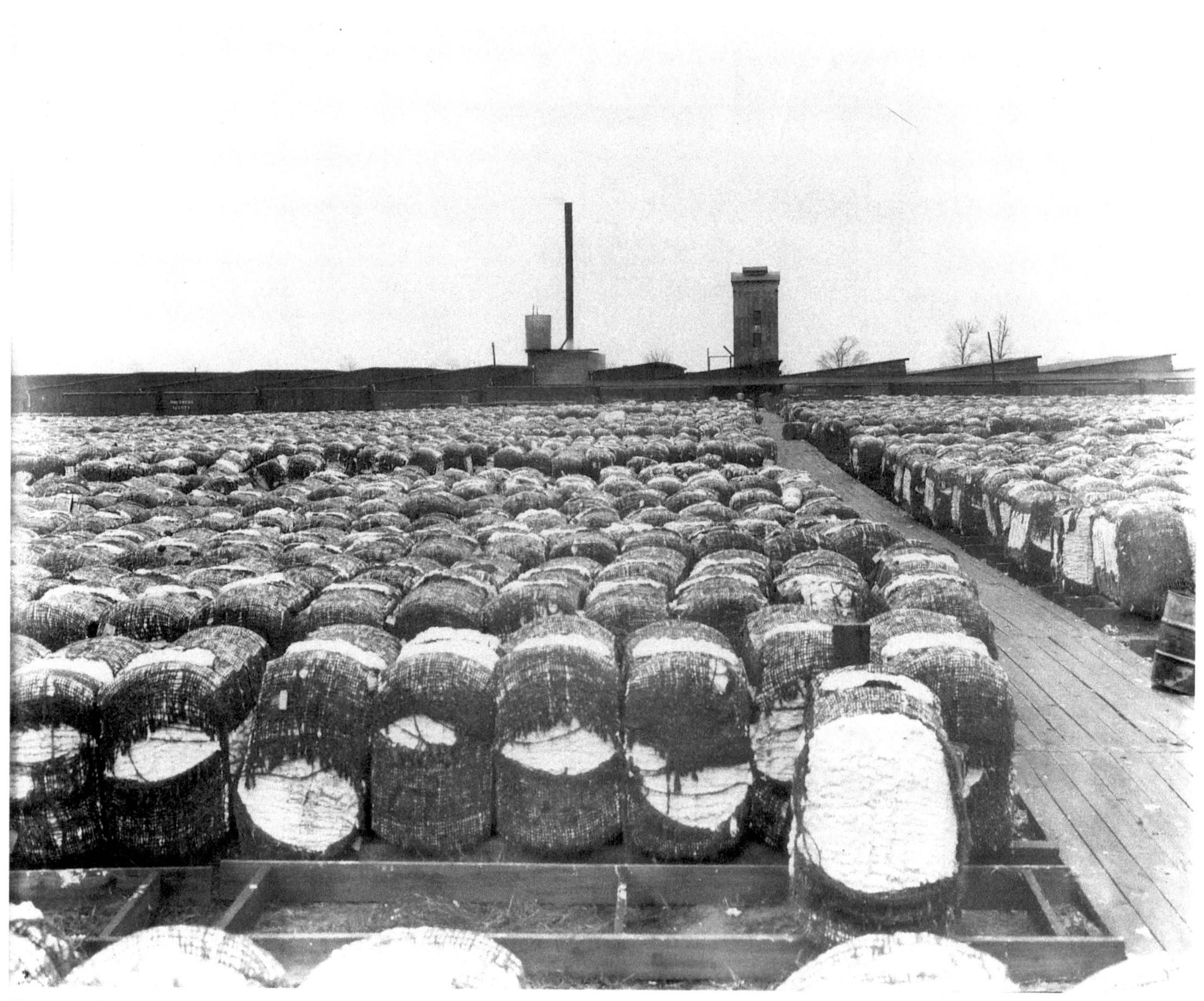

Cotton bales.

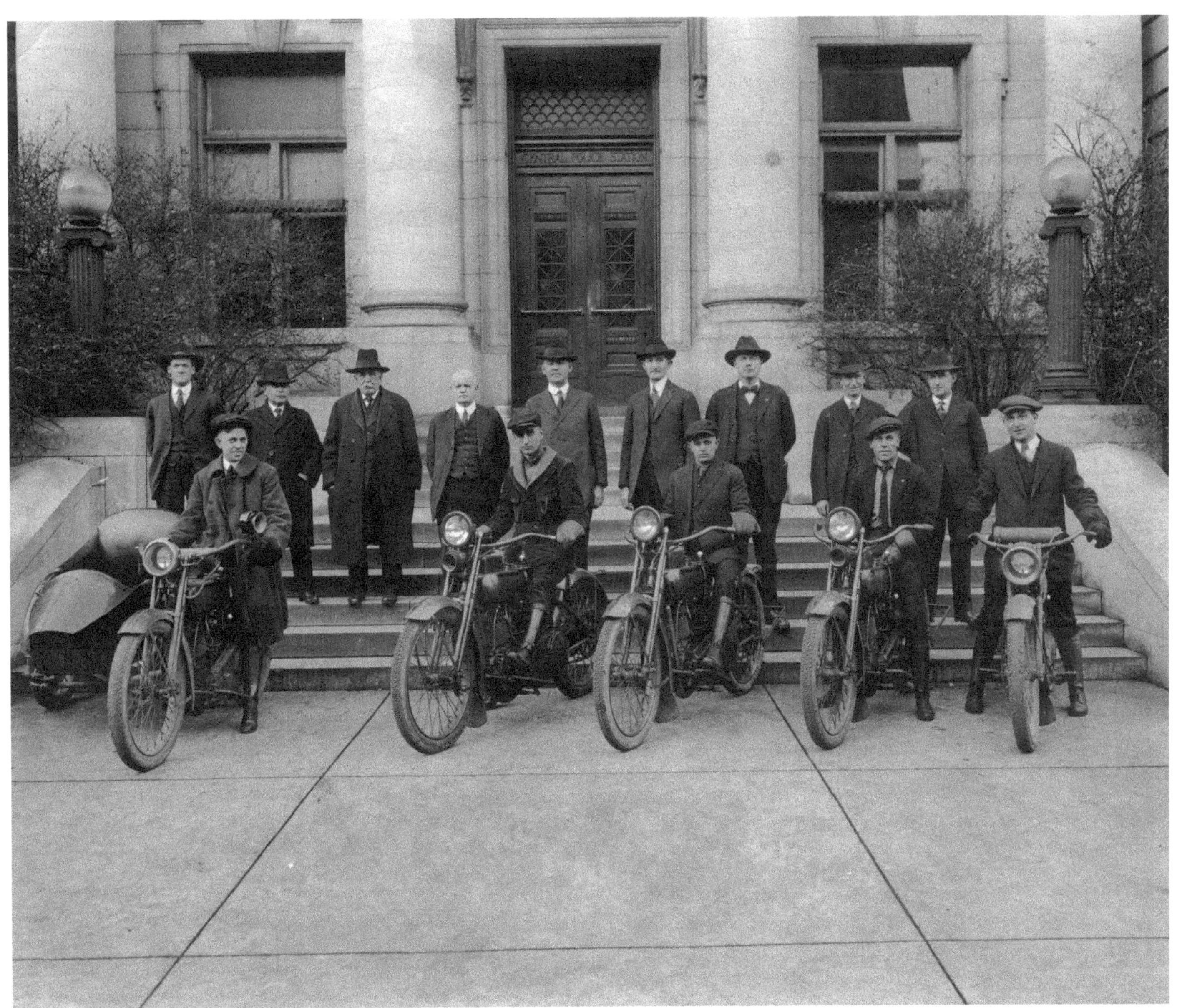

The Motor Cycle and Auto Department of the Metropolitan Police Department pictured in front of the Central Police Station, 1920.

City Beautiful Commission exhibit in Court Square, 1937. The Memphis City Beautiful Commission was founded in 1930, and inspired Memphians to improve the city with their slogan, "Clean Up, Paint Up, Fix Up." The commission is the oldest city beautification organization in the country.

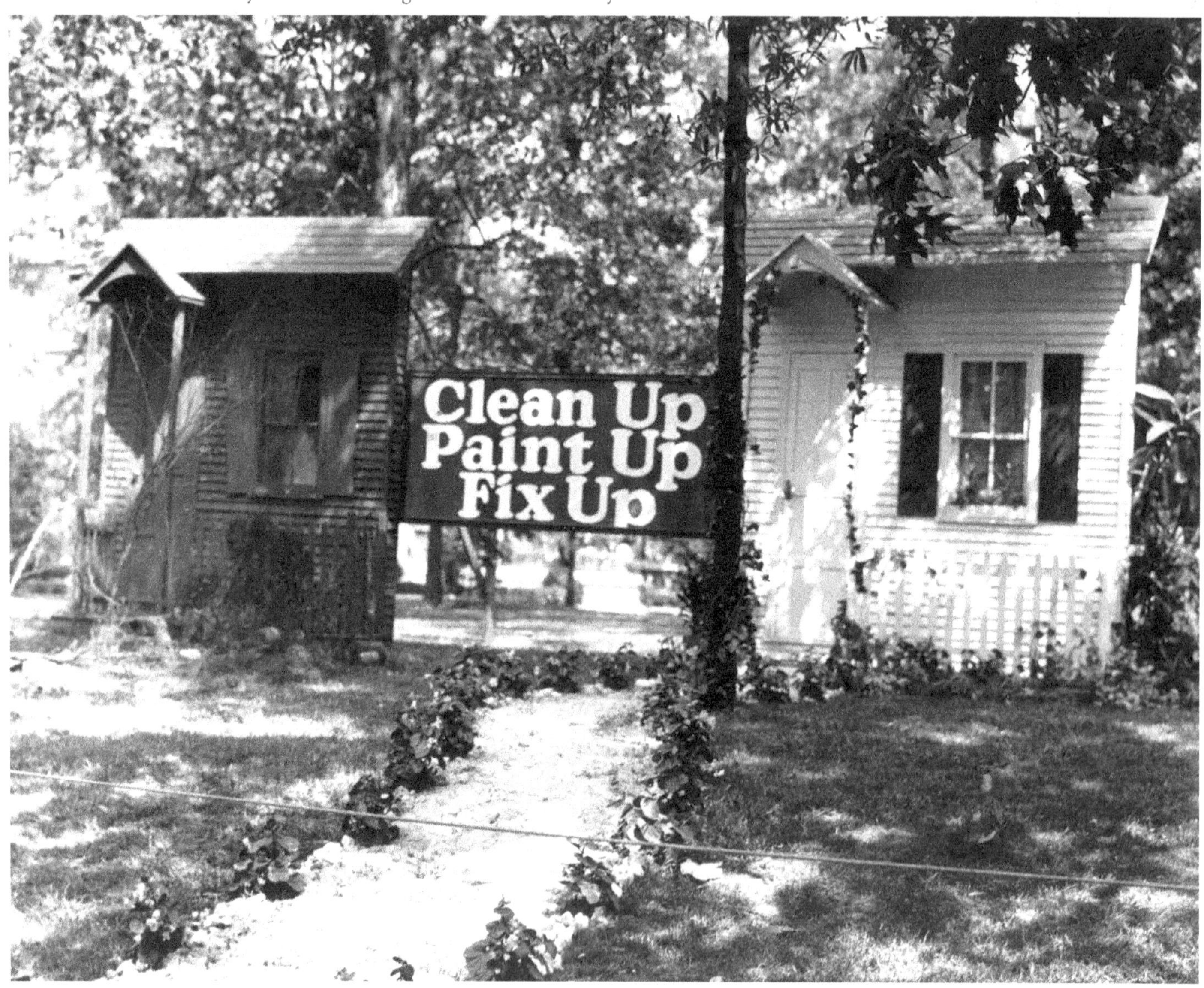

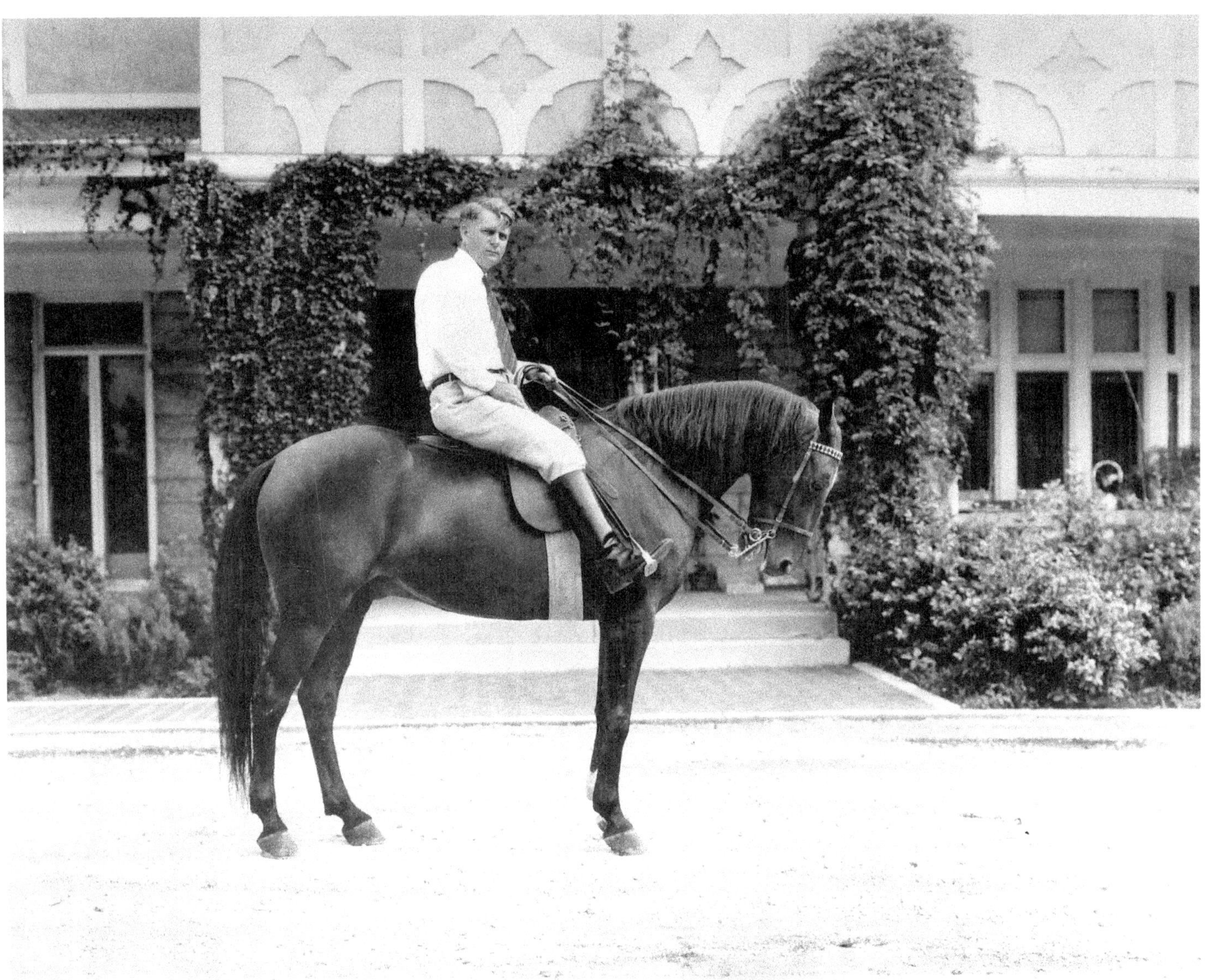

Clarence Saunders, the founder of Piggly Wiggly. Saunders founded his business with one store in 1916, and by 1922, the chain had grown to include over 1,200 stores nationwide.

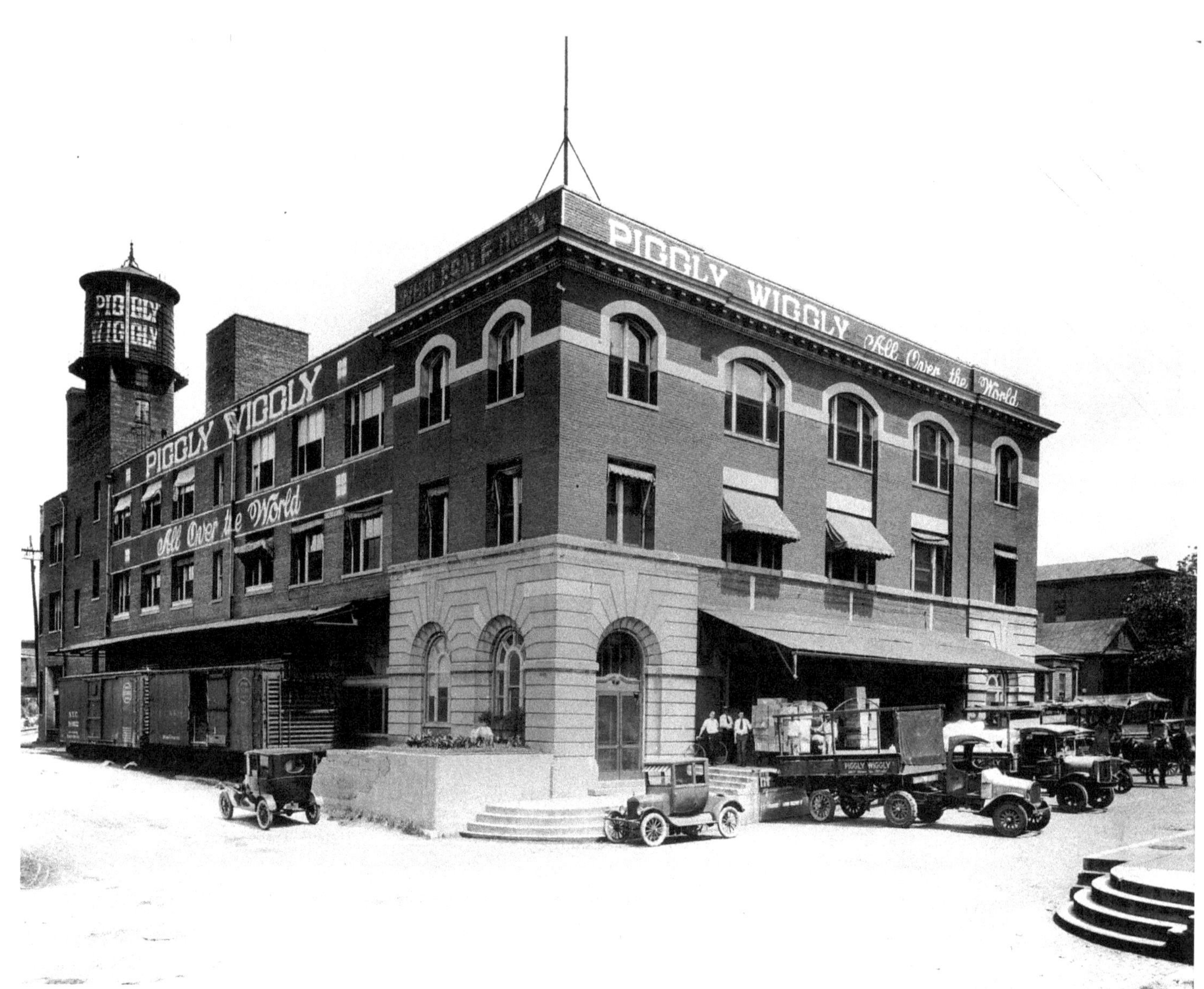

Piggly Wiggly warehouse.

The Pink Palace was originally the home of Clarence Saunders. The city came into possession of the property after Saunders lost his fortune, and it was turned into a museum in 1930.

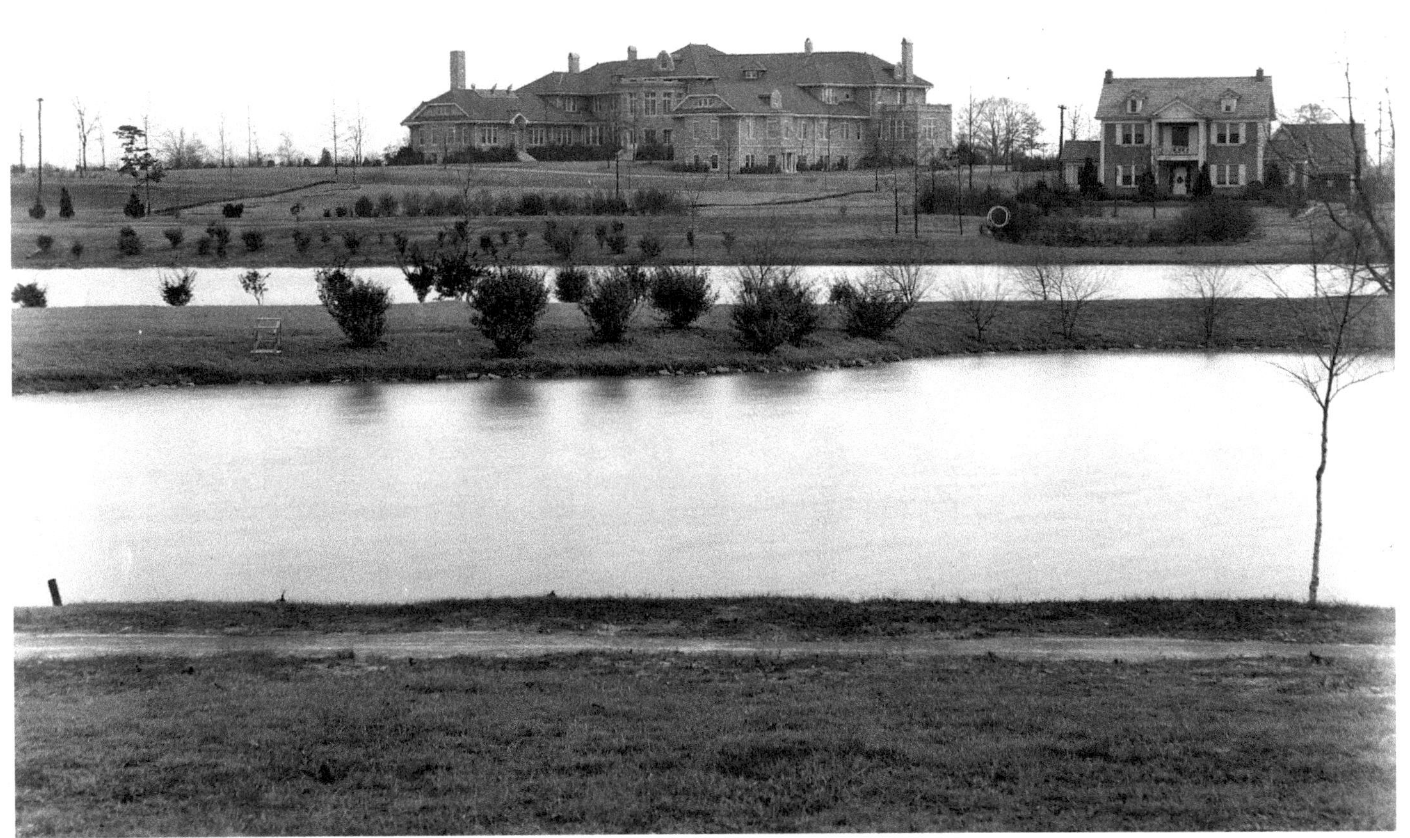

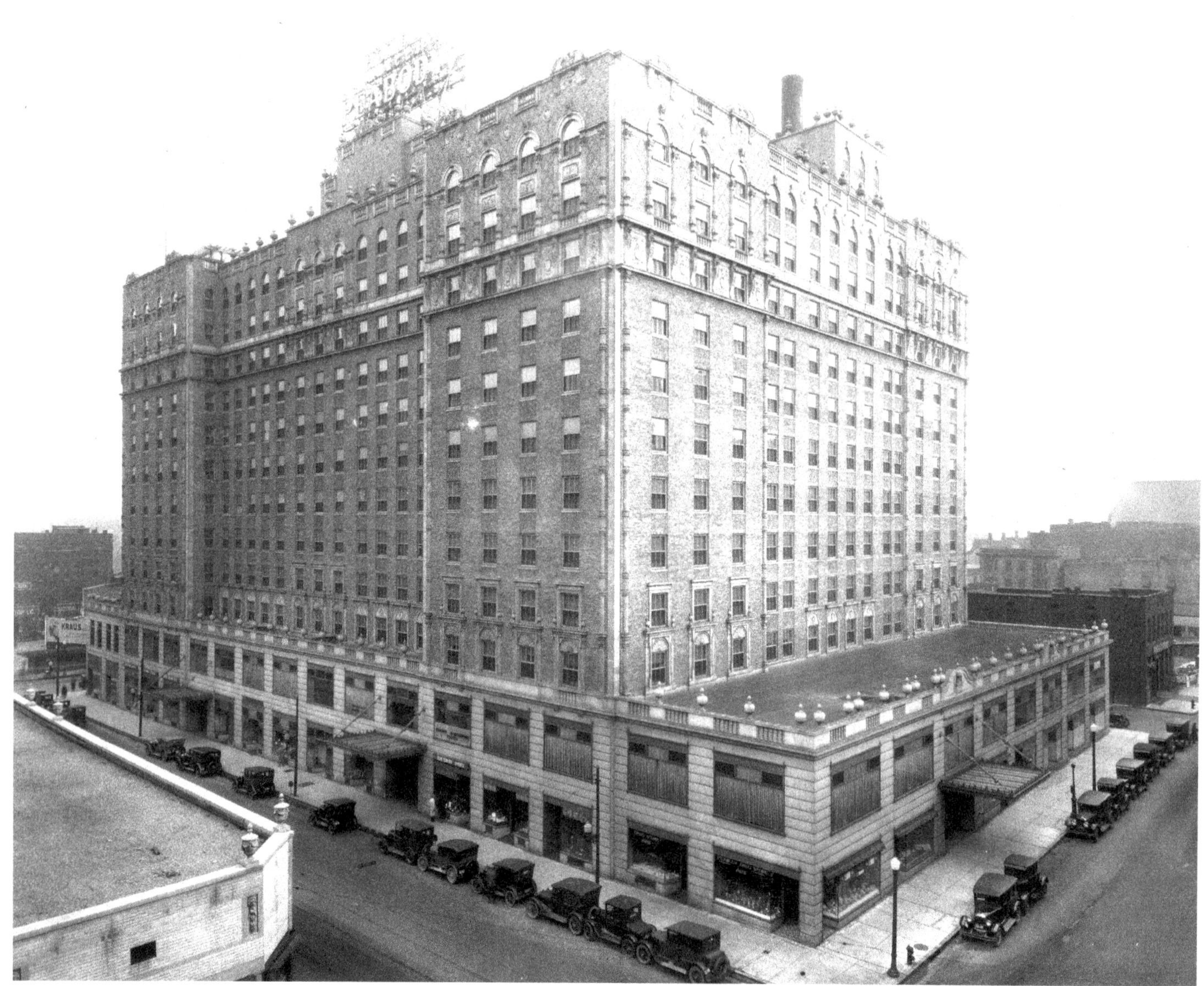

The current incarnation of the Peabody Hotel opened at 149 Union Avenue in 1925.

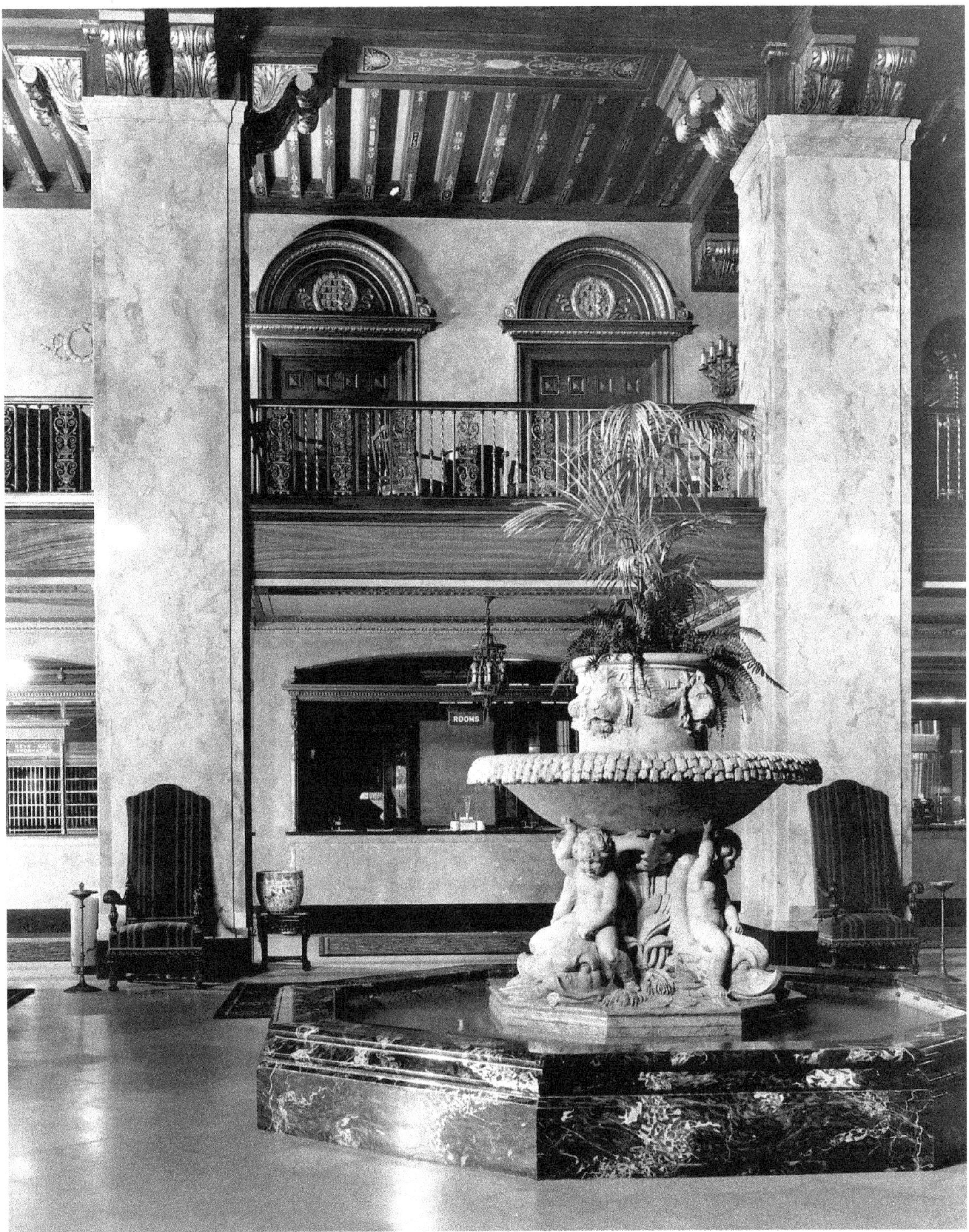

The Peabody Hotel lobby features a Bernini-inspired fountain occupied by live ducks who are escorted from their roof-top roost every morning.

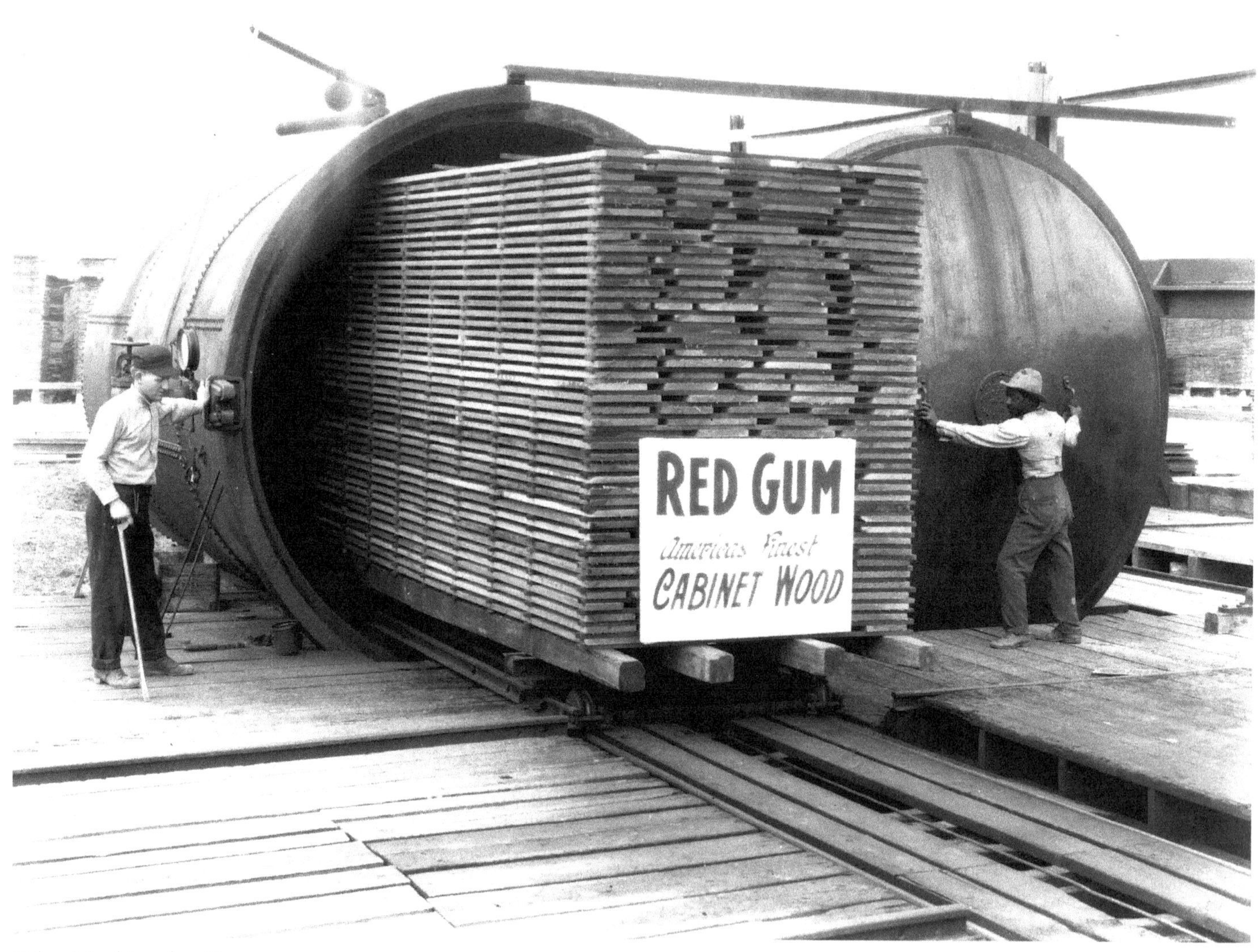

Fisher-Hurd Lumber Company.

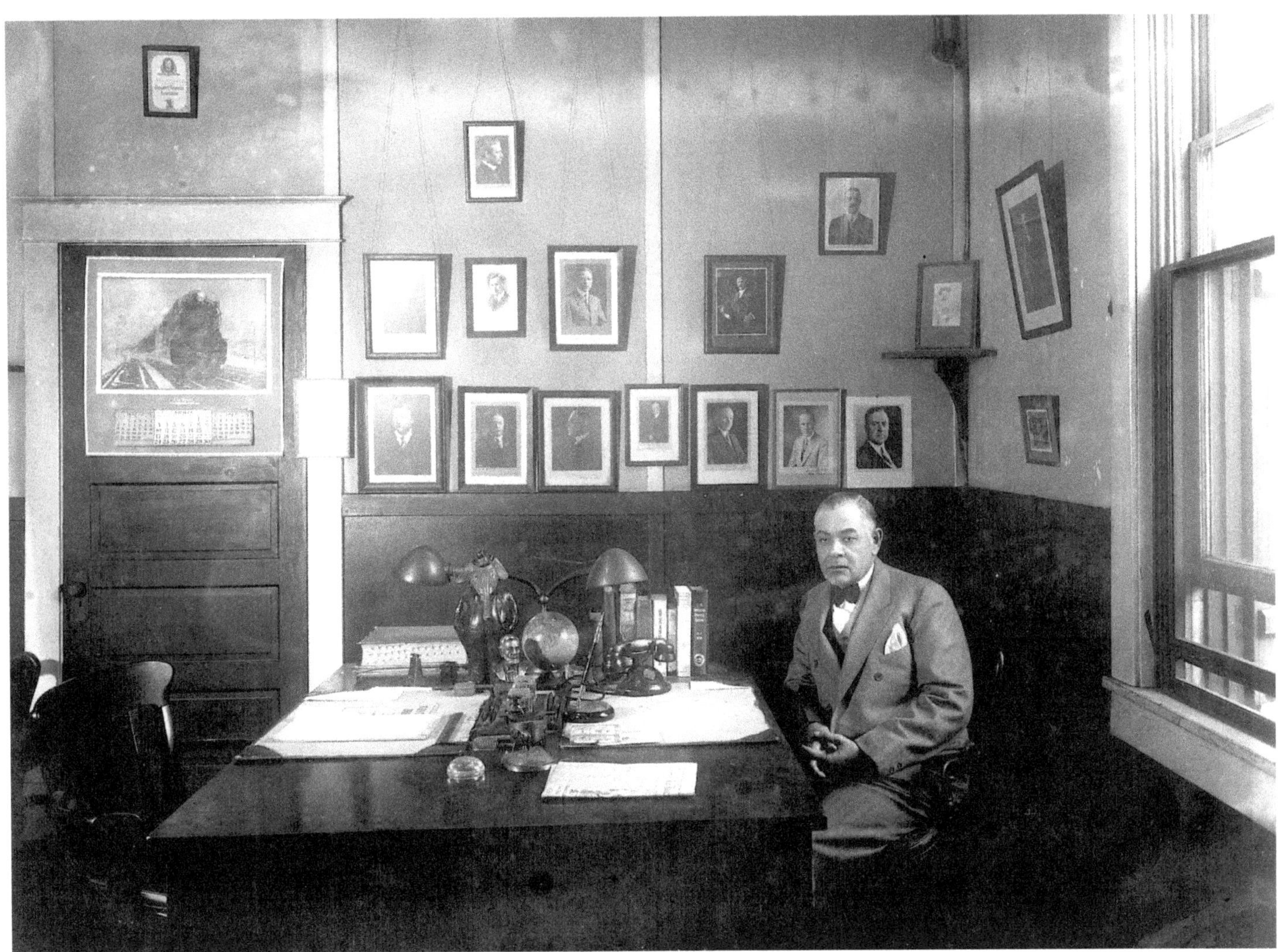

Robert R. Church, Jr., founded the Lincoln League and the Memphis branch of the NAACP. Church also served as a delegate to the Republican National Convention from 1912 to 1940.

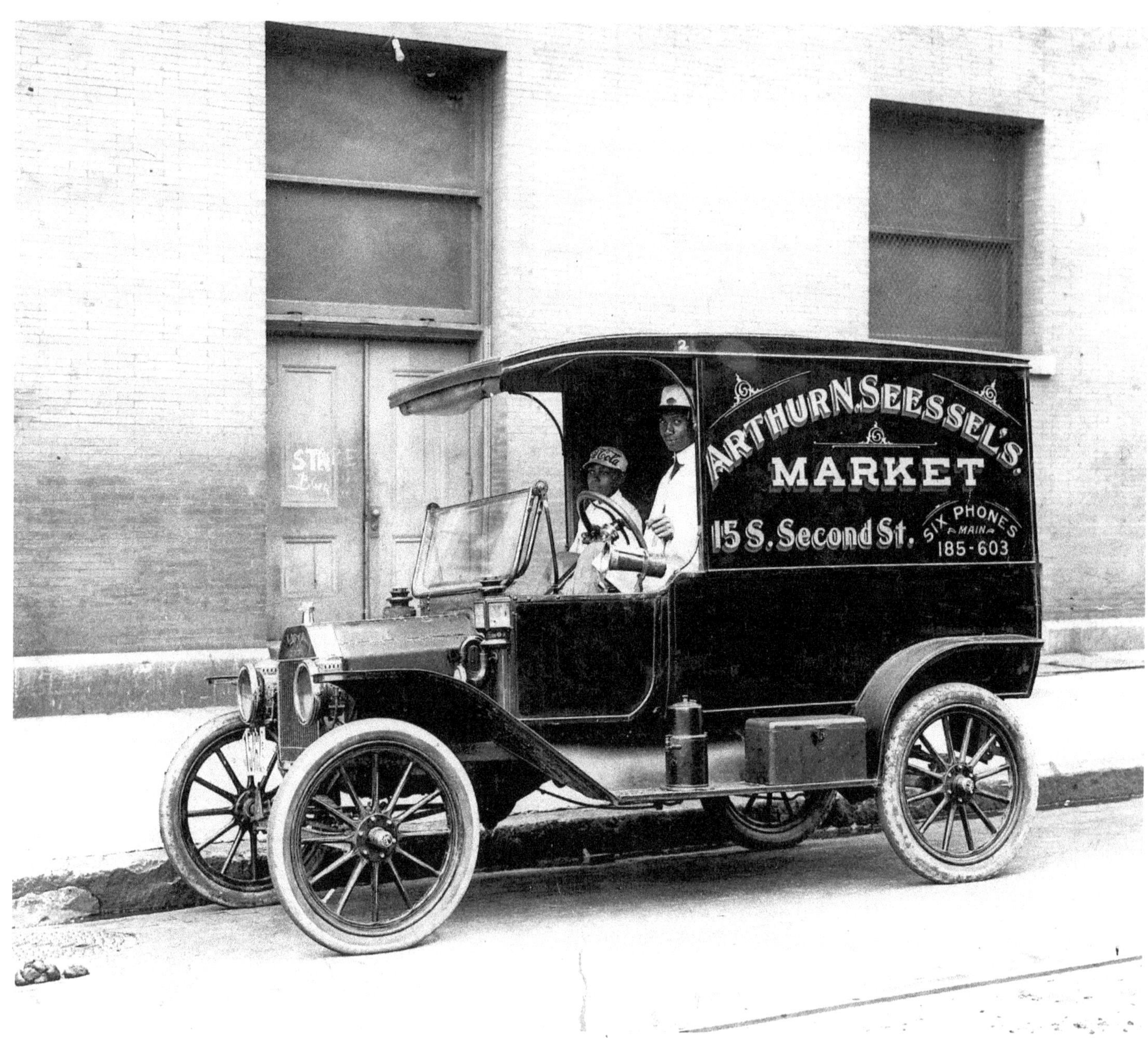

Arthur Seessel moved his family's butcher business to 15 South Second Street in 1909. In 1912, he began using gasoline-powered trucks to deliver his goods. Seessel's Grocery stores continued to deliver items to customers' homes until 1965.

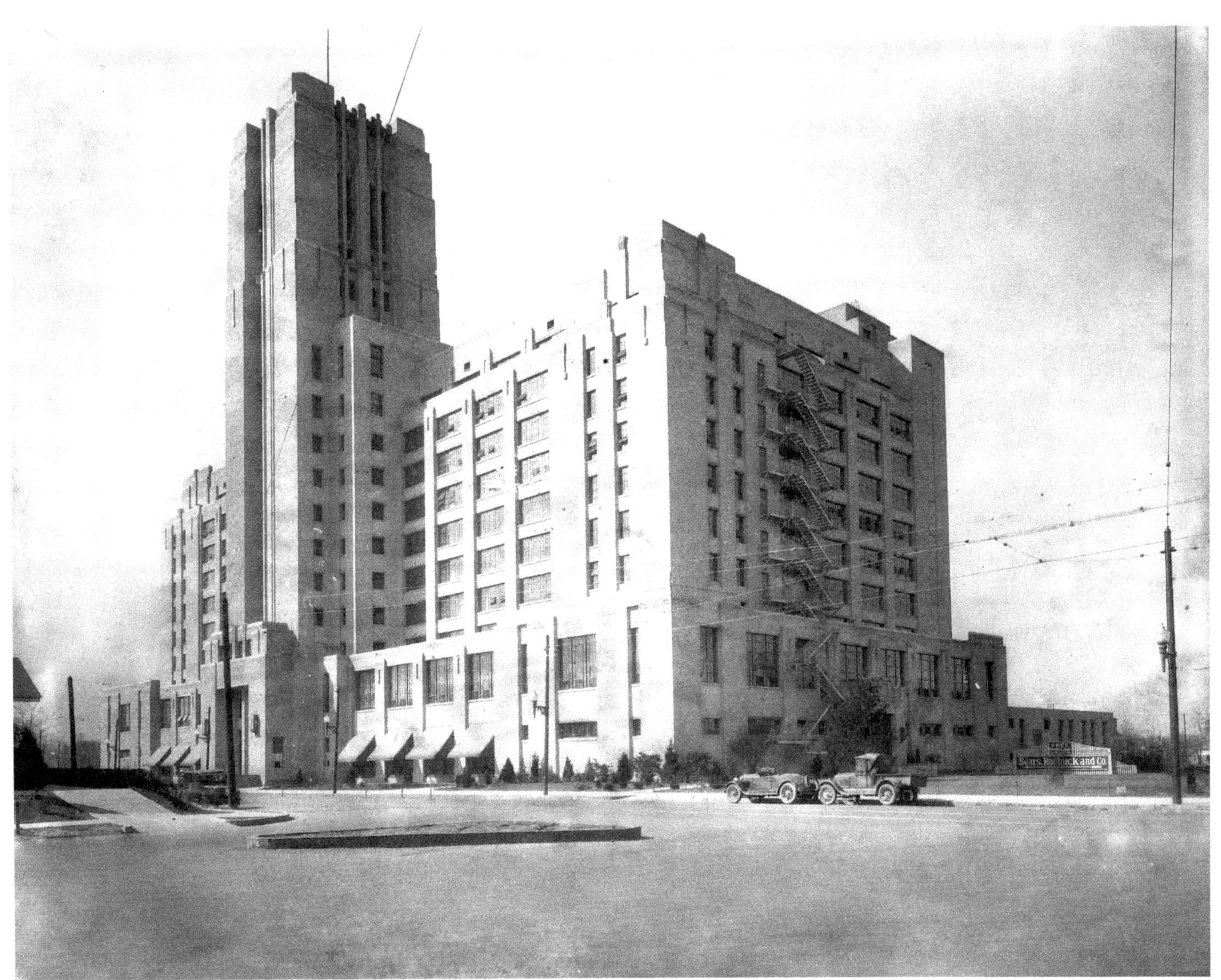

Sears and Roebuck opened this building at 497 Watkins in 1927. It was used as a credit operations and catalog merchandise distribution center in addition to operating as a retail store.

A typical cotton gin where cotton was processed and packaged.

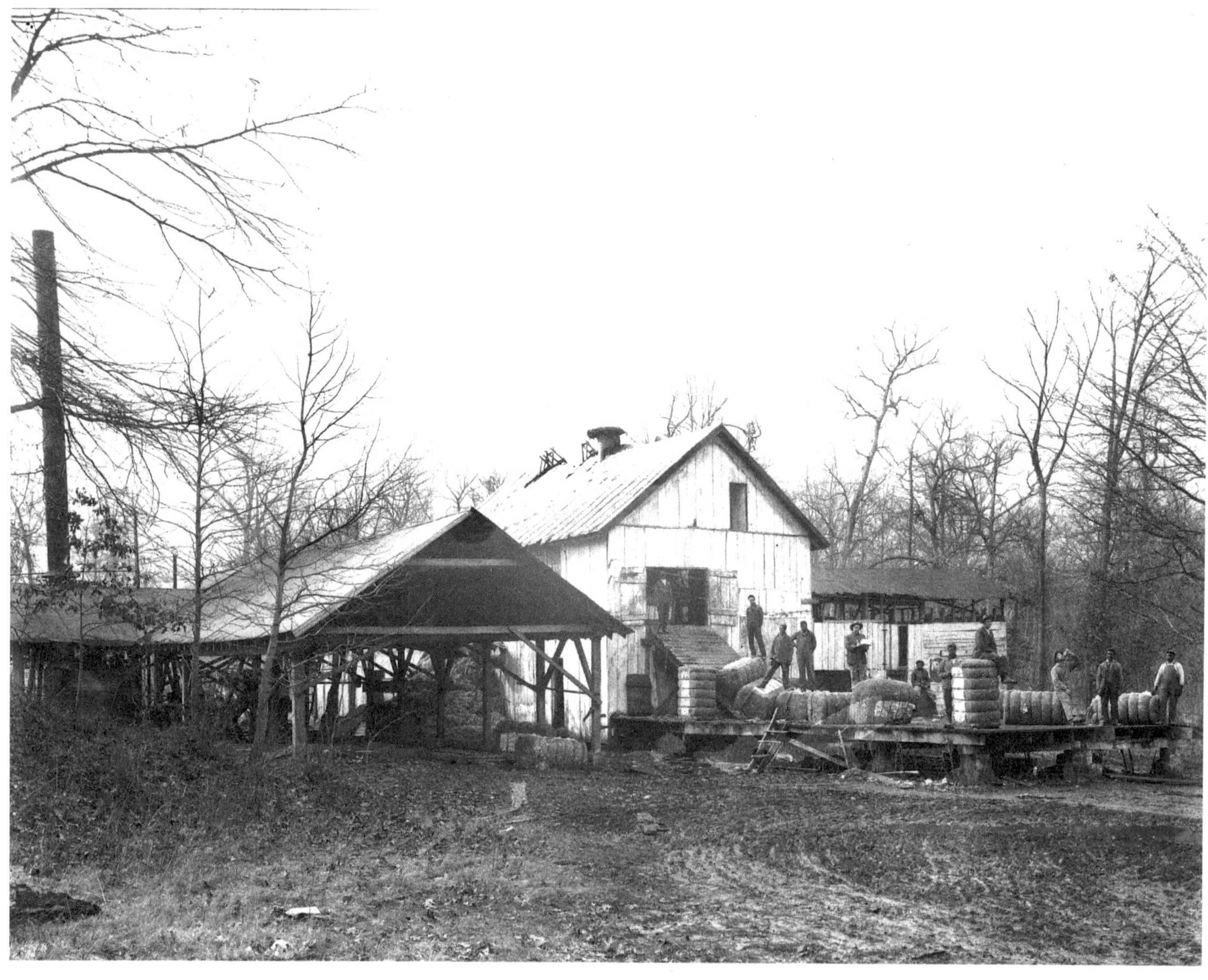

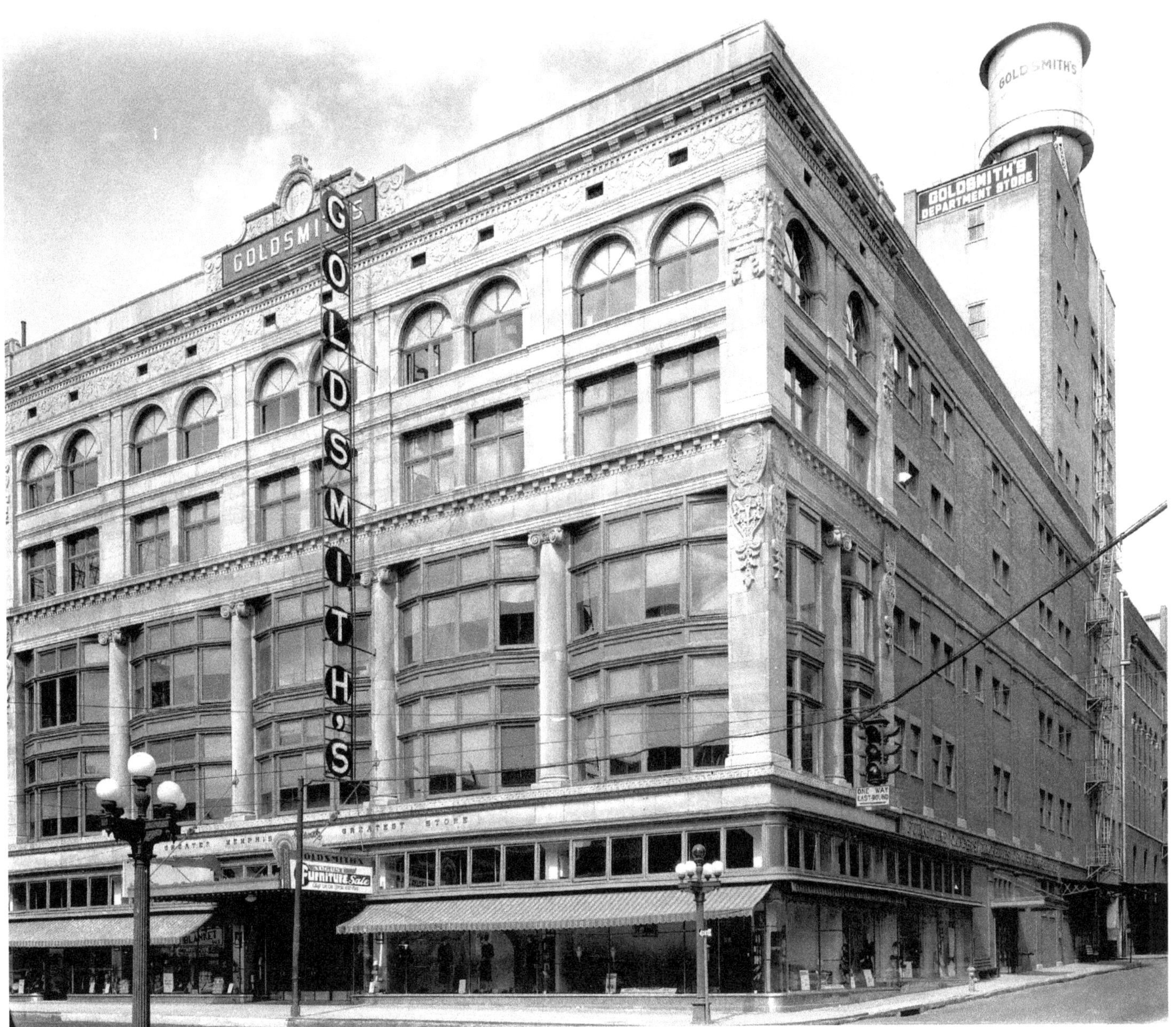

German-born Jacob and Isaac Goldsmith bought their first store on Beale Street in 1870 and a second on Main in 1881. In 1901, Jacob moved operations into this building at 123 South Main after Isaac's death.

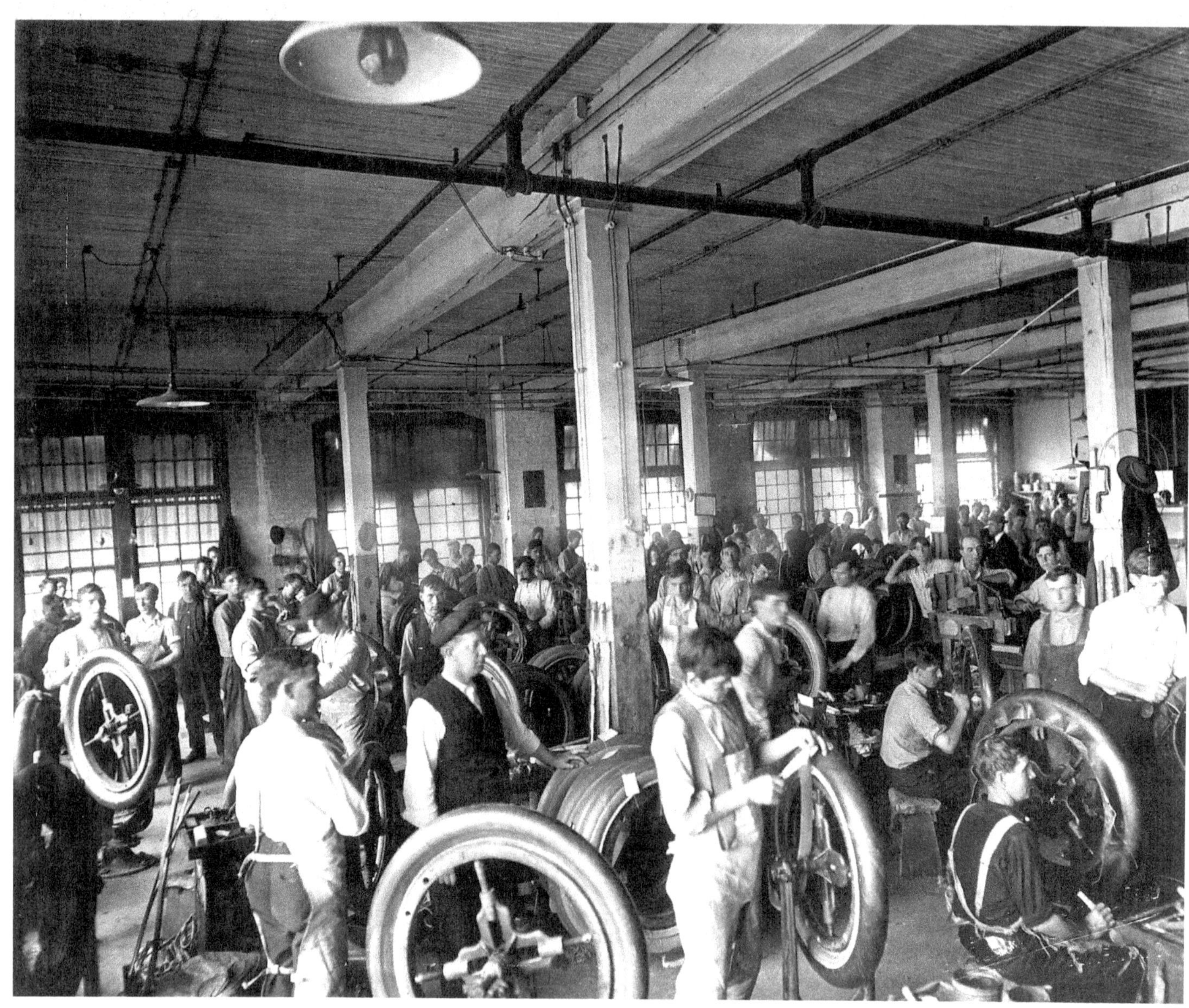

Firestone Tire and Rubber Company made its first tire on January 19, 1937. The eighty-five acre North Memphis facility operated until 1983.

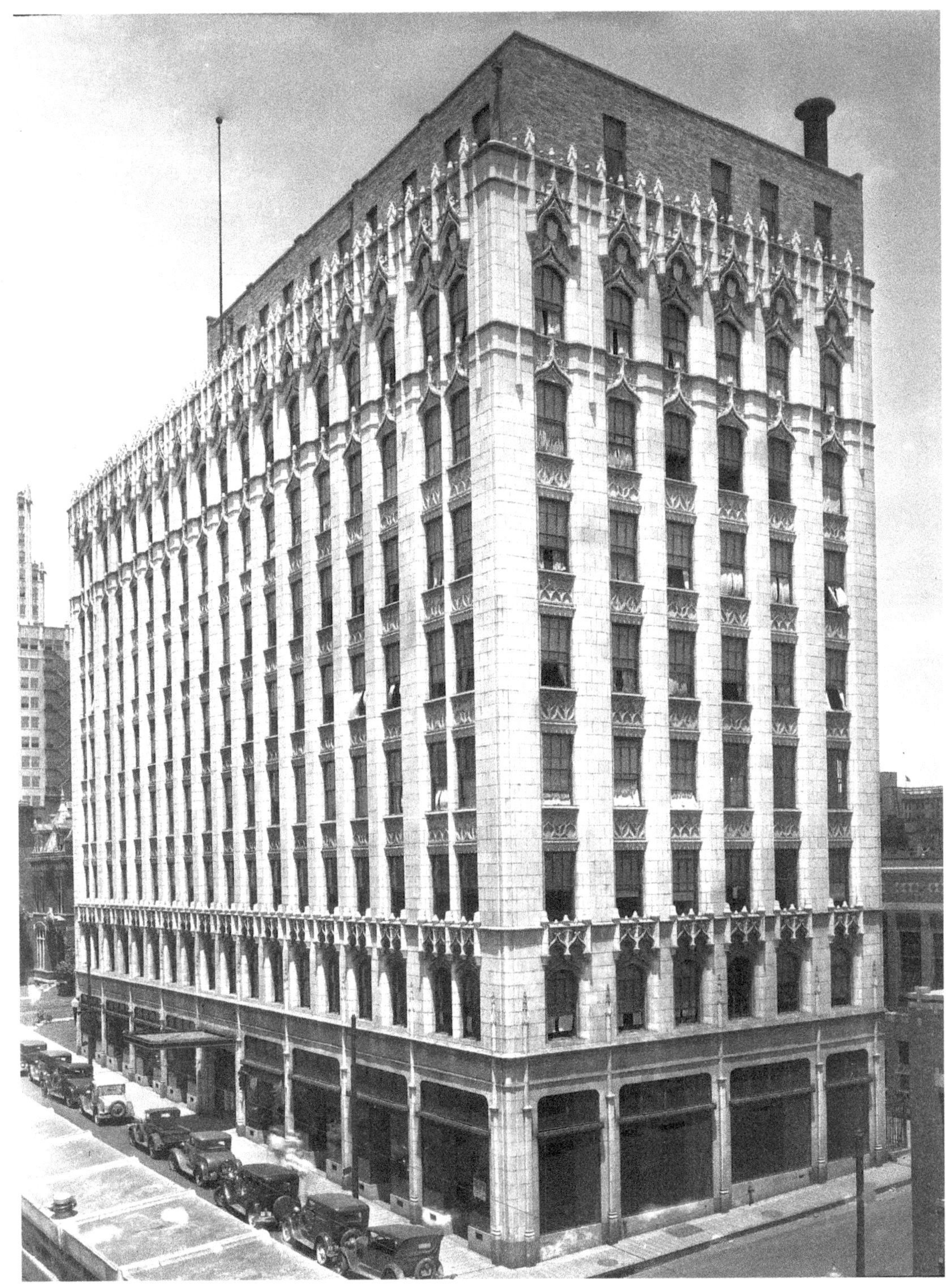

The Medical Arts Building was built in 1924. It was purchased in 1952 and renamed the Hickman Building by *Cotton Trade Journal* president Francis Hickman and his sister Jane Hickman.

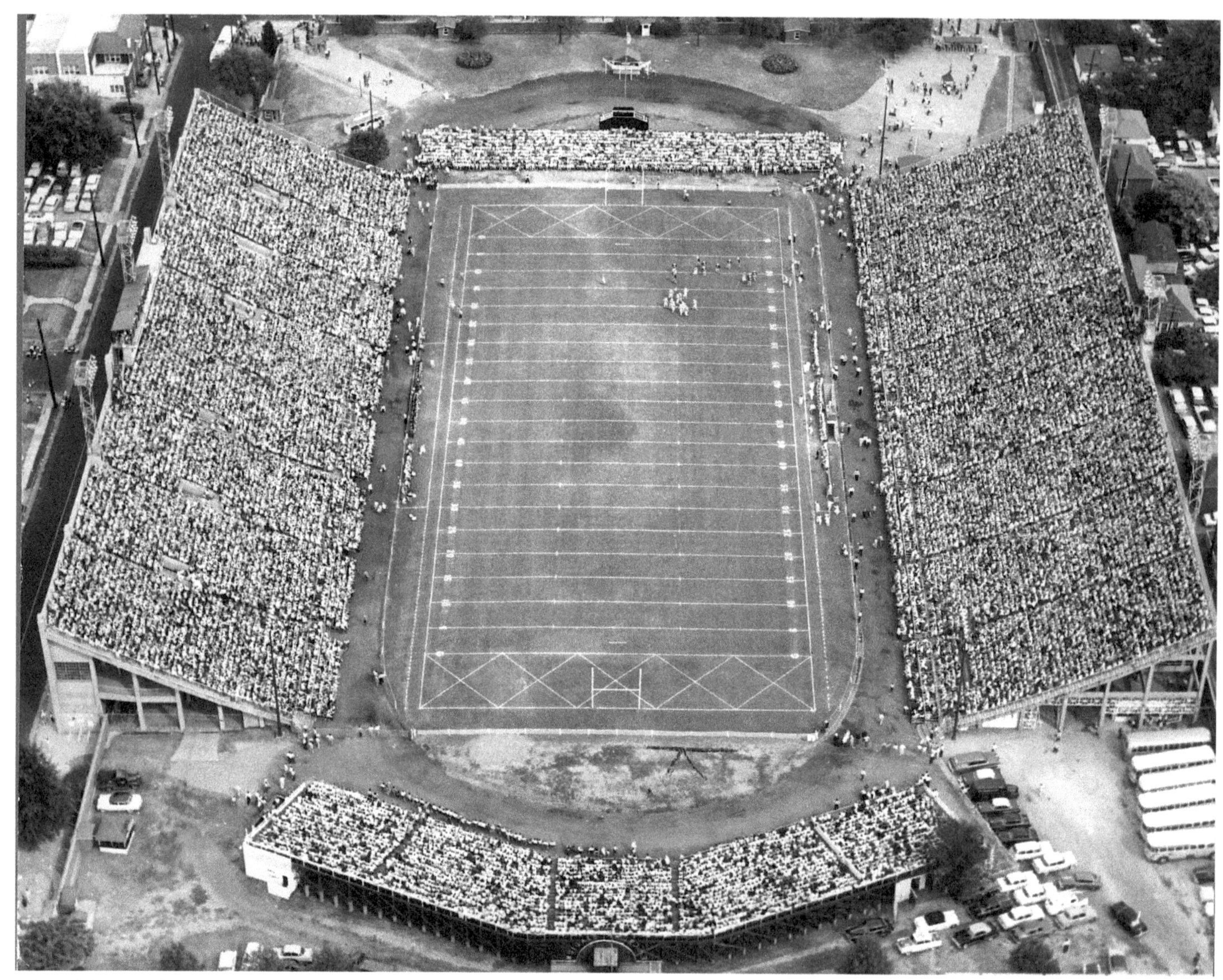

The Athletic Stadium was renamed Crump Stadium in honor of E. H. Crump shortly after its completion in 1934.

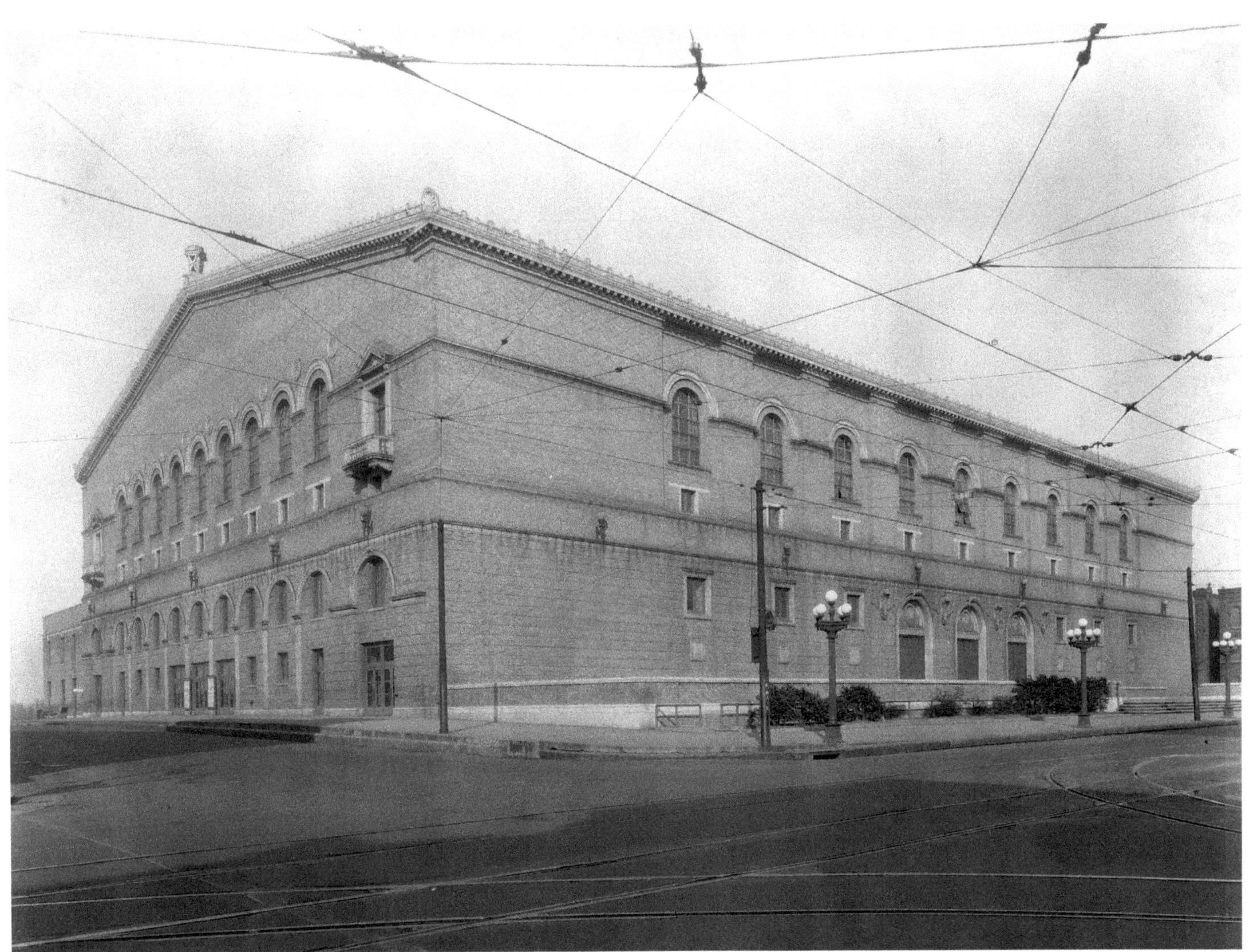

Ellis Auditorium was built on the site of Market Square. John Philip Sousa led the band at the opening ceremony on October 17, 1924. The last performance was given by Bruce Springsteen on November 19, 1996.

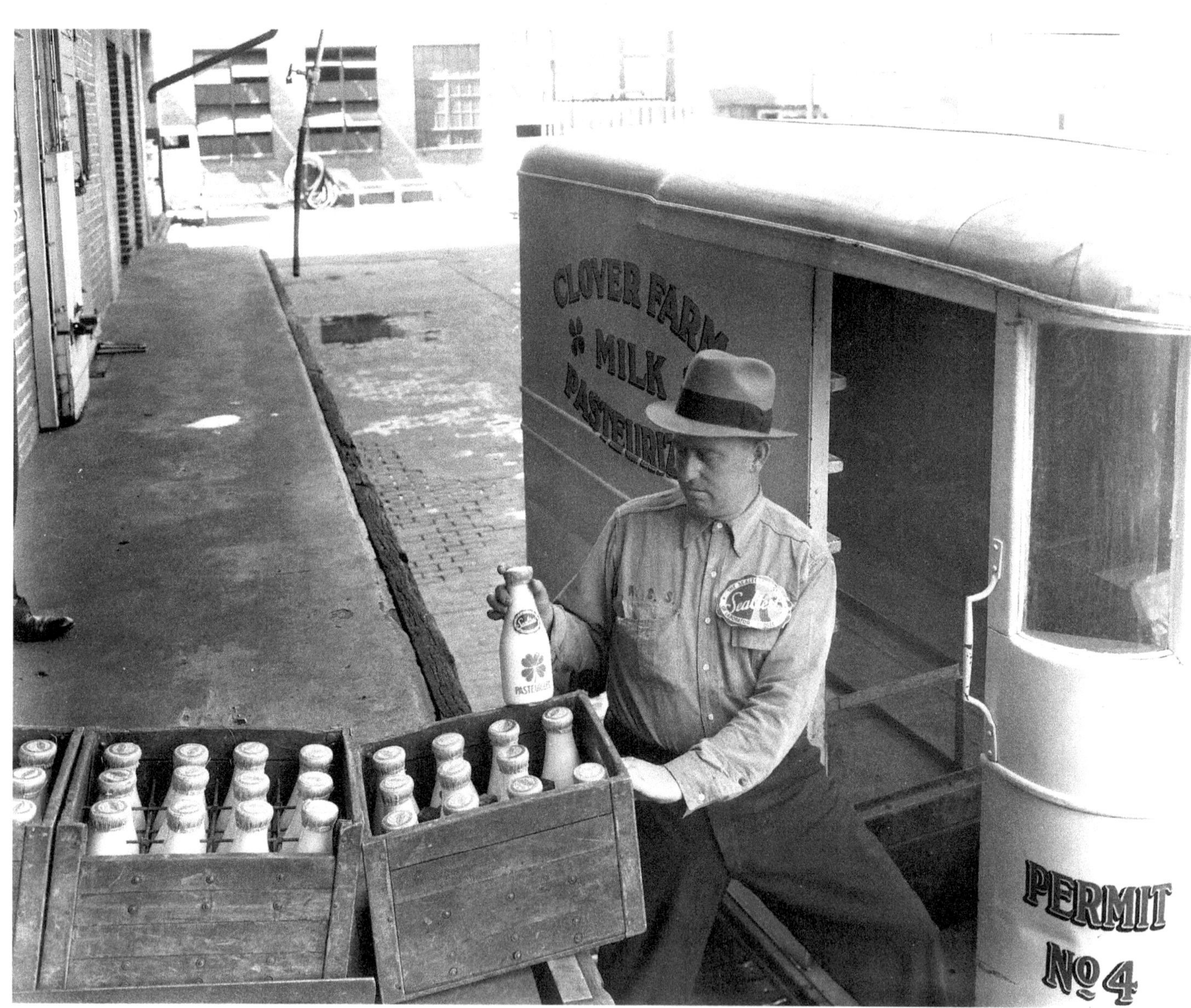

Clover Farm Dairy Company traced its origins back to Major Thompson's 1871 dairy farm. The Memphis Pure Milk Company bought the operation in 1905 and pioneered local efforts in dairy pastuerization and refrigeration.

First National Bank, now First Tennessee, occupied this building until 1961. The Goodwyn Institute moved into the old bank building, while the bank bought the institute's property, demolished the building, and built a new bank on the site.

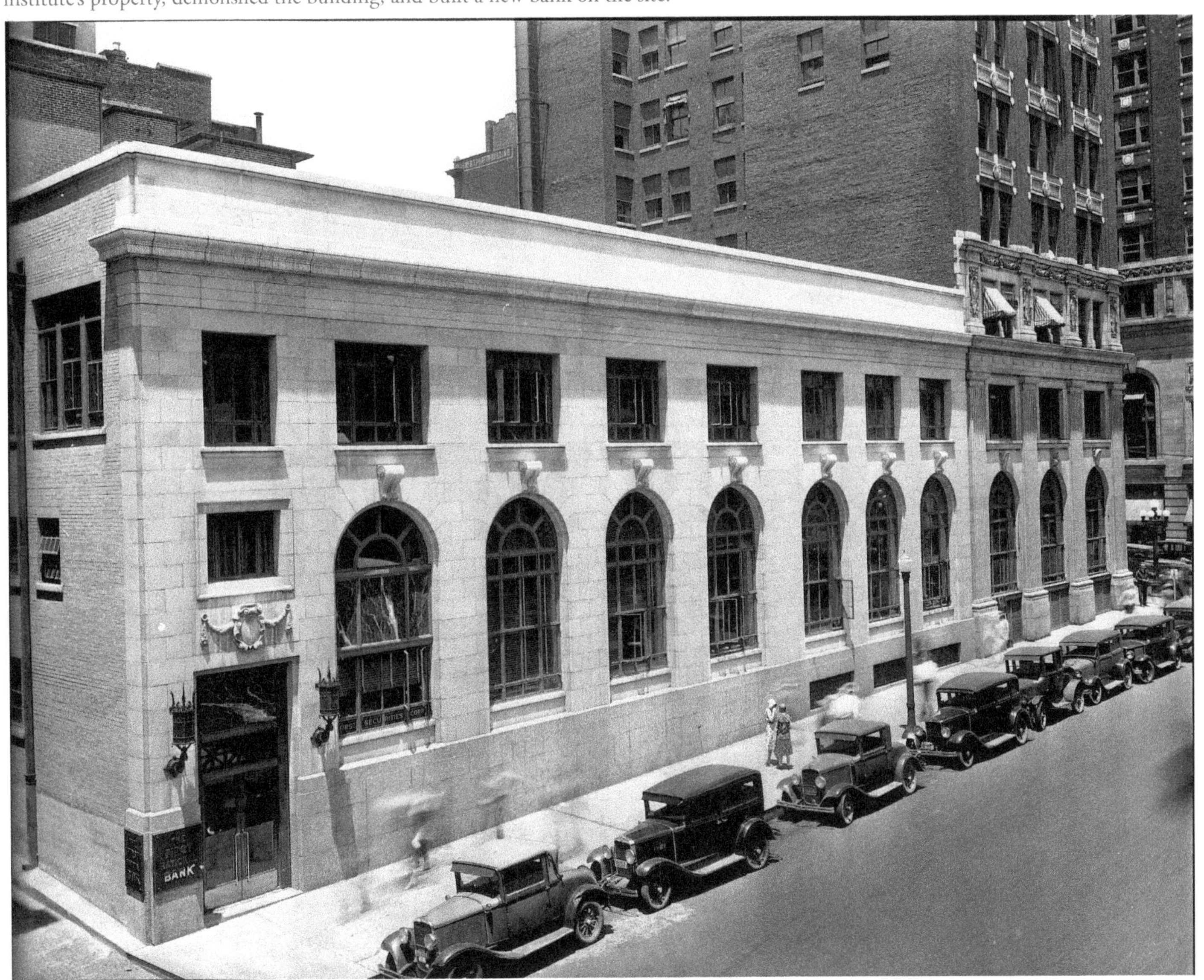

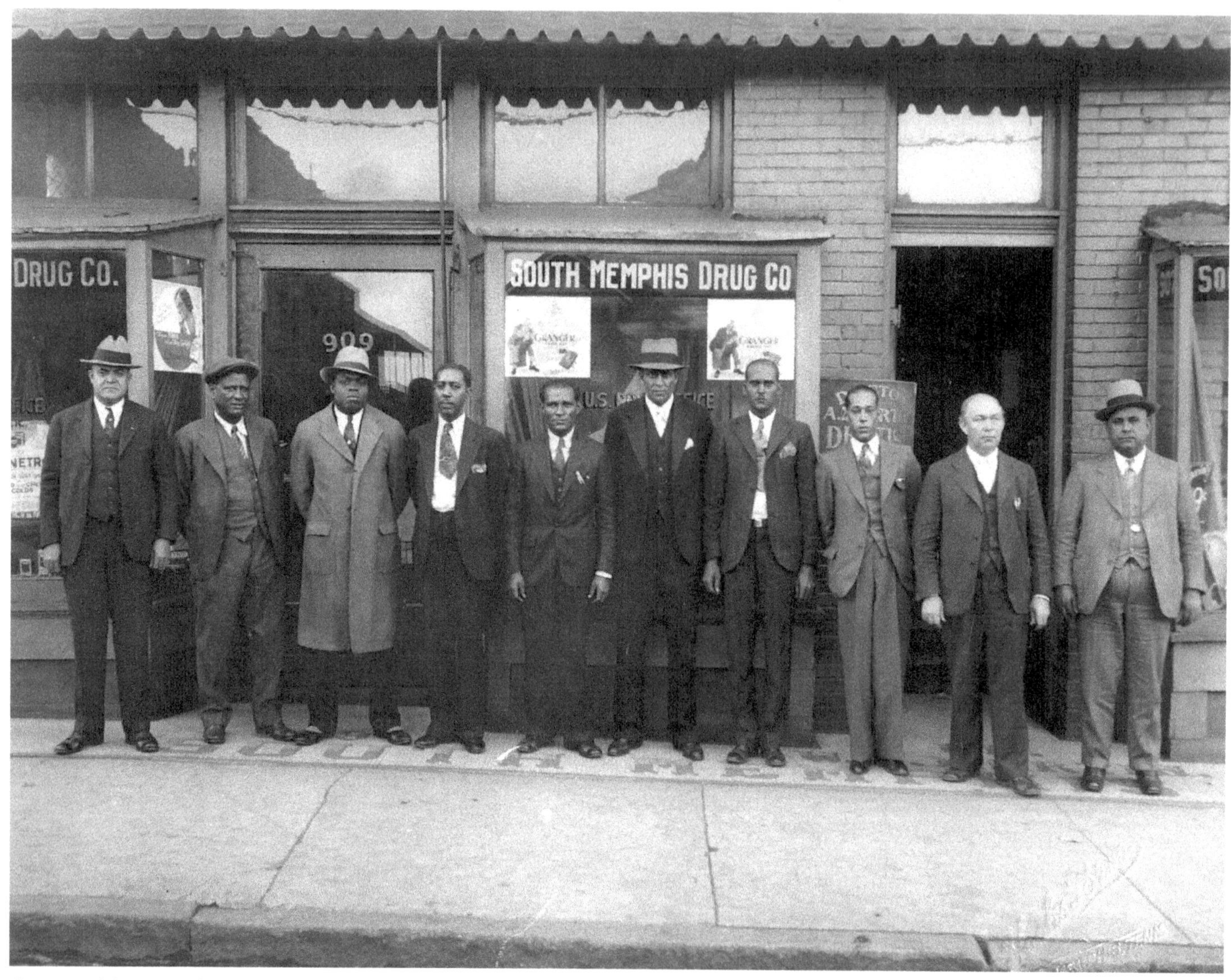

Owners of the Memphis Red Sox baseball team in front of Dr. J.B. Martin's South Memphis Drug Company on Florida Street.

The Shelby County Court House at 140 Adams, completed in 1909.

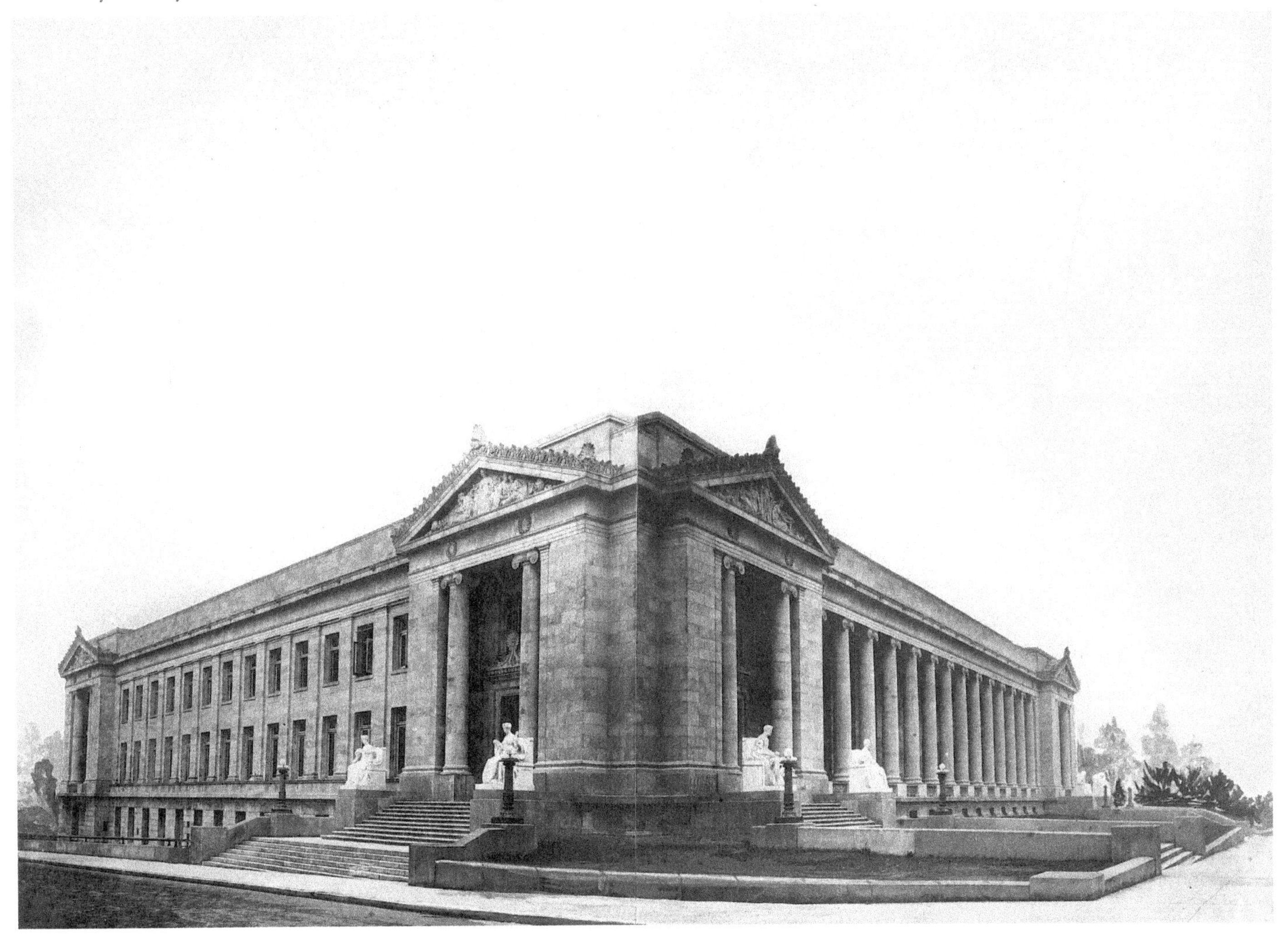

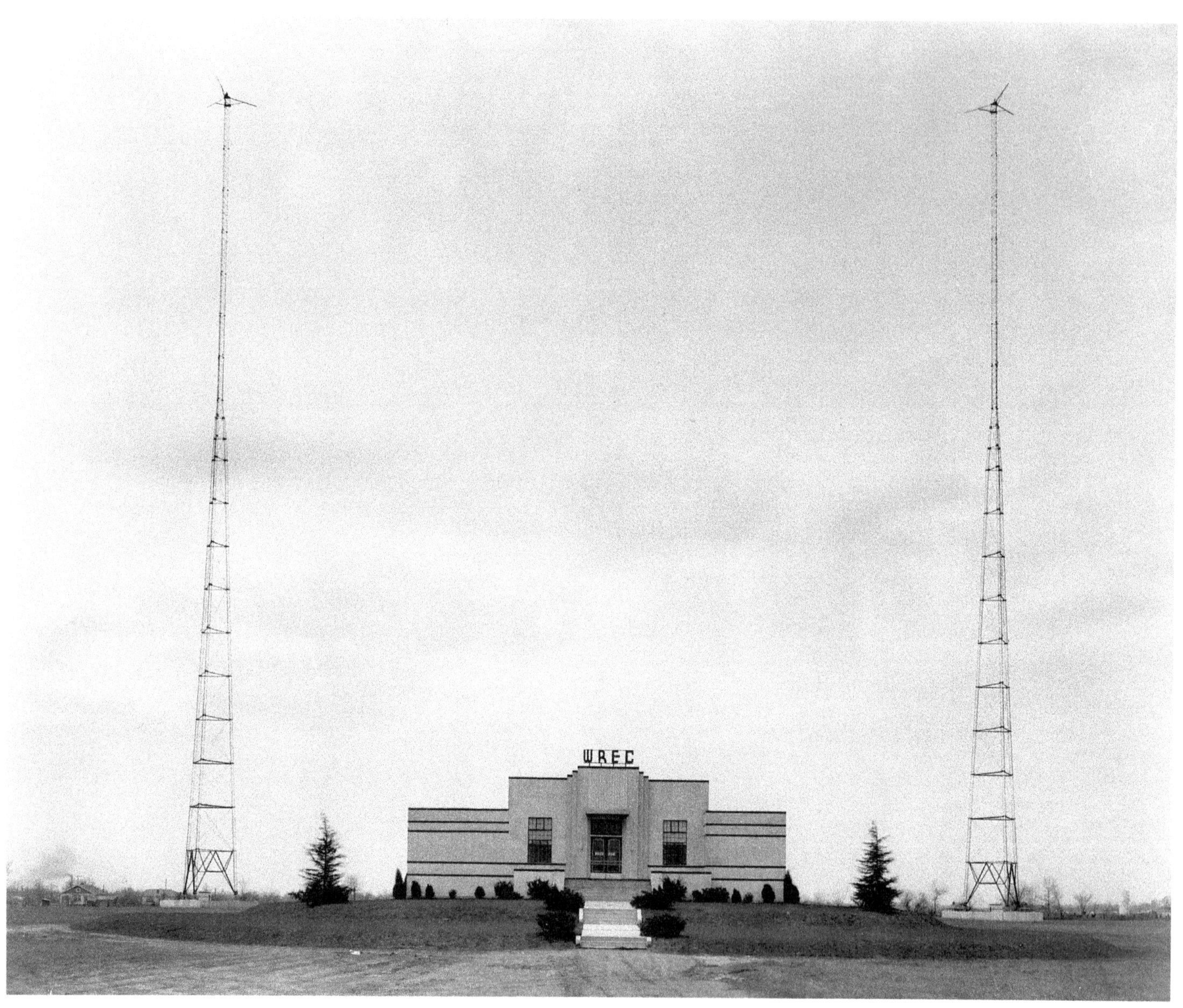

WREC Radio Station at Payne Avenue and Hindman Ferry Avenue, circa 1936.

The Beale Street Markethouse and Cold Storage Plant was razed and replaced by Beale Street Park in 1930. In 1931, the park was renamed Handy's Park in honor of the famous composer W.C. Handy.

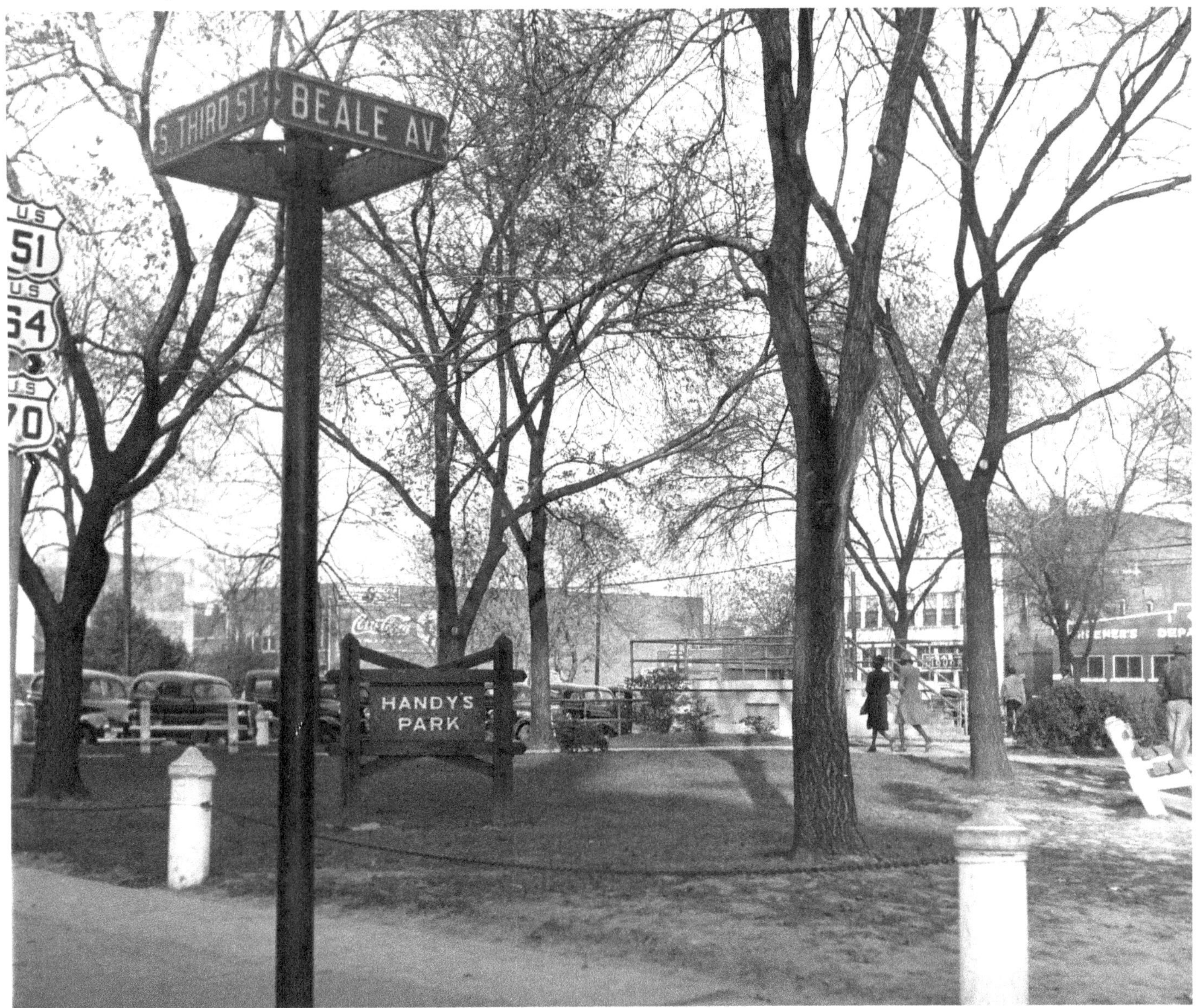

The Colored Old Folks Home was built by Dave Washington, who was the first African American Memphian appointed to the U.S. Postal Service.

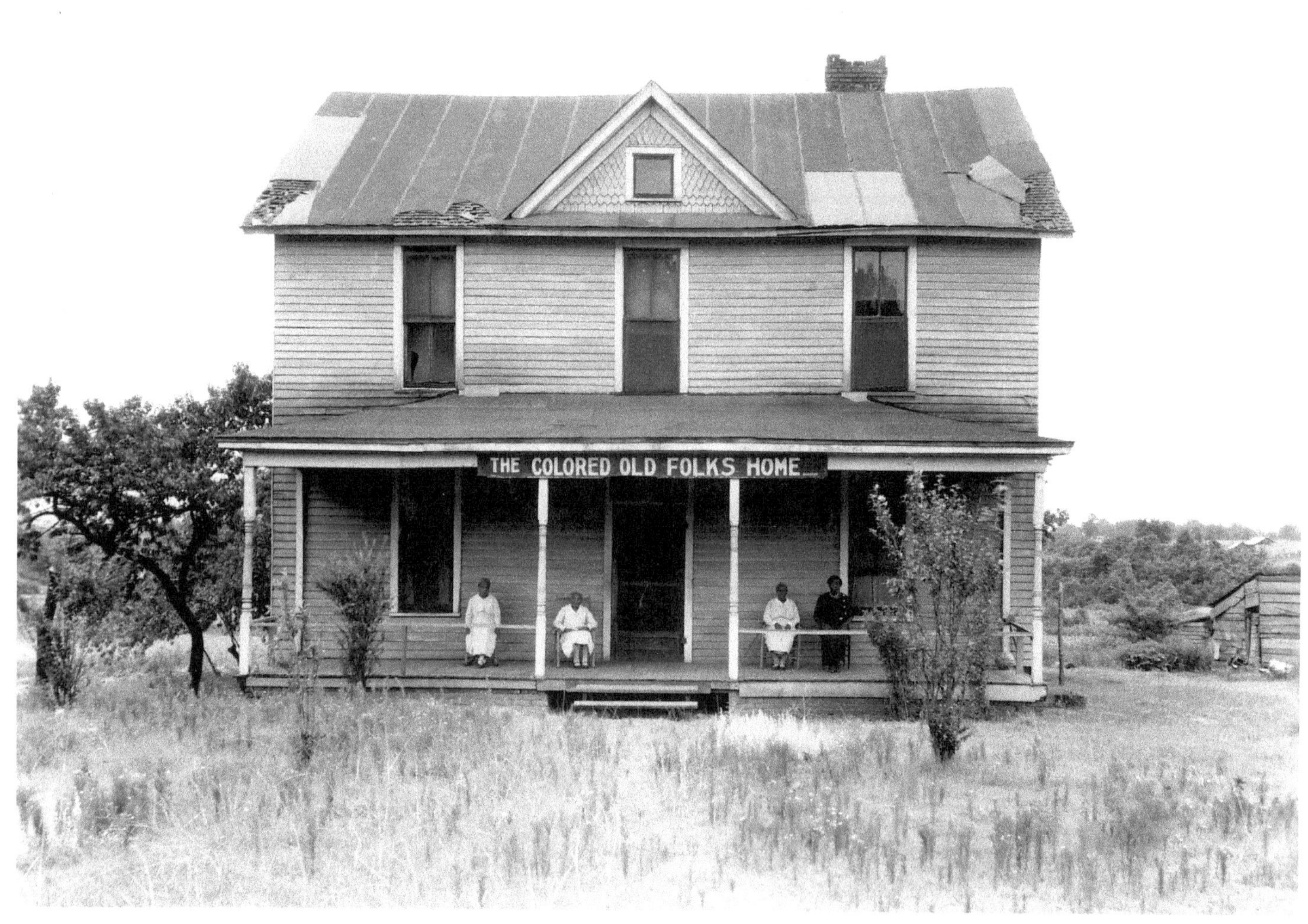

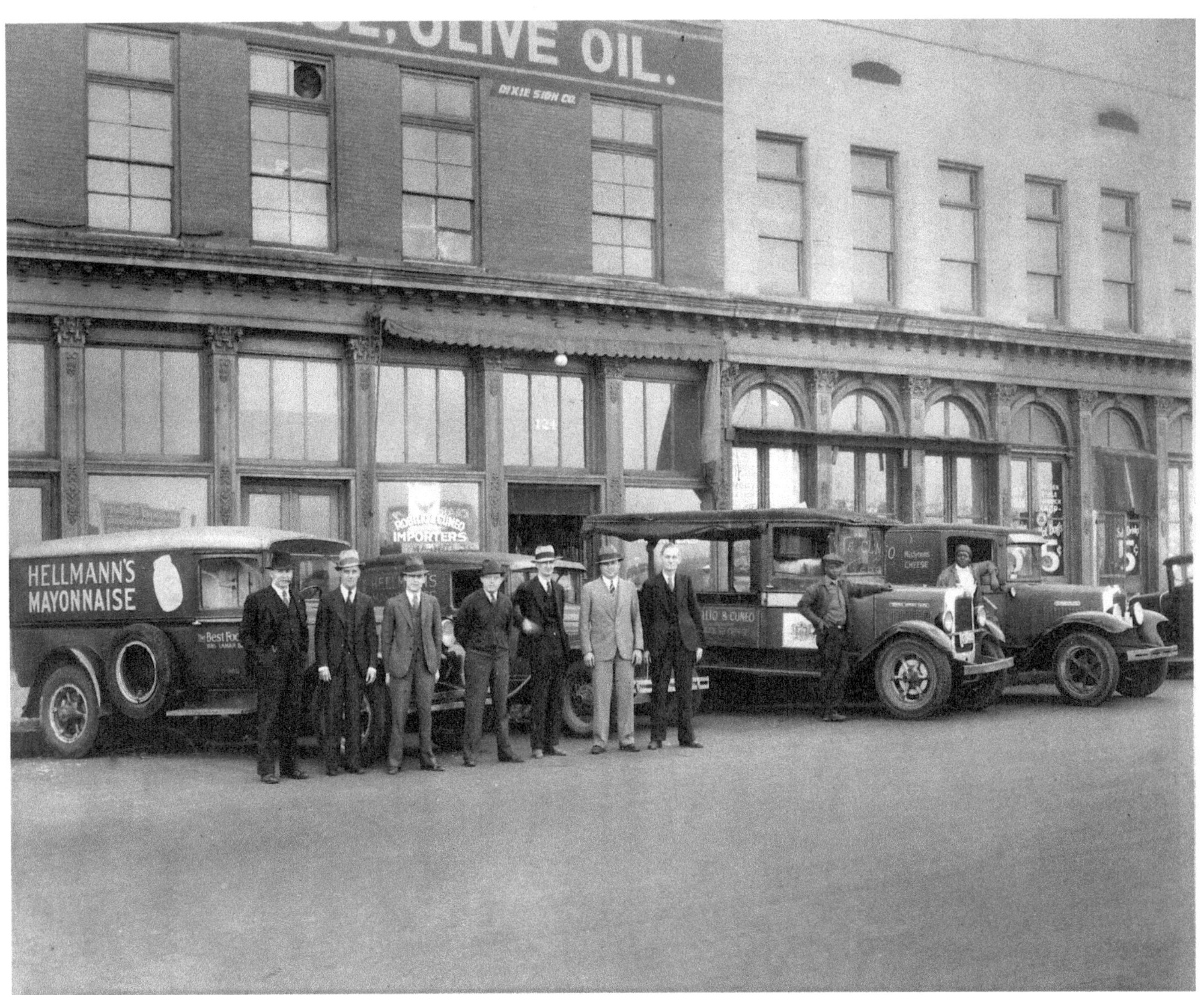

Robilio and Cuneo Importers at 124 North Front Street, circa 1931. John Robilio opened his first grocery store at Jackson and Alabama in 1909, two years after arriving from Italy. He partnered with Thomas Cuneo in 1929 to form Ronco, a pasta manufacturer and import business.

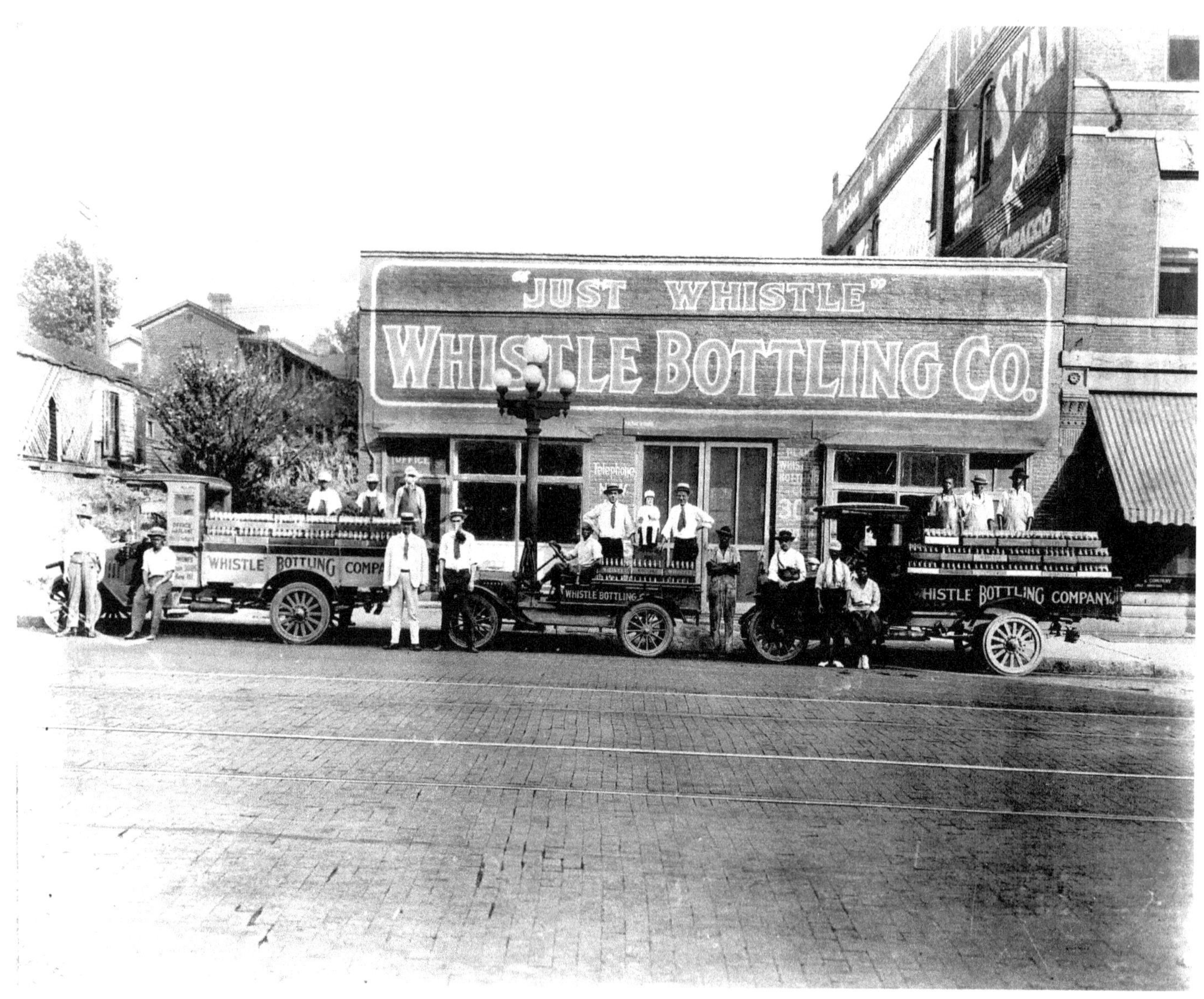

Whistle Bottling Company at 303-307 South Main, circa 1919.

A Cotton Carnival procession passing Court Square in 1937.

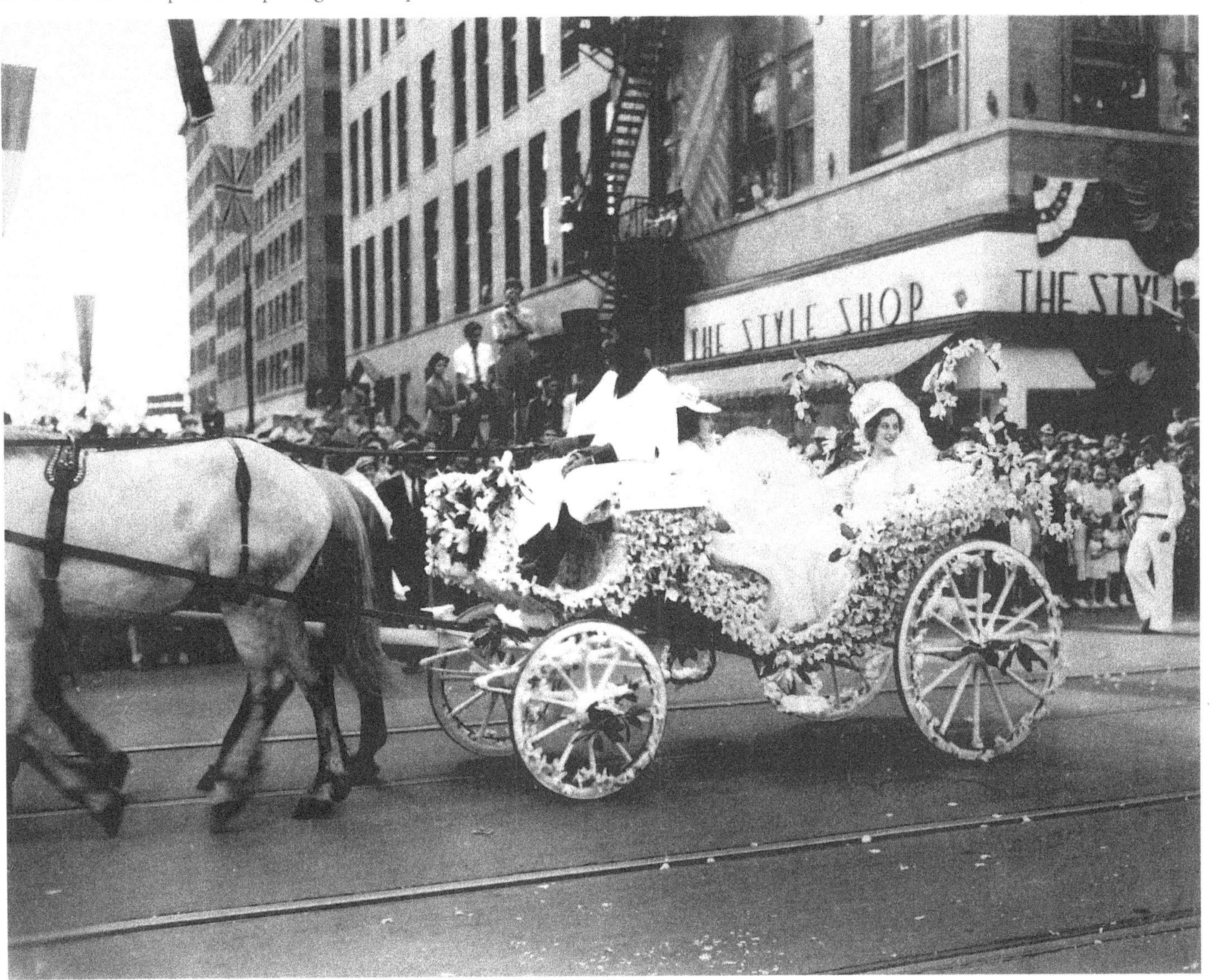

The Cotton Carnival King and Queen escorted by Boy Scouts, 1937.

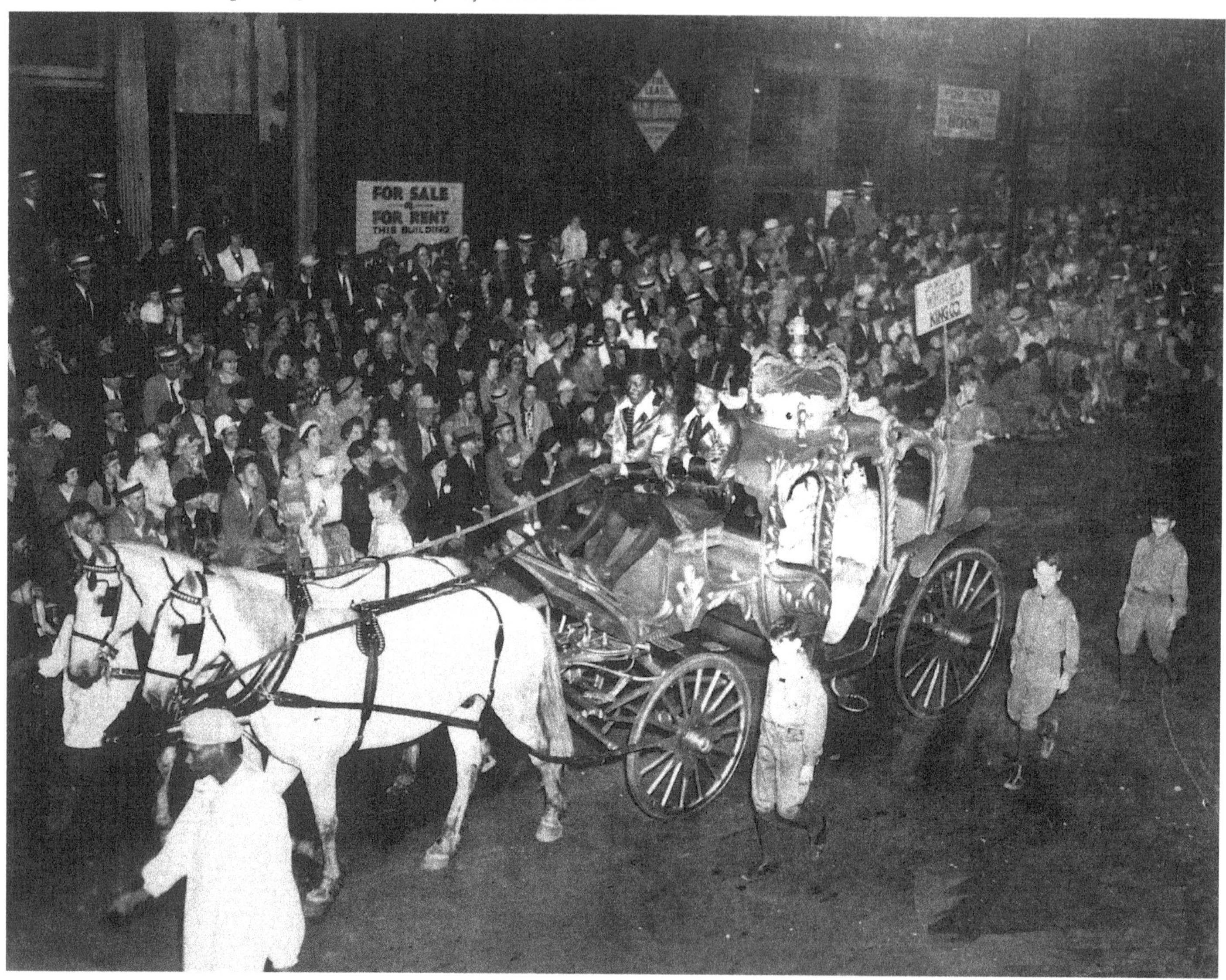

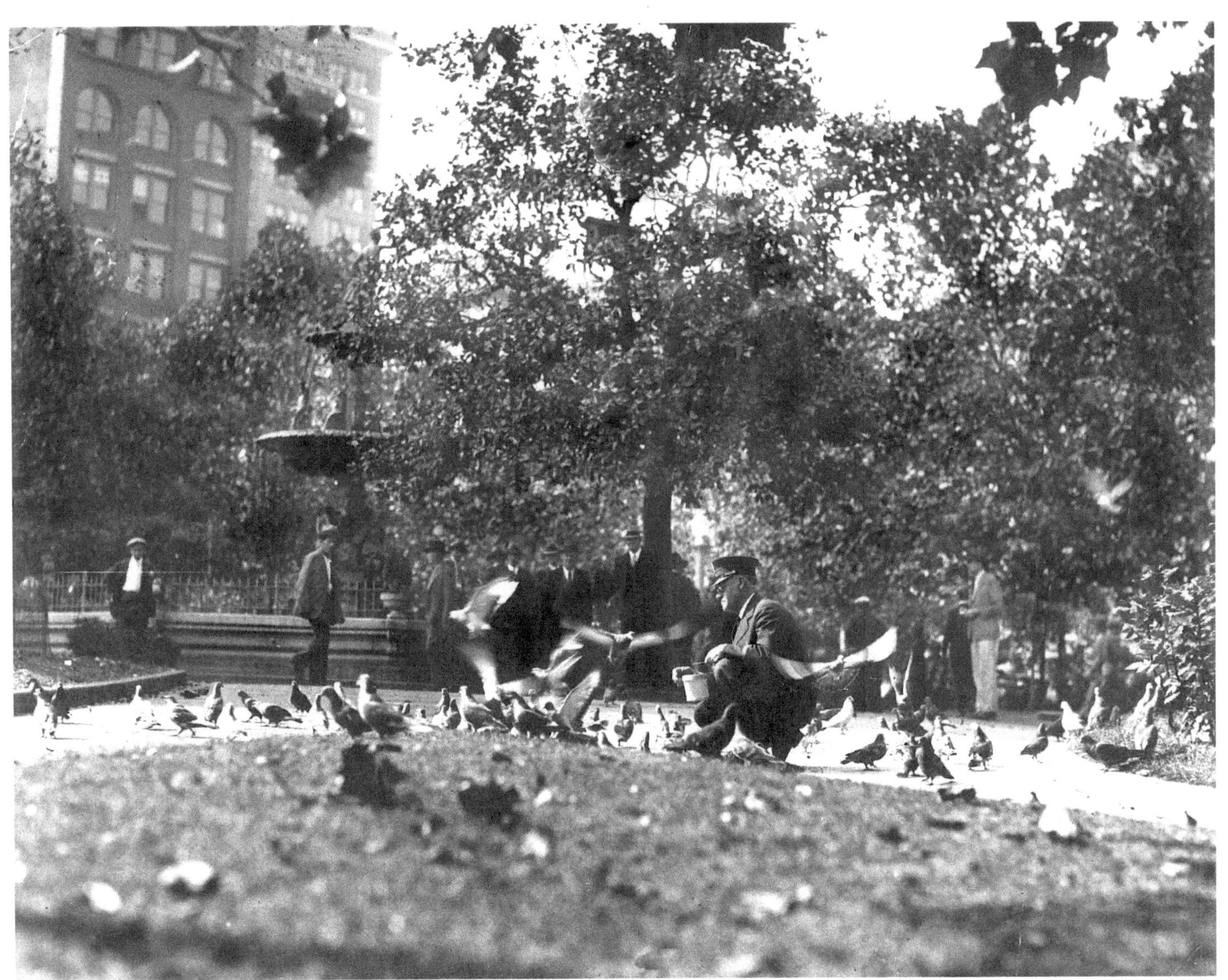

Scene from Court Square, 1932.

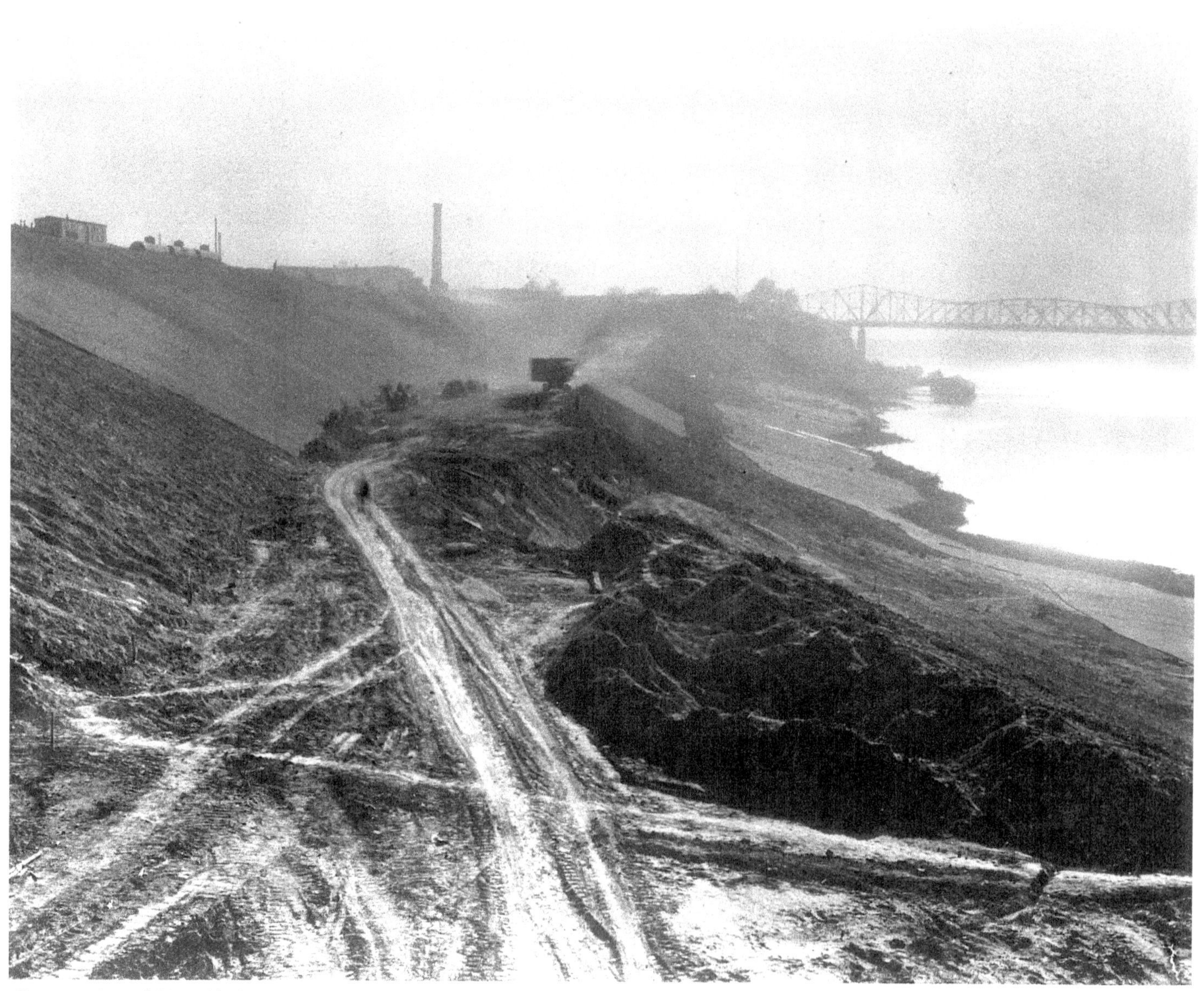

Construction of Riverside Drive.

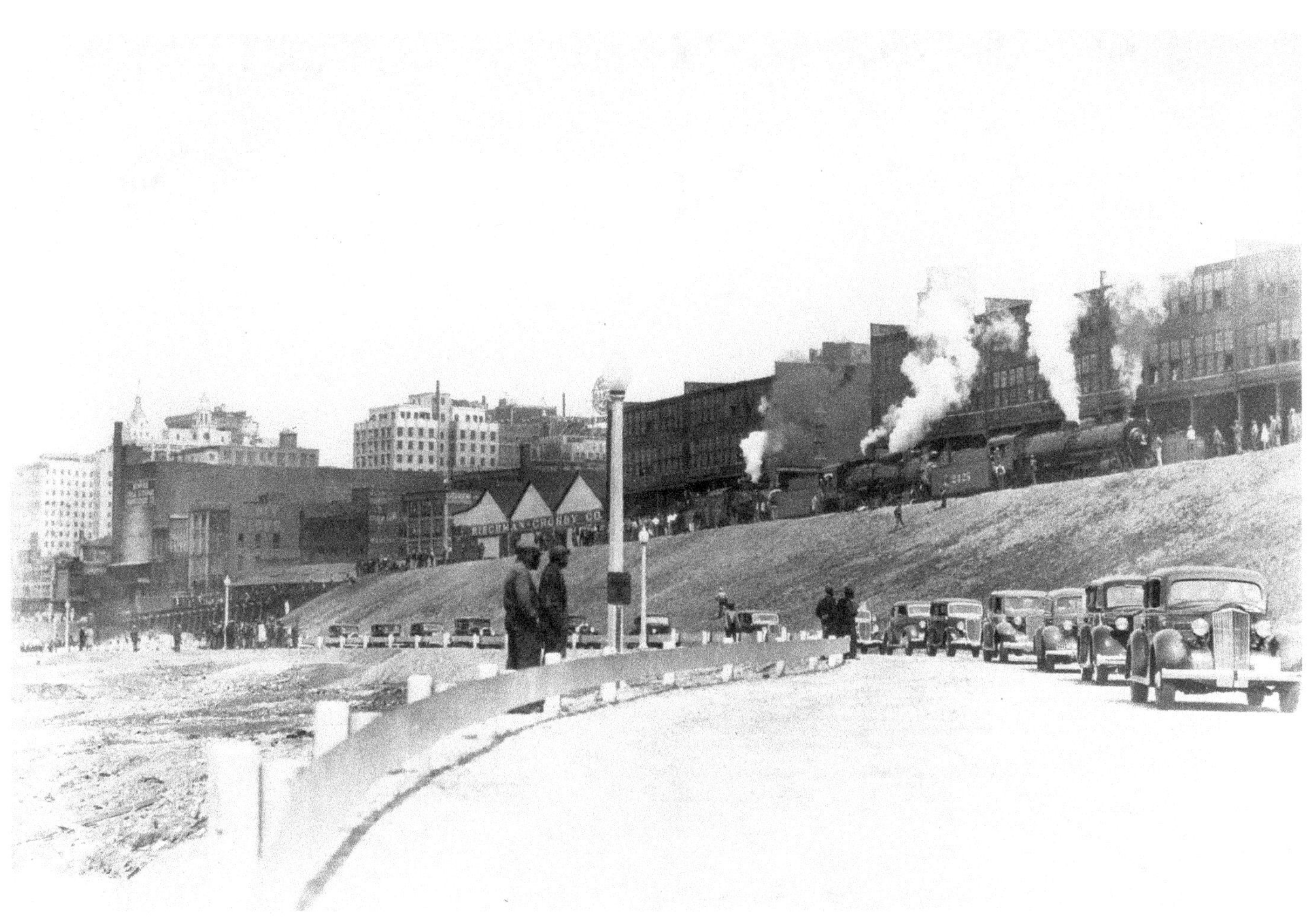

View of Memphis from Riverside Drive in the 1930s.

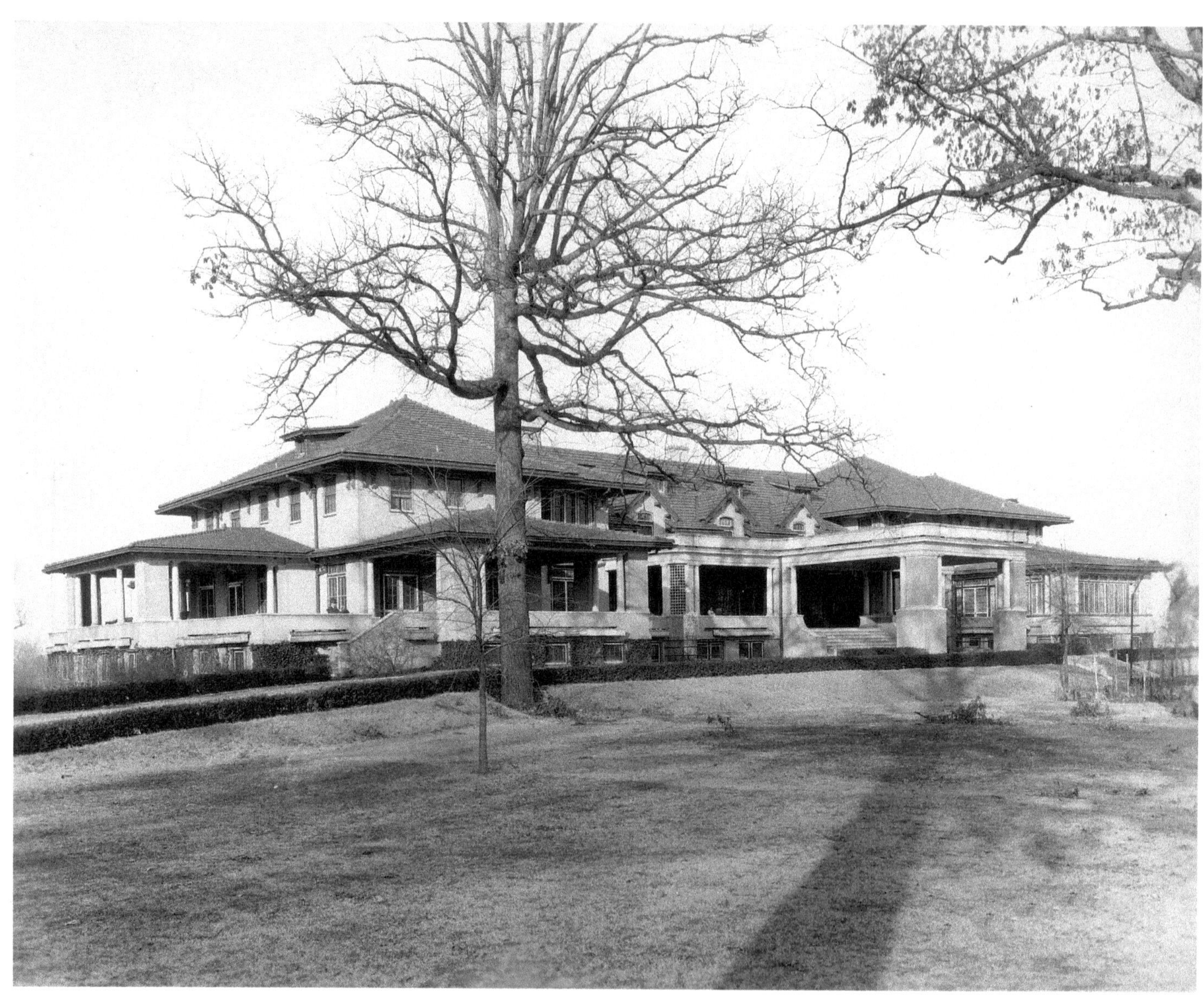

The Memphis Country Club, incorporated in 1905, was first located in the former home of Geraldus Buntyn. The second club building, pictured here, was built after the first burned in 1910. This facility was demolished and replaced by a new building in 1958.

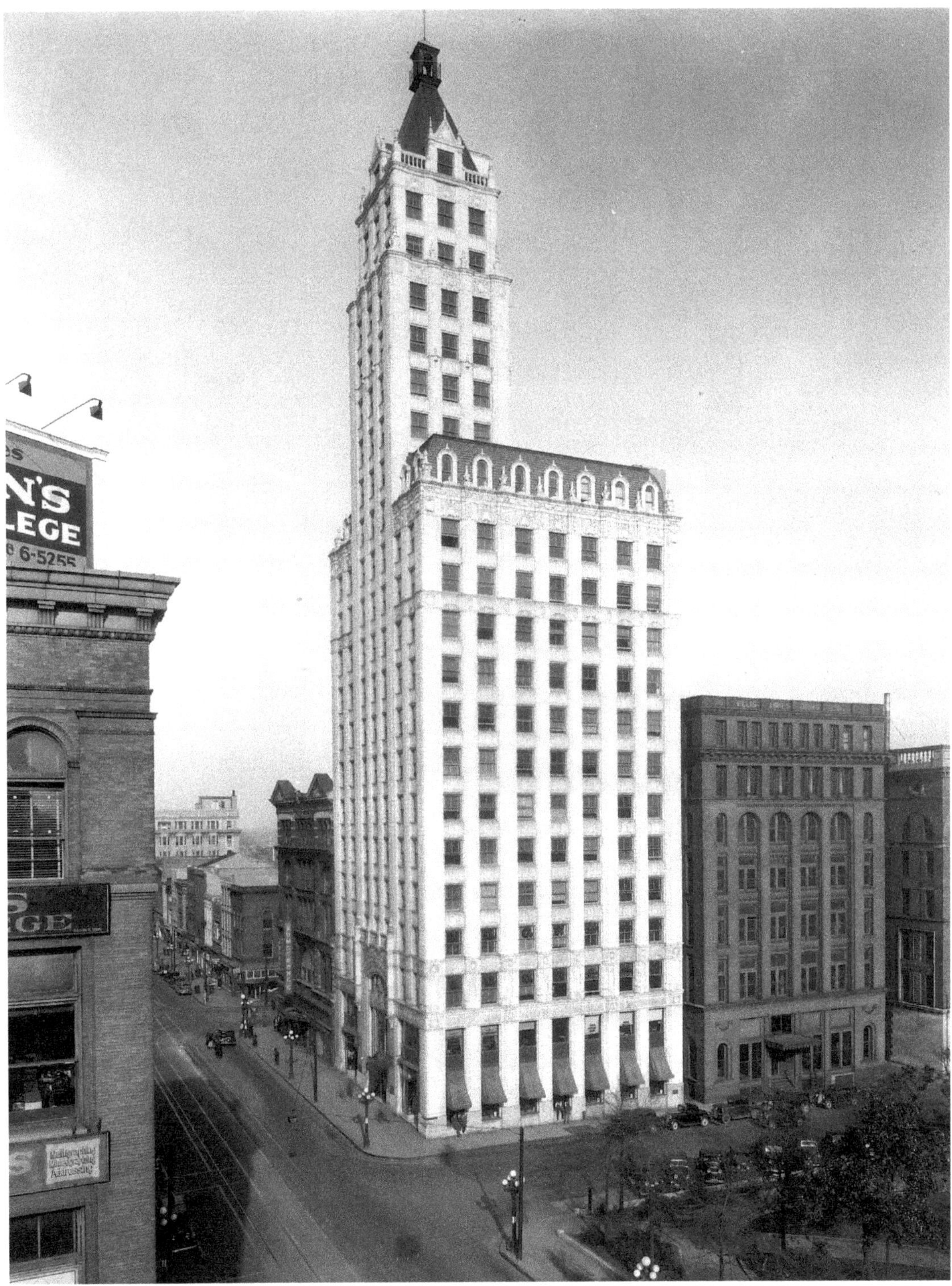

The Columbia Mutual Tower, later named the Lincoln-America Tower, 1935.

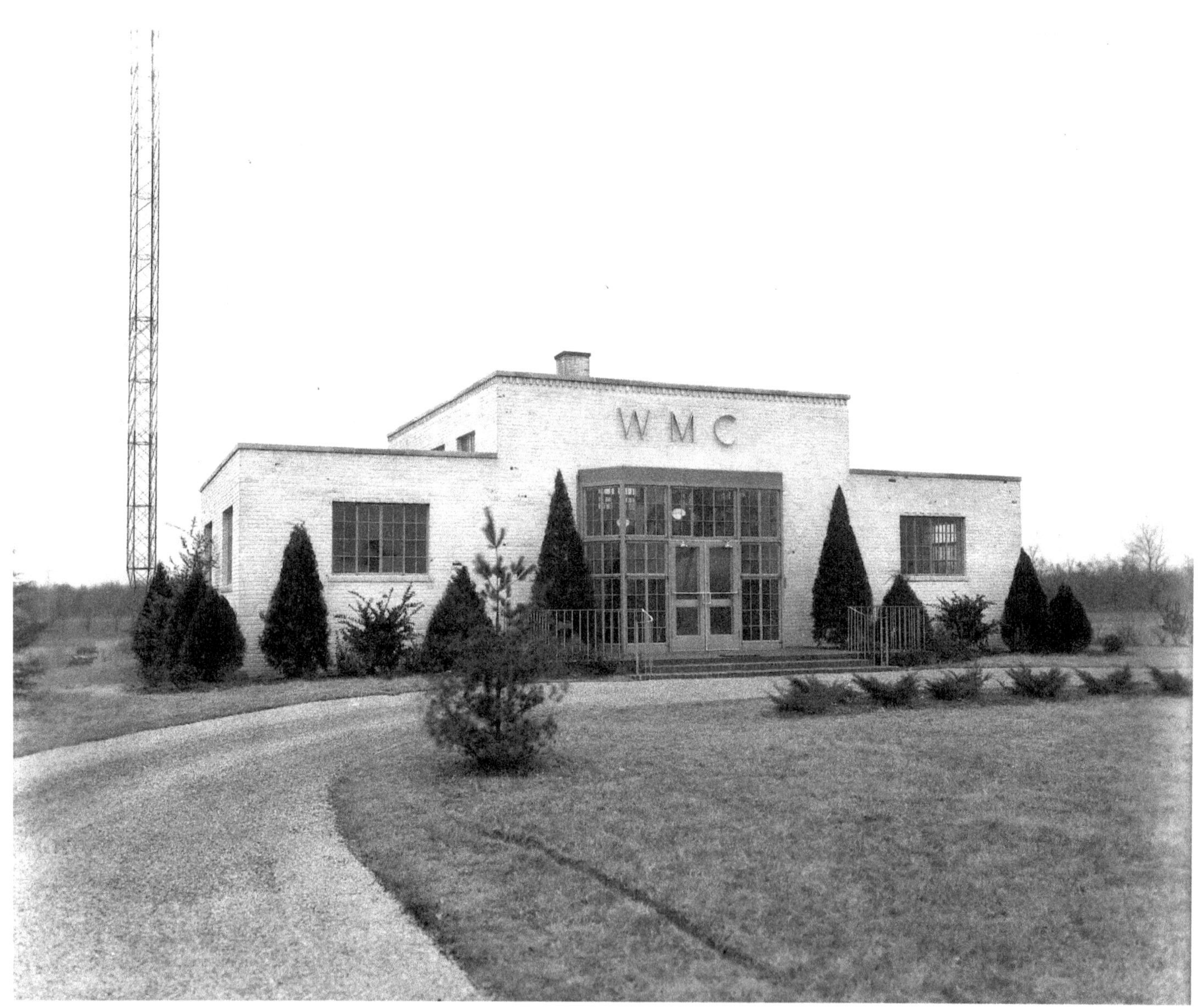

WMC Radio began operating in 1923 from the Commercial Appeal Building and moved into a facility on Highway 70, pictured here, in January 1930. The FCC forced the station to close in December of 1930, but it was able to resume operations from the Gayoso Hotel in September 1931.

Bry's Department Store, 1936.

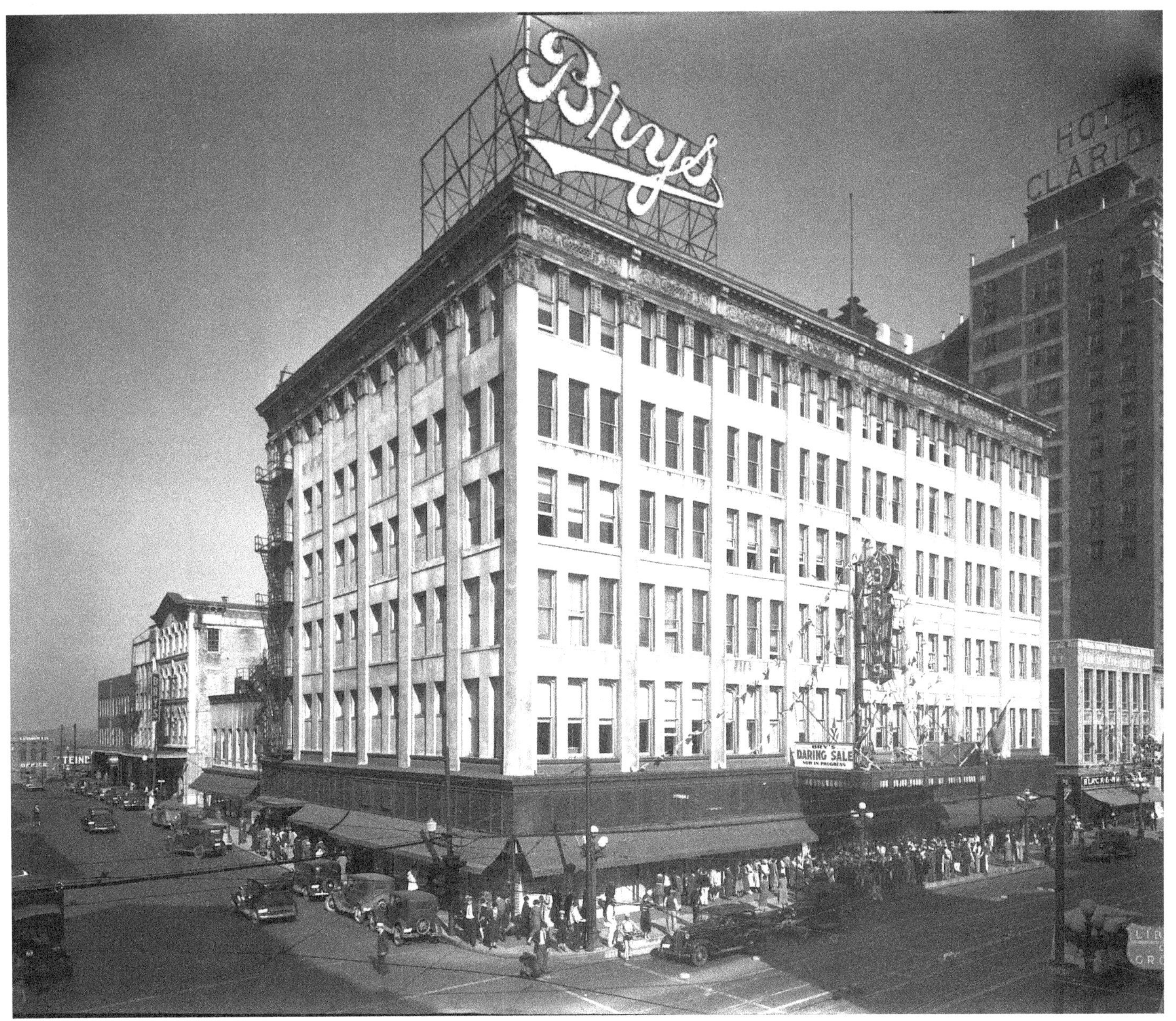

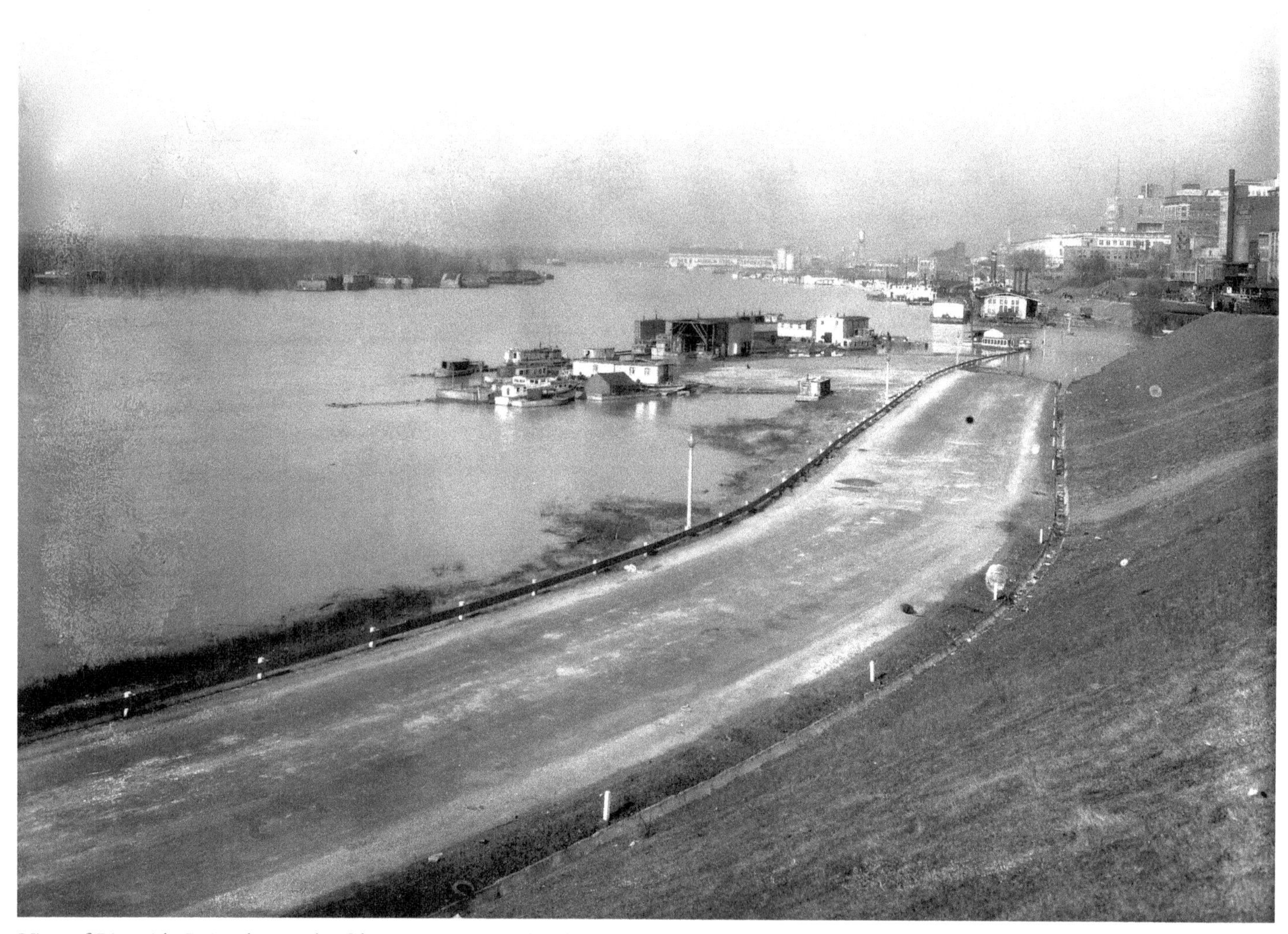

View of Riverside Drive during the Ohio-Mississippi Valley flood of 1937. Water covered Riverside where it meets Beale Street.

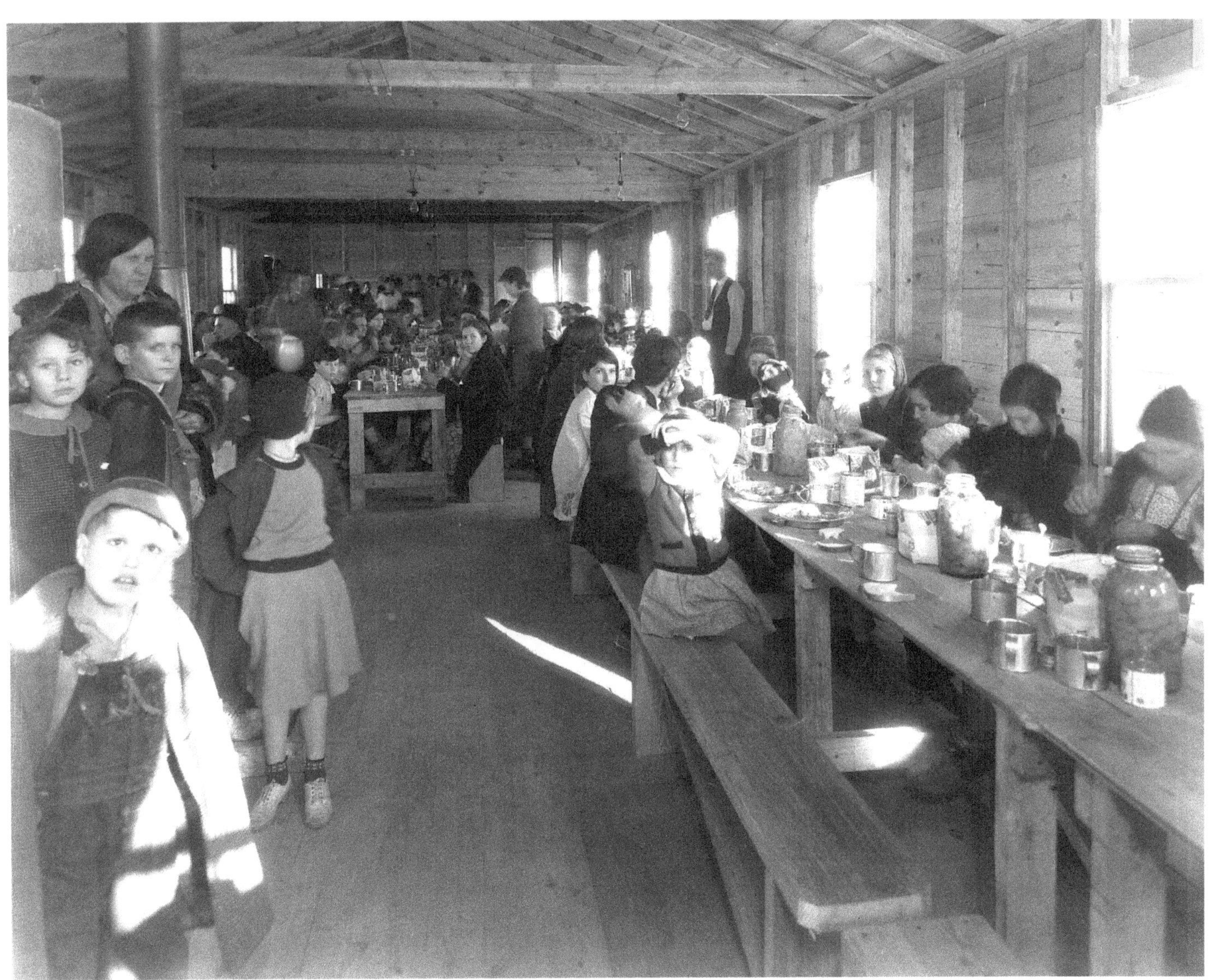

A view of the mess hall at the make-shift refugee camp at the Fairgrounds during the flood of 1937.

Main and McCall, circa 1939.

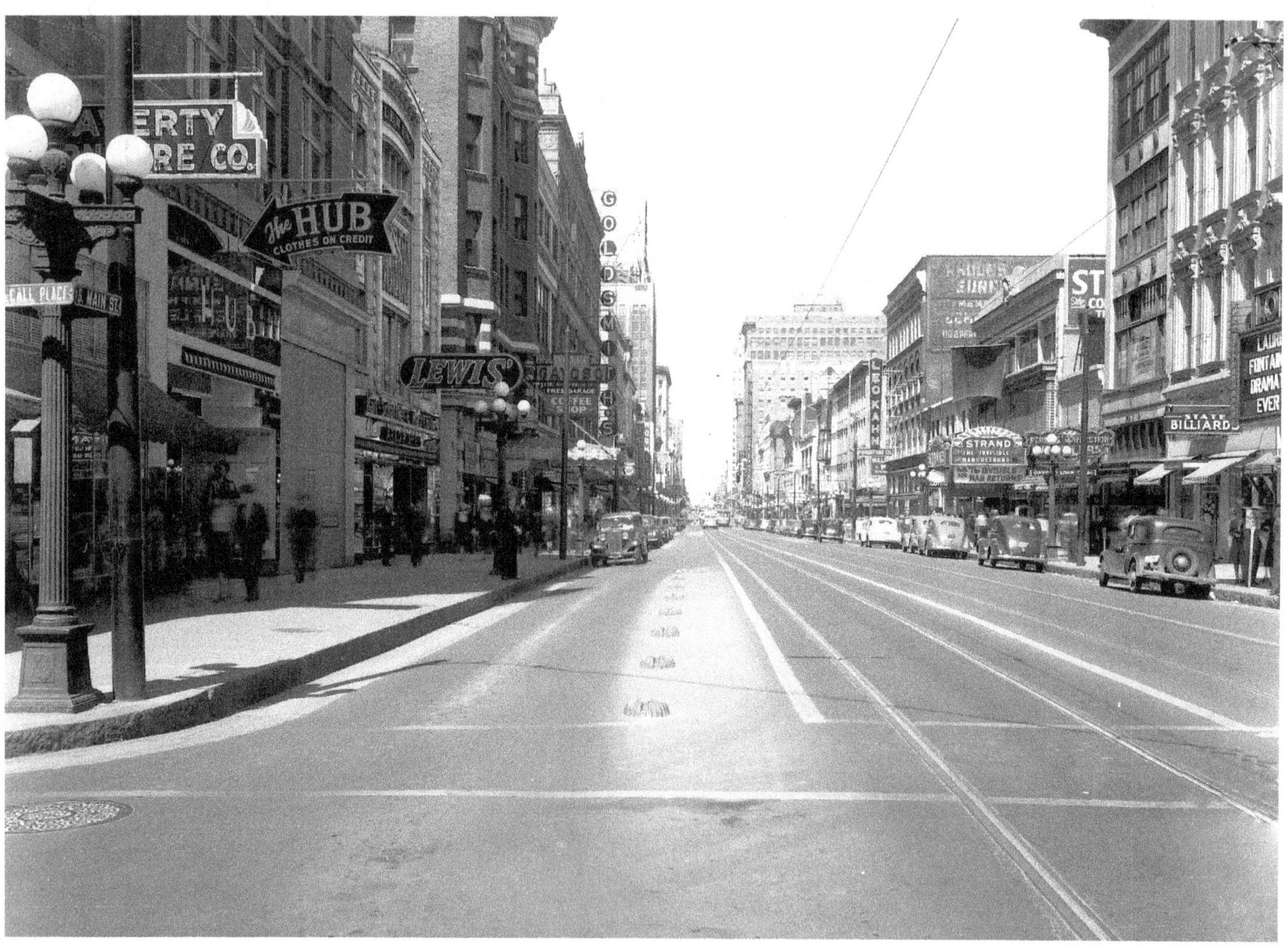

A City on the Move

1940-1959

Memphis and Shelby County played a major role in U.S. efforts during WWII. Chickasaw Ordnance Plant was built in 1940 and a naval air station was opened in Millington in 1942. The next year, the Army Defense Depot and Mallory Air Force Depot were built. Local companies including Firestone Rubber Company, Ford Motor Company and Fisher Auto Plant were converted to war material production. Lieutenant George Lee raised money in the African American community to purchase a bomber named *The Spirit of Beale Street.* A number of aircraft were named for a city by their crews, but the most famous was the *Memphis Belle.* She was the first B-17 to complete 25 missions over Europe with her original crew.

The city grew as a distribution hub in the post-war years. In 1948, President's Island was transformed from an untamed river island into a multi-million dollar industrial complex. River commerce increased from 3.5 million tons per year to approximately eight million tons over the next twenty years. By 1952, there were nine railroad trunk lines, seventeen rail lines, eighty trucking lines and seven airlines operating out of Memphis. Boosters proudly advertised the city's hospitable business environment and high standard of living to encourage businesses to expand or relocate to Memphis. Memphis was named America's quietest, cleanest and safest city several times in the 1950s.

Ironically, while Memphis was the quietest city, it was also host to a musical revolution. Sam Phillips opened the Memphis Recording Studio, later named Sun Record Company. Phillips recorded African American rhythm and blues music by James Cotton, Rufus Thomas, Rosco Gordon, Little Milton, Bobby Blue Bland, B.B. King and Howlin' Wolf. The studio continued its success with Charlie Rich, Jerry Lee Lewis, Johnny Cash, Roy Orbison, Carl Perkins, and of course, Elvis Presley.

This music revolution began in the 1950s and continued through the following decades. The 1960s and 1970s saw the rise of a number of influential recording studios. Stax, began in 1958 and was home to the Mar-Keys, Booker T and the MGs, Sam and Dave, Otis Redding and Isaac Hayes. Willie Mitchell of Hi Studio recorded Al Green and Ann Peebles in the 1970s, while Ardent recorded Alex Chilton and Big Star and remains a popular studio today.

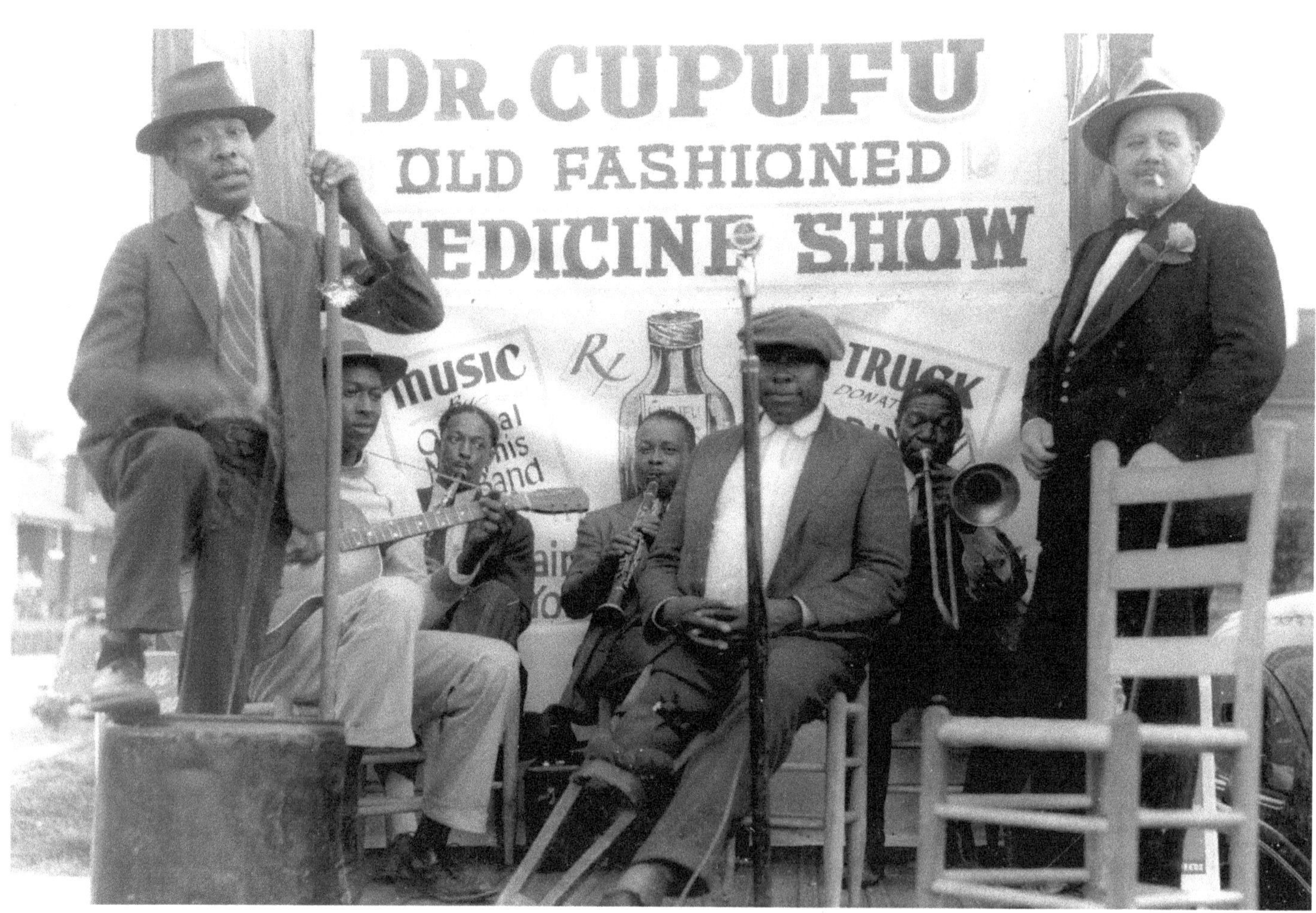

The Dr. Cupufu Old Fashioned Medicine Show at a City Beautiful rally in 1942. Dr. Cupufu stands for the organization's slogan, "Clean Up, Paint Up, Fix Up."

Main and Beale Street, 1940.

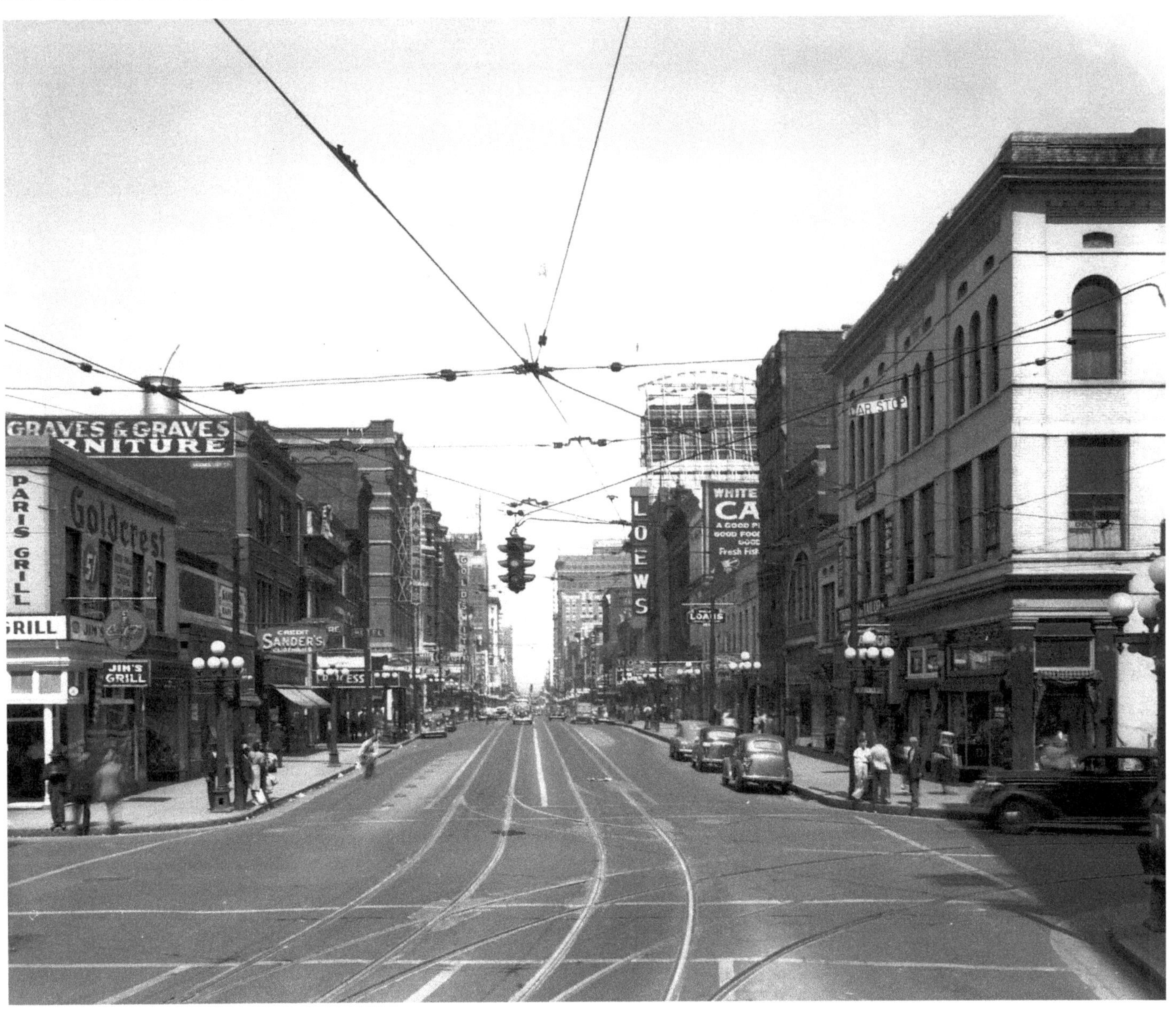

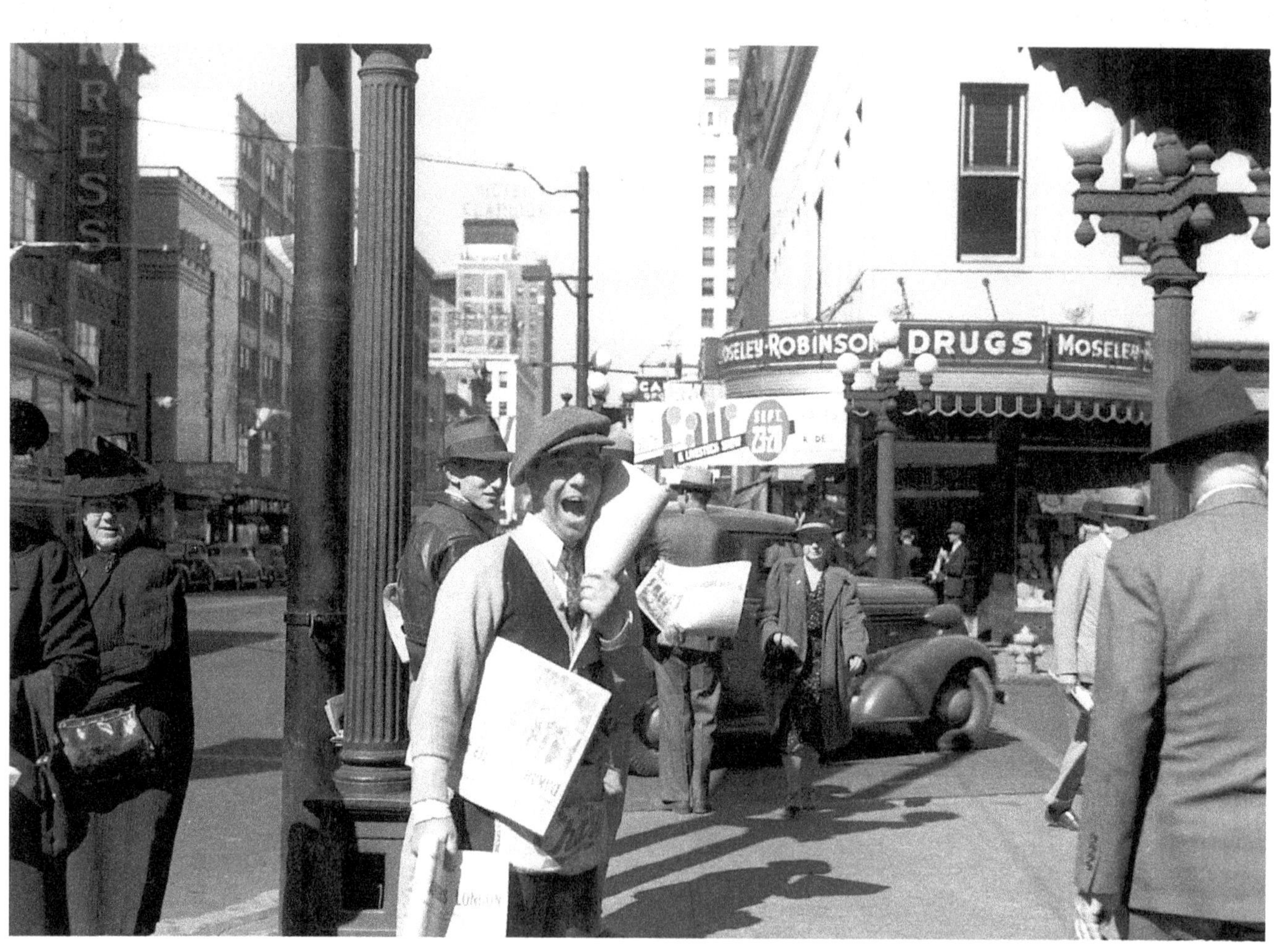

Newspaper boy on the corner of Main and Madison Avenue, 1940.

W.C. Handy wrote some of his most memorable songs while in Memphis. A park on Beale Street was named in his honor, as well as a theater in the Orange Mound neighborhood.

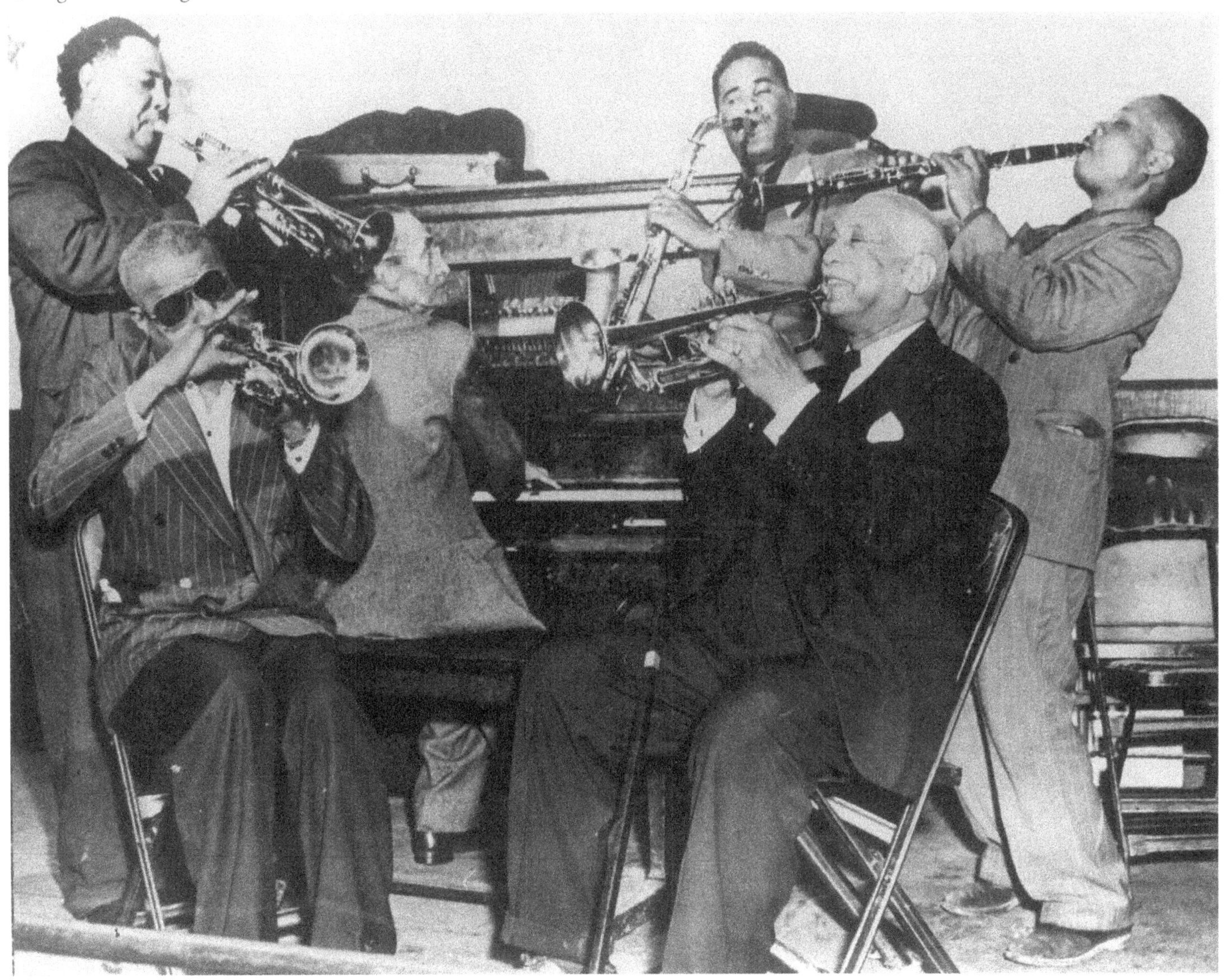

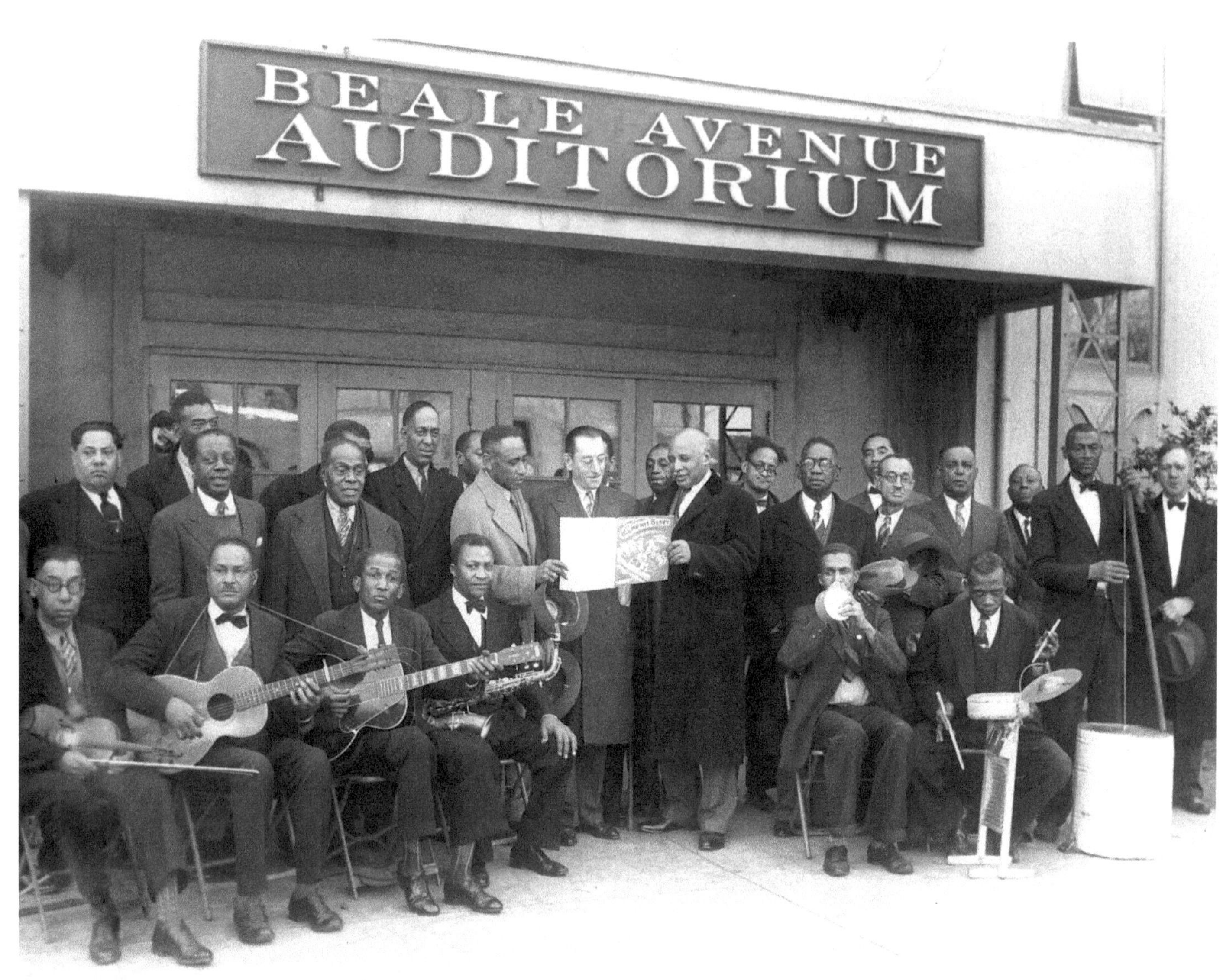

Lt. George W. Lee, W.C. Handy and others in front of Beale Avenue Auditorium in the 1940s. In 1909, W.C. Handy wrote "Mister Crump" about mayoral candidate E.H. Crump. It became his first important song when it was published in 1912 as "Memphis Blues."

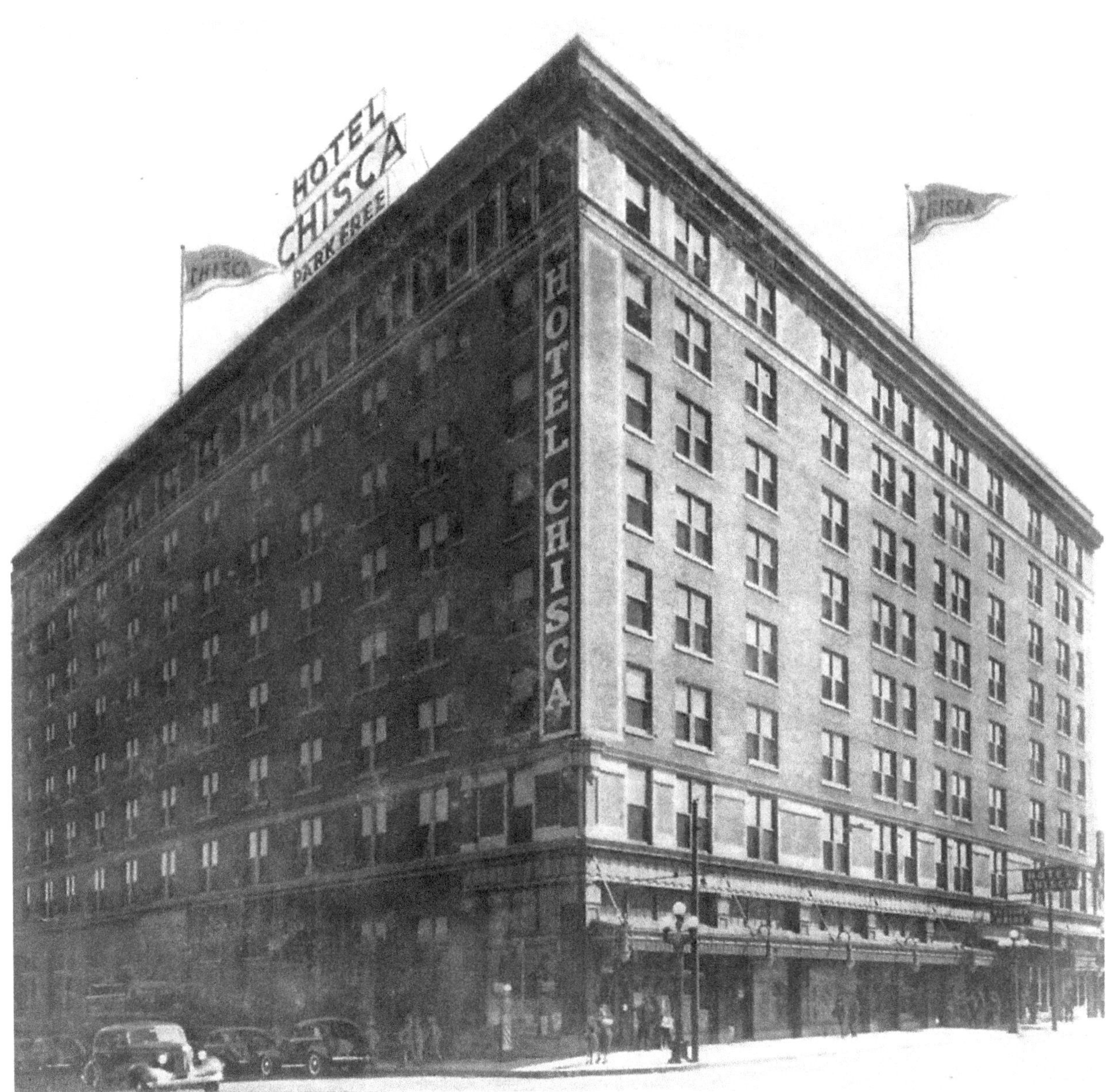

The Hotel Chisca, 1940. The Chisca opened in 1913 and expanded in 1959. The Church of God in Christ acquired it in 1972.

East Memphis Motor Company, formerly East End Motor Company, 1940s.

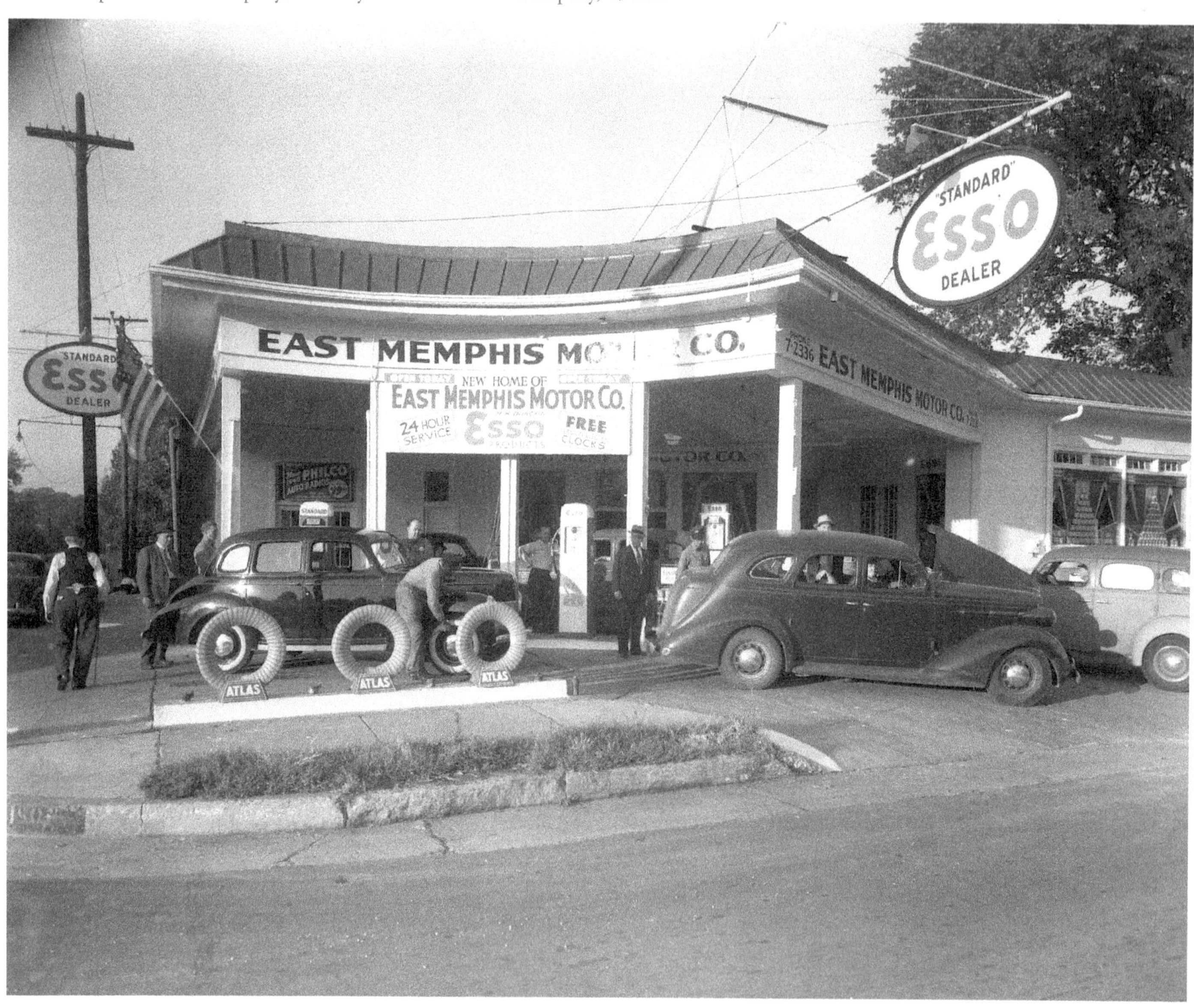

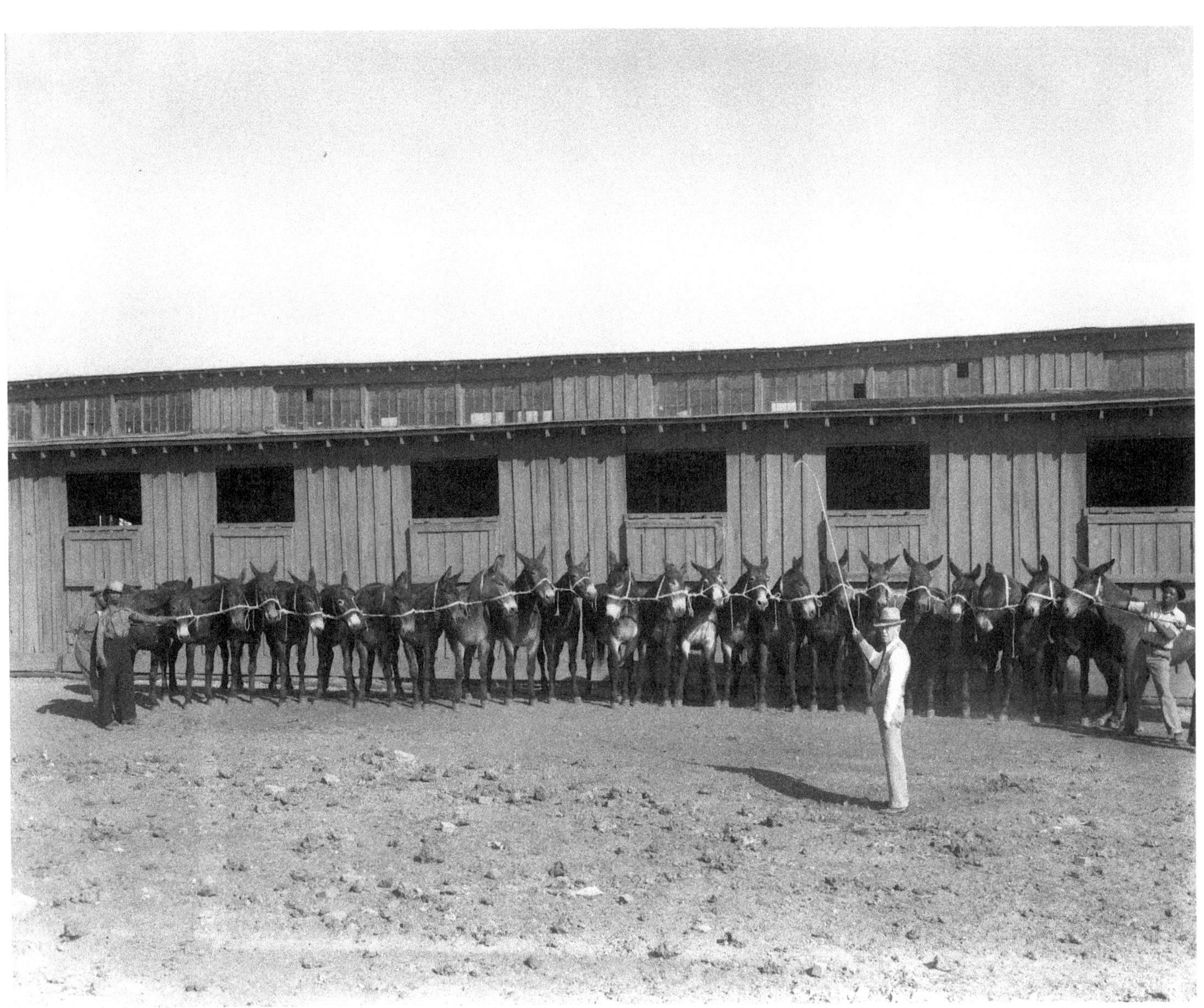

Smith-Podesta Horse and Mule Company at 190 McLemore, 1940. Memphis was considered the largest mule trading market in the country during the first part of the twentieth century.

Streetcar passing Bry's Department Store, 1940.

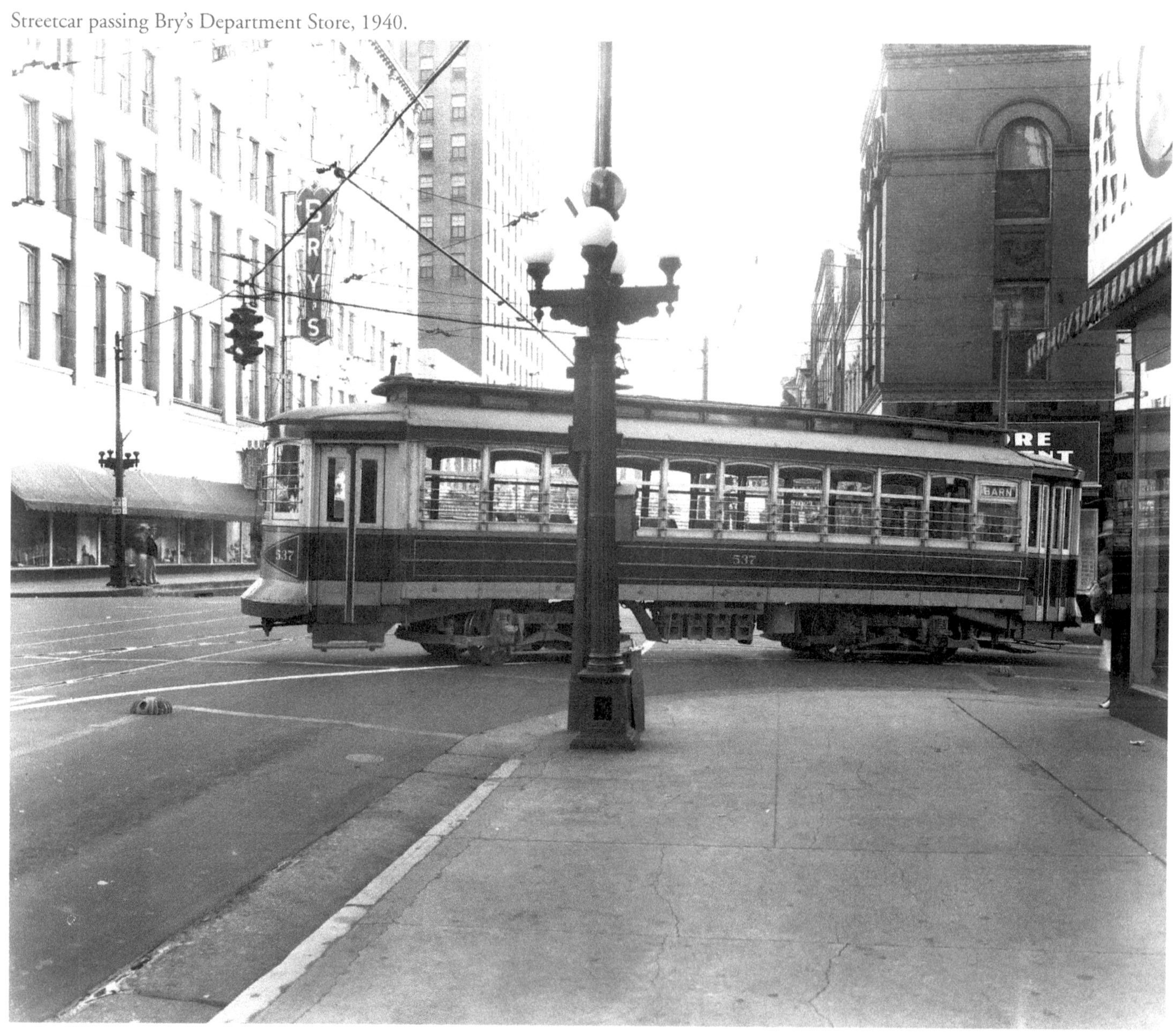

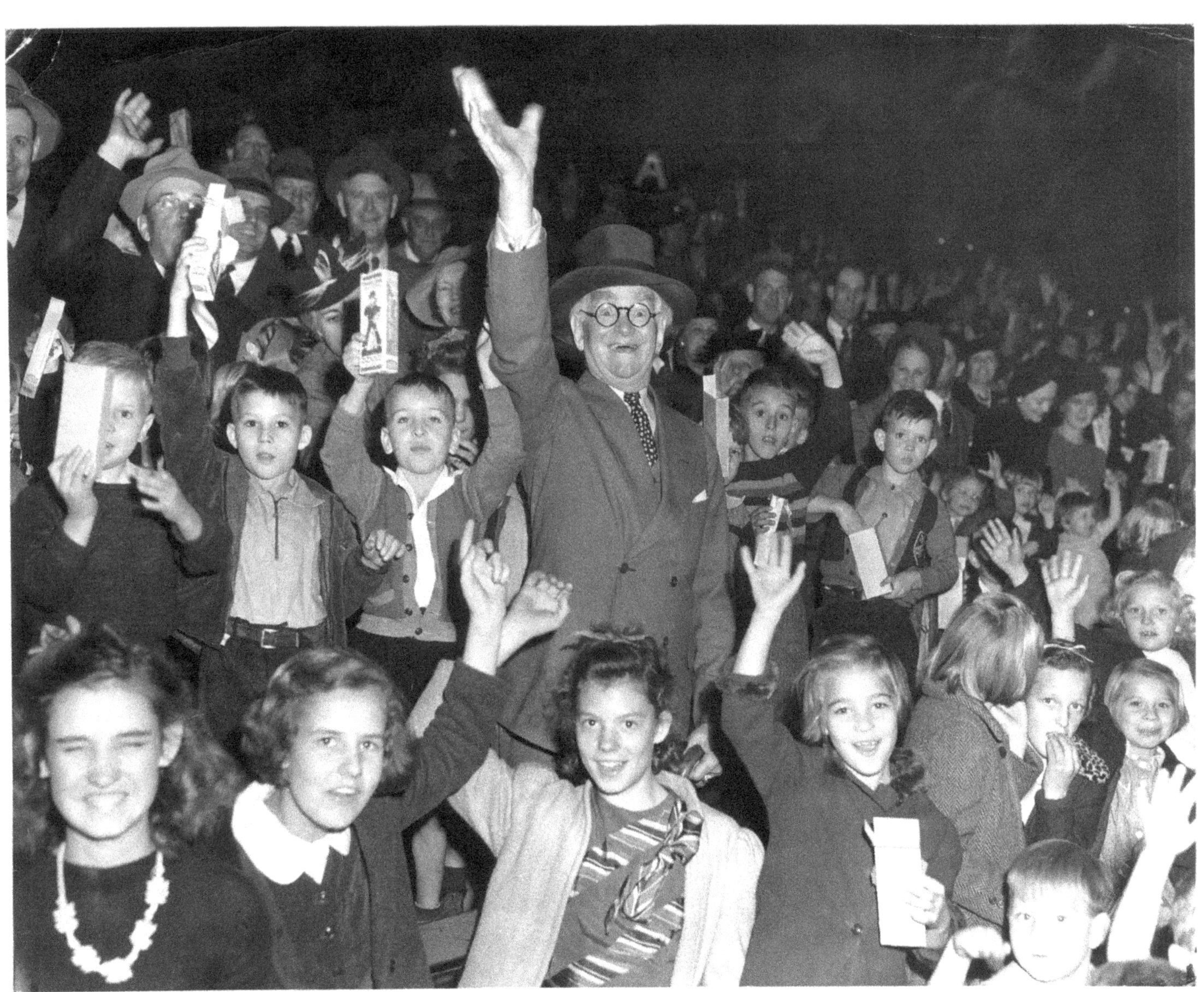

Edward Hull "Boss" Crump attending the circus with school children, 1942.

Workers making repairs to streetcar lines, circa 1946.

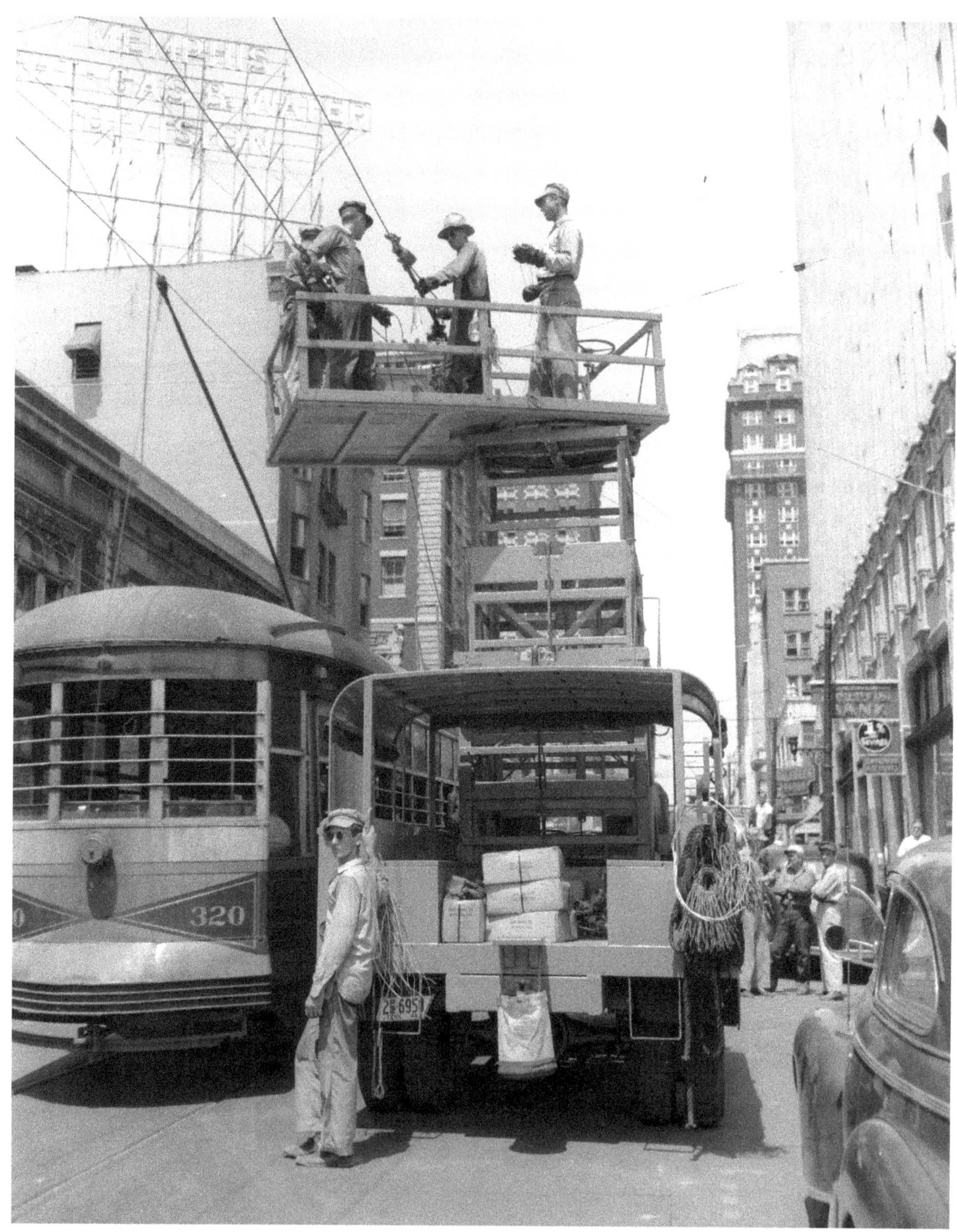

Booker T. Washington High School marching band, 1943.

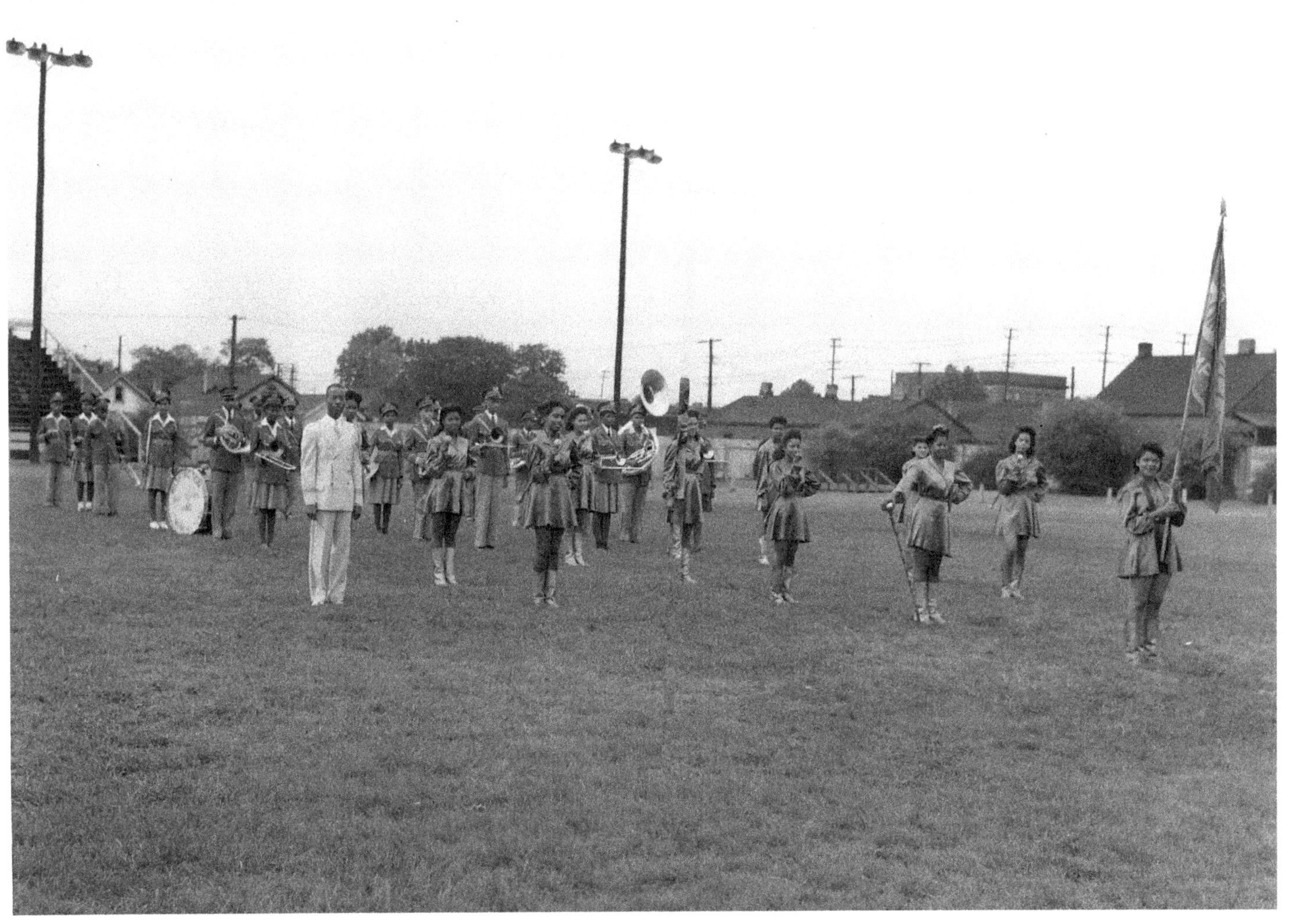

The B-24 Liberator purchased through a fund-raiser led by Lt. George W. Lee during World War II.

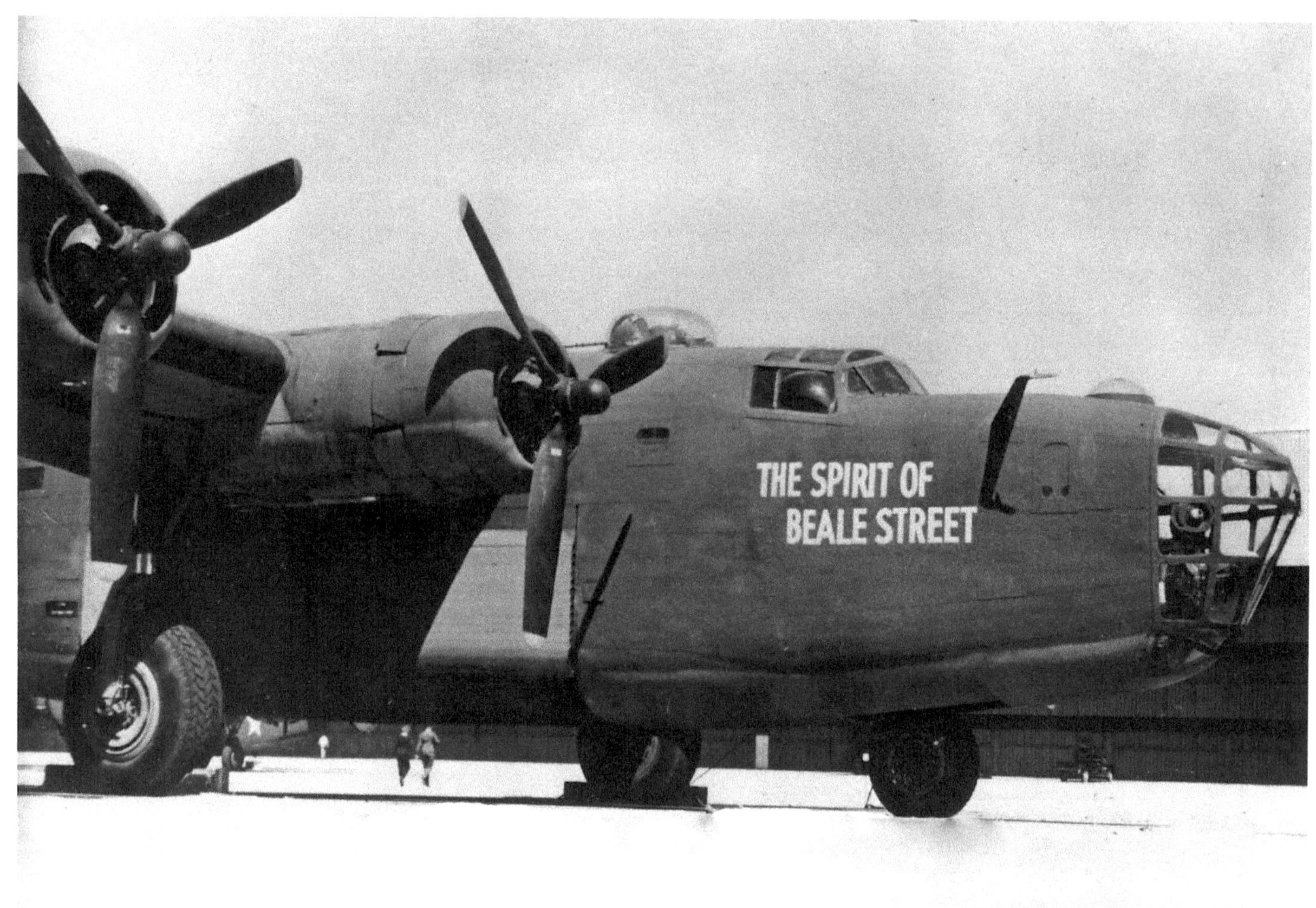

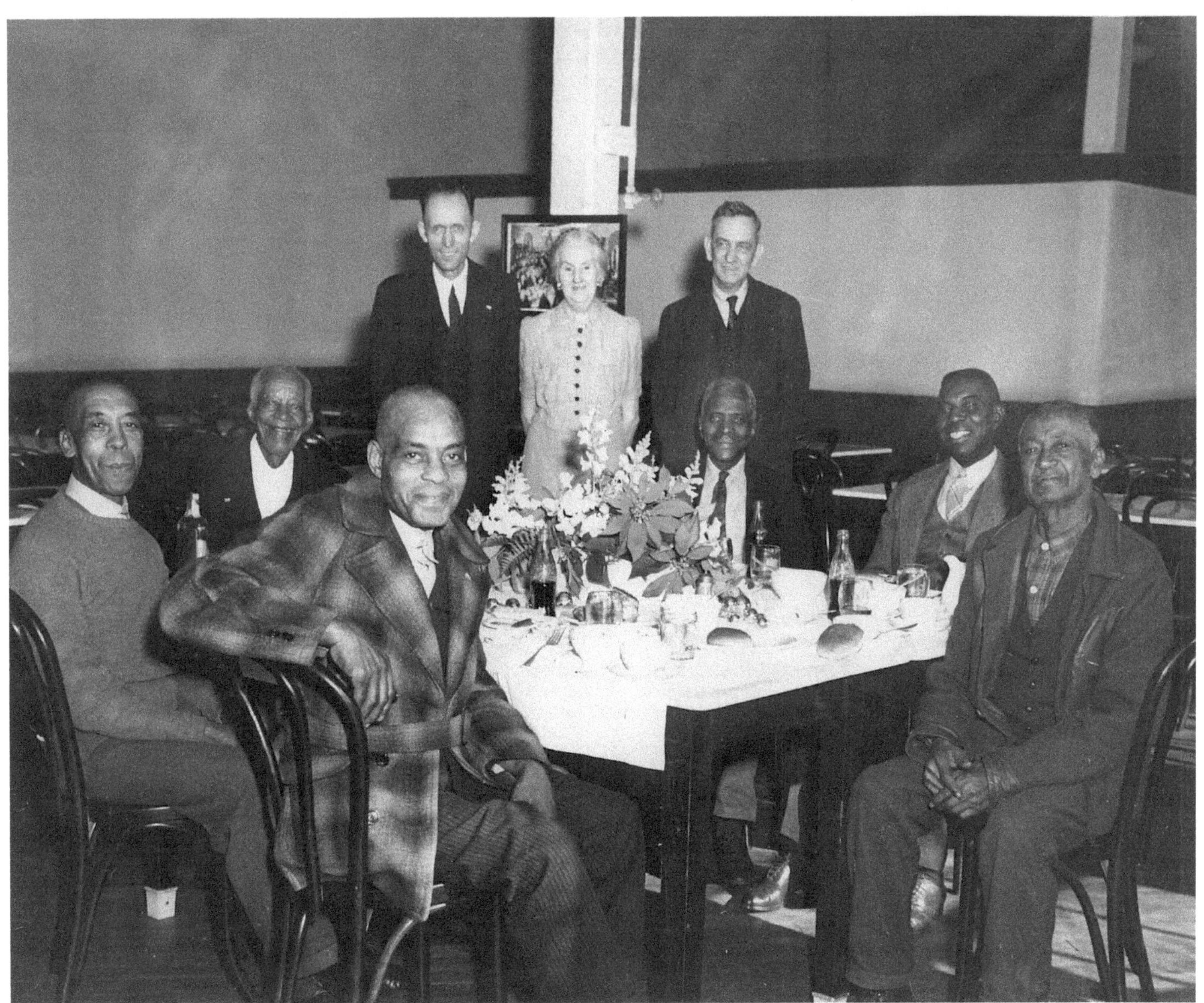

Bemis Brothers Bag Company, 1943. The St. Louis-based company opened a bag factory in Memphis in 1900.

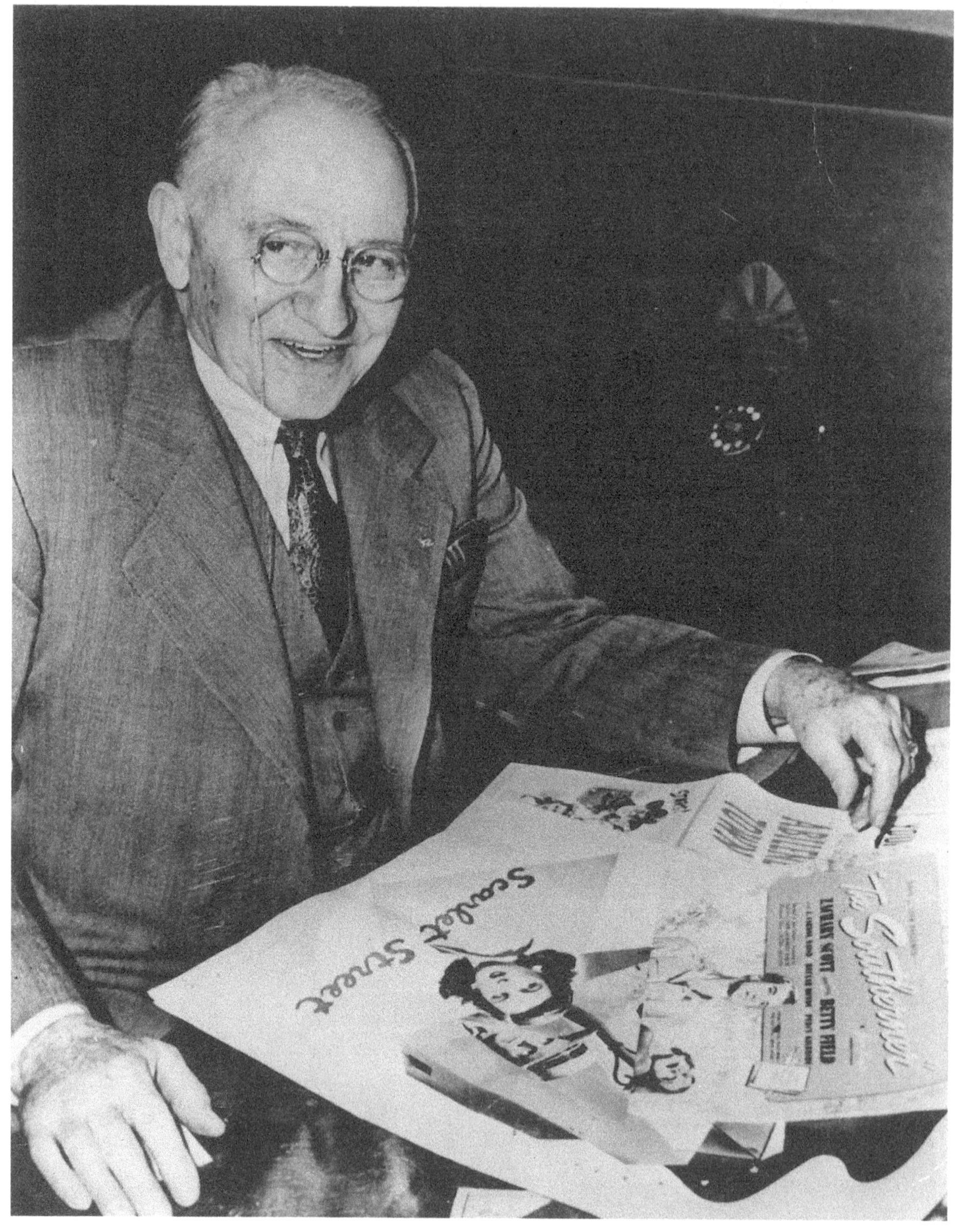

Mayor Watkins Overton appointed Lloyd T. Binford to the Shelby County Board of Censors in 1928. Binford was notorius for banning films based on his personal prejudices during his 25 years of service on the board.

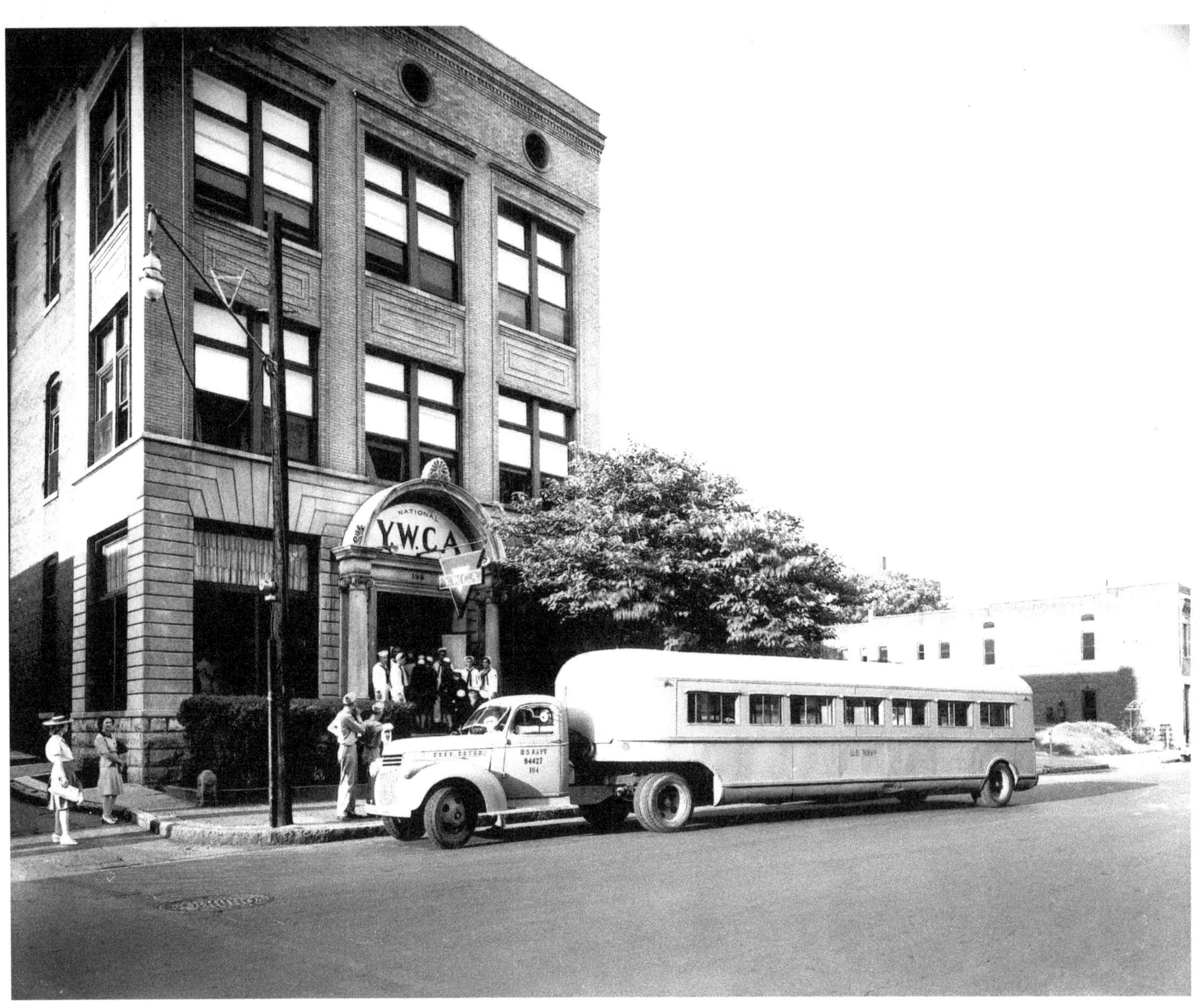

The YWCA Building at 196 Monroe Avenue, 1943. A new building was completed in 1951 at 200-202 Monroe Avenue, which later became home to the Salvation Army.

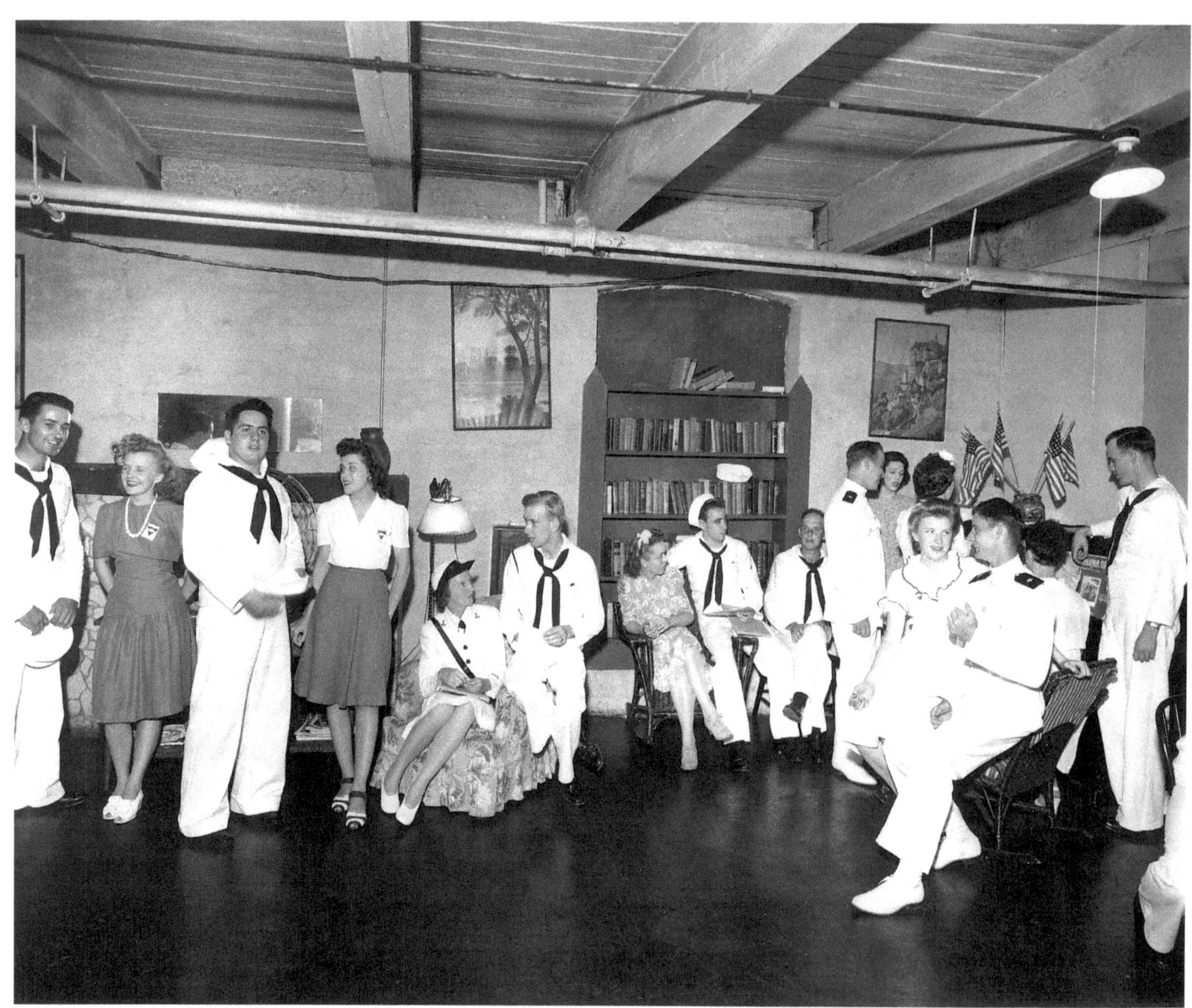

A social gathering at the YWCA in 1943.

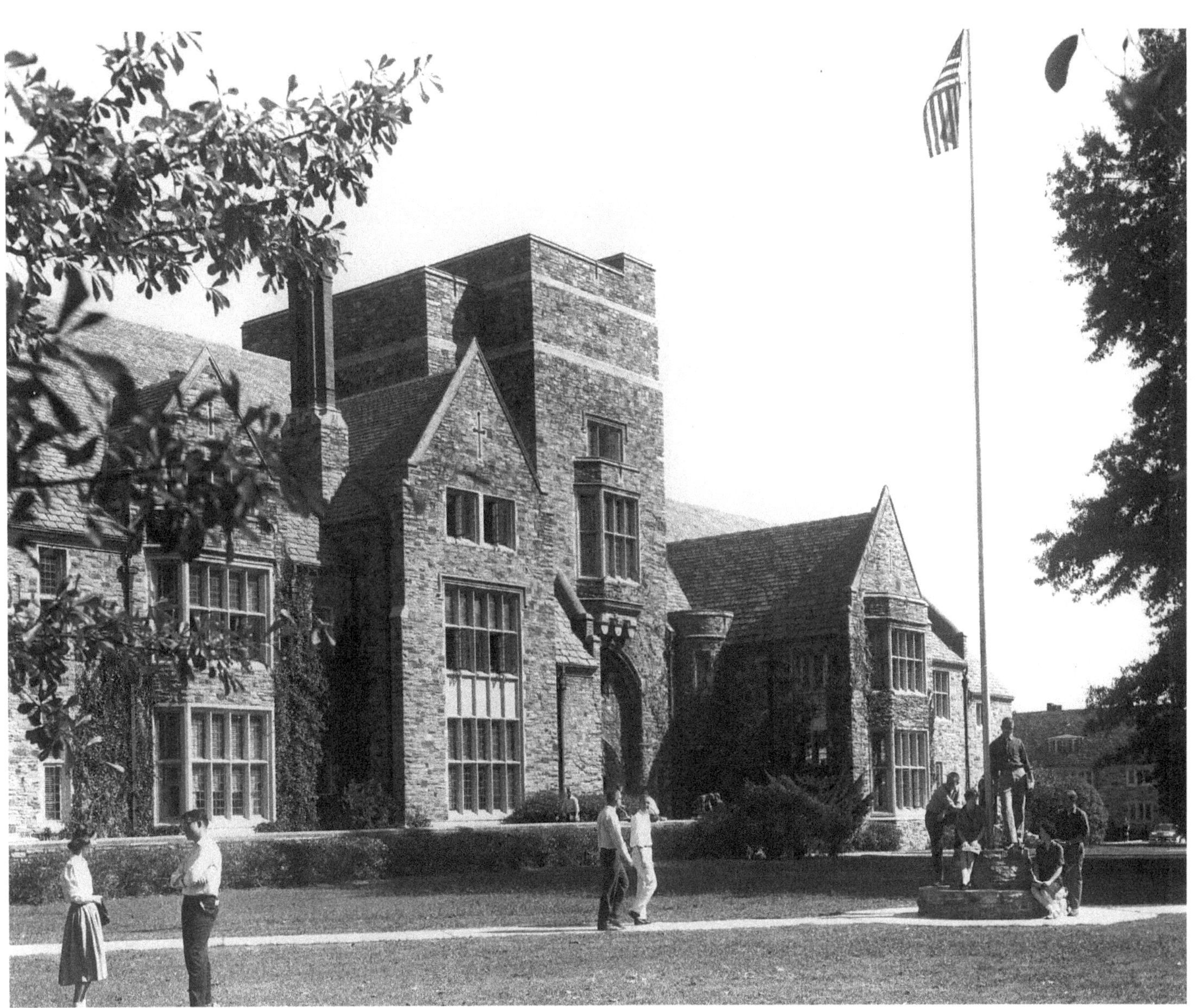

Southwestern College at 2000 North Parkway opened in 1925. The name was changed to Rhodes College in 1984.

View of Union Avenue and Riverside Drive near the Mississippi River in 1944.

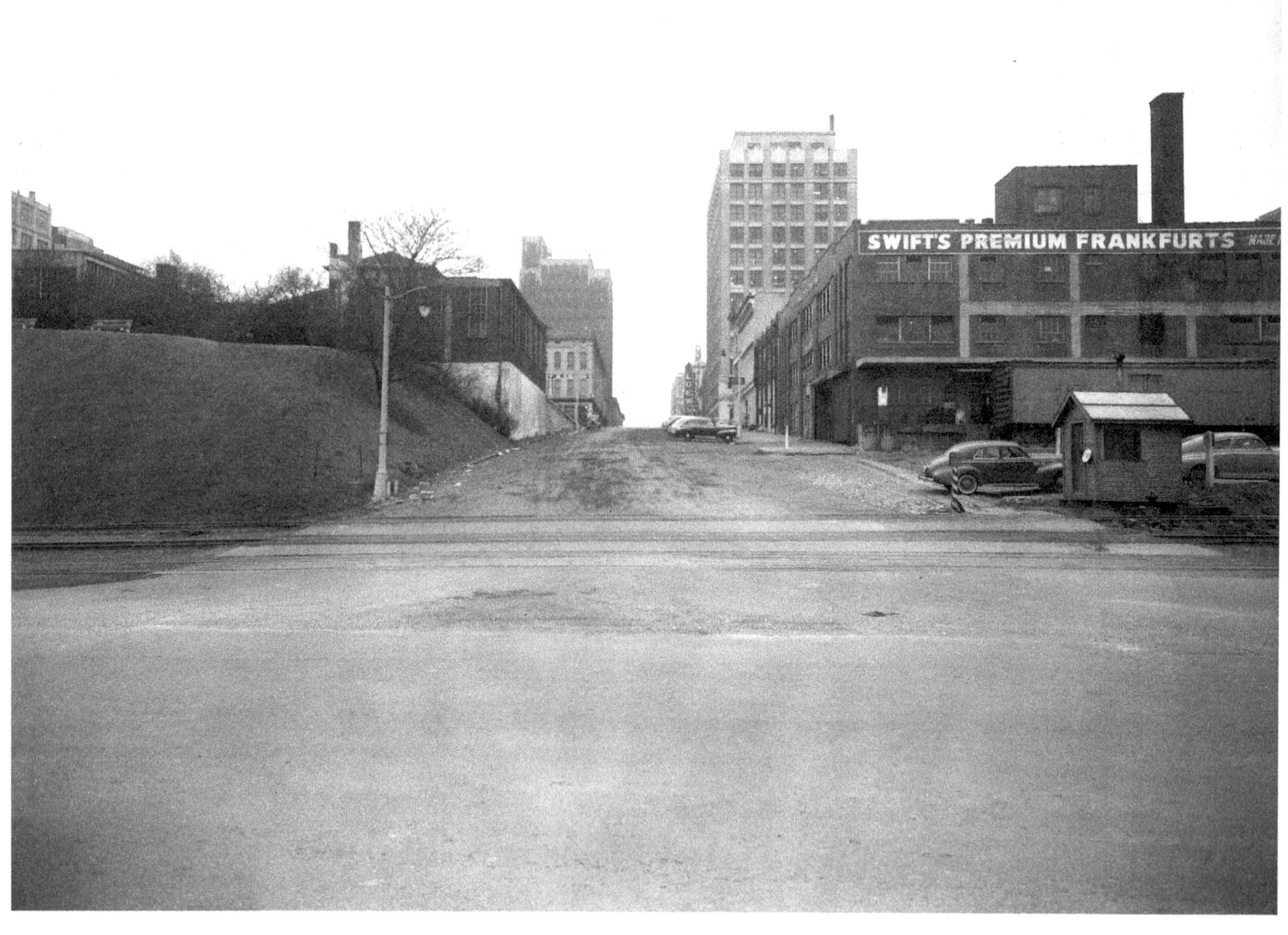

Cotton Exchange, 1944.

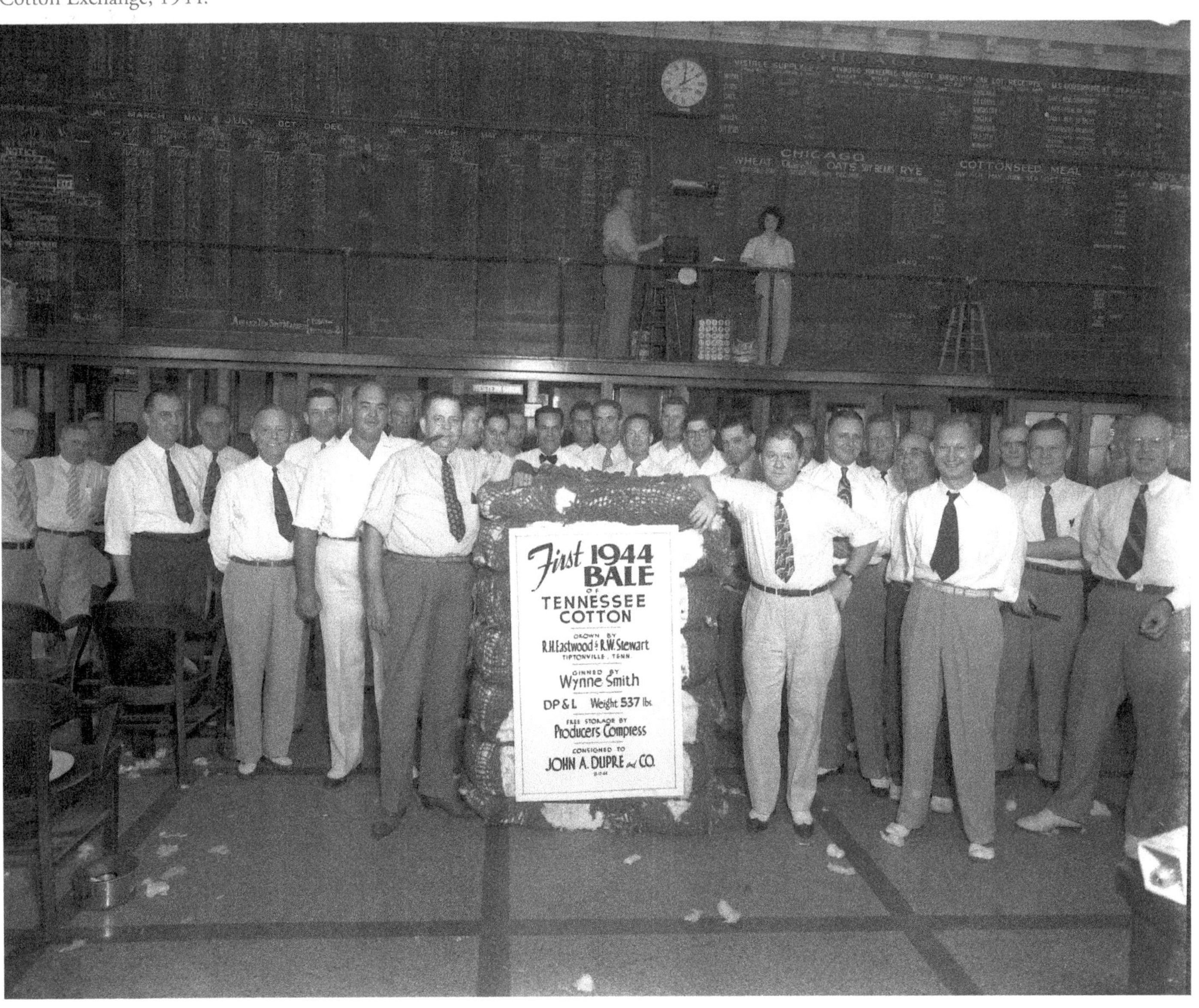

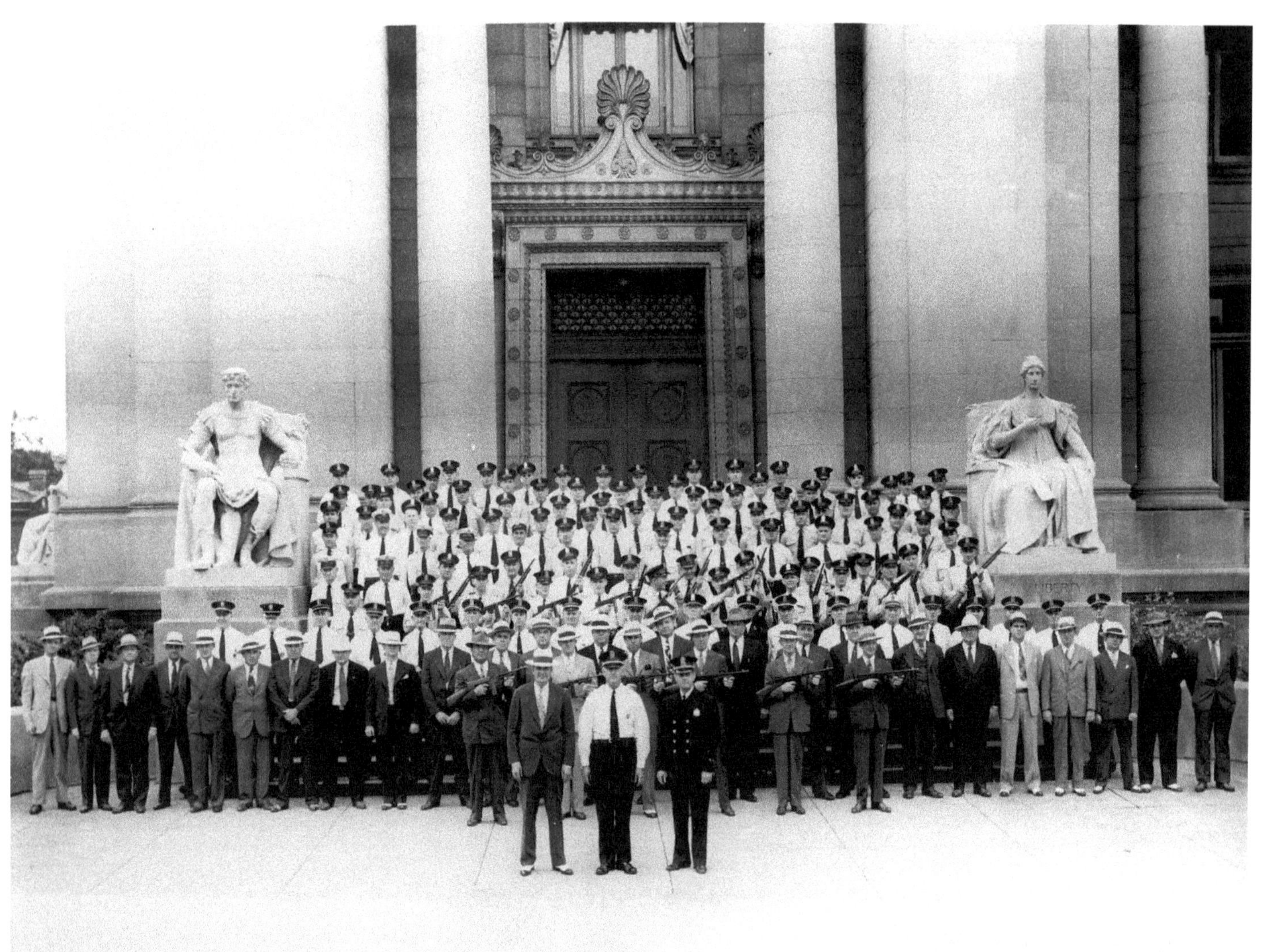

Memphis Police Department, 1944.

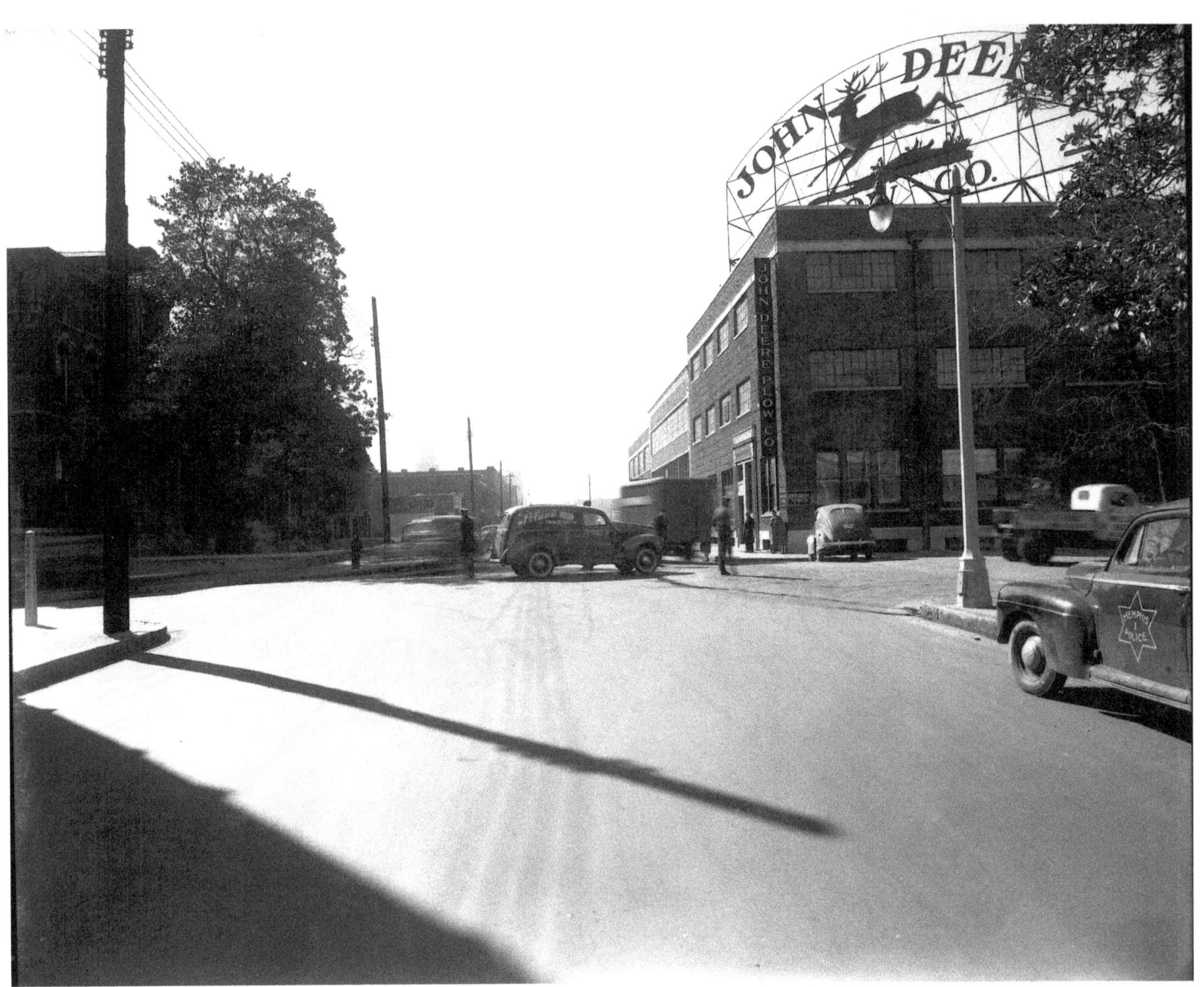

John Deere Company at Front Street and Vance Avenue, 1944.

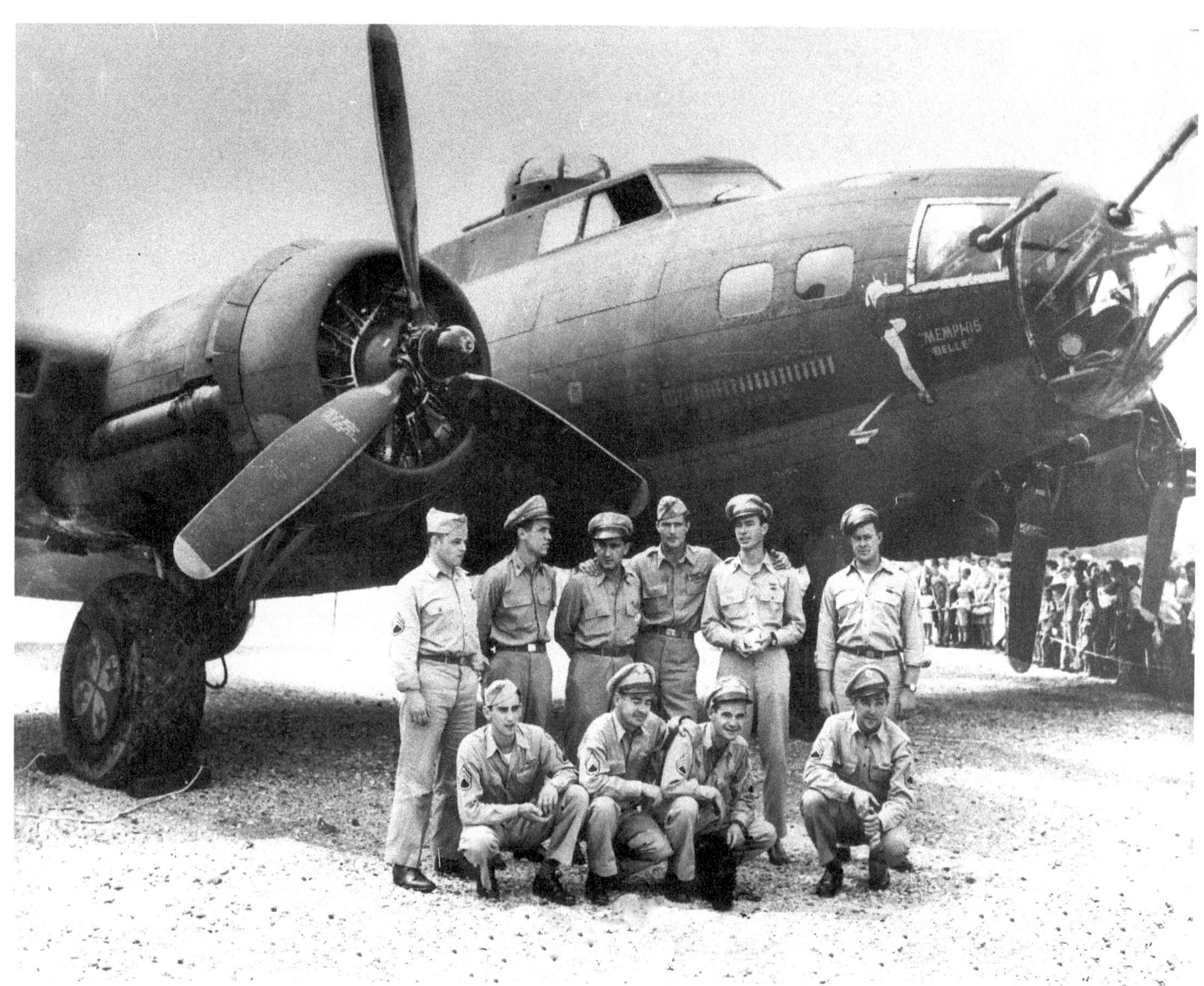

The *Memphis Belle* and her crew after their return from Europe.

Mrs. Christine Parker, who served as librarian for the Mobile Book Service for the Cossitt Library and Shelby County Libraries, 1947.

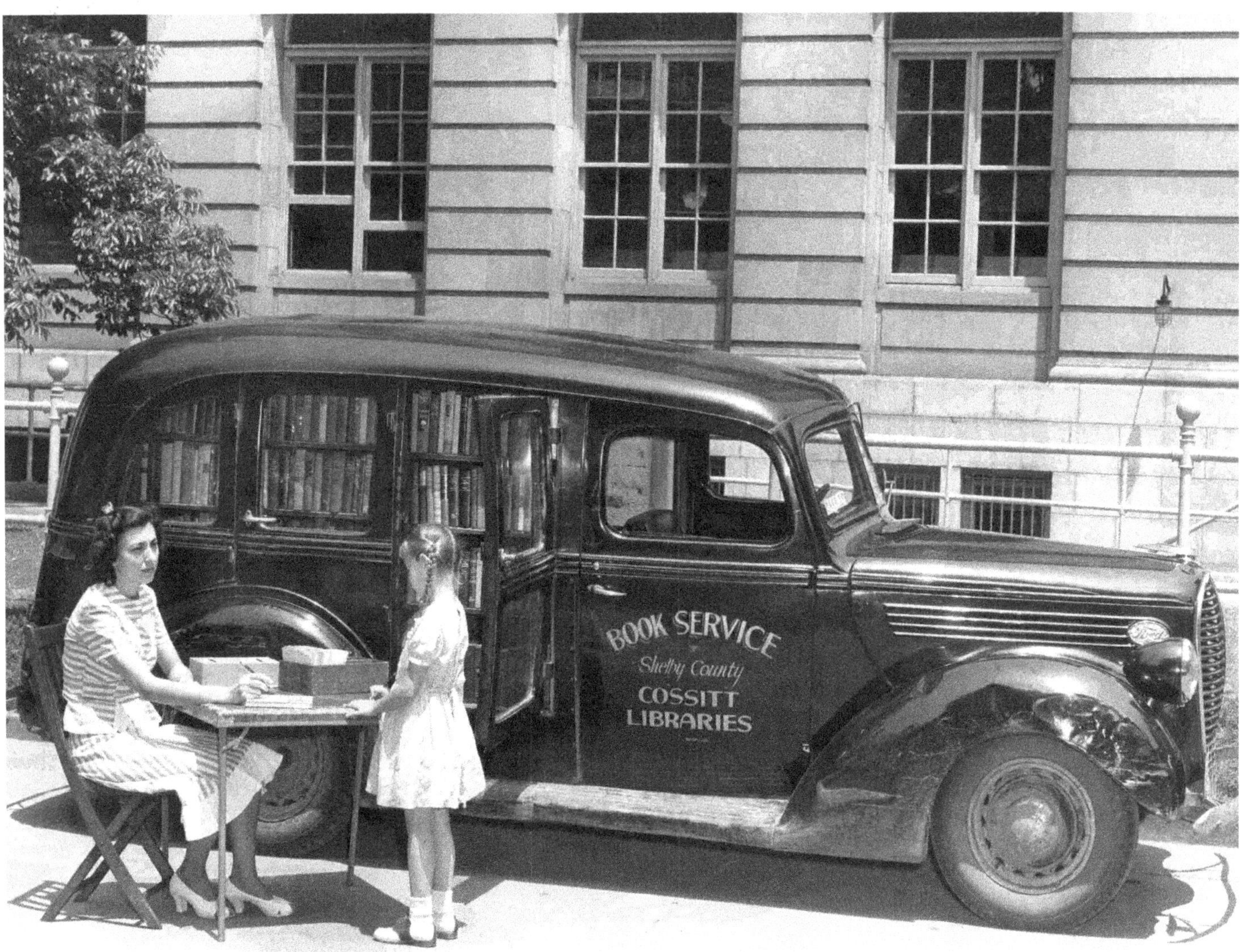

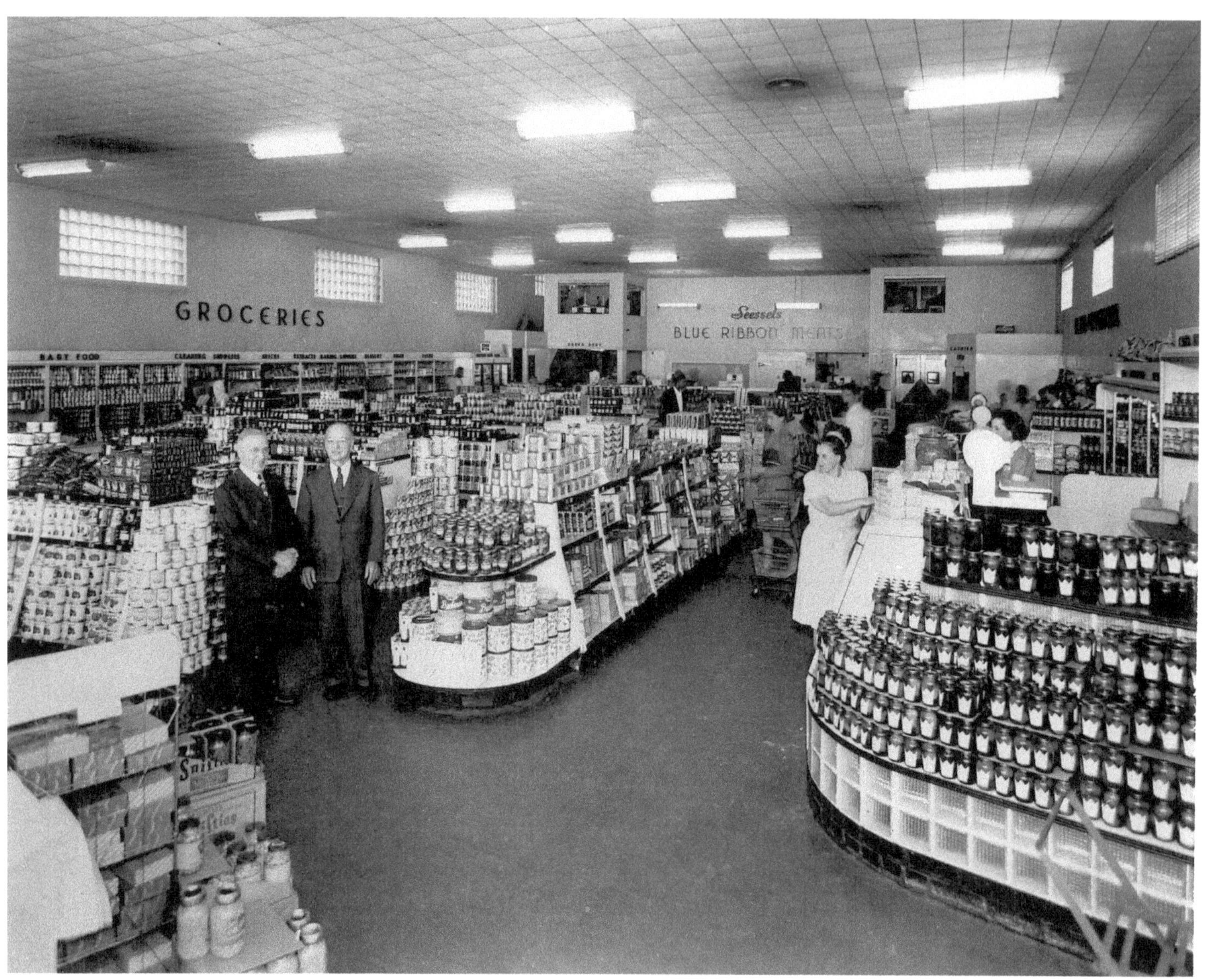

Interior of Seessel's Grocery Store.

Aerial view of the Sterick Building, 1947.

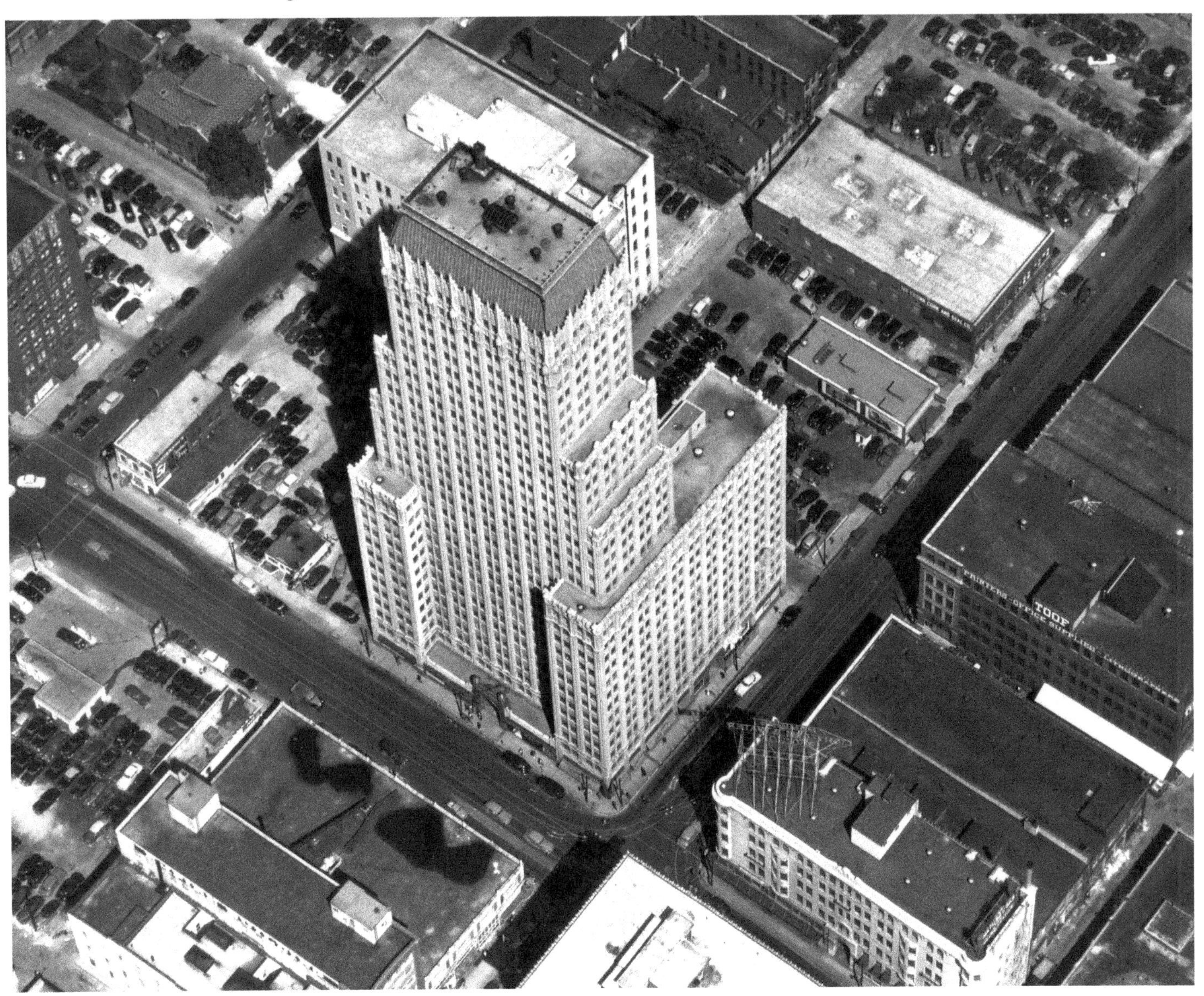

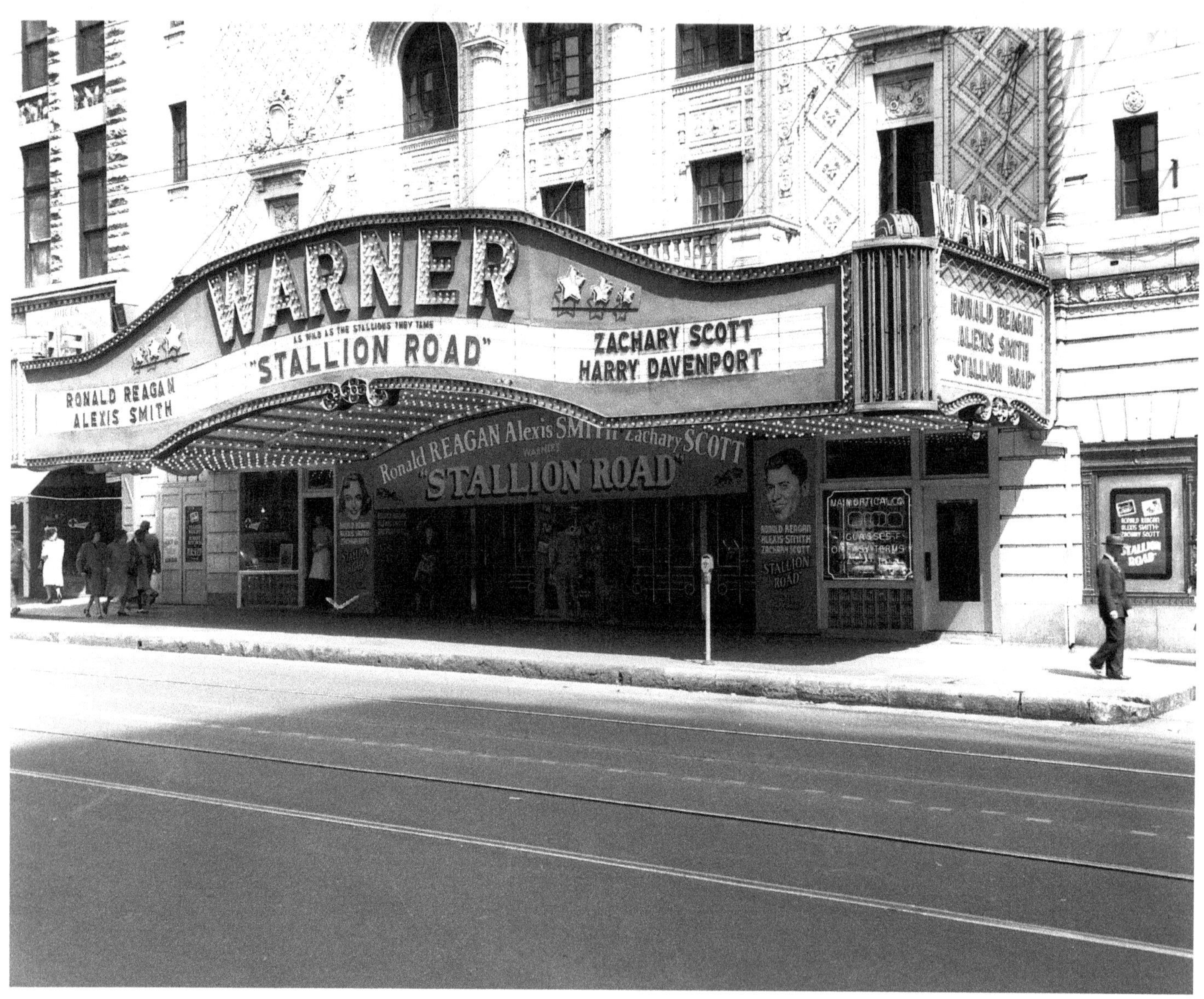

The Warner Theater at 52 South Main Street, 1947. This was one of a number of theaters in the vicinity including Loew's State, The Strand, Princess and Loew's Palace.

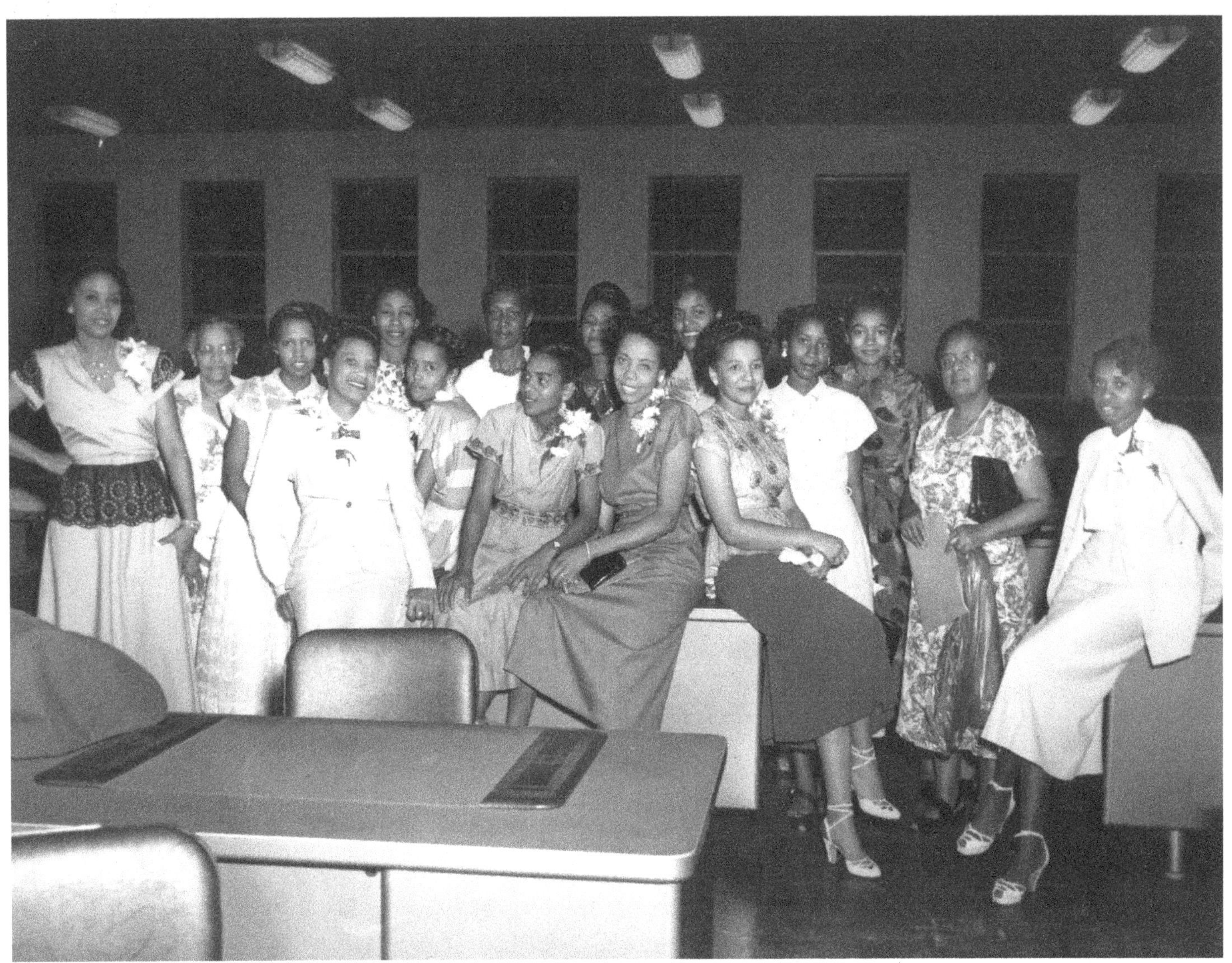

The secretarial staff of Universal Life Insurance Company, 1949. Universal Life Insurance Company was founded by Dr. J.E. Walker in 1923 and operated on the third floor of the Fraternal Bank Building on Beale Street before moving to 234 Hernando in 1930. The company moved again in 1949 into a new building at 480 Linden.

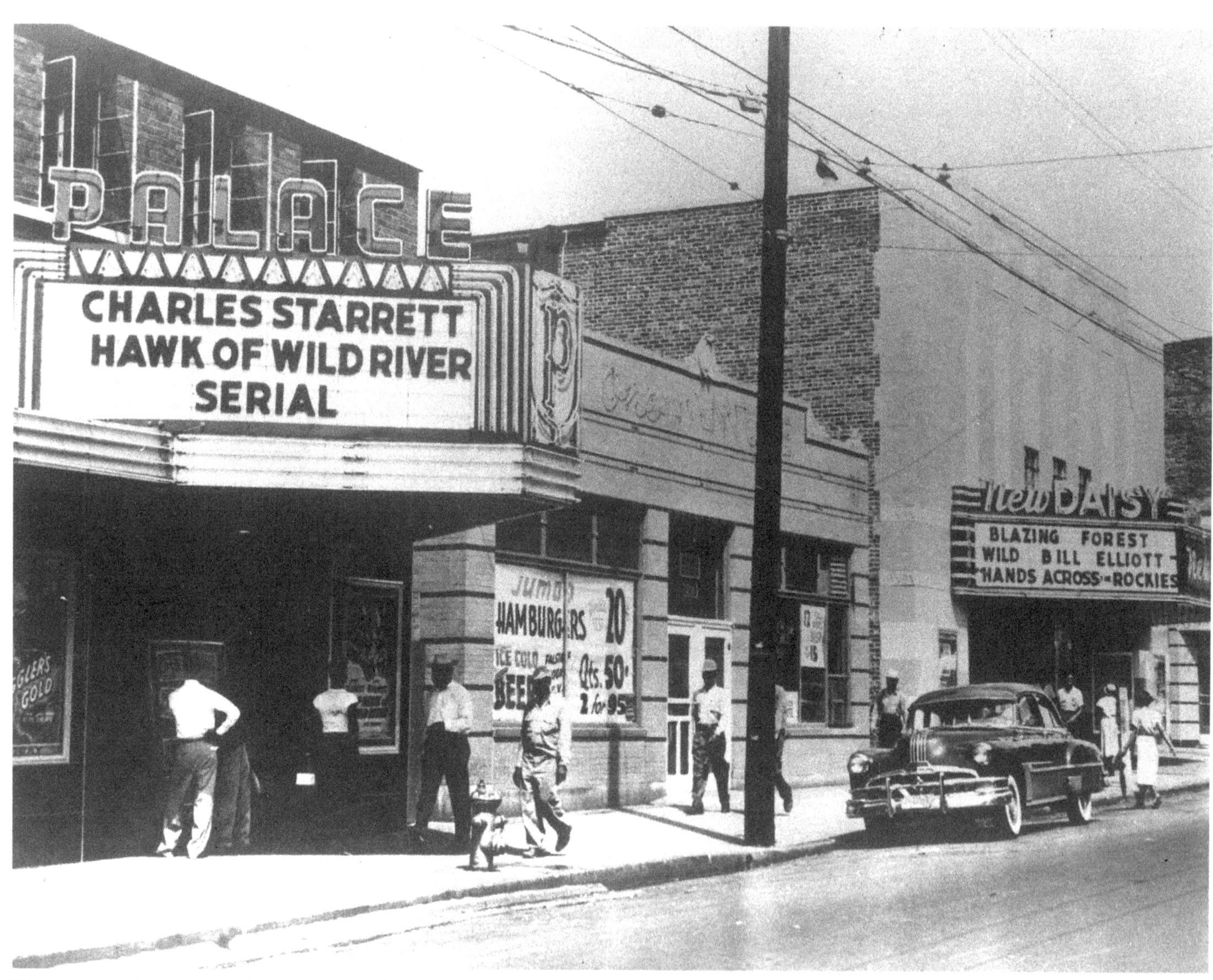

The Palace and New Daisy Theaters on Beale Street, circa 1950.

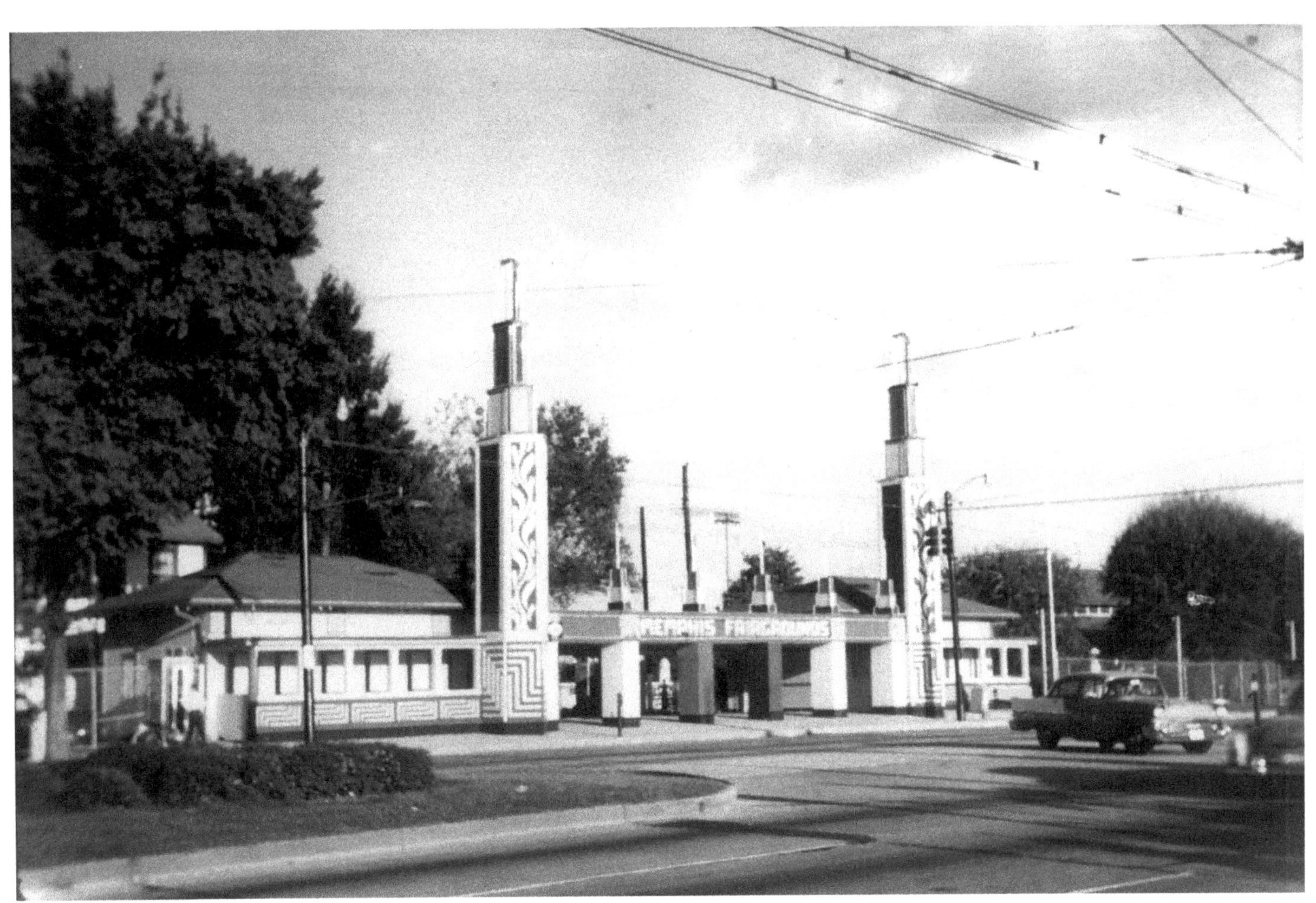

The Main Gate of the Fairgrounds Amusement Park, 1958.

The Pippin Roller Coaster at the Fairgrounds Amusement Park, 1974.

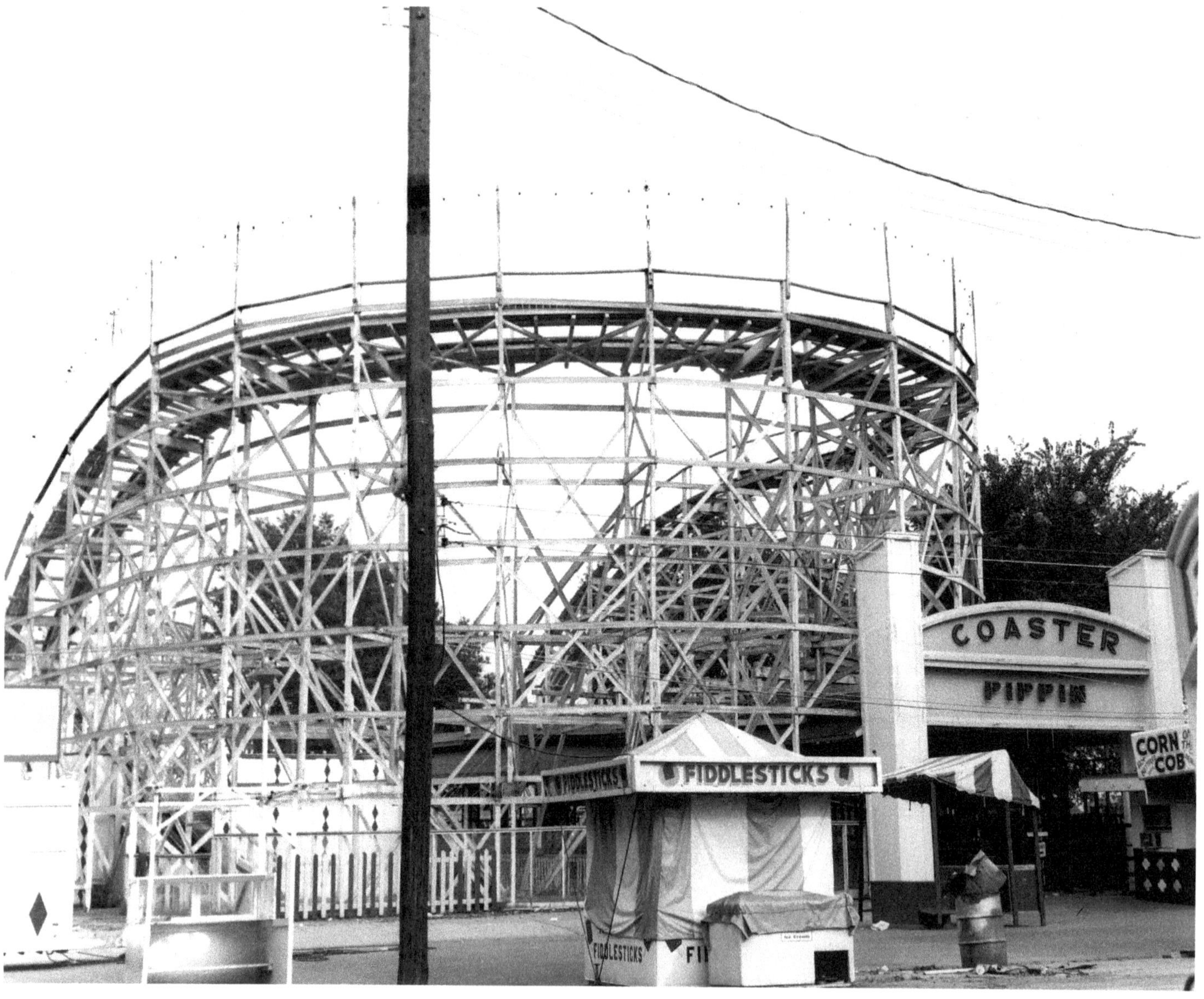

Union Avenue and South Front Street, 1954.

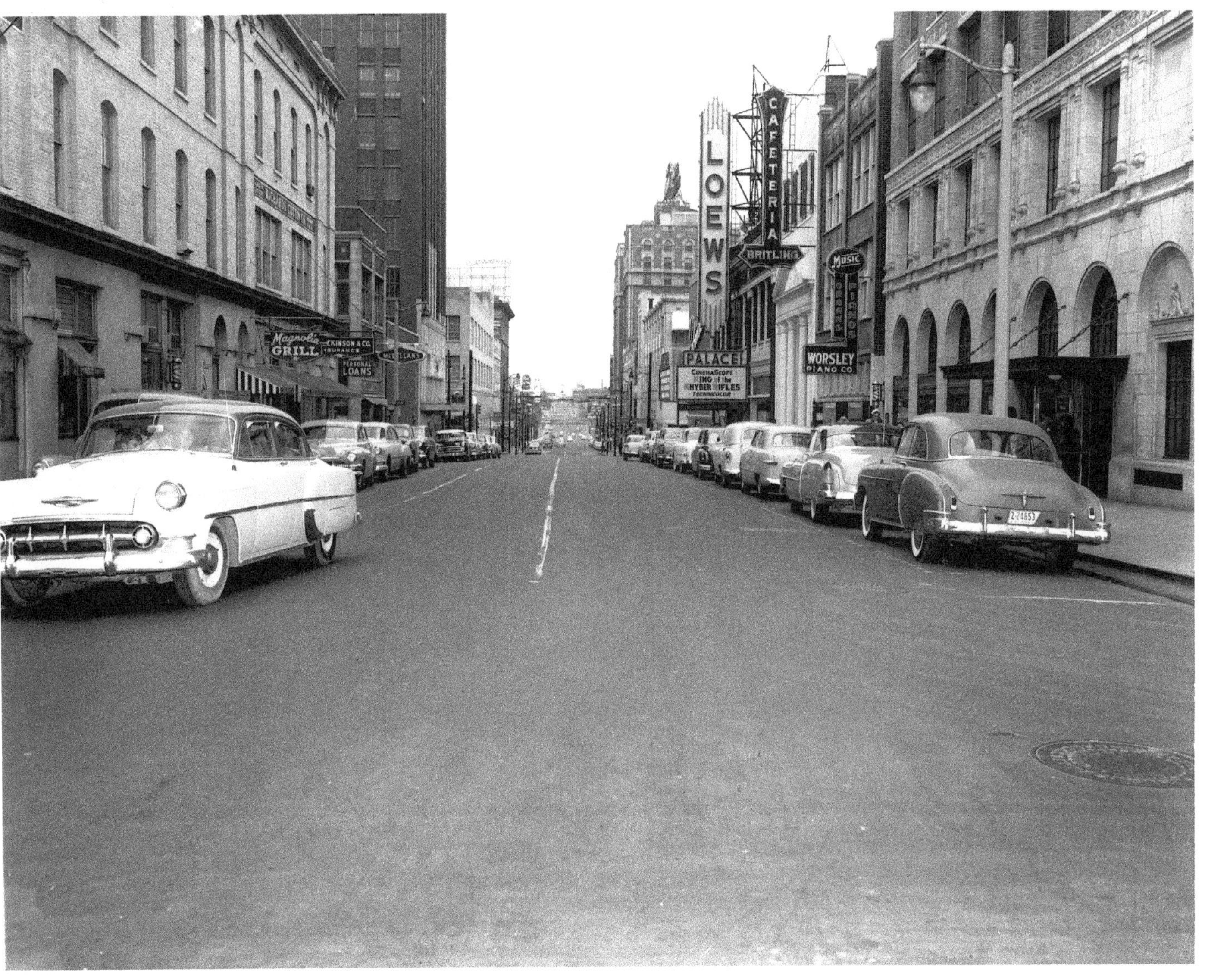

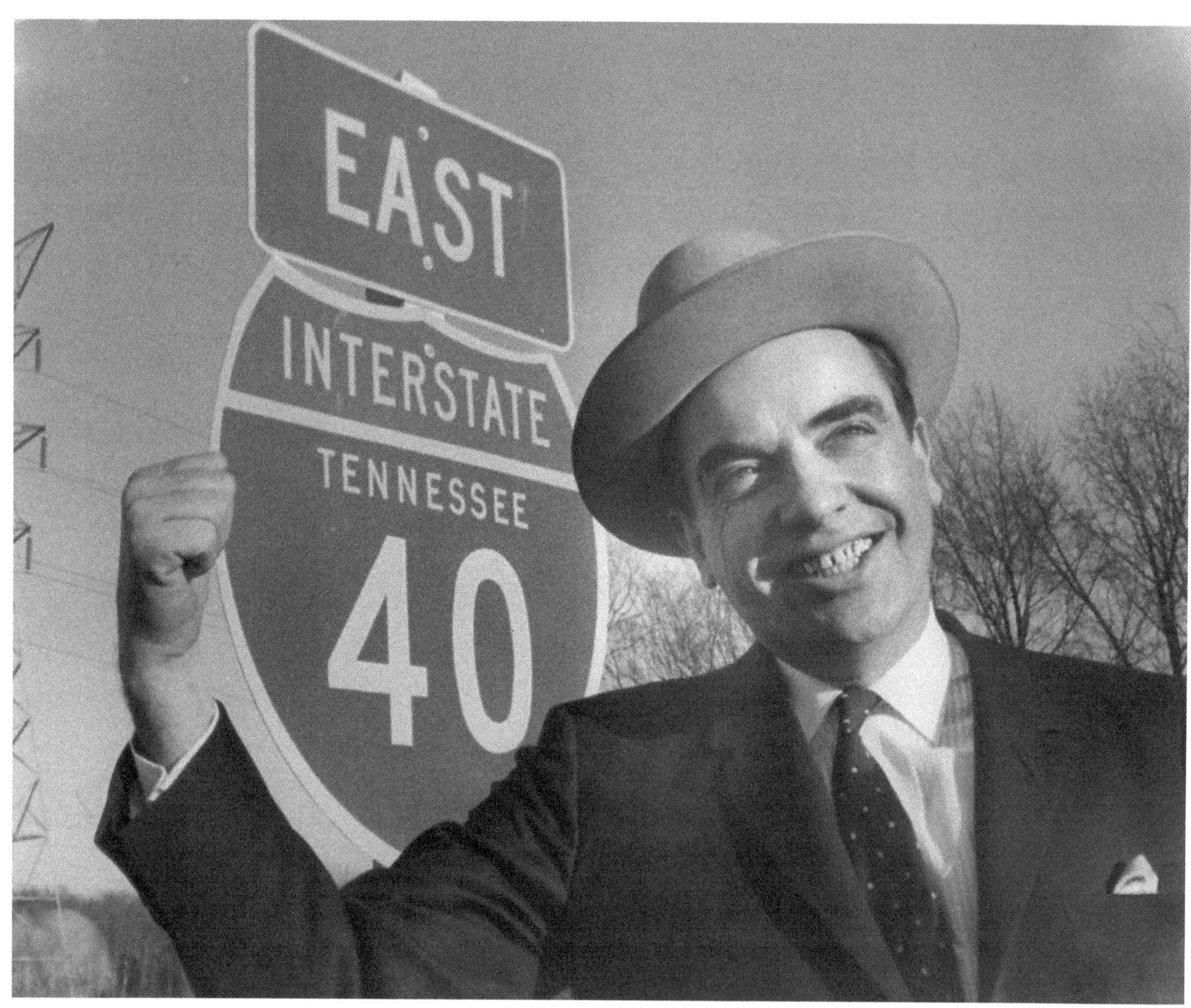

Governor Frank Clement of Tennessee in front of an Interstate 40 sign, circa 1957. I-40 was originally intended to go through Overton Park in Memphis, but public opposition forced the plan to be abandoned. Traffic was rerouted through the northern portion of the I-240 loop, which was redesignated as I-40.

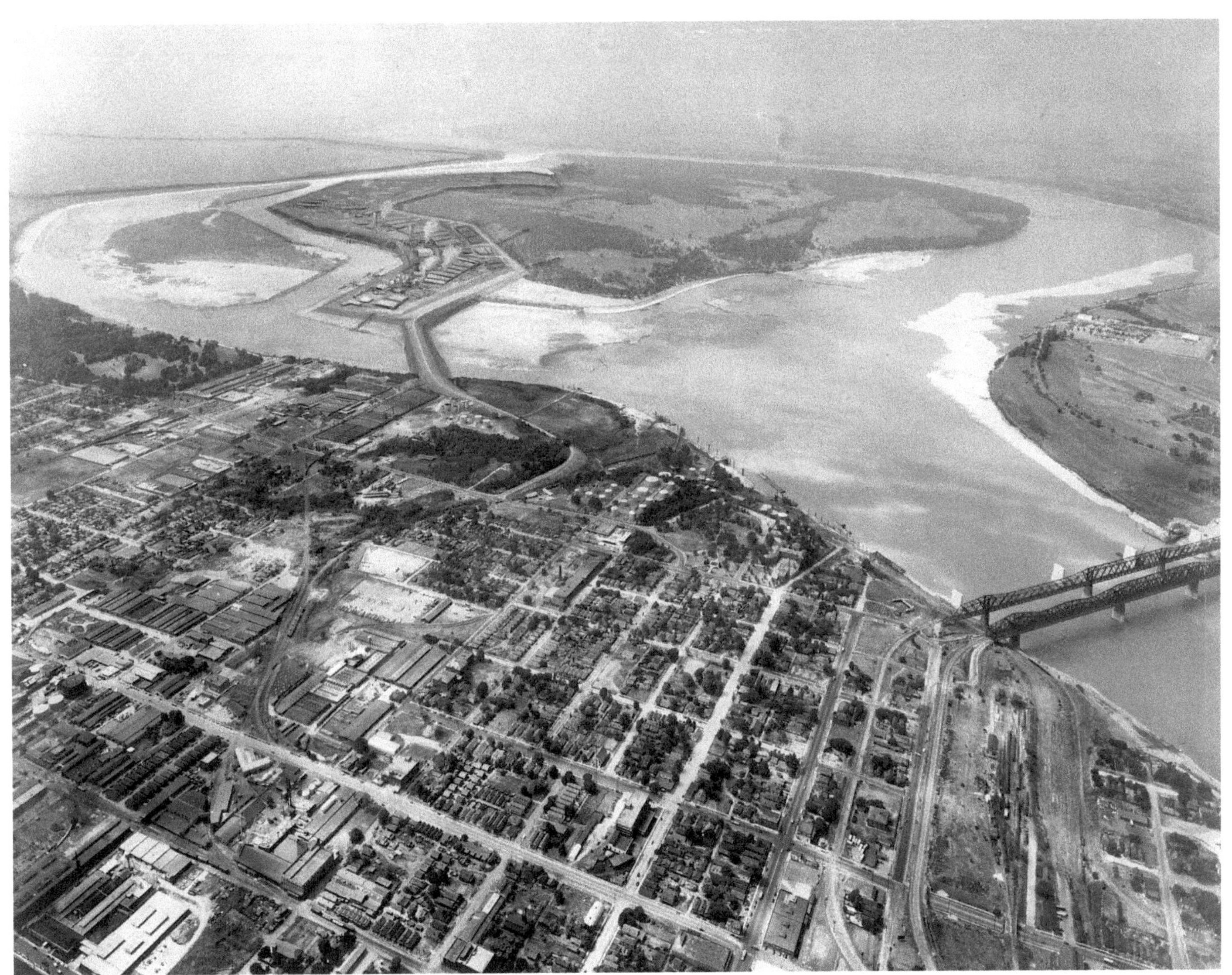

View of Memphis and President's Island, 1948.

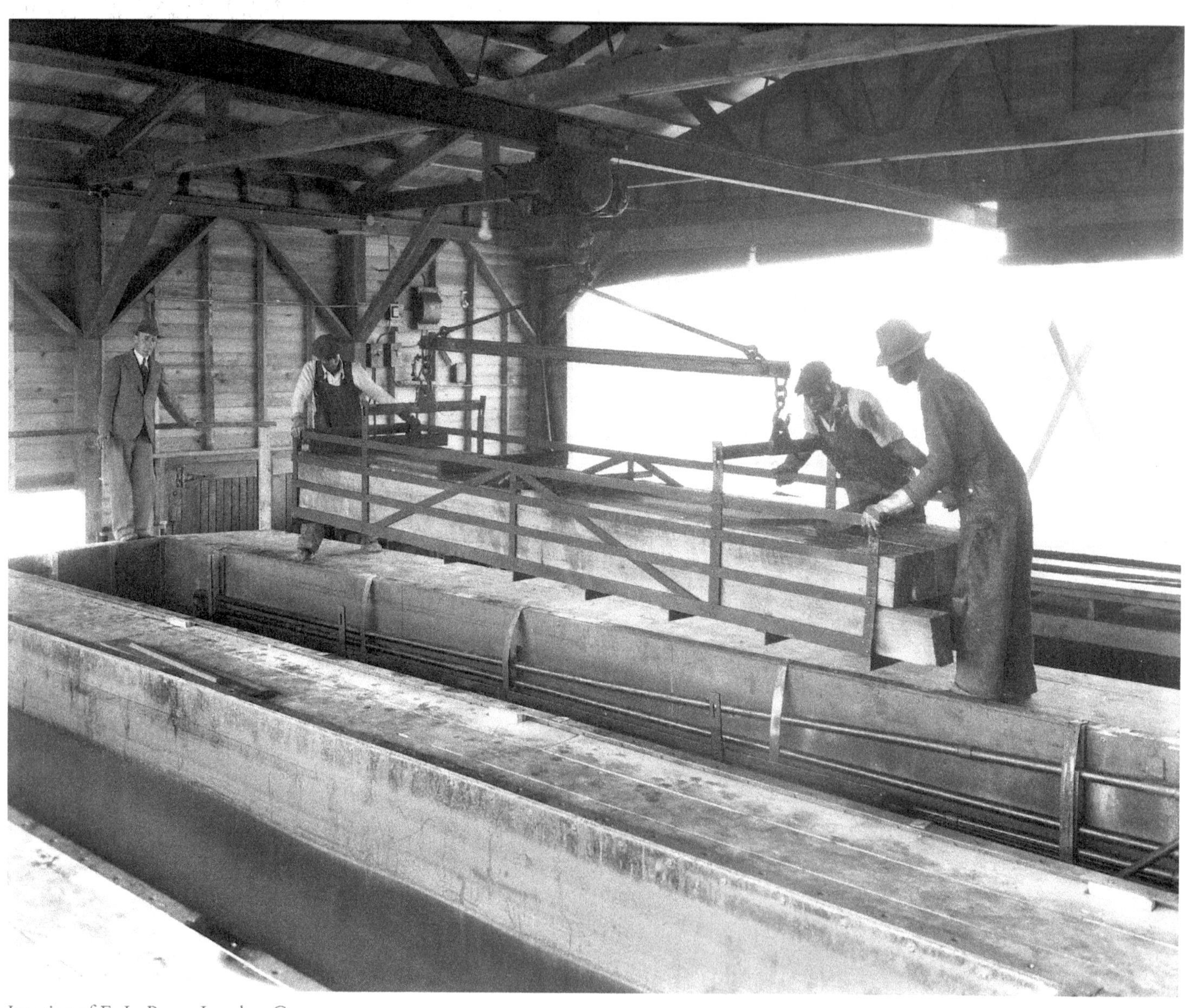

Interior of E. L. Bruce Lumber Company.

Roy Rogers at Ellis Auditorium in 1950.

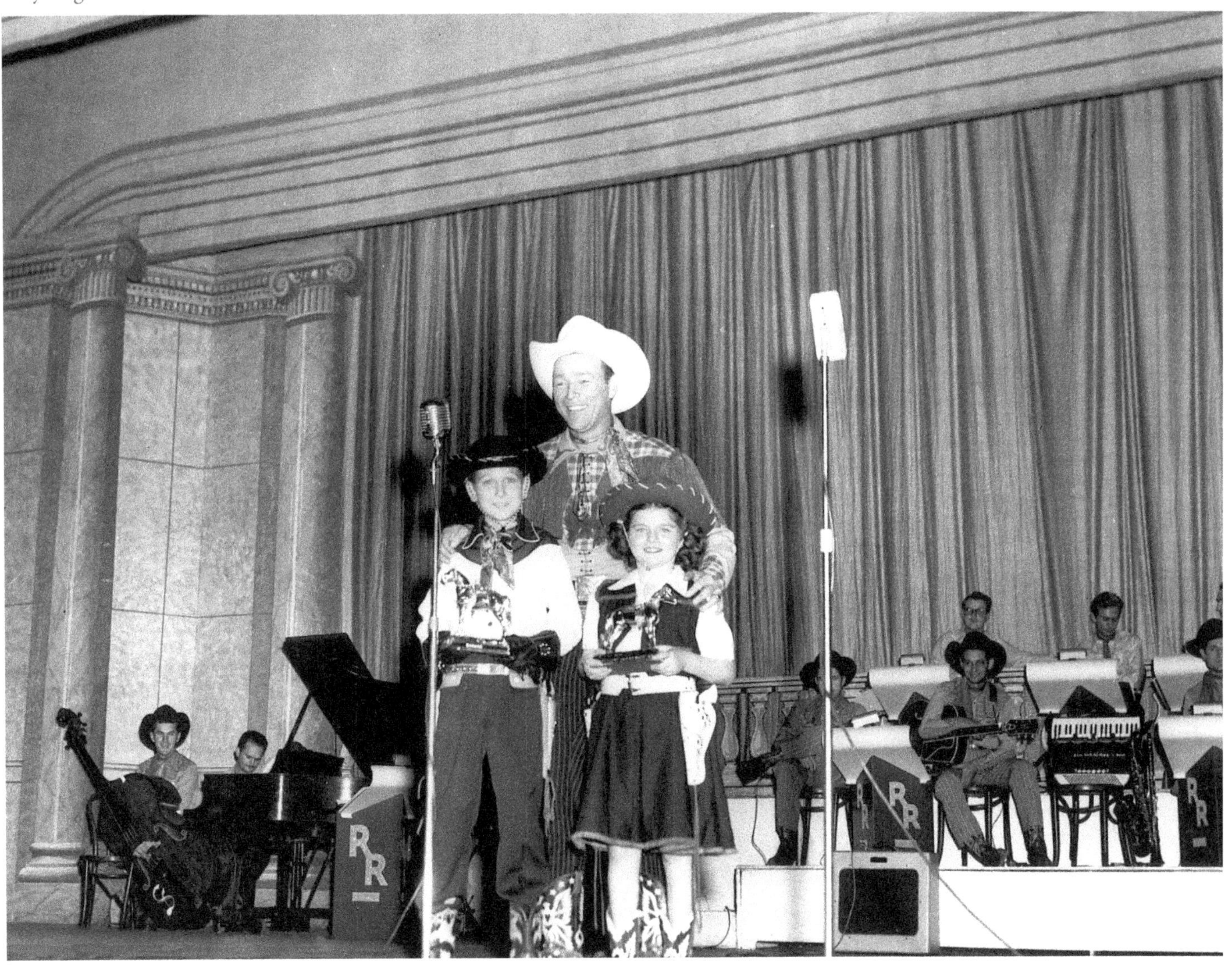

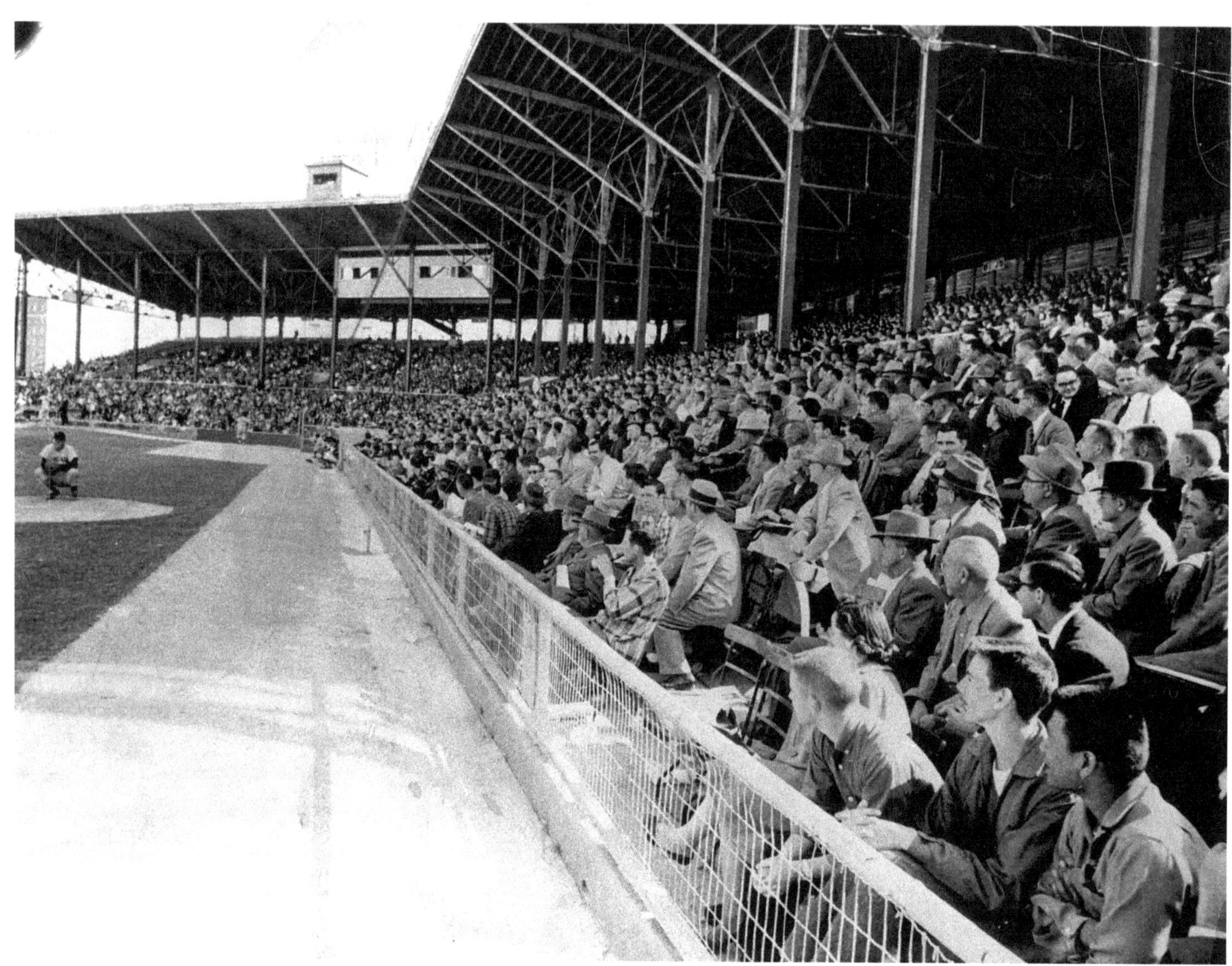

Russwood Park, 1960. Originally named Red Elm Park, the stadium's name was changed in honor of owner Russell E. Gardner by his son-in-law Thomas Watkins in 1915. The park was home to the Memphis "Chicks" baseball team until it was destroyed by fire April 17, 1960.

1960 TO A MODERN CITY

1960-1983

A struggling actor, Amos Joseph Alphonsus Jacobs, vowed to the patron saint of the hopeless that if he found success, he would build a shrine to him. Jacobs found success and became Danny Thomas. Thomas kept his promise by opening a children's hospital. St. Jude Children's Research Hospital opened in 1962 and became a respected international center for the study and treatment of pediatric illnesses. In its first forty years, the hospital treated over sixteen thousand children from the United States and sixty other countries.

However, a number of events shook Memphis in the 1960's and 1970's. While supporting striking sanitation workers, Dr. Martin Luther King, Jr., was assassinated in Memphis on the balcony of the Lorraine Motel on April 4, 1968. Memphis headlines were dominated by battles regarding school desegregation, the proposal of I-40 going through Overton Park, crime, police corruption and teachers, police officers and firefighters striking. On August 16, 1977, the world's attention was drawn to Memphis again when Elvis Presley died at his home, Graceland.

There were a number of other notable Memphians who made advances as well. Fred Smith created Federal Express in 1972, adding another dimension to the city's role as a distribution center. In 1976, Benjamin L. Hooks was elected executive director of the NAACP. Jesse H. Turner became the first African American to serve as chairman of the Shelby County Board of Commissioners in 1983. Dr. Willie Herenton became the first African American superintendent of the Memphis City Schools in 1979 and later became the first African American to be elected mayor in Memphis.

Memphis suffered from a number of setbacks as it did a century before, but once again, the city not only recovered but thrived. Fortunately, a number of successful efforts were made to improve the conditions of the city and its image. The Memphis in May International Festival began in the 1970s and now features local and national entertainment, international cultural exchange and the World Championship Barbecue Cooking Contest. The renovation of the Peabody Hotel was undertaken in the 1980s. In 1982, the Graceland Museum and the Mud Island Park and River Walk were opened. In 1983, the redeveloped Beale Street opened as a major tourist attraction. The 1990s saw the opening of the Memphis Children's Museum, the Pyramid Arena, the National Civil Rights Museum and a revived trolley system.

Wilson Drug Store at 350 Beale Street, 1964.

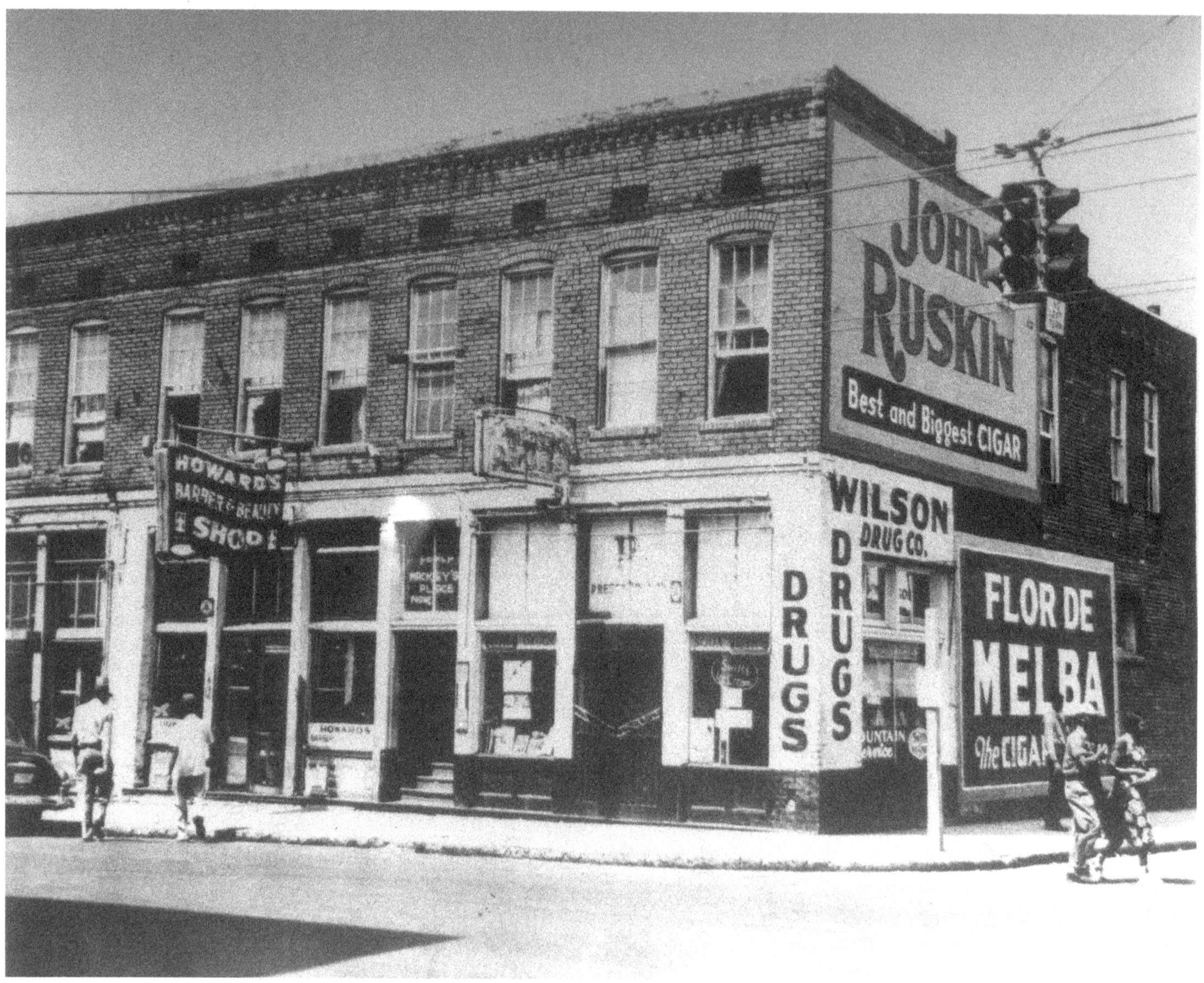

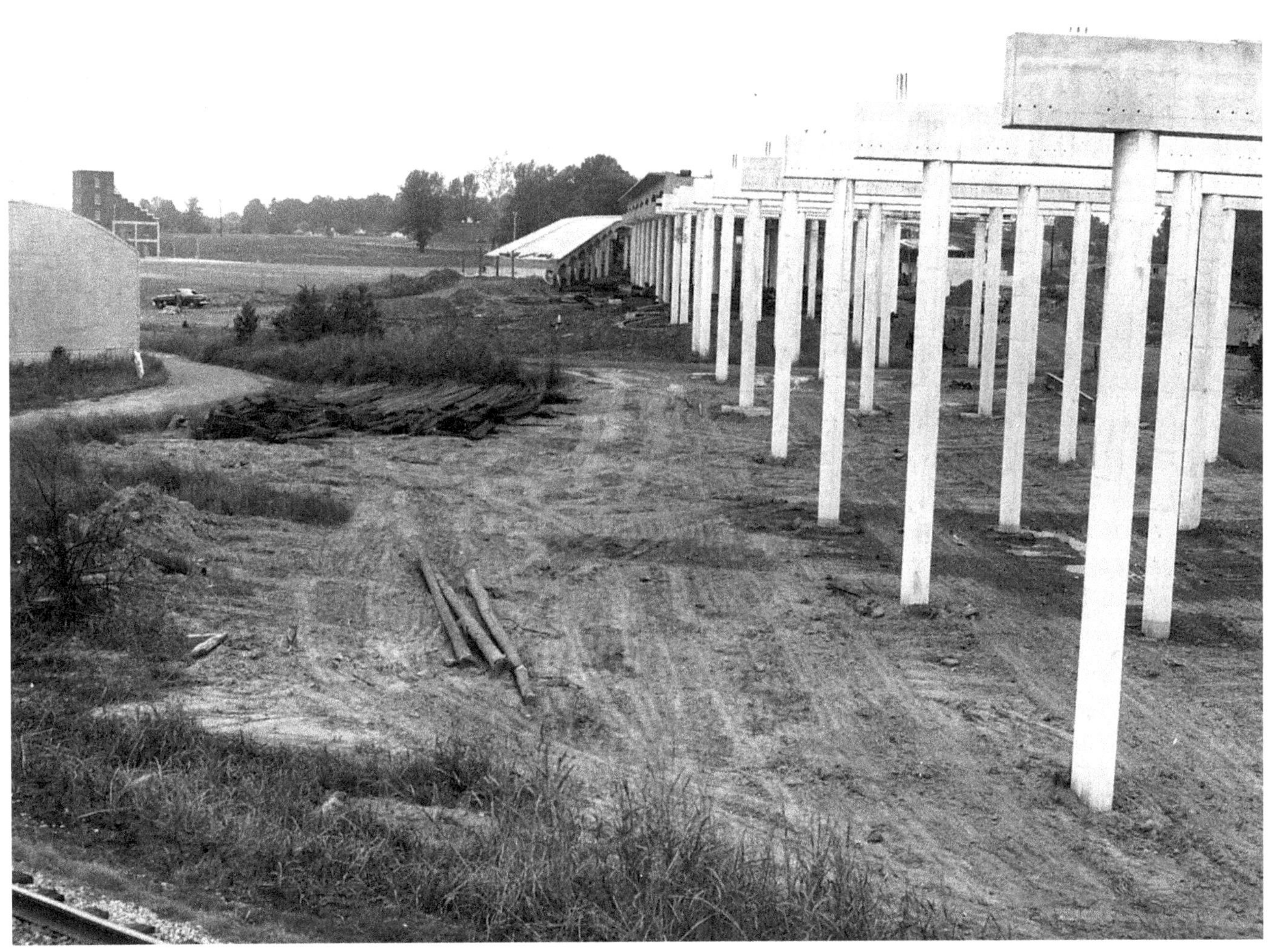

Union Avenue Extended, circa 1961.

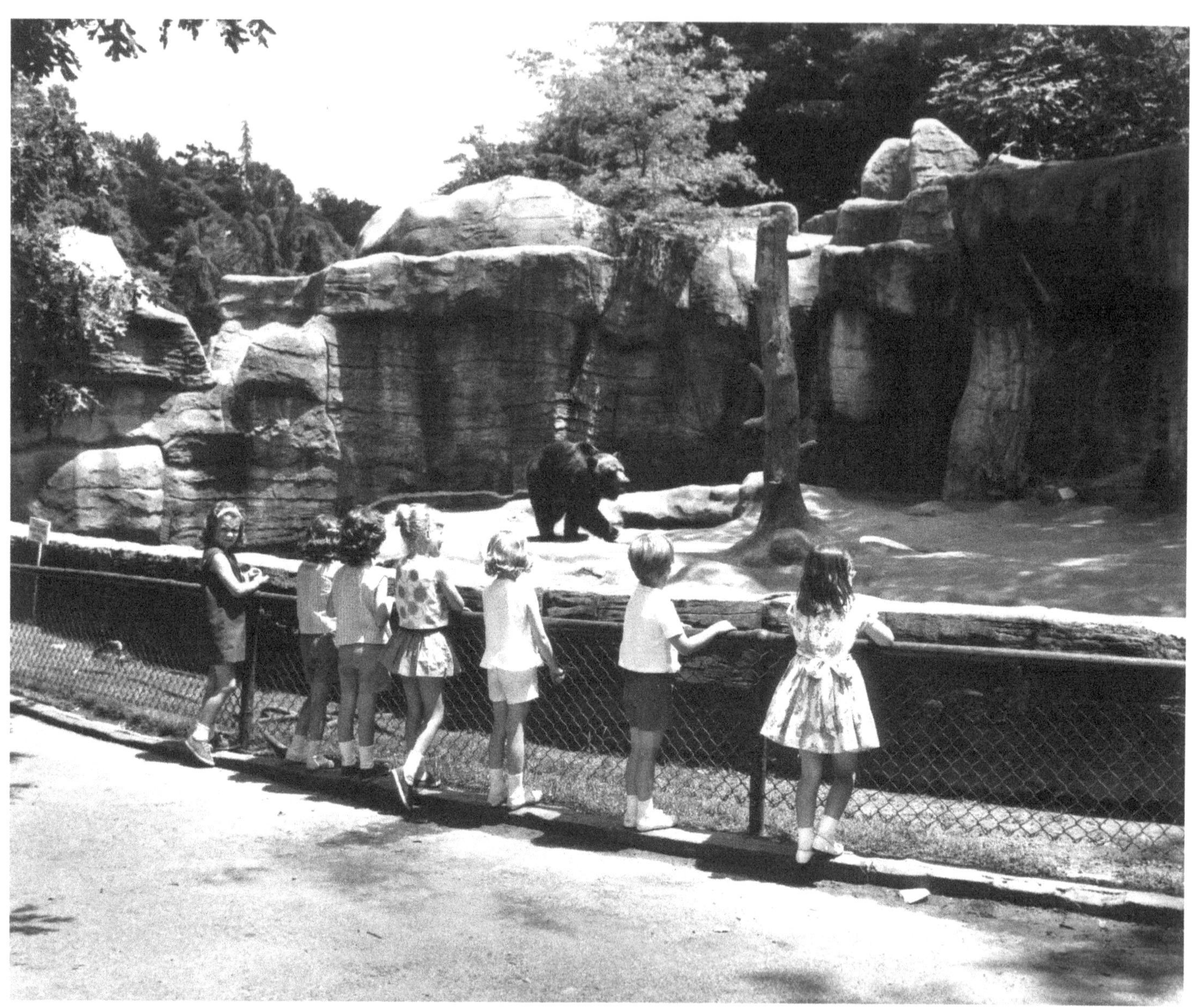

The Memphis Zoo in Overton Park, 1965.

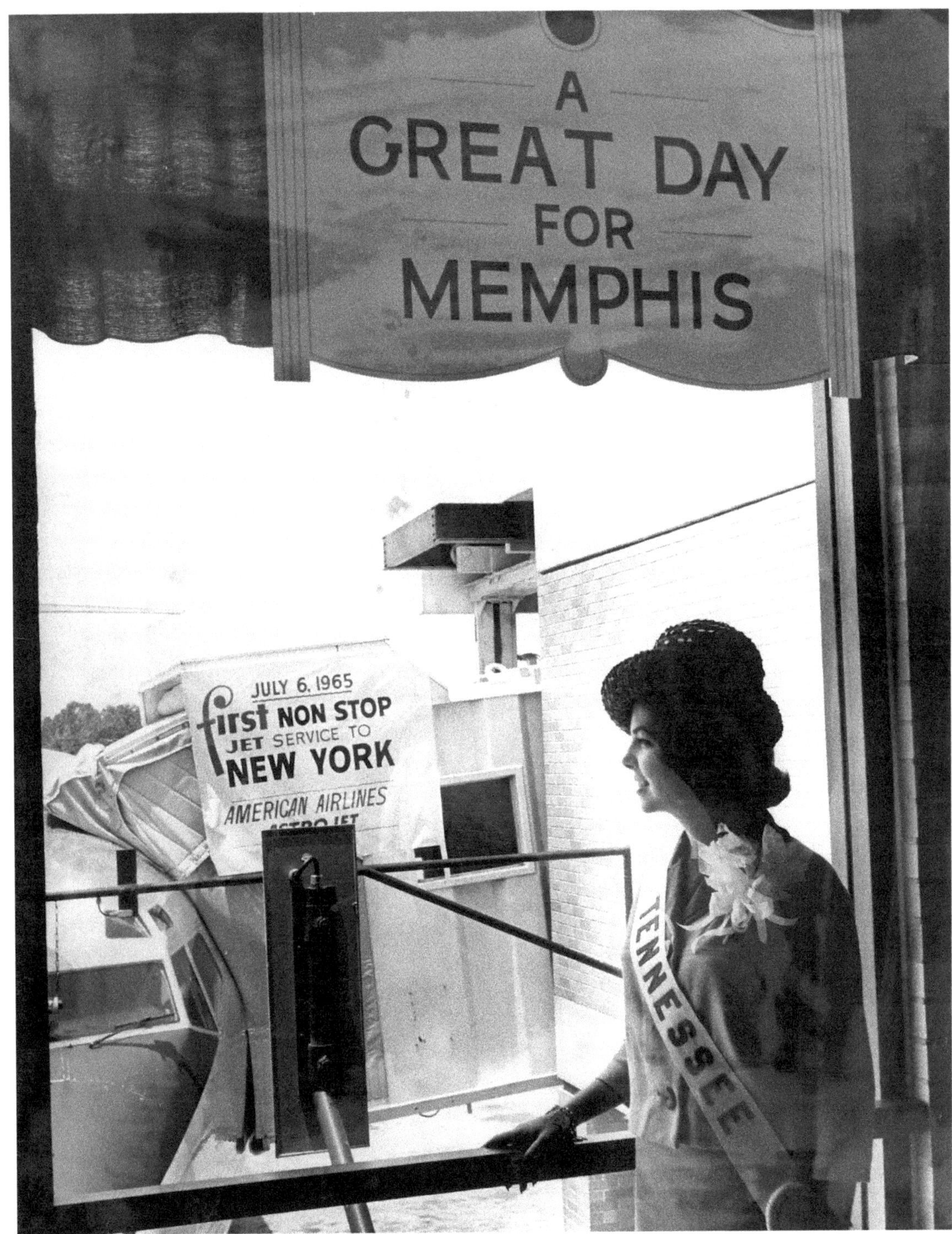

Memphis Metropolitan Airport, 1965. American Airlines offered the first non-stop flight to New York from Memphis beginning July 6, 1965. It was an important step for the airport which at the time was the 27th-busiest in the country.

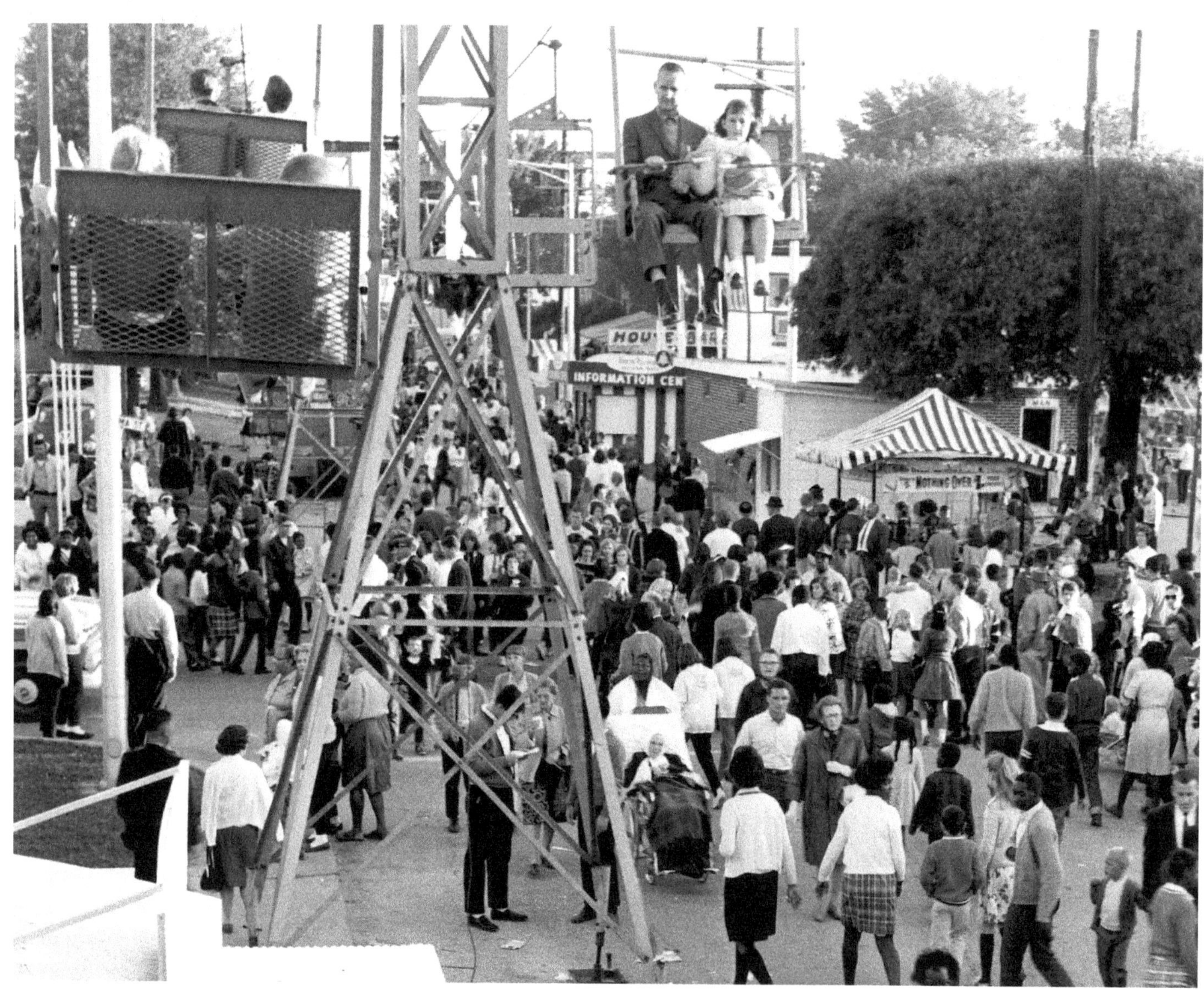

The Mid-South Fair, 1965. The annual Mid-South Fair began in 1856. The fair runs from late September to early October and features shows, livestock exhibits, rides and concession stands.

The final stages of construction of City Hall, 1965.

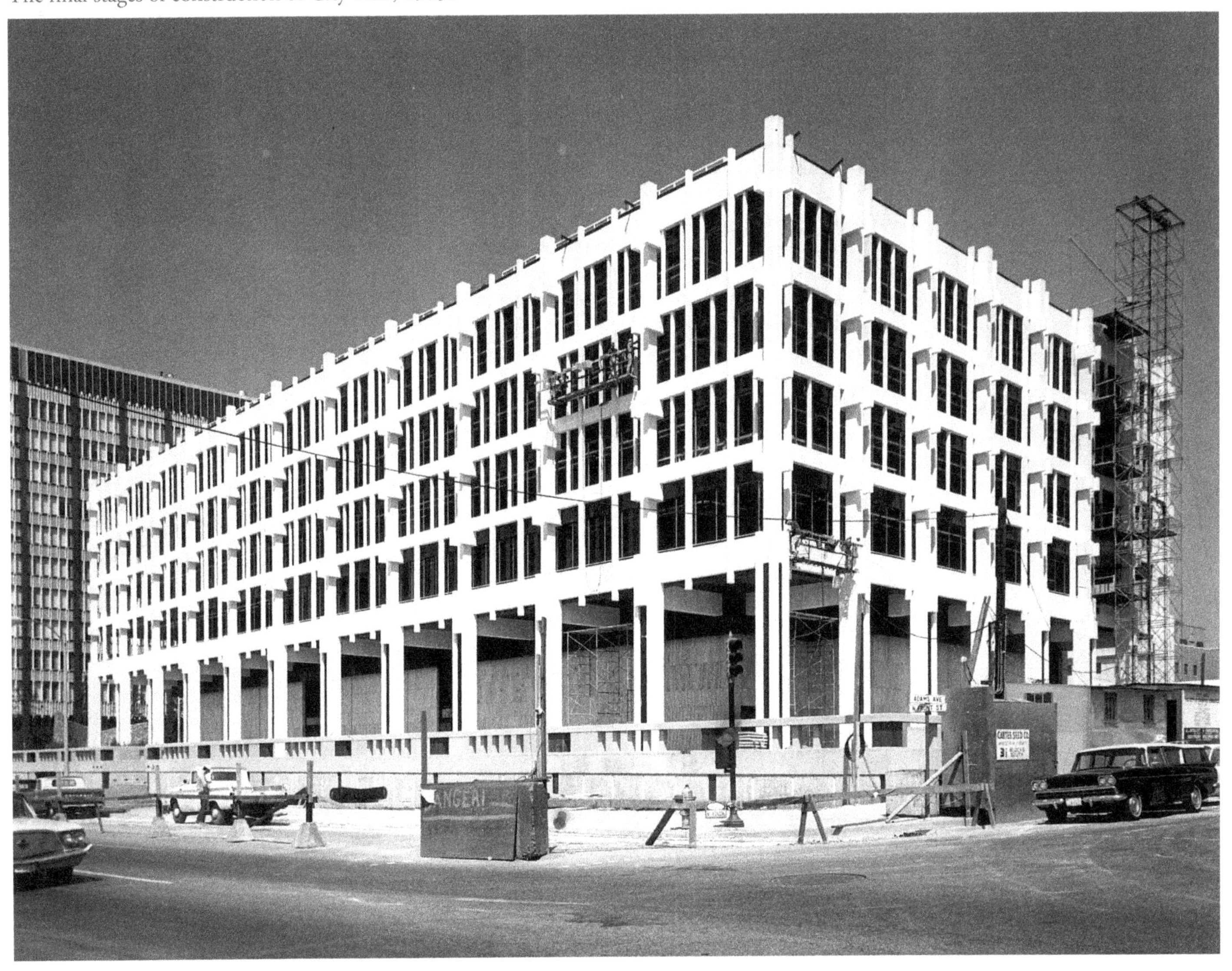

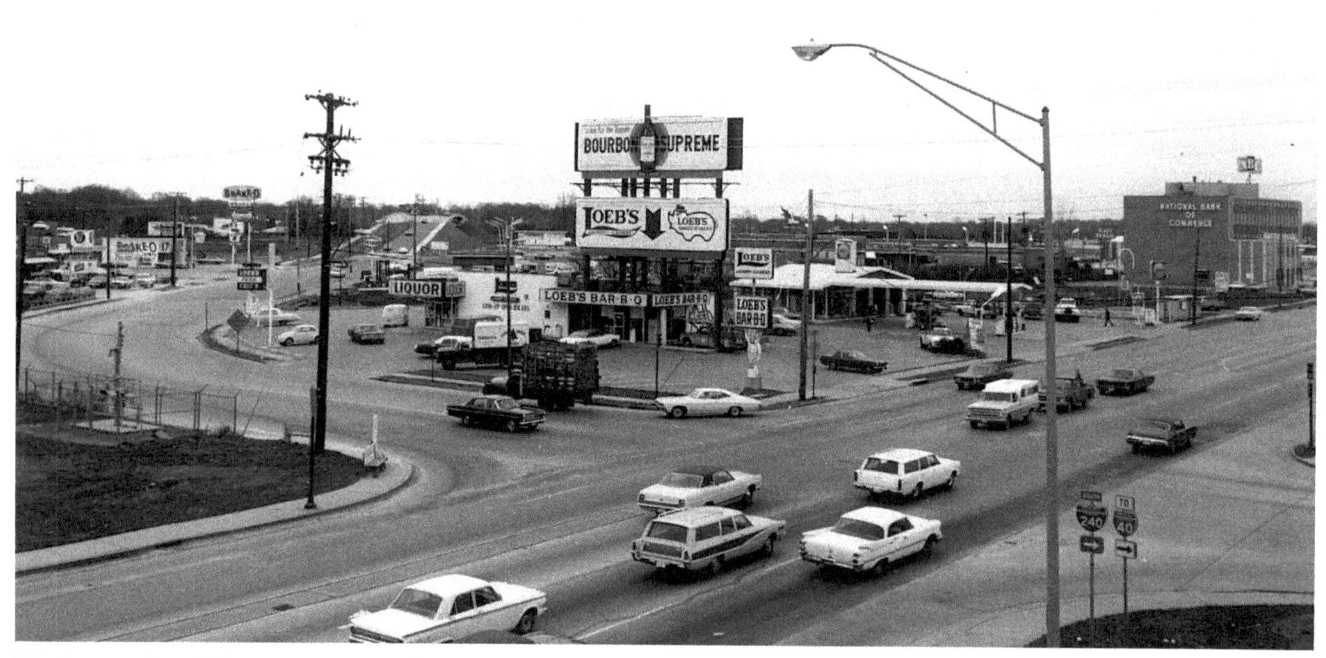

The intersection of Summer Avenue and White Station Road, 1960s.

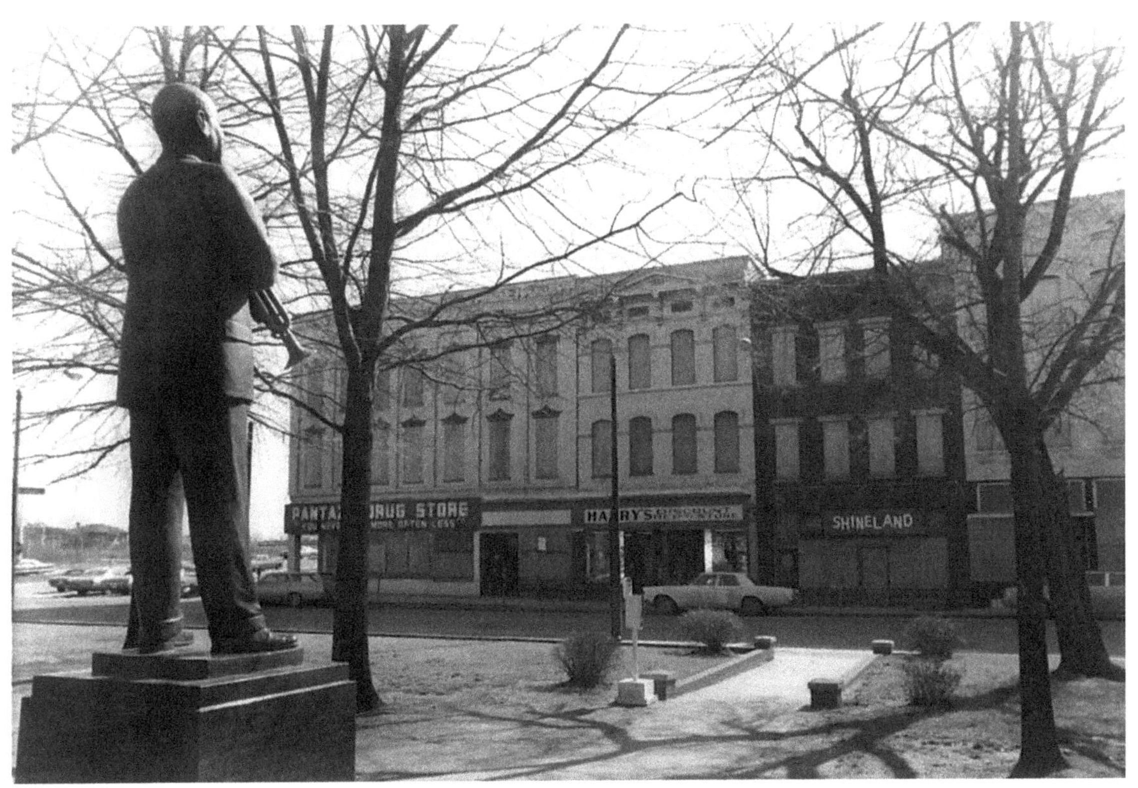

The W.C. Handy Monument on Beale Street, 1970s.

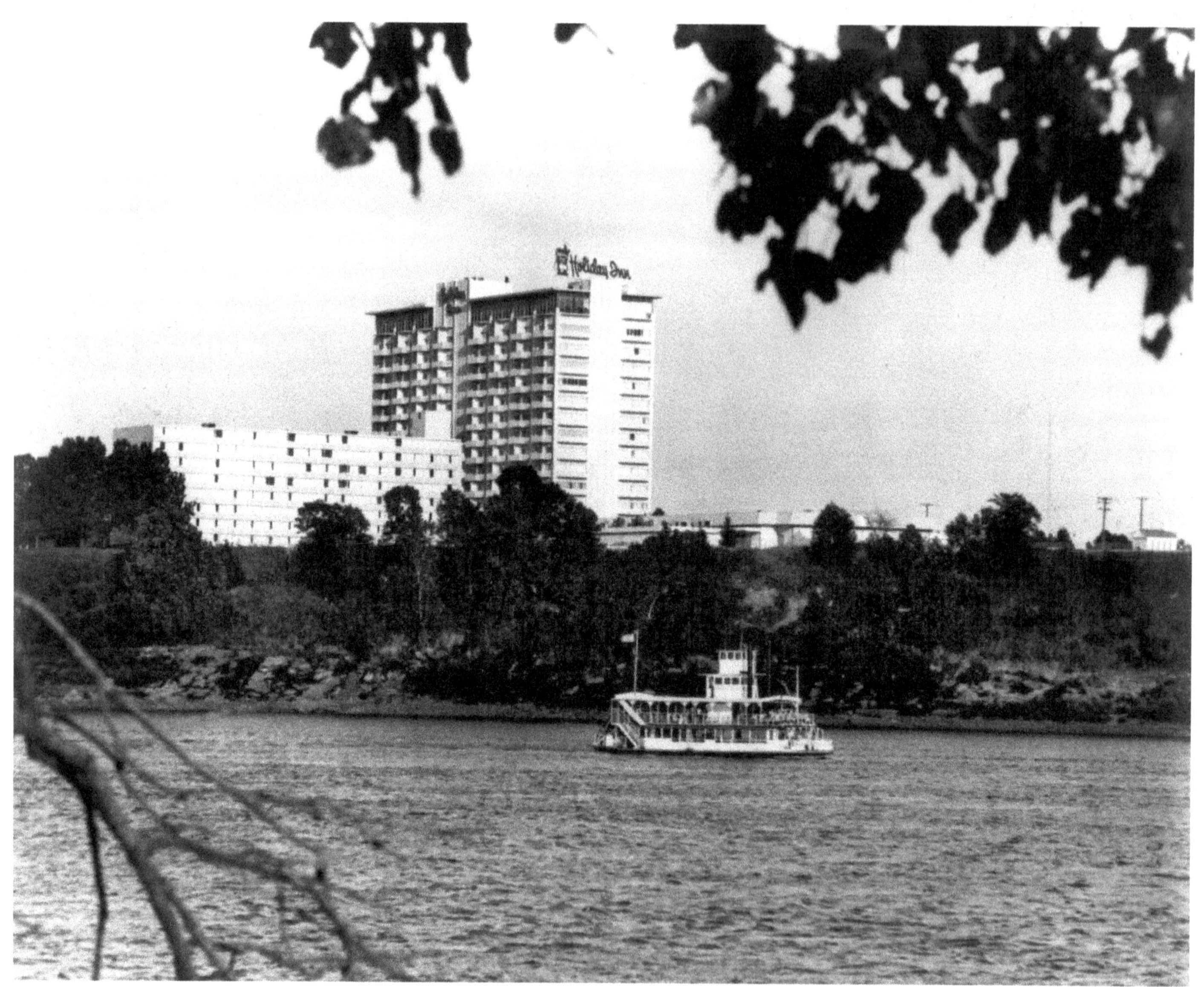

The Holiday Inn Rivermont was open from 1964 until 1984. Its guests included Walter Mondale, Richard Nixon and the Osmonds. The hotel was host to a variety of events including dog shows, Cotton Carnival Balls, boxing matches and NAACP events.

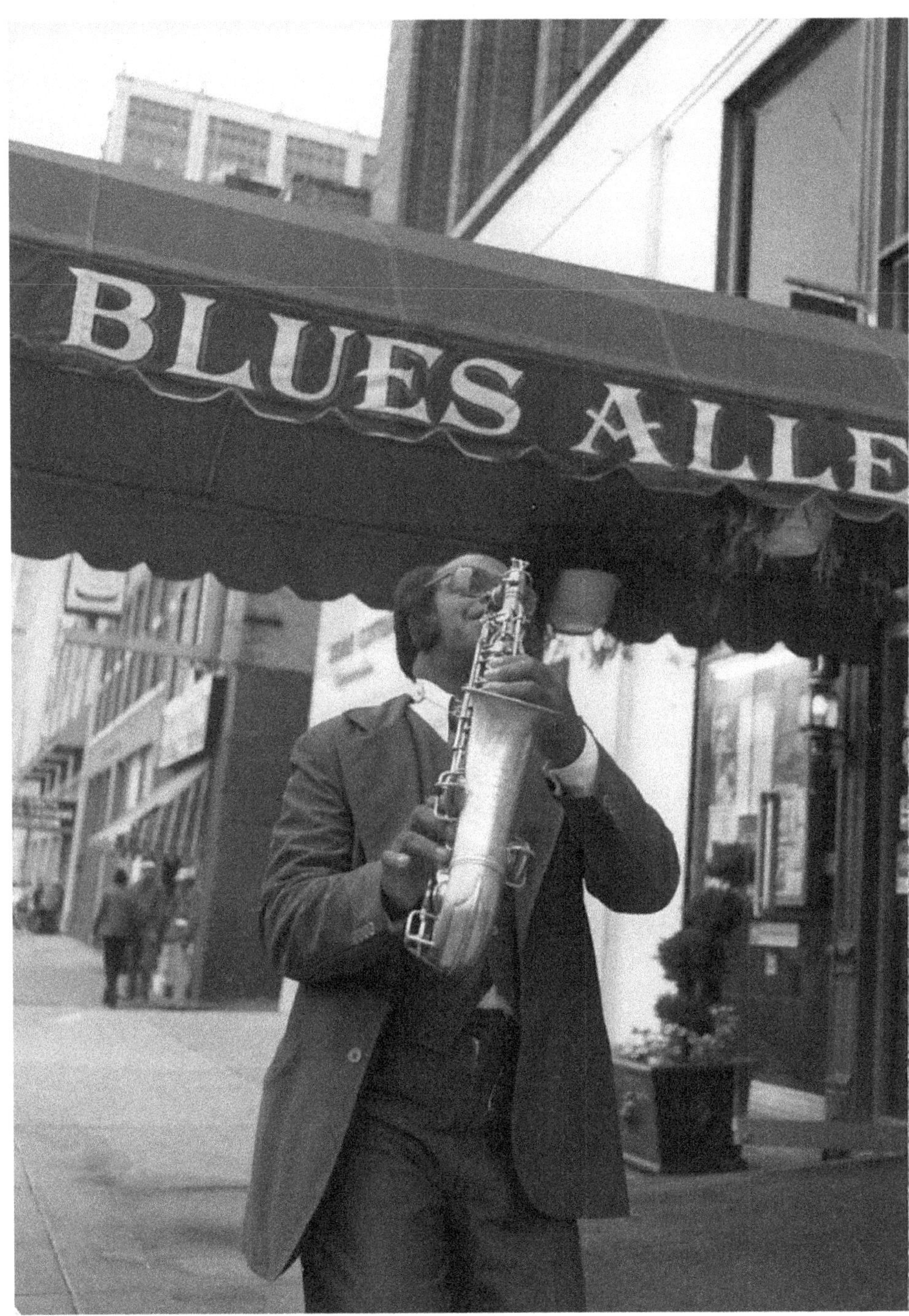

Edward Kirby, a.k.a. Prince Gabe, and his band The Millionaires were known for performing in area night clubs and for leading New Orleans-style funeral processions down Beale Street from the 1960s through the 1980s.

The Schwab family business has been on Beale Street since 1876. Abraham Schwab, pictured here, relocated his dry goods store from 149 to 163 Beale Street in 1912.

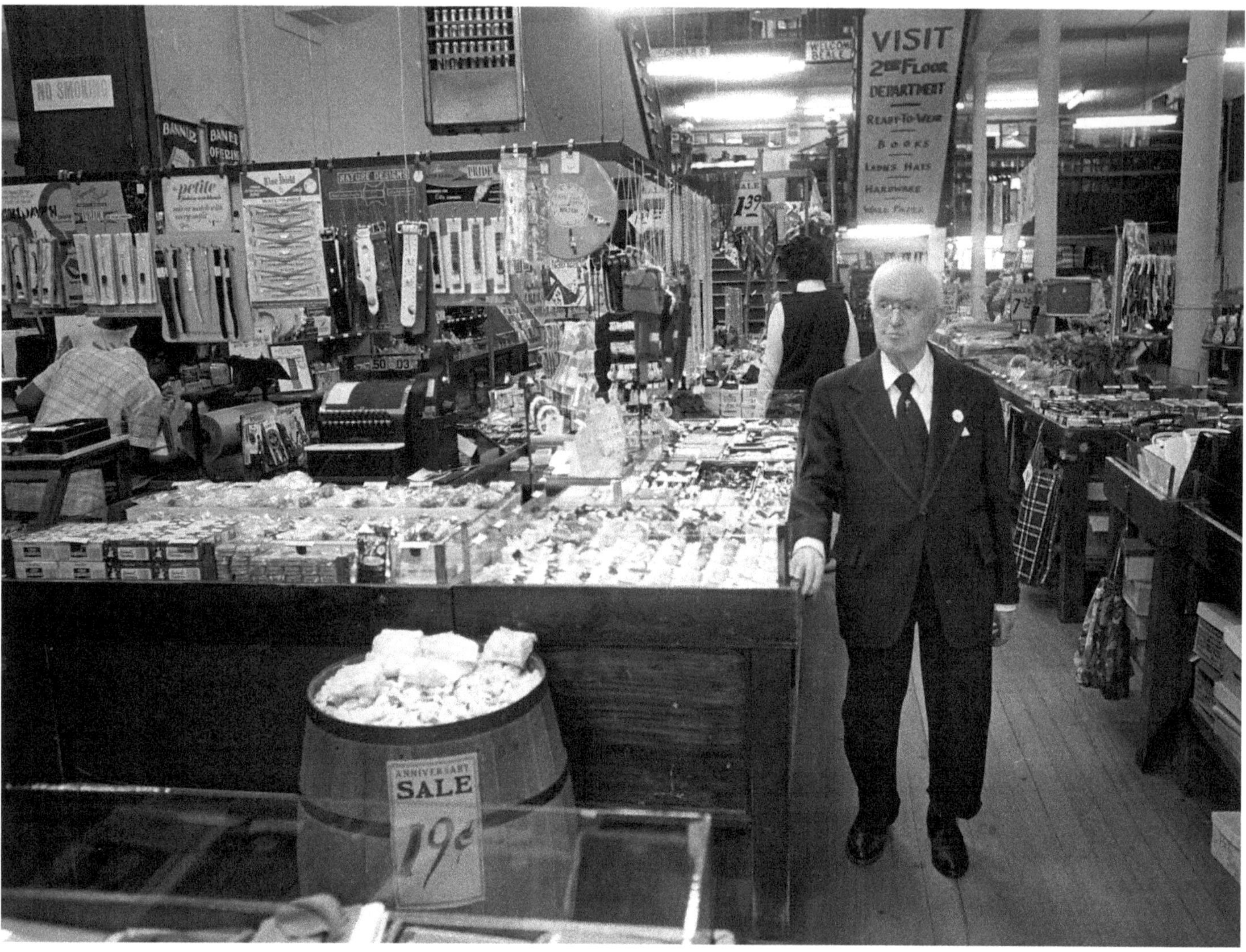

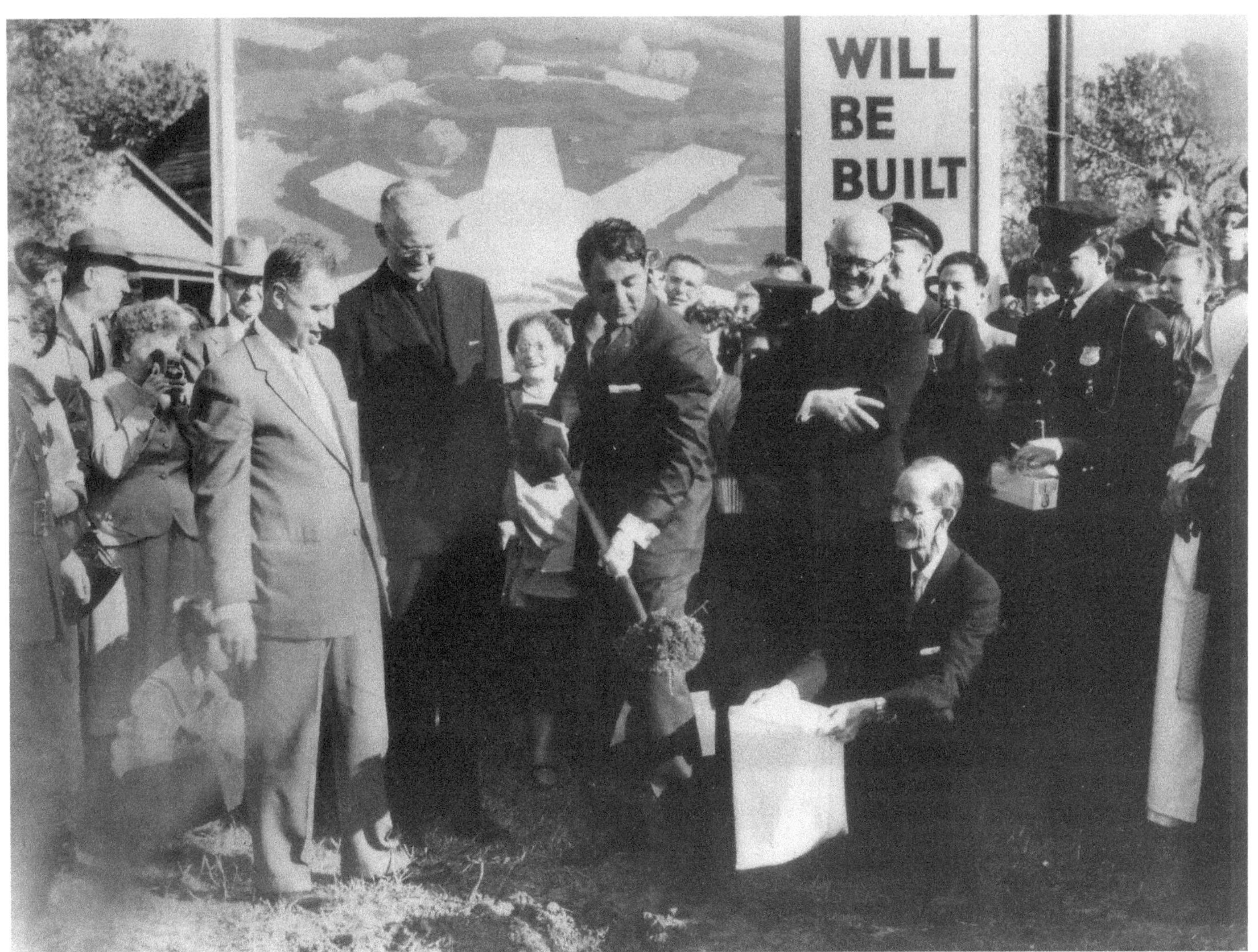

Danny Thomas at the groundbreaking of St. Jude Children's Research Hospital, 1962.

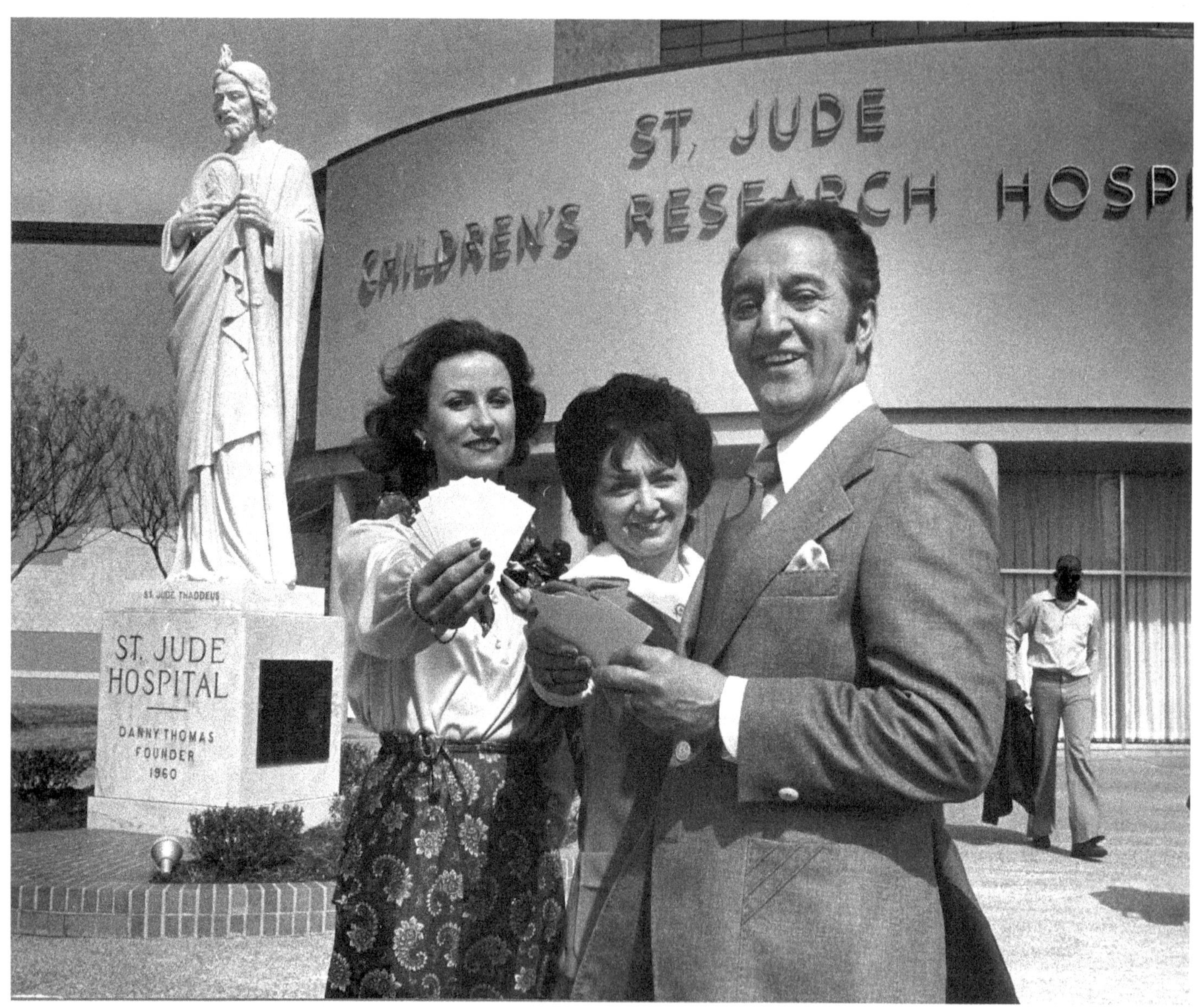

Danny Thomas at St. Jude Children's Research Hospital.

Jackson Mound Park opened in the 1880s and was renamed Desoto Park in 1913. The mound at the back of the picture is known as Chisca's Mound, after a Native American chief encountered by Desoto. The park was named Chickasaw Heritage Park in 1995.

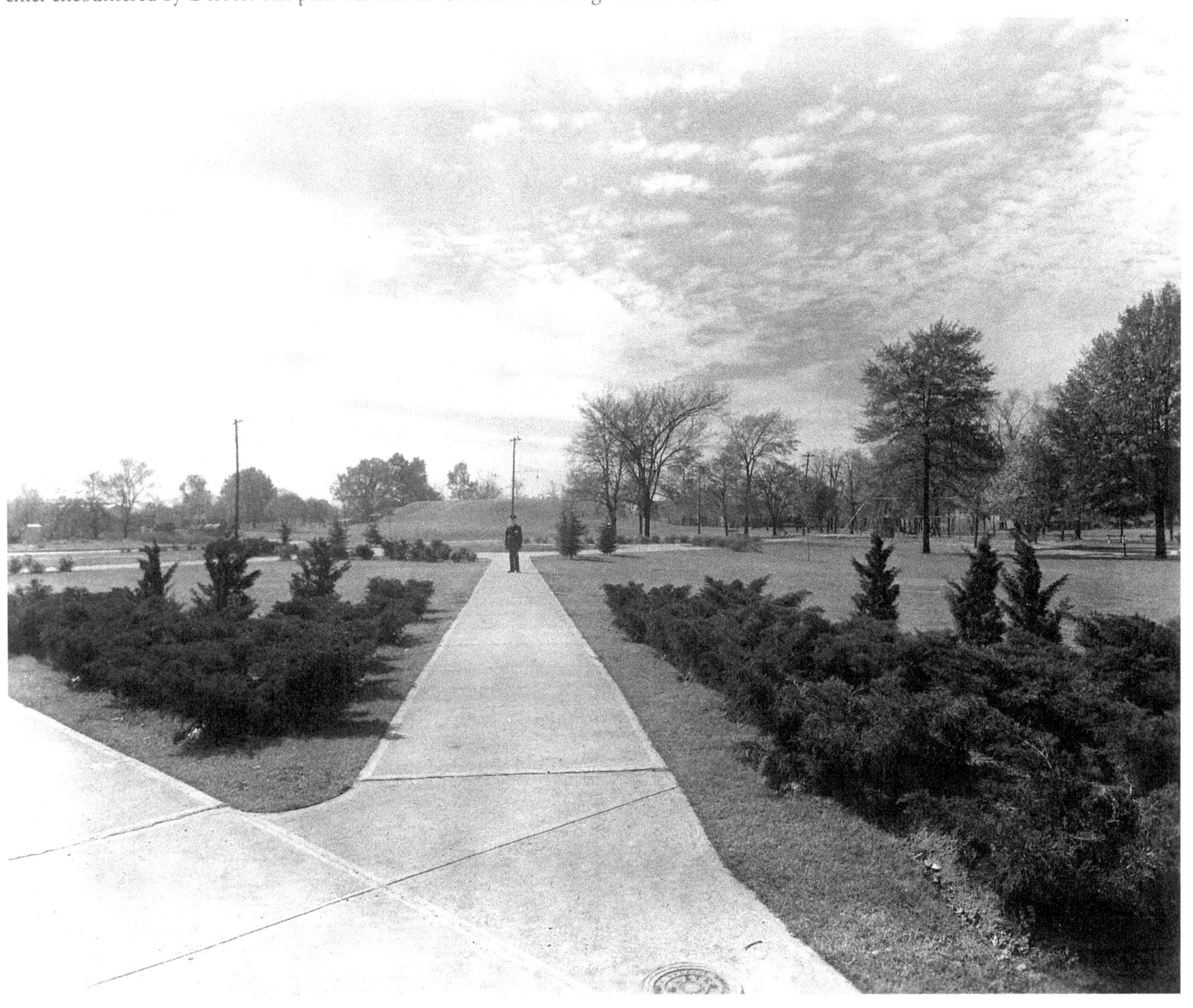

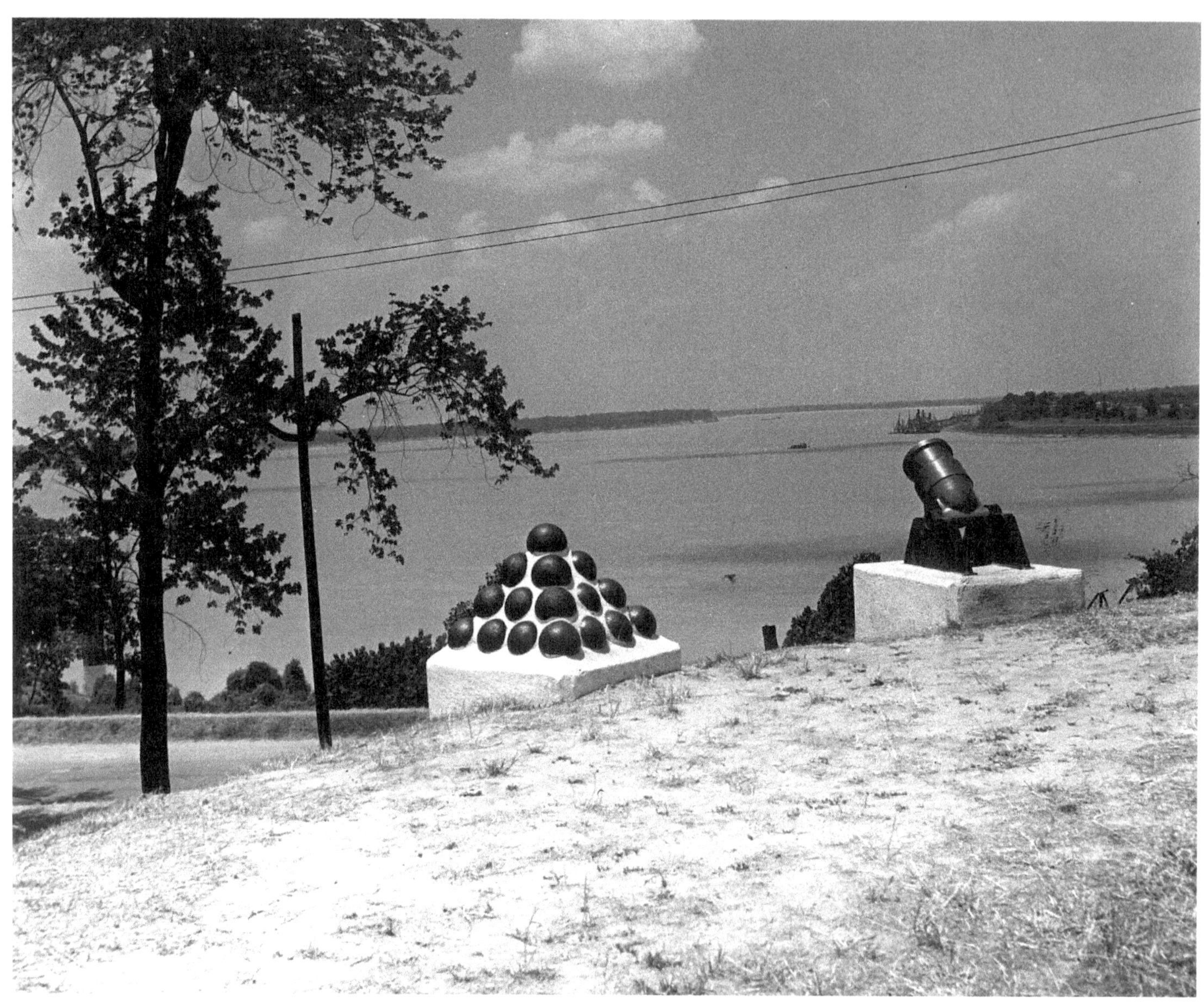

A Civil War cannon and 150 cannonballs were placed in Desoto Park at the request of Congressman Walter Chandler in 1939.

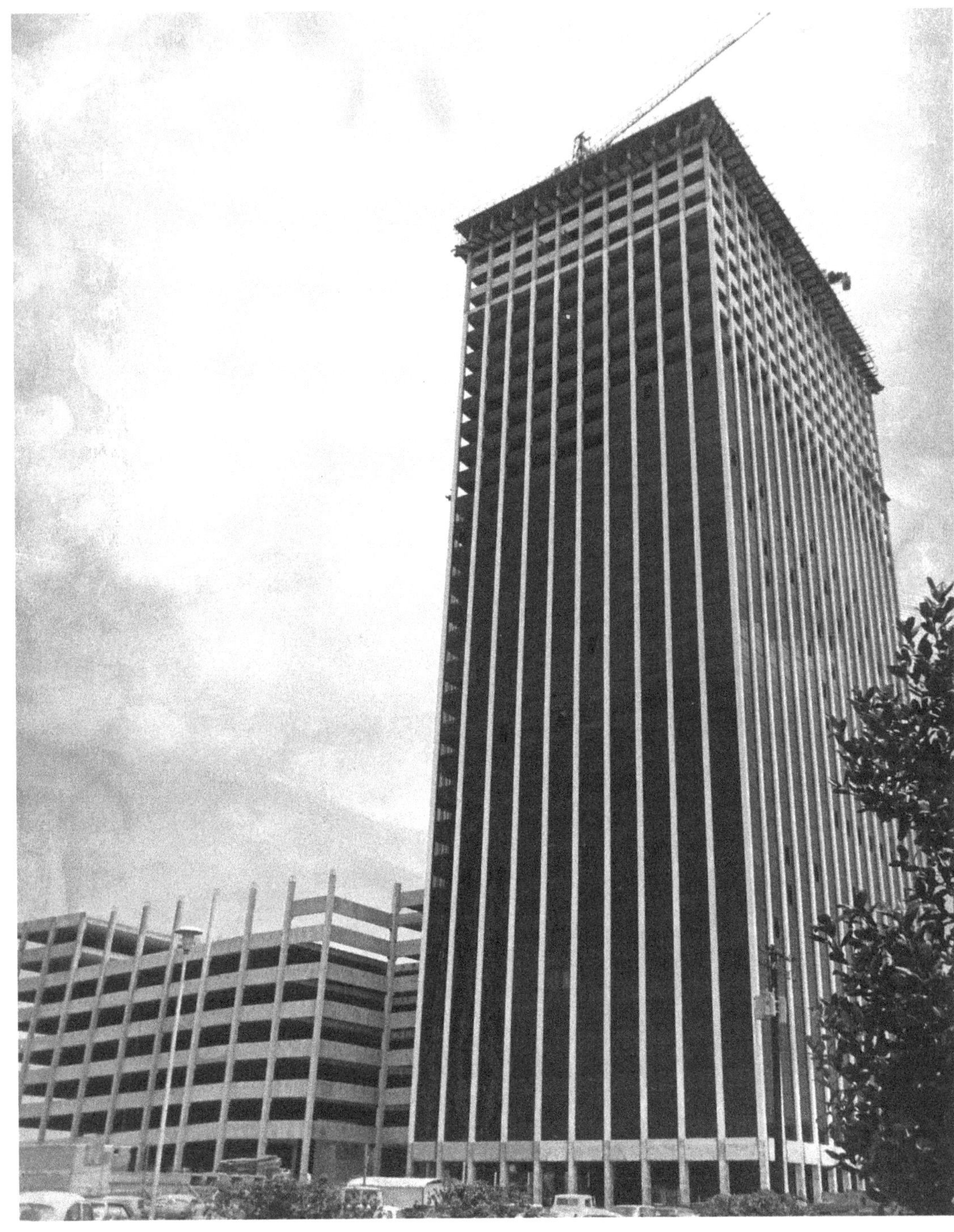

Clark Tower, July 9, 1971. Opened in 1972, The Clark Tower is a 43-floor East Memphis skyscraper named after developer William Benjamin Clark.

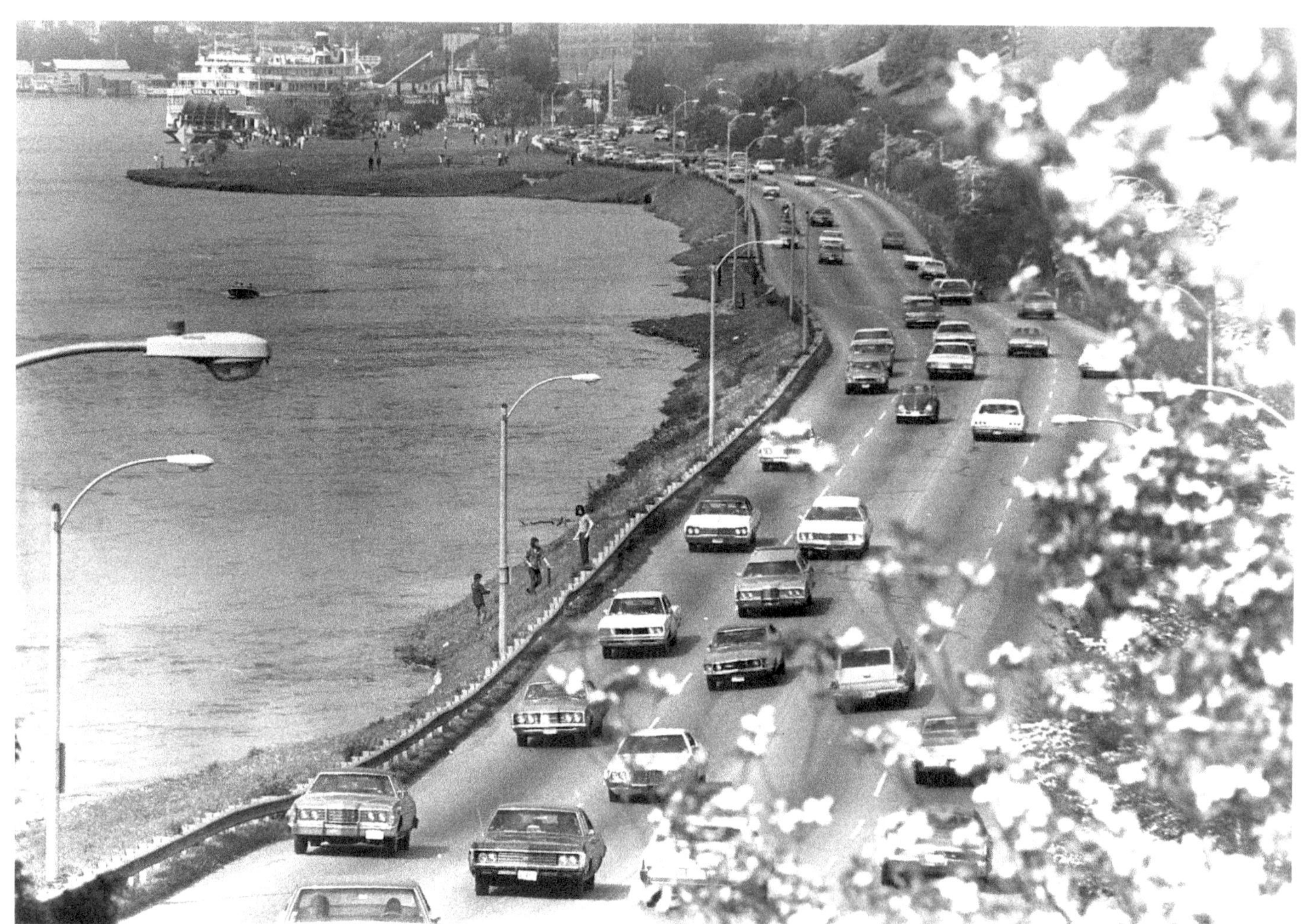

Riverside Drive in the 1970s.

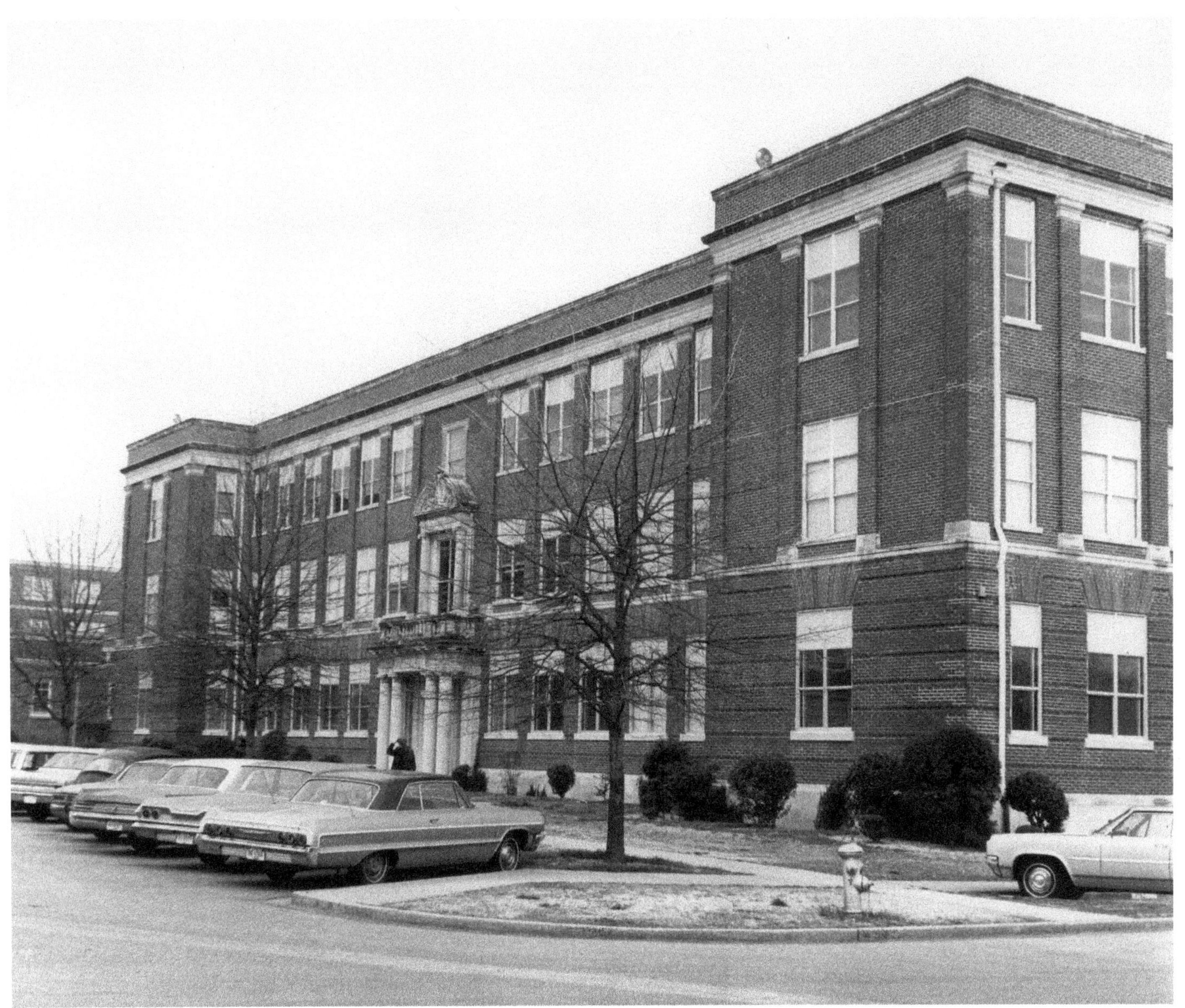

Manning Hall on the campus of Memphis State University, now the University of Memphis, 1968.

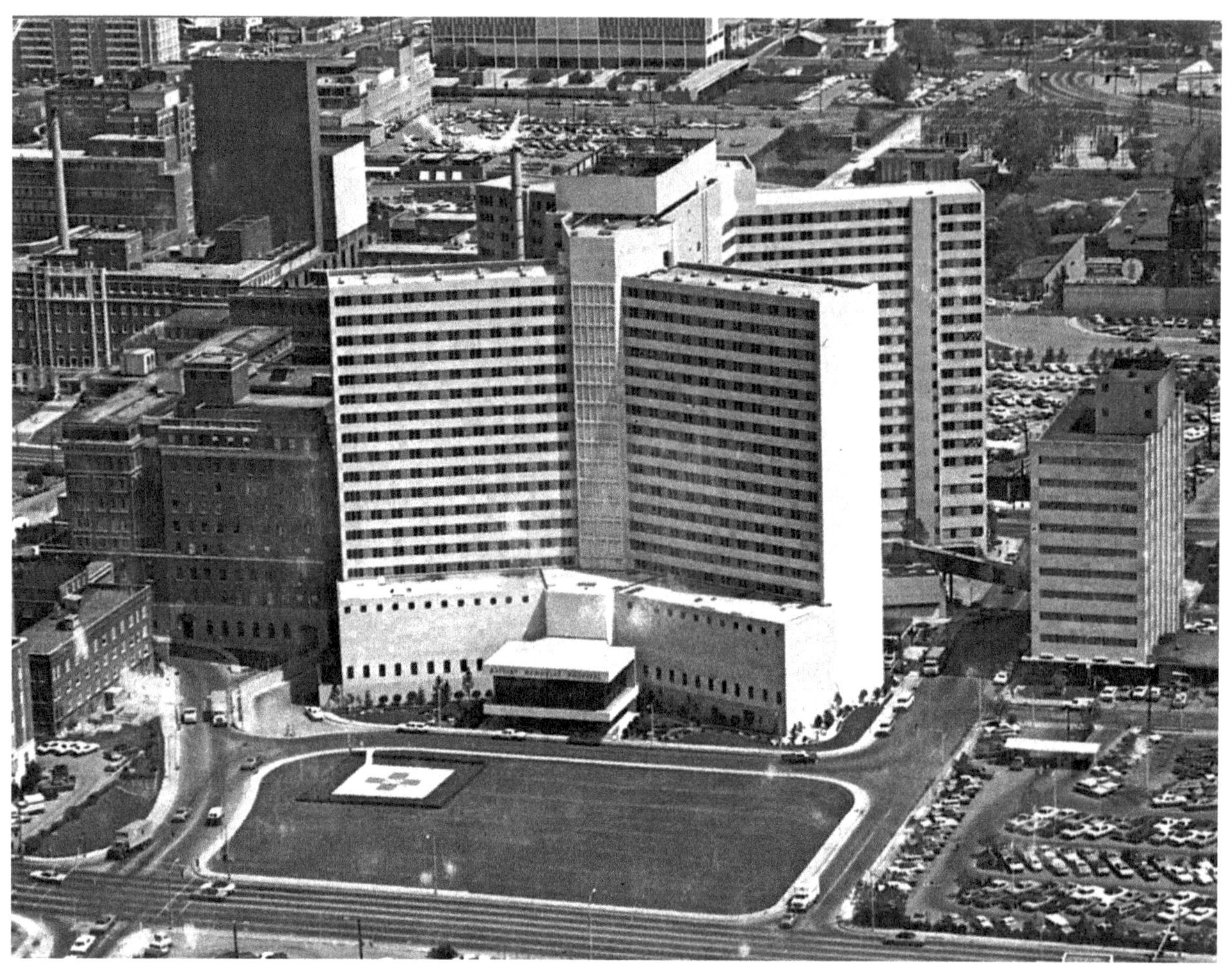

Baptist Memorial Hospital was first constructed in 1955, and an addition was made in 1967. The hospital was demolished in November 2005.

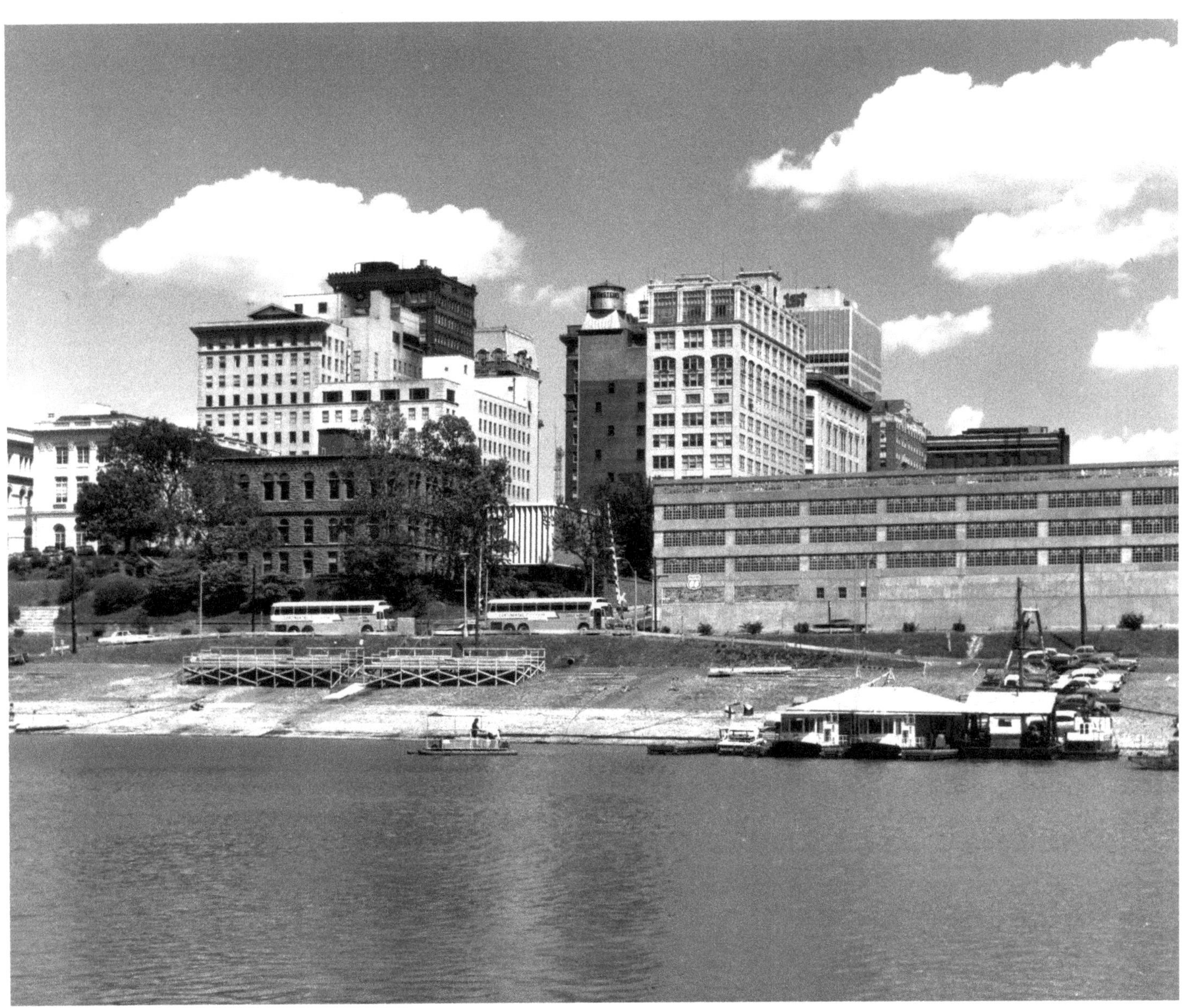

The riverfront at Memphis, 1969.

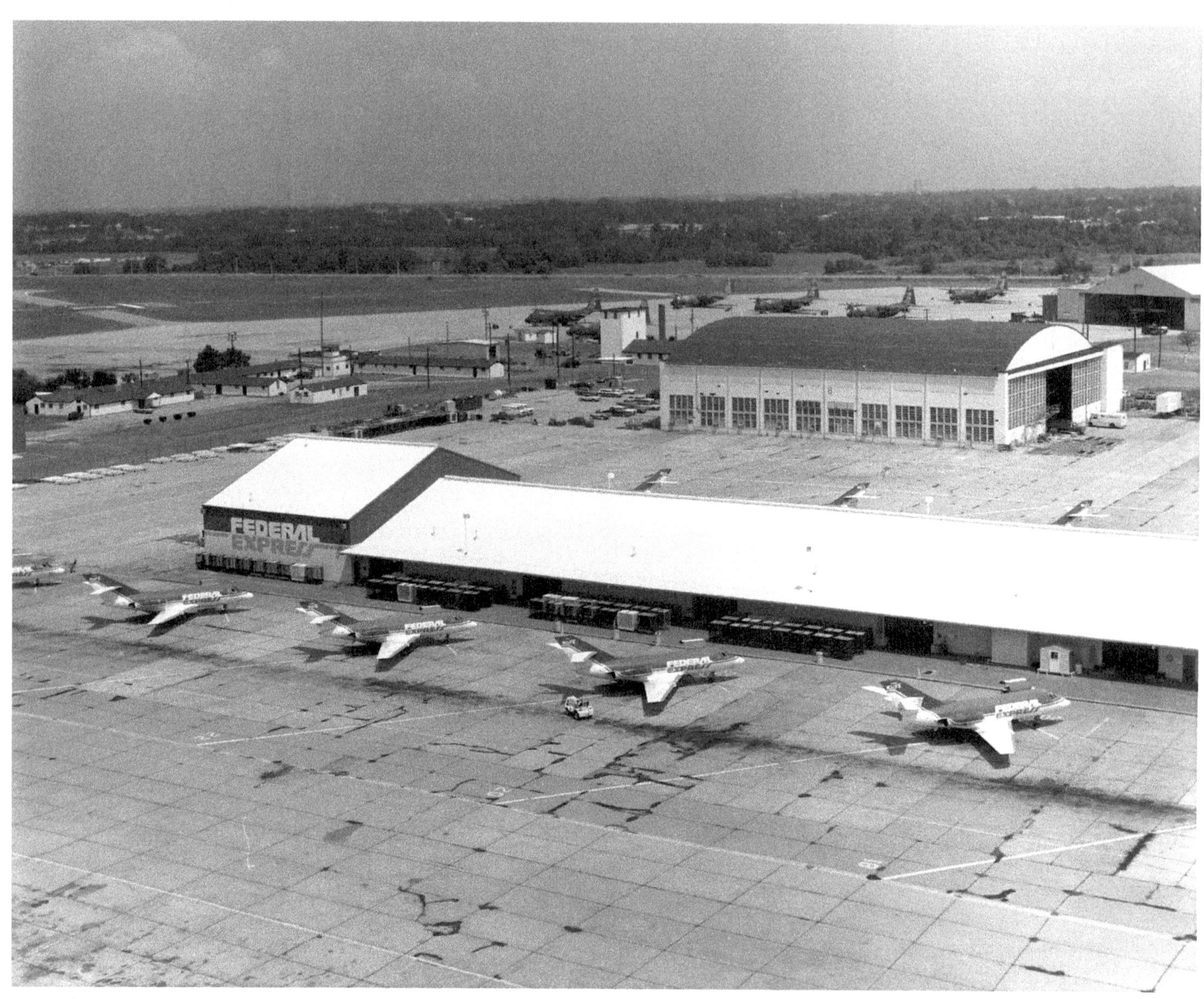

Federal Express, circa 1974.

Notes on the Photographs

These notes, listed by page number, attempt to include all aspects known of the photographs. Each of the photographs are identified by the page number, photograph's title or description, photographer/collection, archive and call or box number when applicable. While every attempt was made to collect all available data, in some cases complete data was unavailable due to the age and condition of some of the photographs and records.

II **King Cotton**
Memphis Public Library
Memphis and Shelby County Room
Photo by John C. Coovert

VI **Shelby Co. Courthouse Law Library**
Memphis Public Library
Memphis and Shelby County Room
2359C 1147

2 **Home of James Monroe Williamson**
Tennessee State Library and Archives Collection
Drawer 14, Folder 130

3 **Hunt-Phelan House**
Memphis Public Library
Memphis and Shelby County Room
Historic American Buildings Survey

4 **Sultana**
Memphis Public Library
Memphis and Shelby County Room
5109C 6188

5 **Fredrick Cossitt**
Memphis Public Library
Memphis and Shelby County Room
1881C 168
Contributed by W.E.D. Stokes, Jr.

6 **Memphis Boat Club**
Memphis Public Library
Memphis and Shelby County Room
Gift of Dr. J.C. Woosley
5613C 3769

7 **Old Steam Dummy**
Memphis Public Library
Memphis and Shelby County Room
617C 4393
Copy furnished by W.R. McKay

8 **N.W. corner of Main and Jefferson**
Memphis Public Library
Memphis and Shelby County Room
7717C 1578

9 **Goldsmith & Bros.**
Memphis Public Library
Memphis and Shelby County Room
6978S

10 **Frisco Bridge**
Memphis Public Library
Memphis and Shelby County Room
4523C 1297
Apply for copies to Pink Palace
Accession no. 1961.12.272/68c

11 **Frisco Bridge**
Memphis Public Library
Memphis and Shelby County Room
6052NC 1337

12 *Belle of the Bend* at Memphis Wharf
Memphis Public Library
Memphis and Shelby County Room
3409C 5415

13 Frisco Bridge Opening
Memphis Public Library
Memphis and Shelby County Room
4076C 1292
Apply for copies to Pink Palace
Accession no. 1961.12.31/68c

14 Street Scene
Memphis Public Library
Memphis and Shelby County Room
Gift of Henry Frank
5592NC 132

15 Court Square 1895
Memphis Public Library
Memphis and Shelby County Room

16 Masonic Temple
Memphis Public Library
Memphis and Shelby County Room
660C 1543

17 St. Brigid's Church
Memphis Public Library
Memphis and Shelby County Room
139C 4035

18 Cossett Library
Memphis Public Library
Memphis and Shelby County Room
1839C 3470

19 Street Workers
Memphis Public Library
Memphis and Shelby County Room

20 Memphis Firehouse
Memphis Public Library
Memphis and Shelby County Room
1678N

21 Fontaine House
Memphis Public Library
Memphis and Shelby County Room
1391C 223

22 Latham Avenue at Trigg circa 1895
Memphis Public Library
Memphis and Shelby County Room

23 Memphis Firefighters
Memphis Public Library
Memphis and Shelby County Room
Gift of Ruth Wyckoff Hunt
7478C 1361

24 Early Fire Engine
Memphis Public Library
Memphis and Shelby County Room
774C 2372
Gift of W.R. McKay

25 Appeal Building, 1895
Memphis Public Library
Memphis and Shelby County Room
683C 948

26 East End Park, 1895
Memphis Public Library
Memphis and Shelby County Room
689NC 4291

27 Tennessee Brewing Company, 1895
Memphis Public Library
Memphis and Shelby County Room
715C 5923

28 Hill Residence
Memphis Public Library
Memphis and Shelby County Room
1486C 210

29 Main Street, 1880's
Memphis Public Library
Memphis and Shelby County Room
3710C 5198
Wyckoff

30 Raleigh Springs Car Line
Memphis Public Library
Memphis and Shelby County Room
1911N

31 Lee House
Memphis Public Library
Memphis and Shelby County Room
3568C 52
From the Municipal Reference Library

32 Front Street, c. 1895-1900
Memphis Public Library
Memphis and Shelby County Room
4

33 Orgill Brothers on Front Street
Memphis Public Library
Memphis and Shelby County Room
3658C 468
Courtesy of Henry Frank, c. 1915

34 Mallory-Neely House
Memphis Public Library
Memphis and Shelby County Room
7339C 1557
Gift of Ed Cooper

35 Bohlen-Huse Ice Company
Memphis Public Library
Memphis and Shelby County Room
1543

36 Gayoso Hotel
Memphis Public Library
Memphis and Shelby County Room
1797C 3026

37 Illinois Central Depot
Memphis Public Library
Memphis and Shelby County Room
876NC 2211

38 McLean Avenue, c. 1890
Memphis Public Library
Memphis and Shelby County Room
6299C 4876
Copy of the Gift of Mrs. Samuel J. Hays

39 Pillow-McIntyre House
Memphis Public Library
Memphis and Shelby County Room
2189

40 Union Avenue, 1895
Memphis Public Library
Memphis and Shelby County Room
605C 5252

41 The *Peters Lee* Riverboat
Memphis Public Library
Memphis and Shelby County Room
2436
Donated by Miss Bert Wade
Photo by Coovert, No 1206

42 President William McKinley, 1901
Memphis Public Library
Memphis and Shelby County Room
7811C 6719
Apply for copies to Pink Palace
Accession no.; 194

43 The *John A. Wood* Riverboat
Memphis Public Library
Memphis and Shelby County Room
6961C 5383
Gift of Mrs. Al Groce

44 The Cotton Exchange Building
Memphis Public Library
Memphis and Shelby County Room
1461C 1183

45 *Katie Robbins*
Memphis Public Library
Memphis and Shelby County Room
2417C 5407
Donated by Miss Bert Wade
Photo by Coovert, No 305

46 Hardwood Capitol of the World
Memphis Public Library
Memphis and Shelby County Room

48 The *Katie Adams* III, ca. 1903
Memphis Public Library
Memphis and Shelby County Room
2459C 5475

49 Main Street, 1900
Memphis Public Library
Memphis and Shelby County Room
1458C 5135

50 St. Peter's Catholic Church
Memphis Public Library
Memphis and Shelby County Room
1396C 1934

51 St. Peter's Catholic Church Interior
Memphis Public Library &
Information
Center
Memphis and Shelby County Room
6661NC 1935
Photo by Poland

52 South Main Street and Union
Memphis Public Library
Memphis and Shelby County Room

53 First Methodist Episcopal Church, 1900
Memphis Public Library
Memphis and Shelby County Room
1502C 1857

54 Raleigh Springs
Memphis Public Library
Memphis and Shelby County Room
2932C 4313

55 Raleigh Springs Resort
Memphis Public Library
Memphis and Shelby County Room
1474

56 Bell Tavern
Memphis Public Library
Memphis and Shelby County Room
220C 3126

57 Mule-drawn Coca-Cola Wagon
Tennessee State Library and Archives
Looking Back at Tennessee
TP106, Accession No. 1988-017

58 Local Baseball Team
Memphis Public Library
Memphis and Shelby County Room
7917C 984
Gift of Memphis Police Department

59 Montgomery Park
Memphis Public Library
Memphis and Shelby County Room
5936C 2840
Gift of Henry Frank

60 Nickey and Sons Company, 1908
Memphis Public Library
Memphis and Shelby County Room
3992C 3485
Gift of Ed Cooper

61 *Grey Eagle* and *Alton*
Memphis Public Library
Memphis and Shelby County Room
Robert J. Gasper Collection

62 **T. H. Hayes and Sons Funeral Home**
Memphis Public Library
Memphis and Shelby County Room

64 **Main Street**
Memphis Public Library
Memphis and Shelby County Room
1970C 5114

65 **First School Bus**
Memphis Public Library
Memphis and Shelby County Room
1925

66 **Nat Edwards and Co. Livery Stables**
Memphis Public Library
Memphis and Shelby County Room
3548C 3757

67 **Grover Cleveland Sherrod**
Tennessee State Library and Archives
Looking Back at Tennessee,
File Location: BG255, Accession No. 1988-017

68 **Business Men's Club**
Memphis Public Library
Memphis and Shelby County Room
3554C 3999

69 **East End Park Merry-Go-Round**
Memphis Public Library
Memphis and Shelby County Room
4395C 4293
Gift of Mrs. Patricia Stegall Kolwyck

70 **Main & Madison, 1912**
Memphis Public Library
Memphis and Shelby County Room
4443C 5108
Donated by Miss Roberta Wade.
Photo by Coovert

71 **Court Square, 1912**
Memphis Public Library
Memphis and Shelby County Room
2148N

72 **Flood, 1912**
Memphis Public Library
Memphis and Shelby County Room
2740C 2497
Photo by Coovert, No 1437

73 **Camp Crump Refugee Camp, 1912**
Memphis Public Library
Memphis and Shelby County Room
7799C 2457
Apply for copies to Pink Palace
Accession no.: 1975.13.694/68c

74 **Camp Crump Refugee Camp, 1912**
Memphis Public Library
Memphis and Shelby County Room
9059

75 **Seessel's**
Memphis Public Library
Memphis and Shelby County Room
6205
Gift of John Malmo

76 **Shelby County Court House**
Memphis Public Library
Memphis and Shelby County Room
167C 1466

77 **Germania Bank Building**
Memphis Public Library
Memphis and Shelby County Room
87C 1226

78 **Beale Street and Hernando, ca 1915**
Memphis Public Library
Memphis and Shelby County Room
2869

79 **Hadden's Horn**
Memphis Public Library
Memphis and Shelby County Room
5872NC 2747

80 **Wolf River**
Memphis Public Library
Memphis and Shelby County Room
4693C 5151
Apply for copies to Pink Palace
Accession no. 1975.13.341/68c

81 **Sinking of *DeSoto* and *Georgia Lee***
Memphis Public Library
Memphis and Shelby County Room
1991C 5831

82 **Harahan Bridge, 1914**
Memphis Public Library
Memphis and Shelby County Room
4526C 1420
Apply for copies to Pink Palace
Accession no. 1961.12.55/68c

83 **Schwab's on Beale Street Memphis**
Memphis Public Library
Memphis and Shelby County Room
3006C 363
Gift of The Schwab Family

84 **Cordova Hotel**
Memphis Public Library
Memphis and Shelby County Room
295C 3071
MaCallum & Robinson Inc.

85 **Memphis Women's Club, 1904**
Memphis Public Library
Memphis and Shelby County Room

86 **Cotton Warehouse Interior**
Memphis Public Library
Memphis and Shelby County Room
5869C 2074

88 **Cotton Bales**
Memphis Public Library
Memphis and Shelby County Room
2031C 1783
Wyckoff

89 **Federal Barge Line**
Memphis Public Library
Memphis and Shelby County Room
8019C 1401P
Photo by Poland

90 **Cotton Bales**
Memphis Public Library
Memphis and Shelby County Room
5444C 1760
Photo by Poland

91 **Metropolitan Police Department**
Tennessee State Library and Archives
Library Collection.
Drawer 20, Folder 170, Image Number: 3974

92 **City Beautiful Commission**
Memphis Public Library
Memphis and Shelby County Room

93 **Clarence Saunders, founder of Piggly Wiggly**
Memphis Public Library
Memphis and Shelby County Room
7029C 4223

94 **Piggly Wiggly Warehouse**
Memphis Public Library
Memphis and Shelby County Room
6922C 3721
Copy of gift of Mrs. Al Groce

95 **Pink Palace**
Memphis Public Library
Memphis and Shelby County Room
2977C 3628

96 **Peabody Hotel**
Memphis Public Library
Memphis and Shelby County Room
4154NC 3066
Photo by Poland

97 **Peabody Hotel Lobby**
Memphis Public Library
Memphis and Shelby County Room
6817
Photograph by Tebbs & Knell, Inc

98 **Fisher-Hurd Lumber Company**
Memphis Public Library
Memphis and Shelby County Room
4393NC 2359
Photo by Poland

99 **Robert R. Church, Jr.**
Memphis Public Library
Memphis and Shelby County Room
2863C 475
Photo by Hooks Brothers

100 **Seesel's Delivery Vehicle**
Memphis Public Library
Memphis and Shelby County Room
6568C 4714
Gift of Sam Seessel

101 **Sears, Roebuck and Company**
Memphis Public Library
Memphis and Shelby County Room
4156NC 4707
Photo by Poland

102 **Cotton Gin**
Memphis Public Library
Memphis and Shelby County Room
5712NC 1989
Photo by Poland

103 **Goldsmith's**
Memphis Public Library
Memphis and Shelby County Room
5774C 2885

104 **Firestone Tire and Rubber Company**
Memphis Public Library
Memphis and Shelby County Room
7351C 1546
Gift of Pink Palace

106 **Crump Stadium**
Memphis Public Library
Memphis and Shelby County Room
7059C 4183

105 **Medical Arts Building**
Memphis Public Library
Memphis and Shelby County Room
5038NC 1569
Photo by Poland

107 **Ellis Auditorium**
Memphis Public Library
Memphis and Shelby County Room
3318C 1174
From the Municipal Reference Library

108 **Clover Farm Dairy Company**
Memphis Public Library
Memphis and Shelby County Room
5778C 1687

109 **First National Bank**
Memphis Public Library
Memphis and Shelby County Room
5897C 1227

110 **Red Sox Baseball Team's Owners**
Memphis Public Library
Memphis and Shelby County Room
2879C 4202

111 Shelby County Court House
Memphis Public Library
Memphis and Shelby County Room
3847C 1593
Photo by Poland

112 WREC Radio Station
Memphis Public Library
Memphis and Shelby County Room
5449NC 6951

113 Handy's Park
Memphis Public Library
Memphis and Shelby County Room
3567C 4058
From the Municipal Reference Library

114 The Colored Old Folks Home
Memphis Public Library
Memphis and Shelby County Room
2870C 1945

115 Robilio and Cuneo Importers
Memphis Public Library
Memphis and Shelby County Room
9067

116 Whistle Bottling Company
Memphis Public Library
Memphis and Shelby County Room
6874C 5326

117 Cotton Carnival, 1937
Memphis Public Library
Memphis and Shelby County Room
1634C 1821
Contributed by Bert Wade

118 Cotton Carnival, 1937
Memphis Public Library
Memphis and Shelby County Room
1649C 1805
Contributed by Bert Wade

119 Scene from Court Square
Memphis Public Library
Memphis and Shelby County Room
363C 3379

120 Riverside Drive Construction
Memphis Public Library
Memphis and Shelby County Room
3155C 4814
Gift of the Memphis Police Department

121 Memphis from Riverside Drive
Memphis Public Library
Memphis and Shelby County Room
3379C 5163
From the Municipal Reference Library

122 Memphis Country Club
Memphis Public Library
Memphis and Shelby County Room
7044C 4316
Photo by Poland

123 Columbia Mutual Tower Building
Memphis Public Library
Memphis and Shelby County Room
3258C 1182
Gift of the Memphis Police Department

124 WMC Radio Station Transmitter Site
Memphis Public Library
Memphis and Shelby County Room
4656NC 6675
Photo by Poland

125 Bry's Department Store
Memphis Public Library & Information Center
Memphis and Shelby County Room
6108NC 945

126 Riverside Drive during 1937 Flood
Memphis Public Library
Memphis and Shelby County Room
3147
Gift of the Memphis Police Department

127 Fairgrounds Refugee Camp, 1937
Memphis Public Library
Memphis and Shelby County Room
3673C 2544
From the Municipal Reference Library

128 Main and McCall, 1940
Memphis Public Library
Memphis and Shelby County Room
6893NC 5107

130 Dr. Cupufu Old Fashioned Medicine Show
Memphis Public Library
Memphis and Shelby County Room

131 Main and Beale, 1940
Memphis Public Library
Memphis and Shelby County Room
6895NC 5278

132 Newspaper Boy on Main and Madison
Memphis Public Library
Memphis and Shelby County Room
7587NC 1104

133 W. C. Handy
Memphis Public Library & Information Center
Memphis and Shelby County Room
6671NC 498

134 W. C. Handy/Beale Ave. Auditorium
Memphis Public Library
Memphis and Shelby County Room
2875
Gift of The Links, Inc. Photo by Hooks Brothers

135 CHISCA HOTEL, 1940
Memphis Public Library
Memphis and Shelby County Room
2203C 3095

136 EAST MEMPHIS MOTOR COMPANY
Memphis Public Library
Memphis and Shelby County Room
8230N

137 PODESTA MULE COMPANY
Memphis Public Library
Memphis and Shelby County Room
4502NC 4488
Photo by Poland

138 STREETCAR, 1940
Memphis Public Library
Memphis and Shelby County Room
6782

139 EDWARD HULL "BOSS" CRUMP
Memphis Public Library
Memphis and Shelby County Room
From the E.H. Crump Collection

140 REPAIRING STREETCAR LINE
Memphis Public Library
Memphis and Shelby County Room
Pink Palace Collection
Accession No. 1976.24.18/68c

141 BOOKER T. WASHINGTON HIGH SCHOOL BAND
Memphis Public Library
Memphis and Shelby County Room
4853C 7221
From the Municipal Reference Library

142 SPIRIT OF BEALE STREET
Memphis Public Library
Memphis and Shelby County Room
2872C 4682
Gift of The Links, Inc.
Photo by Hooks Brothers

143 BEMIS BROTHERS BAG COMPANY
Memphis Public Library
Memphis and Shelby County Room

144 LLOYD T. BINFORD
Memphis Public Library
Memphis and Shelby County Room
2796C 6099

145 YWCA
Memphis Public Library
Memphis and Shelby County Room
6730NC 5341

146 YWCA SOCIAL GATHERING
Memphis Public Library
Memphis and Shelby County Room
6740NC 7262

147 SOUTHWESTERN COLLEGE
Memphis Public Library
Memphis and Shelby County Room
7077C 4130

148 UNION AVENUE, 1944
Memphis Public Library
Memphis and Shelby County Room
5829NC 4773
Photo by Poland

149 COTTON EXCHANGE, 1944
Memphis Public Library
Memphis and Shelby County Room
4440NC 1675
Photo by Poland

150 MEMPHIS POLICE DEPARTMENT
Memphis Public Library
Memphis and Shelby County Room
8197C 3719
Gift of the Chandler family (by John Chandler)

151 JOHN DEERE COMPANY AT FRONT STREET
Memphis Police Department
4552NC 4613
Photo by Poland

152 THE *MEMPHIS BELLE*
Memphis Public Library
Memphis and Shelby County Room
6795
Gift of Cooper Photographs

153 MOBILE BOOK SERVICE
Memphis Public Library
Memphis and Shelby County Room

154 SEESSEL'S INTERIOR
Memphis Public Library
Memphis and Shelby County Room
6565C 4701
Gift of Sam Seessel

155 AIRVIEW OF THE STERICK BUILDING
Tennessee State Library and Archives
Department of Conservation Photograph Collection
Box 12, File 52, Accession No. RG 82, Negative # CV4371

156 WARNER THEATER
Memphis Public Library
Memphis and Shelby County Room
6274NC 5378

157 UNIVERSAL LIFE INSURANCE COMPANY
Memphis Public Library
Memphis and Shelby County Room
4889C 5352
Gift of Universal Life Insurance Co.
Photo by Hooks Brothers

158 THE PALACE AND NEW DAISY THEATERS
Memphis Public Library
Memphis and Shelby County Room
6091NC 353

159 Fairgrounds Amusement Park
Memphis Public Library
Memphis and Shelby County Room
613C 4487
Gift from John M. Caruthers

160 Fairgrounds Amusement Park
Memphis Public Library
Memphis and Shelby County Room
665C 5316
Gift of Donne Walden

161 Union Ave and S Front St
Memphis Public Library
Memphis and Shelby County Room
6787NC 4976

162 Governor Frank Clement
Memphis Public Library
Memphis and Shelby County Room
773C 465
Picture Credit: Commercial Appeal

163 President's Island, Aerial View
Memphis Public Library
Memphis and Shelby County Room
8028C 1396
From the Fowler Collection

164 E. L. Bruce Lumber Company
Memphis Public Library
Memphis and Shelby County Room
5825NC 951
Photo by Poland

165 Roy Rogers at Ellis Auditorium
Memphis Public Library
Memphis and Shelby County Room
6256N

166 Russwood Park, 1960
Memphis Public Library
Memphis and Shelby County Room
6152C 4584
Gift of John Guinozzo

168 Wilson Drug Store
Memphis Public Library
Memphis and Shelby County Room
6092NC 379

169 Union Avenue Extended
Memphis Public Library
Memphis and Shelby County Room
8349C 5604
Gift of Mr. and Mrs. James R. Webb in honor of Lisa Hilary Webb

170 Overton Park Zoo
Tennessee State Library and Archives
Department of Conservation
Photograph Collection
Box 16, File 123, Accession No. RG 82, Negative # CV9916

171 America Airlines
Memphis Public Library
Memphis and Shelby County Room
724C 1258

172 Mid-South Fair, 1965
Memphis Public Library
Memphis and Shelby County Room
7435C 4421

173 City Hall, 1965
Memphis Public Library
Memphis and Shelby County Room
8688

174 Summer Ave and White Station Rd
Memphis Public Library
Memphis and Shelby County Room
8309C 5540
Gift of Mr. and Mrs. James R. Webb in honor of Lisa Hilary Webb

175 W. C. Handy Monument
Memphis Public Library
Memphis and Shelby County Room
7171C 238
Duplicate print from the urban Renewal Files

176 Holiday Inn Rivermont
Memphis Public Library
Memphis and Shelby County Room
6348C 3022
Gift of Holiday Inn Rivermont

177 Edward Kirby, a.k.a. Prince Gabe
Memphis Public Library
Memphis and Shelby County Room
7325
Gift of Ed Cooper

178 A. Schwab
Memphis Public Library
Memphis and Shelby County Room
8227C 6515
Gift of Saul Brown

179 St. Jude Groundbreaking
Memphis Public Library
Memphis and Shelby County Room

180 Danny Thomas at St. Jude's Research Center
Memphis Public Library
Memphis and Shelby County Room
8082C 6408
Gift of Saul Brown

181 DeSoto Park
Memphis Public Library
Memphis and Shelby County Room
3732C 4341
From the Municipal Reference Library

182 DeSoto Park
Memphis Public Library
Memphis and Shelby County Room
3336C 7261
From the Municipal Reference Library

183 CLARK TOWER
Memphis Public Library
Memphis and Shelby County Room
7076C 4429

184 RIVERSIDE DRIVE
Memphis Public Library
Memphis and Shelby County Room
30149C 5033
Gift of Saul Brown

185 REMODELED MANNING HALL
Tennessee State Library and Archives
Library Collection
Drawer 14, Folder 105;
Image Number: 2746

186 BAPTIST MEMORIAL HOSPITAL
Memphis Public Library
Memphis and Shelby County Room
777C 3108

187 THE WATERFRONT AT MEMPHIS
Tennessee State Library and Archives
Department of Conservation
Photograph Collection
Box 16, File 146; Accession No. RG 82;
Image No. 15815

188 FEDERAL EXPRESS
Memphis Public Library
Memphis and Shelby County Room

198 MEMPHIS IN MAY
Memphis Public Library
Memphis and Shelby County Room
Gift of Saul Brown

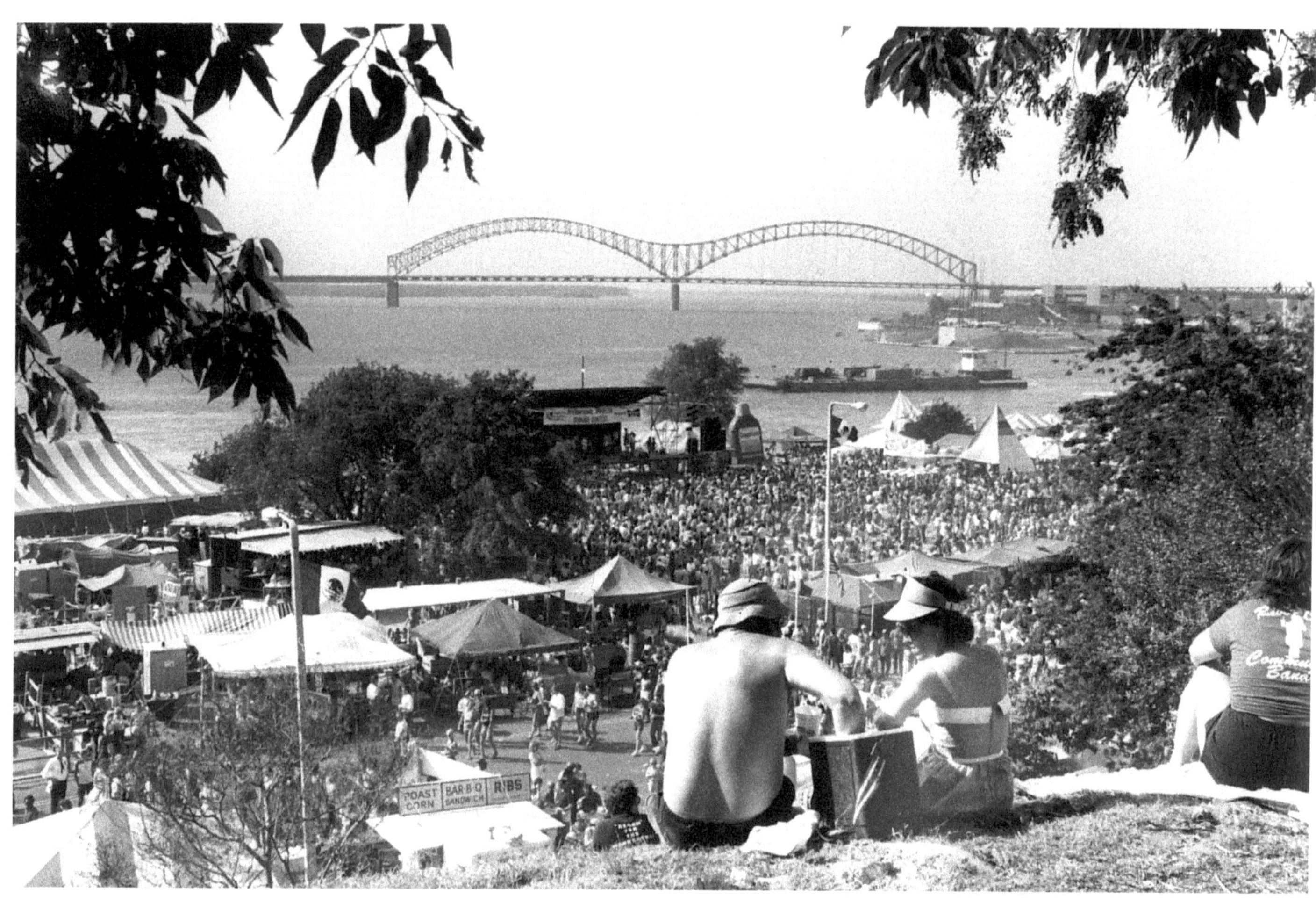

Memphis in May International Festival at Tom Lee Park, circa 1980. The festival was founded in the 1970s to foster relations between the city and foreign countries. Each year, the festival honors a specific country and includes educational programs, the Beale Street Music Festival, the Sunset Symphony and the World Championship Barbeque Cooking Contest.

HISTORIC PHOTOS OF MEMPHIS

Memphis is a resilient and enduring city. From its position on a bluff of the Mississippi River, it has survived fever, flood, and depression. The ever-growing and diverse population has overcome adversity and has made Memphis the most populous and culturally significant city in the region. The people of Memphis have made it the home of the blues, barbecue, business, and so much more. Memphis is today, just as much as ever, a city of change and innovation.

Historic Photos of Memphis captures this journey through still photography from the finest archives of city, state, and private collections. From the Civil War to the building of a modern metropolis, *Historic Photos of Memphis* follows life, government, education, and events throughout the history of Memphis. This book captures unique and rare scenes through the lens of hundreds of historic photographers. Published in striking black and white, these images communicate the historic events and everyday life of two centuries of people building a unique and prosperous city.

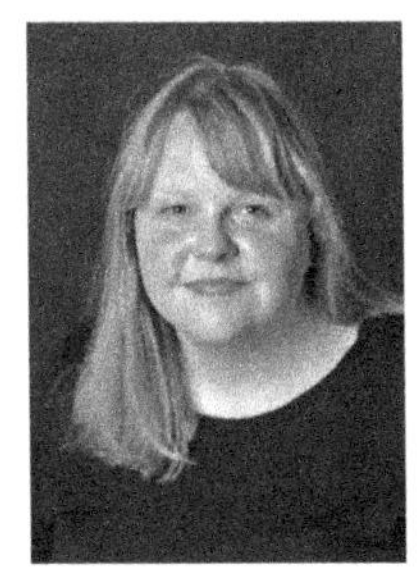

Gina Cordell received a bachelor's and master's degree in sociology from the University of Memphis. She served as a researcher and administrator at the University of Alabama and the University of Memphis before joining the Memphis Public Library and Information Center in 2000 as the social sciences librarian in the History/Social Sciences Department. She has published articles on Memphis history and women and body image and has written and compiled a comprehensive guide to the processed manuscript collections in the Memphis and Shelby County Room. Gina lives in Memphis with her husband, Paul, and Boston terrier, Violet.

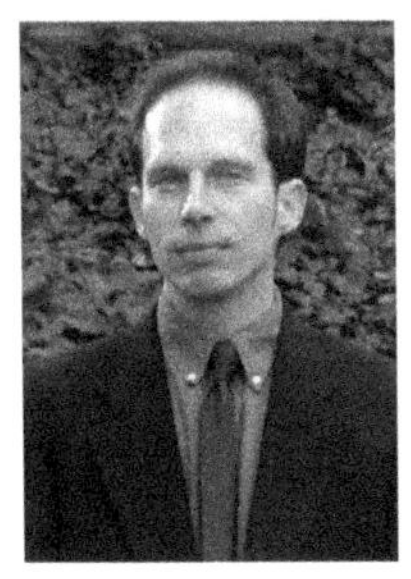

Patrick W. O'Daniel is currently a Librarian/Specialist (Genealogy) with the History/Social Sciences Department of the Memphis Public Library. He has a master's degree in history from the University of Memphis. He studied at Samford University, and is now working toward a master's degree in information sciences from the University of Tennessee, Knoxville. Patrick has presented programs on creating local history and genealogy collections for public libraries at the Public Library Association Conference in Phoenix, Arizona, and the Tennessee Library Association Conference in Chattanooga, Tennessee. He has written articles for the *West Tennessee Historical Society Papers* in 2002 and for the *Tennessee Archivist* in 2006. Patrick lives in Memphis with his wife, Kathy, and daughter, Kelly.

WWW.TURNERPUBLISHING.COM

www.ingramcontent.com/pod-product-compliance
Lightning Source LLC
LaVergne TN
LVHW070459120826
845154LV00019BA/29

* 9 7 8 1 6 8 3 3 6 9 1 3 4 *